IMPROVE

How I Discovered **IMPROV** and Conquered Social Anxiety

by

Alex Graudins

:01

First Second

New York

:01

First Second

Published by First Second
First Second is an imprint of Roaring Brook Press,
a division of Holtzbrinck Publishing Holdings Limited Partnership
120 Broadway, New York, NY 10271
firstsecondbooks.com

The names and identifying characteristics of some persons described in this book have been changed.

Library of Congress Cataloging-in-Publication Data is available.

Our books may be purchased in bulk for promotional, educational, or business use.
Please contact your local bookseller or the Macmillan Corporate and Premium Sales Department
at (800) 221-7945 ext. 5442 or by email at MacmillanSpecialMarkets@macmillan.com.

First edition, 2022
Edited by Calista Brill and Tim Stout
Cover design and interior book design by Molly Johanson
Special thanks to Alex Lu, Veronica Agarwal, and Kyla Smith

Penciled on an iPad Pro with Clip Studio Paint. Printed onto 9"x12" Bristol board and
inked with Winsor & Newton Series 7 #0-2 Kolinsky brushes, Pilot Fude brush pens, and
fine/extra fine Zebra brush pens. Lettered in InDesign and colored digitally in Photoshop.

Printed in China

ISBN 978-1-250-20823-1 (paperback)
10 9 8 7 6 5 4 3 2 1

ISBN 978-1-250-20822-4 (hardcover)
10 9 8 7 6 5 4 3 2 1

Don't miss your next favorite book from First Second!
For the latest updates go to firstsecondnewsletter.com and sign up for our enewsletter.

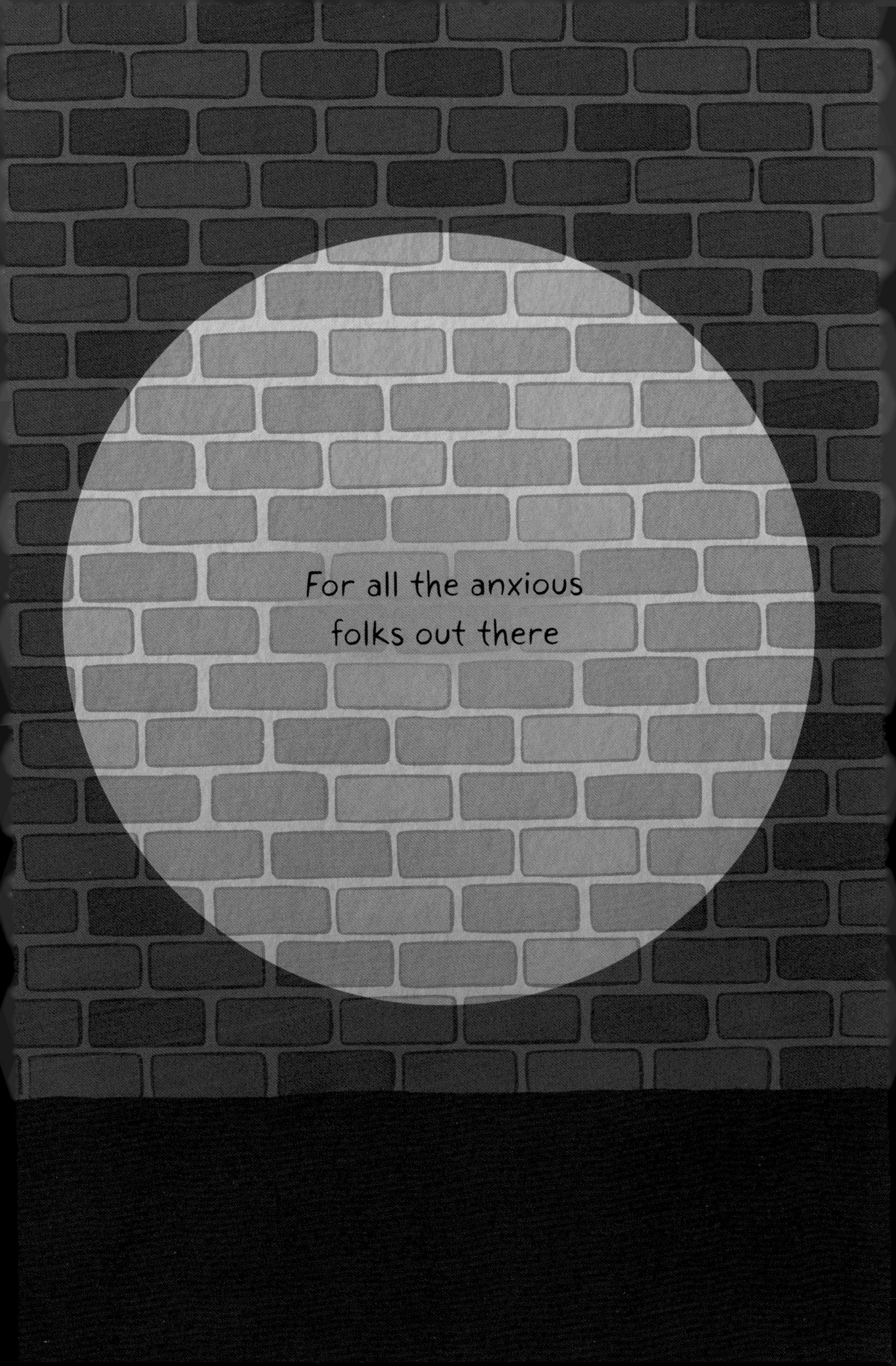
For all the anxious
folks out there

PART 1

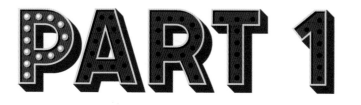

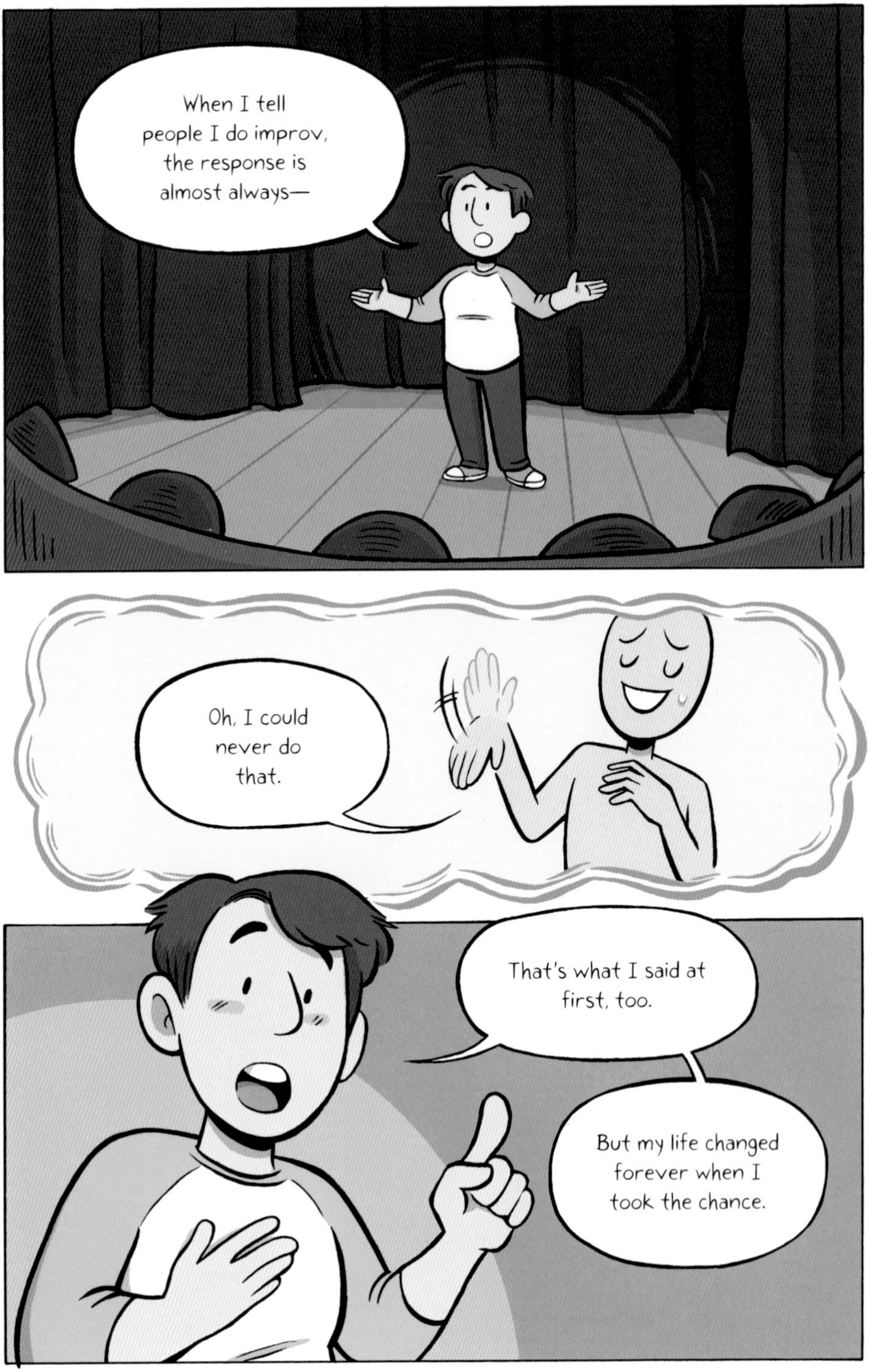
When I tell people I do improv, the response is almost always—
Oh, I could never do that.
That's what I said at first, too.
But my life changed forever when I took the chance.

I've always been interested in telling stories. They were my way of processing the world and my emotions.

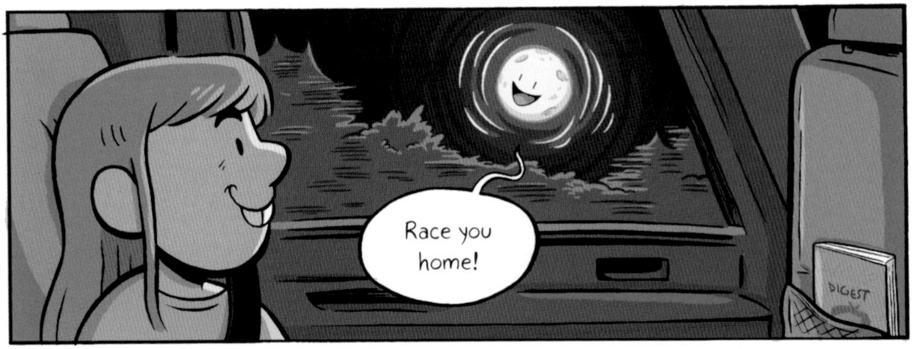
Race you home!
DIGEST

I've been drawing since I was five years old and had decided by seventh grade I wanted to spend my life making cartoons.

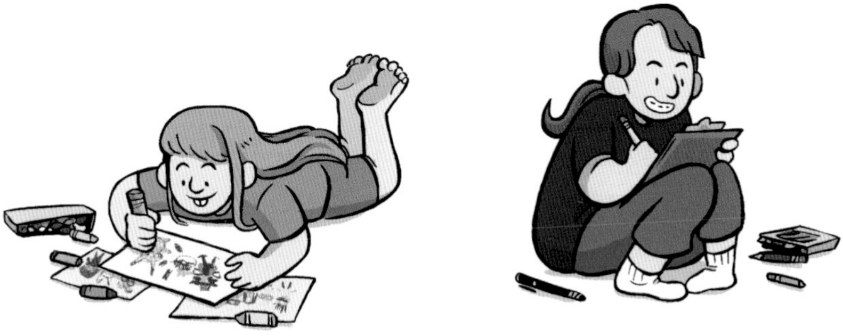

I never saw myself as a performer...though my imagination wasn't shy at dreaming up fantasies.

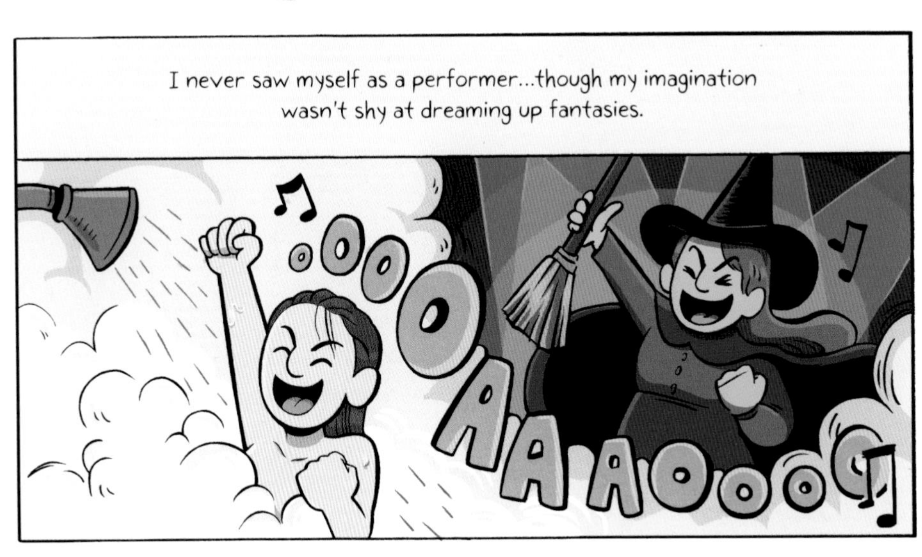

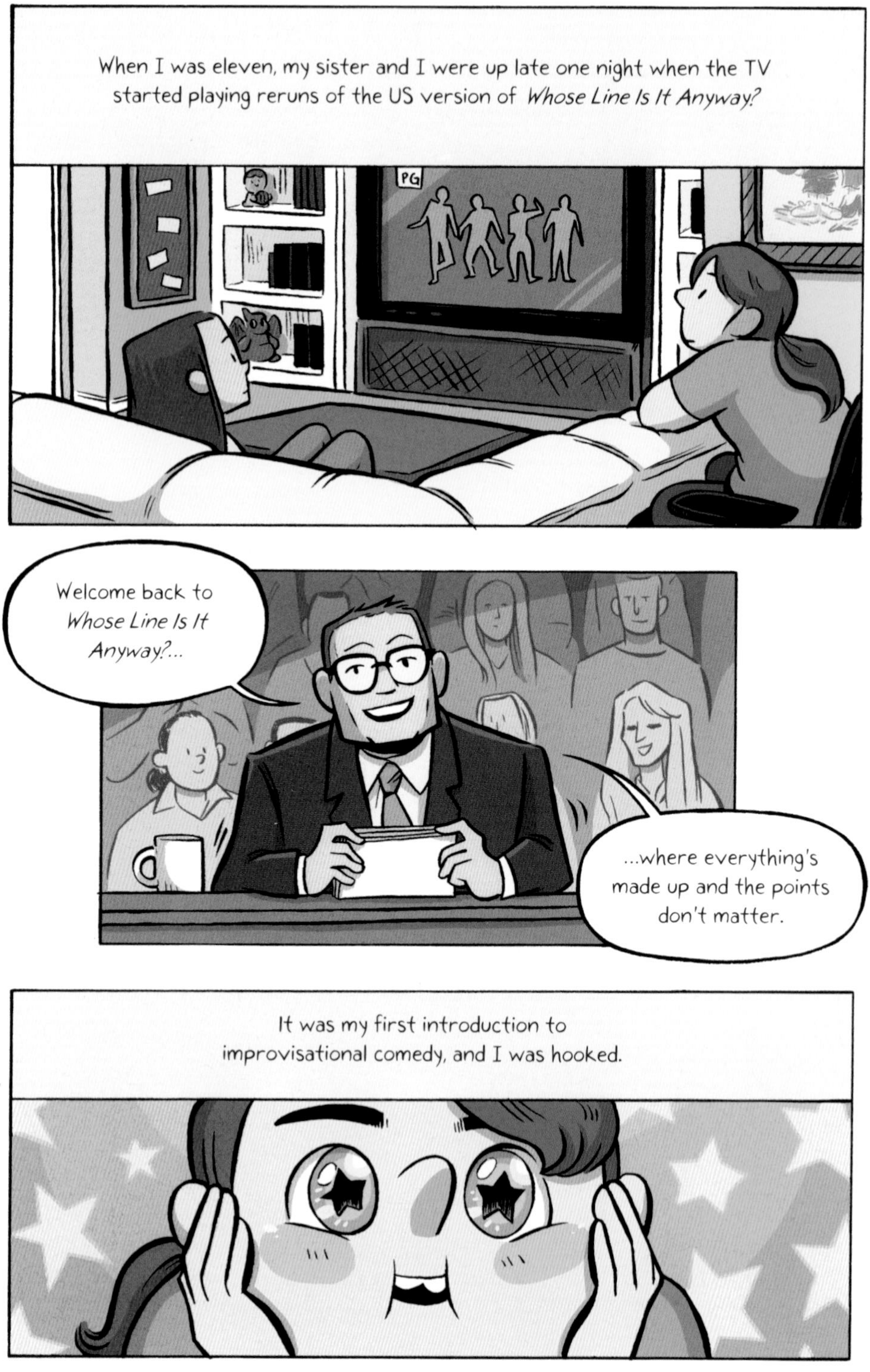
When I was eleven, my sister and I were up late one night when the TV started playing reruns of the US version of *Whose Line Is It Anyway?*
PG
Welcome back to *Whose Line Is It Anyway?*...
...where everything's made up and the points don't matter.
It was my first introduction to improvisational comedy, and I was hooked.

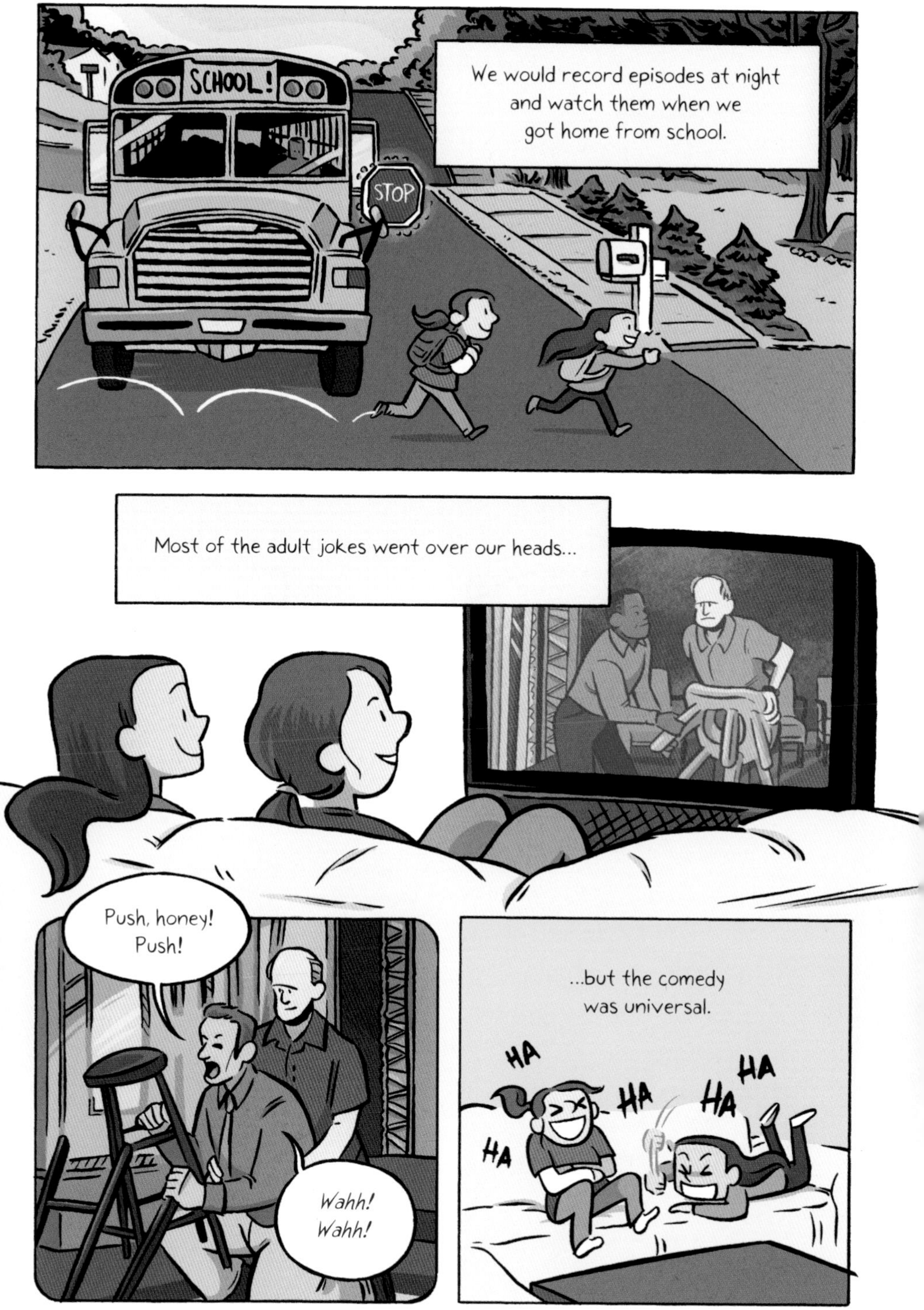
SCHOOL!
STOP
We would record episodes at night and watch them when we got home from school.
Most of the adult jokes went over our heads...
Push, honey! Push!
Wahh! Wahh!
...but the comedy was universal.
HA
HA
HA
HA
HA

I loved it so much, I tried throwing an improv party, but few of my friends had seen the show.

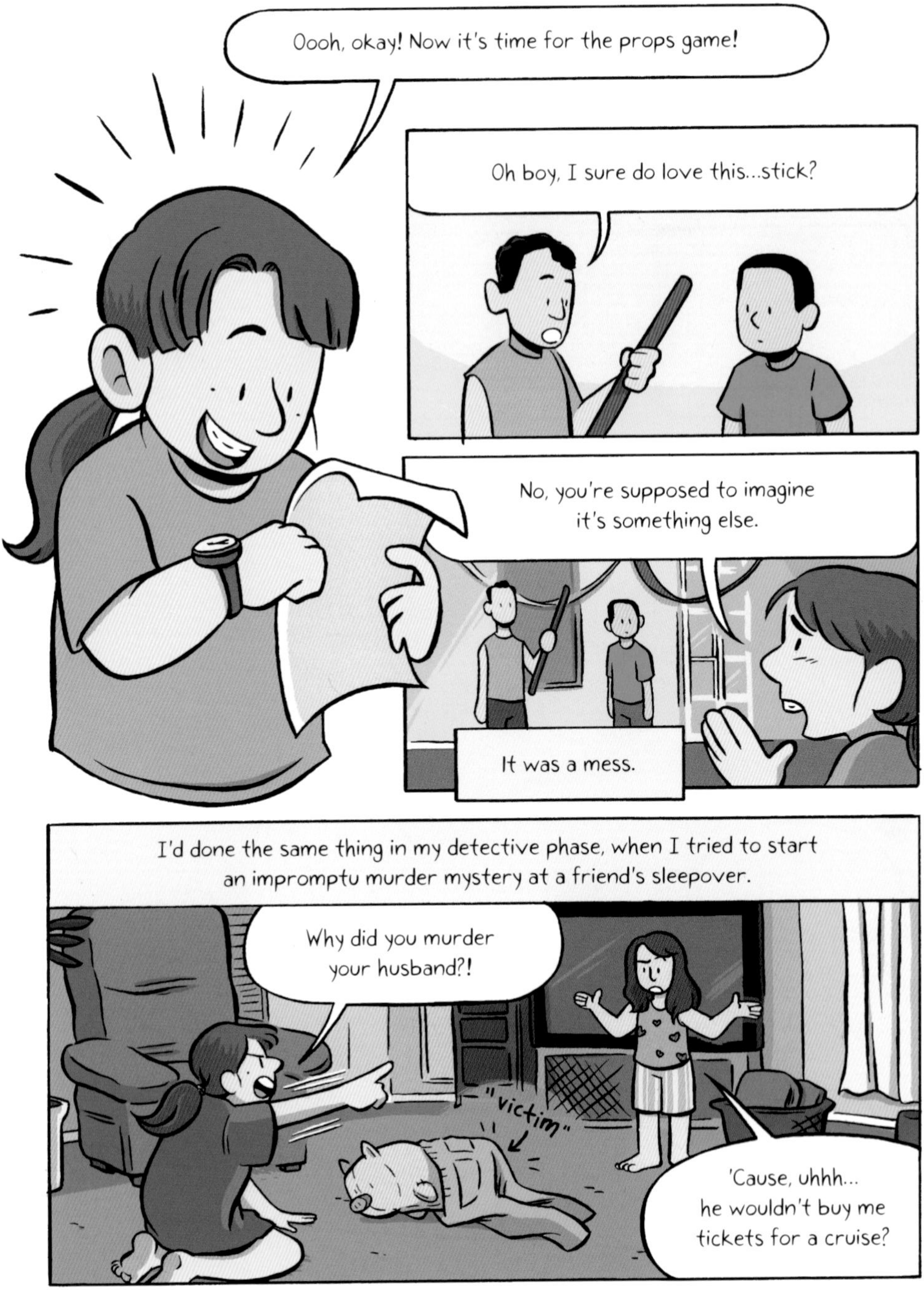
Oooh, okay! Now it's time for the props game!
Oh boy, I sure do love this...stick?
No, you're supposed to imagine it's something else.
It was a mess.
I'd done the same thing in my detective phase, when I tried to start an impromptu murder mystery at a friend's sleepover.
Why did you murder your husband?!
"victim"
'Cause, uhhh... he wouldn't buy me tickets for a cruise?

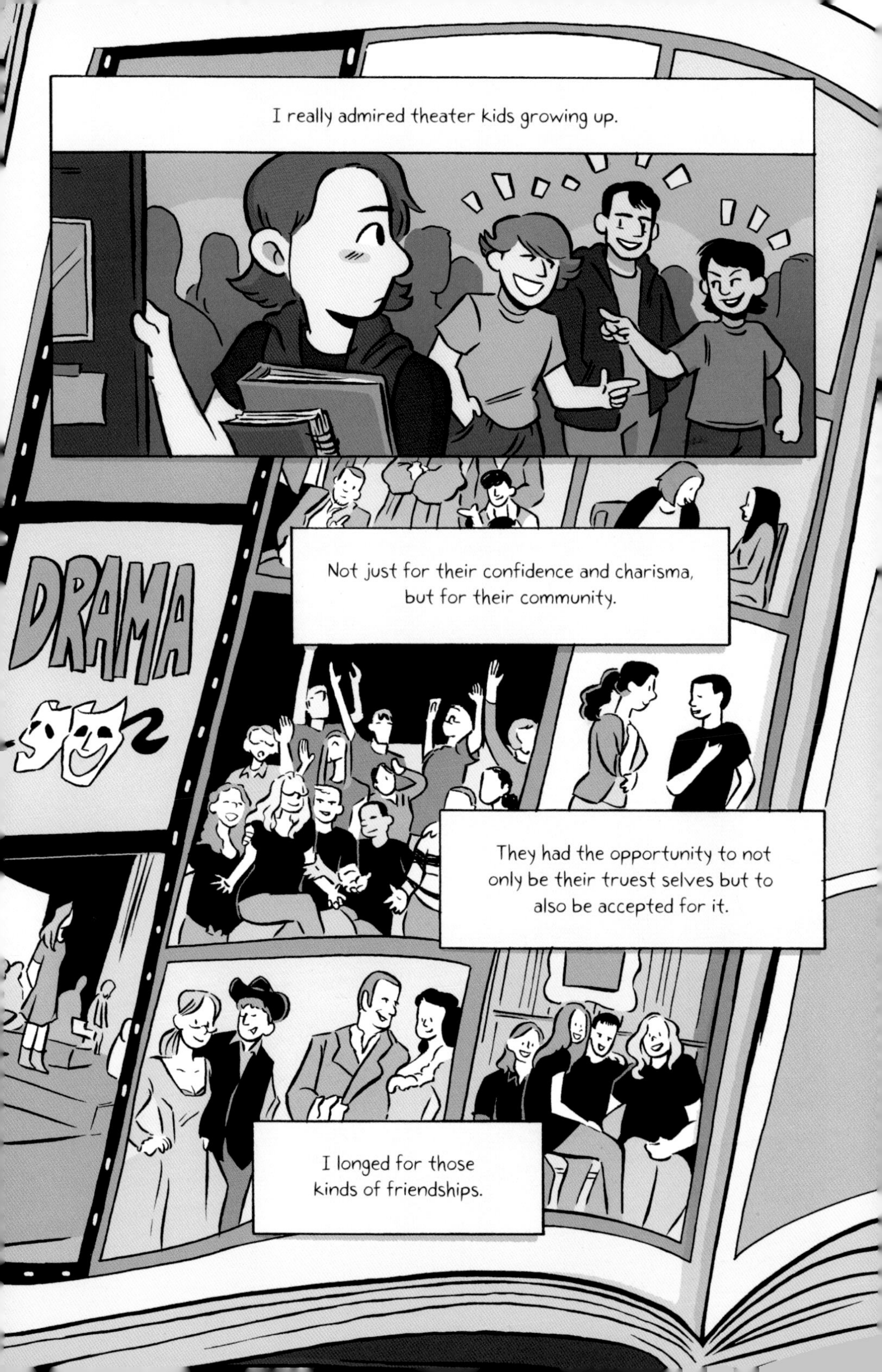
I really admired theater kids growing up.
DRAMA
Not just for their confidence and charisma, but for their community.
They had the opportunity to not only be their truest selves but to also be accepted for it.
I longed for those kinds of friendships.

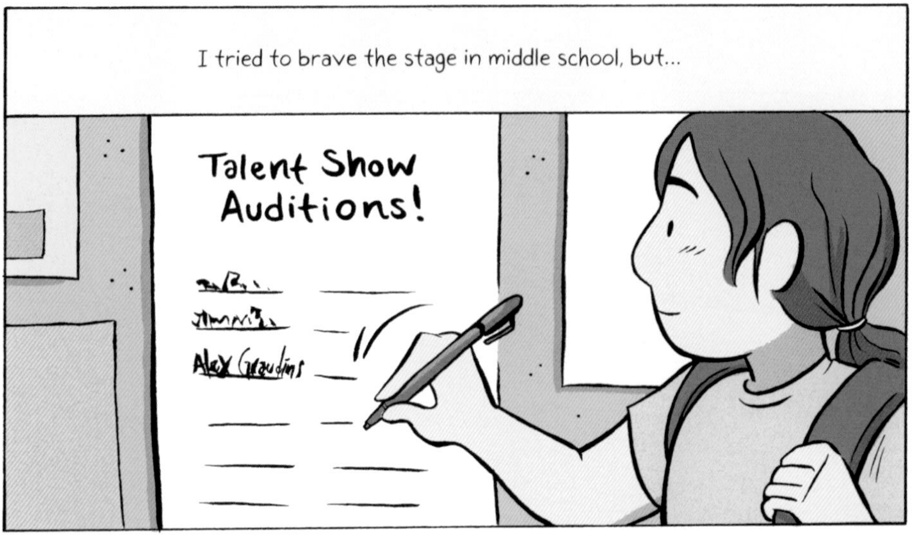
I tried to brave the stage in middle school, but...
Talent Show Auditions!
Alex Graudins

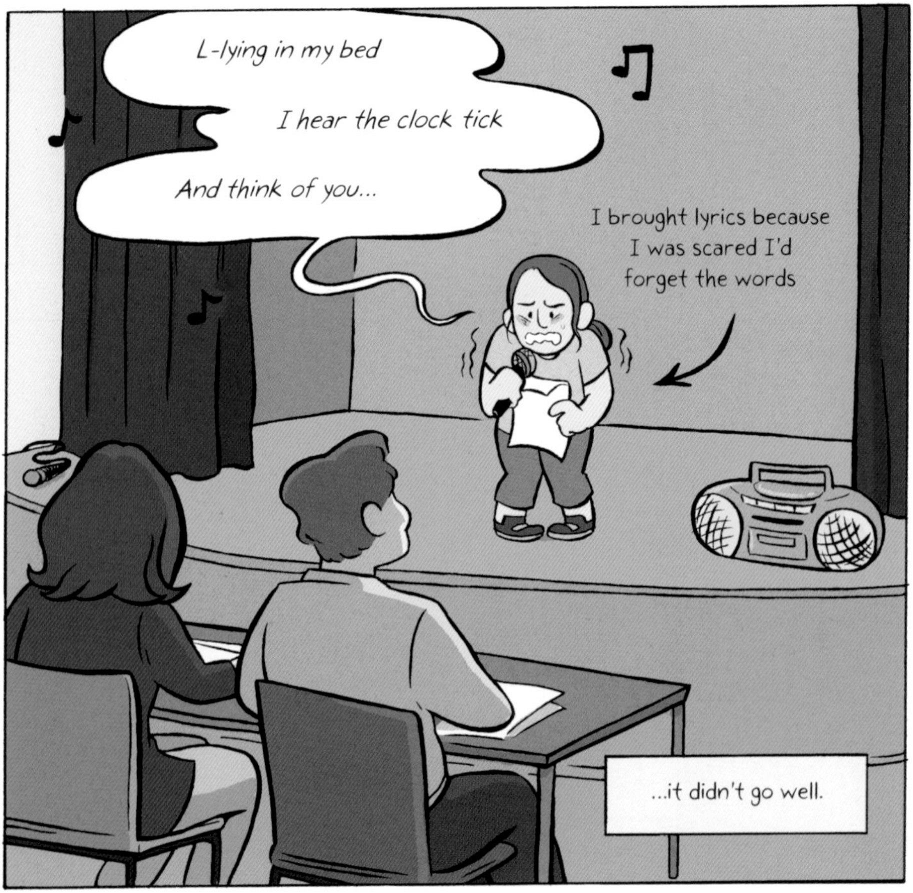
L-lying in my bed
I hear the clock tick
And think of you...
I brought lyrics because I was scared I'd forget the words
...it didn't go well.

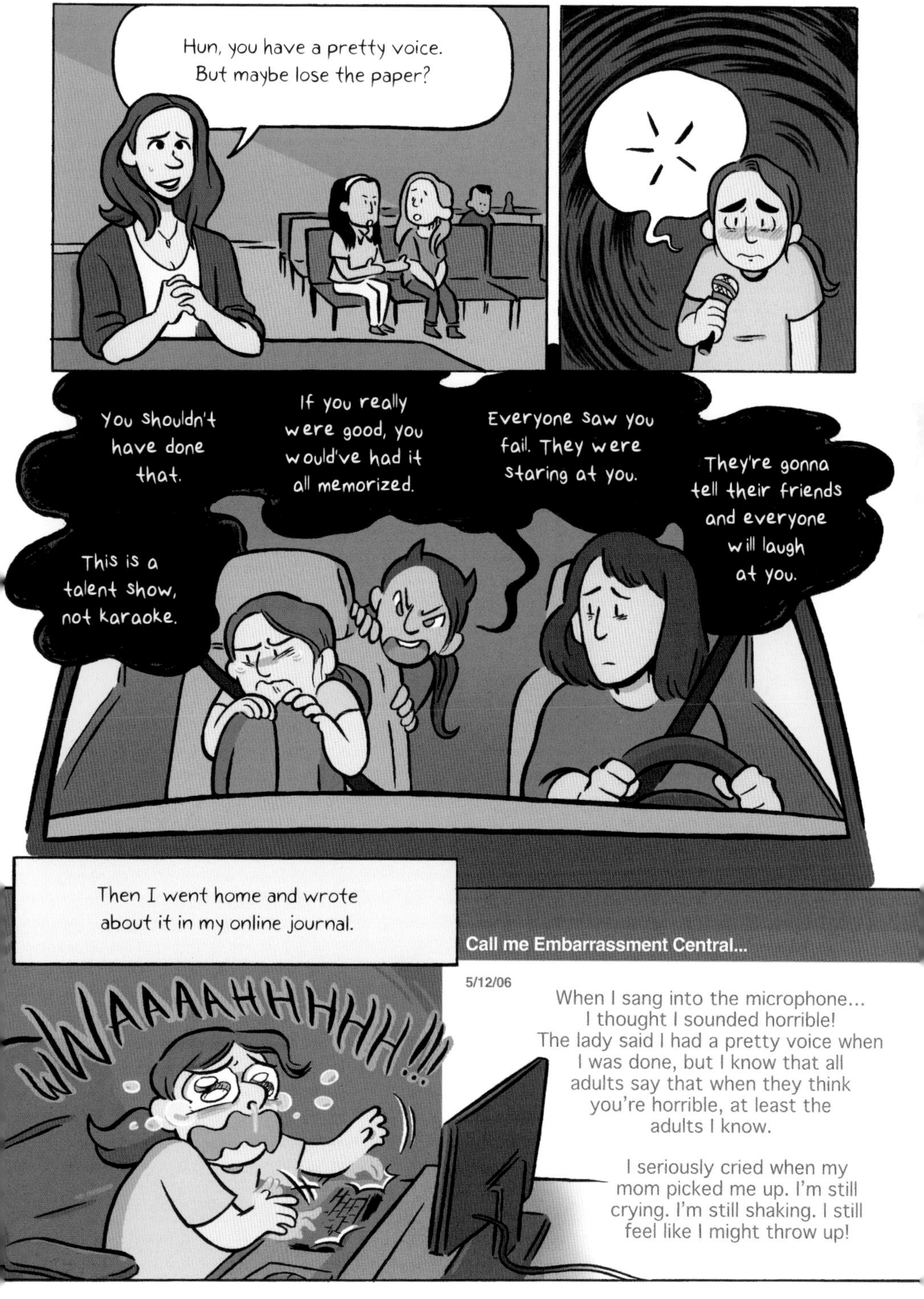
Hun, you have a pretty voice.
But maybe lose the paper?
You shouldn't have done that.
If you really were good, you would've had it all memorized.
Everyone saw you fail. They were staring at you.
They're gonna tell their friends and everyone will laugh at you.
This is a talent show, not karaoke.
Then I went home and wrote about it in my online journal.
Call me Embarrassment Central...
5/12/06
When I sang into the microphone... I thought I sounded horrible! The lady said I had a pretty voice when I was done, but I know that all adults say that when they think you're horrible, at least the adults I know.
I seriously cried when my mom picked me up. I'm still crying. I'm still shaking. I still feel like I might throw up!
WAAAAHHHHH!!!

After that, I spent my school days watching from afar, yearning for a spotlight I thought I didn't belong in.

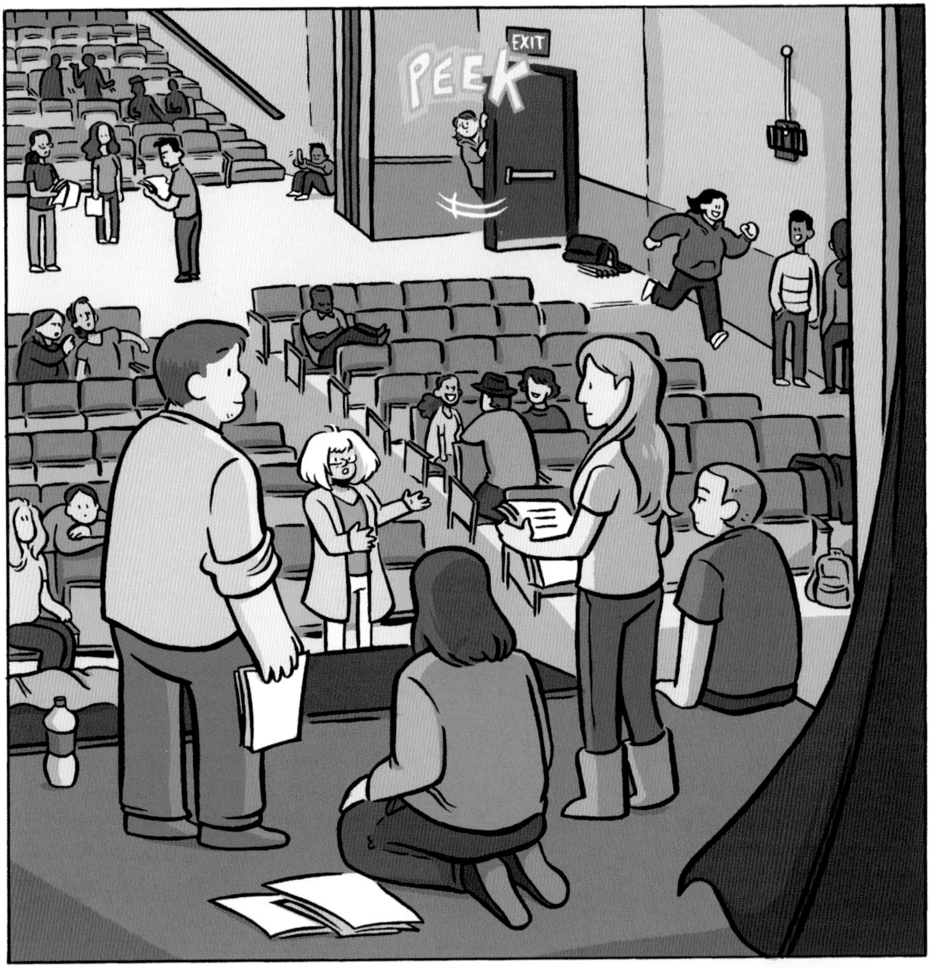
EXIT
PEEK

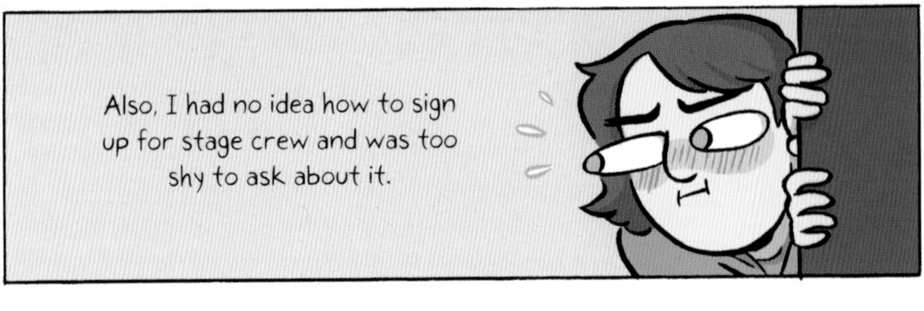
Also, I had no idea how to sign up for stage crew and was too shy to ask about it.

In those years, I noticed I was increasingly sad and scared, more so than I'd ever been before.

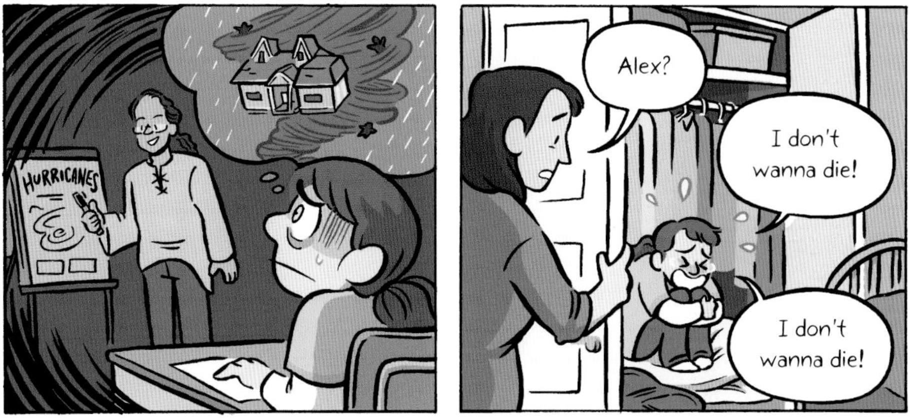
HURRICANES
Alex?
I don't wanna die!
I don't wanna die!

I became self-conscious of how other people saw me.

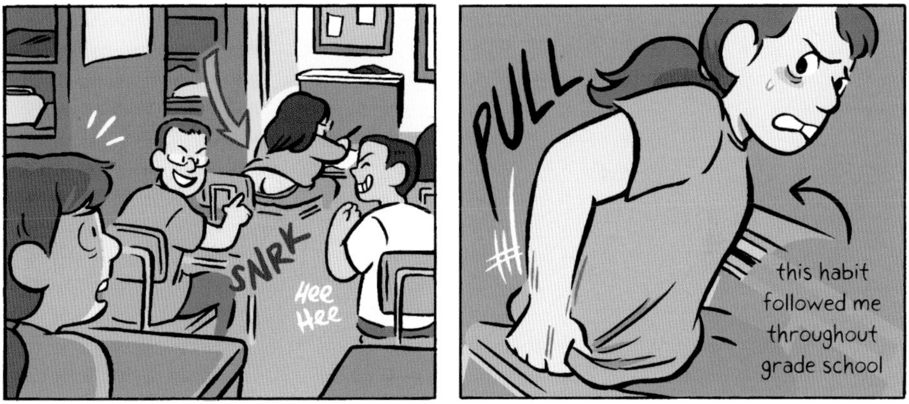
SNRK
Hee Hee
PULL
this habit followed me throughout grade school

Simple, everyday interactions were difficult.

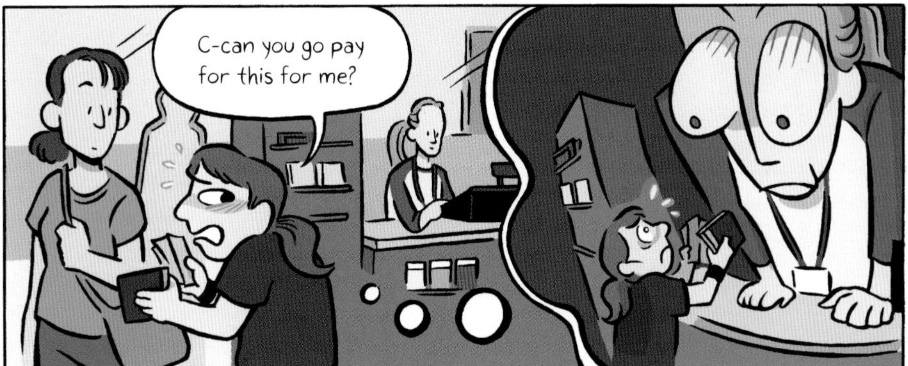
C-can you go pay for this for me?

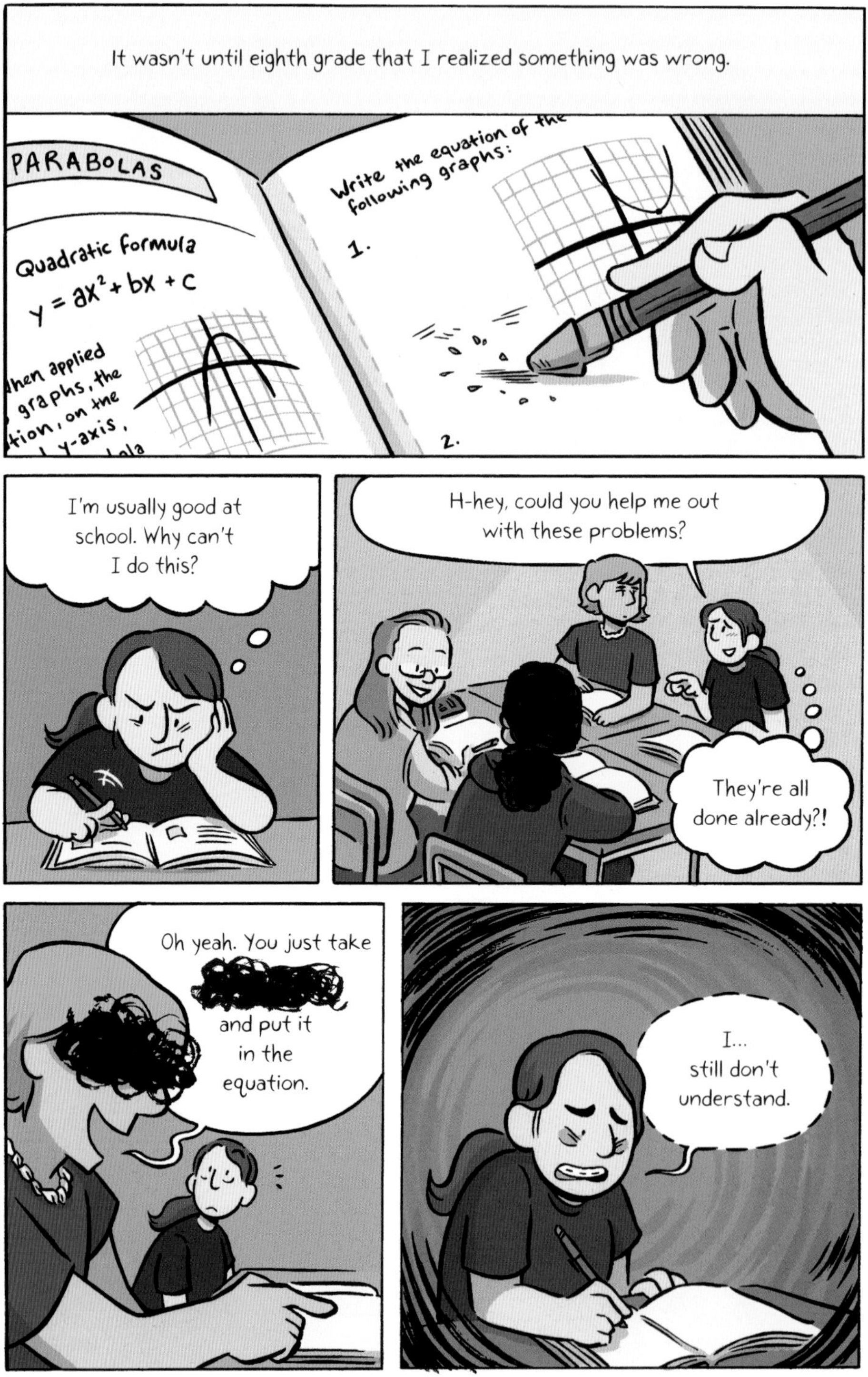

It wasn't until eighth grade that I realized something was wrong.
PARABOLAS
Quadratic formula
y = ax² + bx + c
Write the equation of the following graphs:
1.
2.
I'm usually good at school. Why can't I do this?
H-hey, could you help me out with these problems?
They're all done already?!
Oh yeah. You just take [redacted] and put it in the equation.
I... still don't understand.

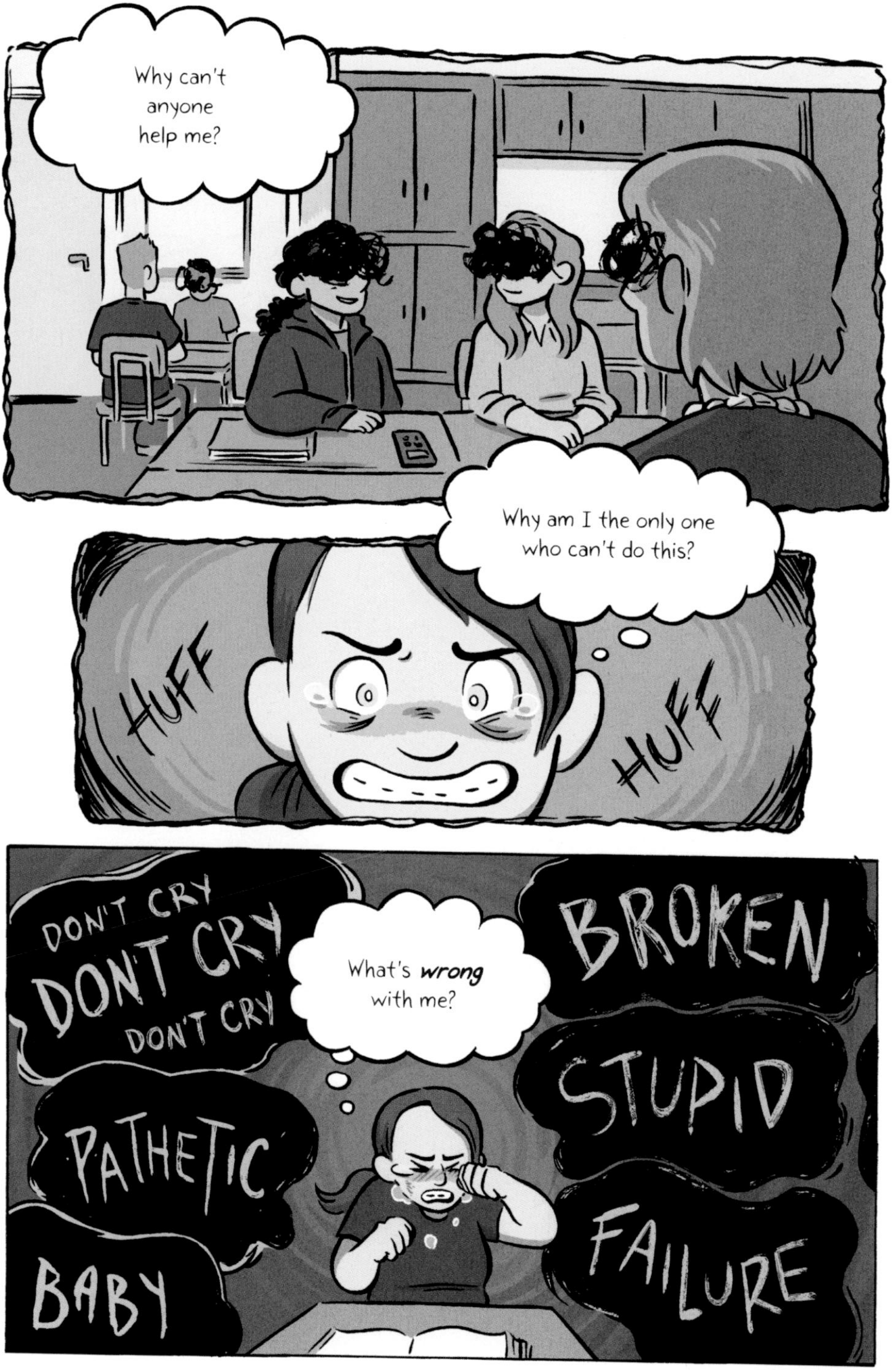
Why can't anyone help me?
Why am I the only one who can't do this?
HUFF
HUFF
DON'T CRY
DON'T CRY
DON'T CRY
What's **wrong** with me?
BROKEN
STUPID
PATHETIC
BABY
FAILURE

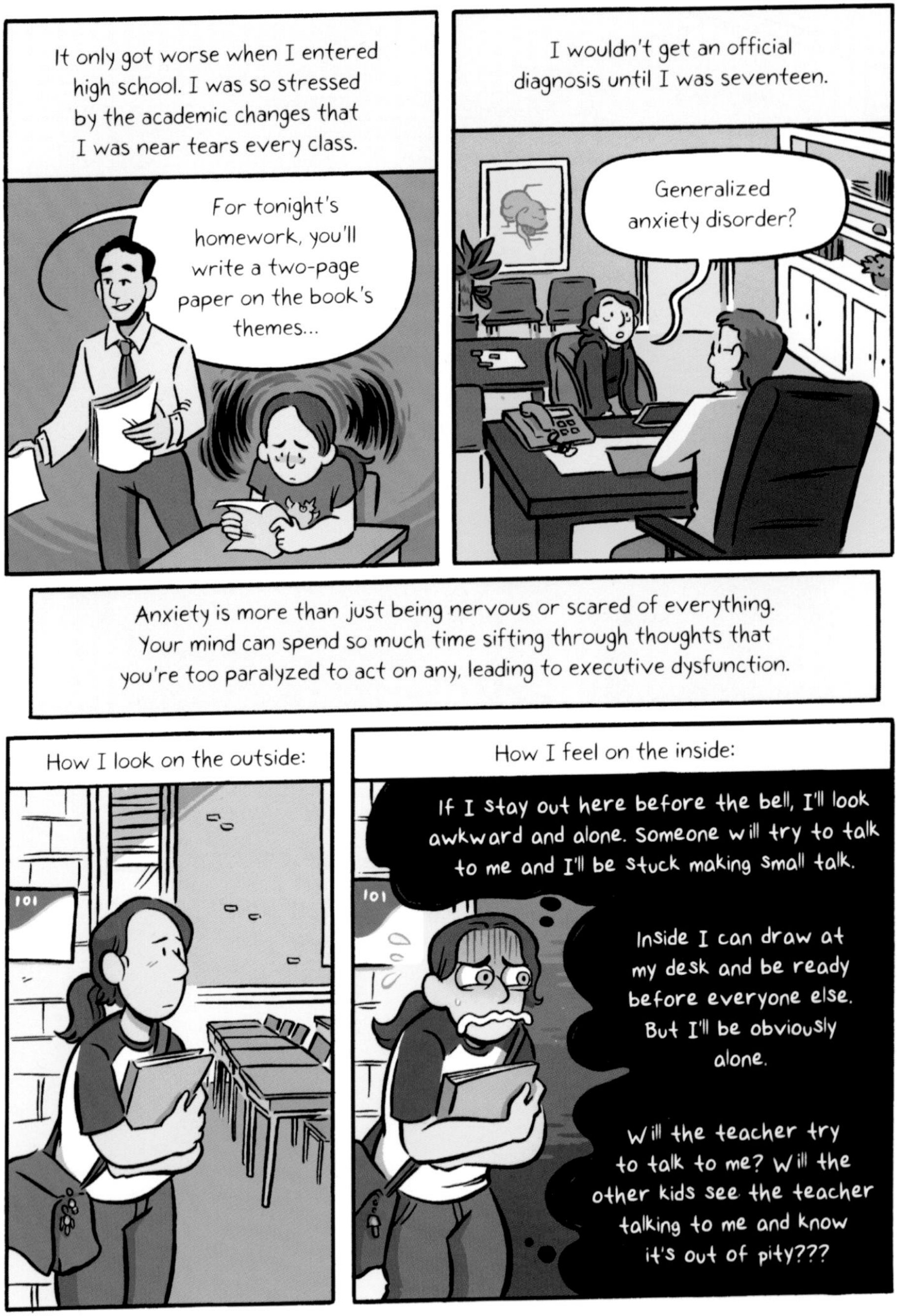

It only got worse when I entered high school. I was so stressed by the academic changes that I was near tears every class.
For tonight's homework, you'll write a two-page paper on the book's themes...
I wouldn't get an official diagnosis until I was seventeen.
Generalized anxiety disorder?
Anxiety is more than just being nervous or scared of everything. Your mind can spend so much time sifting through thoughts that you're too paralyzed to act on any, leading to executive dysfunction.
How I look on the outside:
101
How I feel on the inside:
101
If I stay out here before the bell, I'll look awkward and alone. Someone will try to talk to me and I'll be stuck making small talk.
Inside I can draw at my desk and be ready before everyone else. But I'll be obviously alone.
Will the teacher try to talk to me? Will the other kids see the teacher talking to me and know it's out of pity???

It's ***exhausting.*** Finally, I understood why I often didn't want to leave my bed, or felt tired for no reason—I was using all my energy to deal with these racing thoughts!

My biggest challenges stemmed from social anxiety—all the fun of regular anxiety, now with the constant fear of being judged and the inescapable need to be liked.

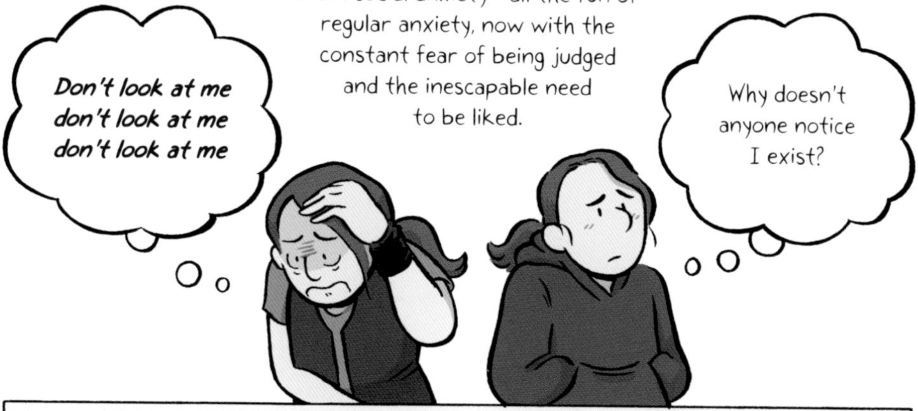
Don't look at me don't look at me don't look at me
Why doesn't anyone notice I exist?

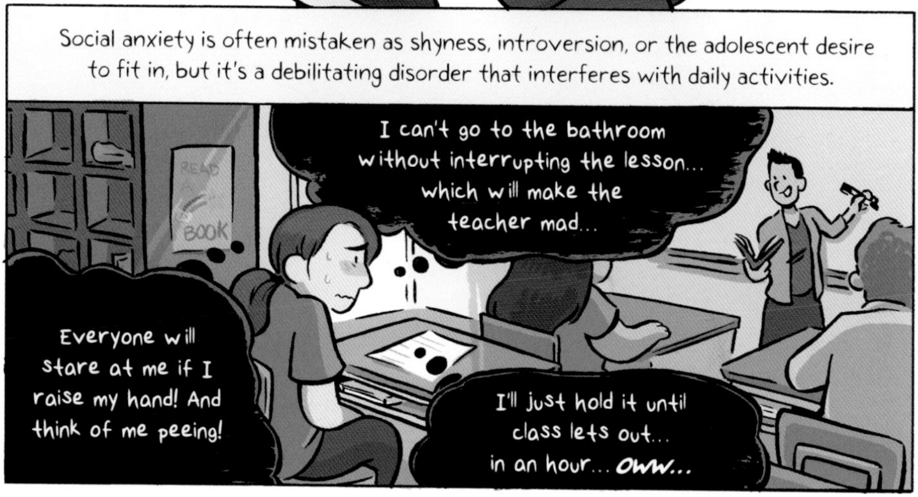
Social anxiety is often mistaken as shyness, introversion, or the adolescent desire to fit in, but it's a debilitating disorder that interferes with daily activities.
I can't go to the bathroom without interrupting the lesson... which will make the teacher mad...
Everyone will stare at me if I raise my hand! And think of me peeing!
I'll just hold it until class lets out... in an hour... ***OWW...***
READ A BOOK

I didn't *want* to care about what other people thought of me, but it was so physically ingrained in me that I couldn't ***not*** care.

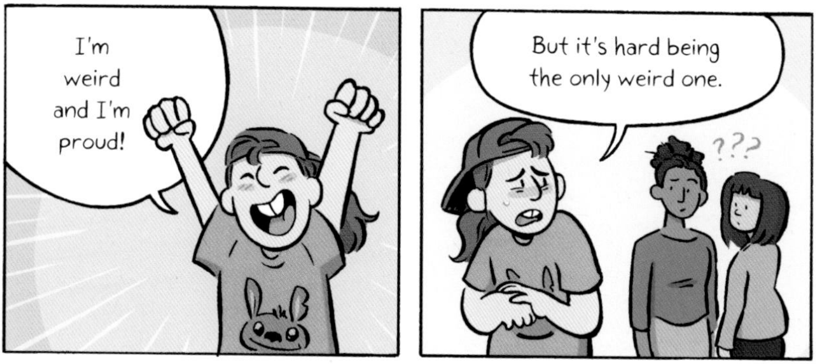
I'm weird and I'm proud!
But it's hard being the only weird one.
???

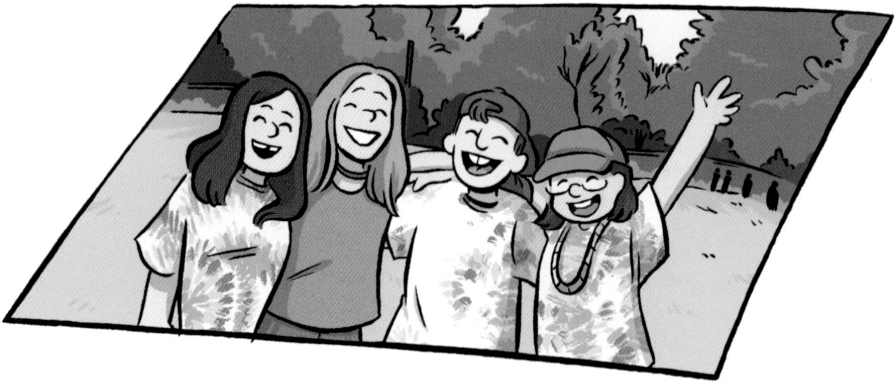

My social anxiety spiked when my core friend group
drifted apart in middle school.

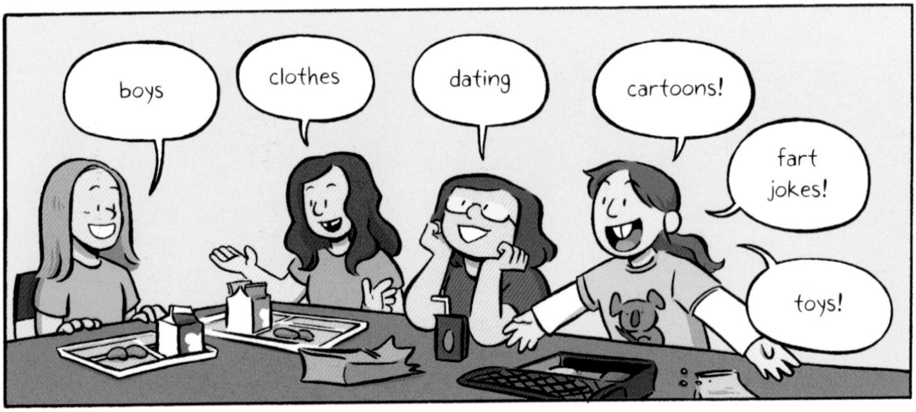
boys
clothes
dating
cartoons!
fart jokes!
toys!

It's natural to grow apart and want different things, but at the time
I could only come up with one reason for the split.

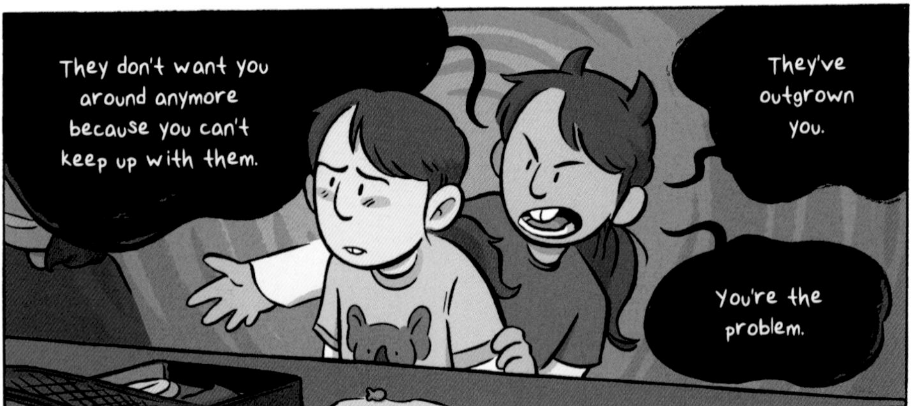
They don't want you around anymore because you can't keep up with them.
They've outgrown you.
You're the problem.

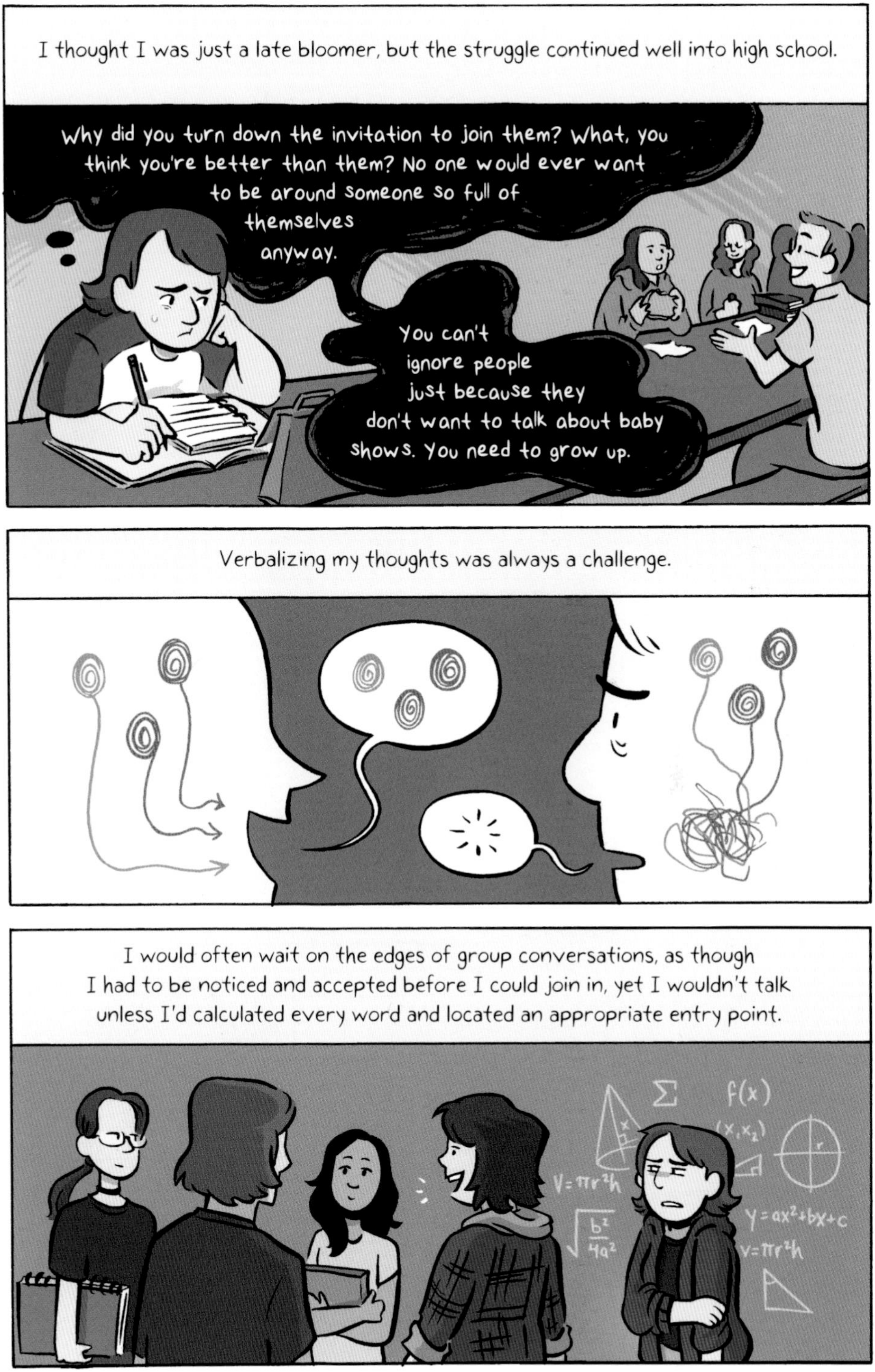
I thought I was just a late bloomer, but the struggle continued well into high school.
Why did you turn down the invitation to join them? What, you think you're better than them? No one would ever want to be around someone so full of themselves anyway.
You can't ignore people just because they don't want to talk about baby shows. You need to grow up.
Verbalizing my thoughts was always a challenge.
I would often wait on the edges of group conversations, as though I had to be noticed and accepted before I could join in, yet I wouldn't talk unless I'd calculated every word and located an appropriate entry point.
Σ
f(x)
V=πr²h
y=ax²+bx+c
V=πr²h

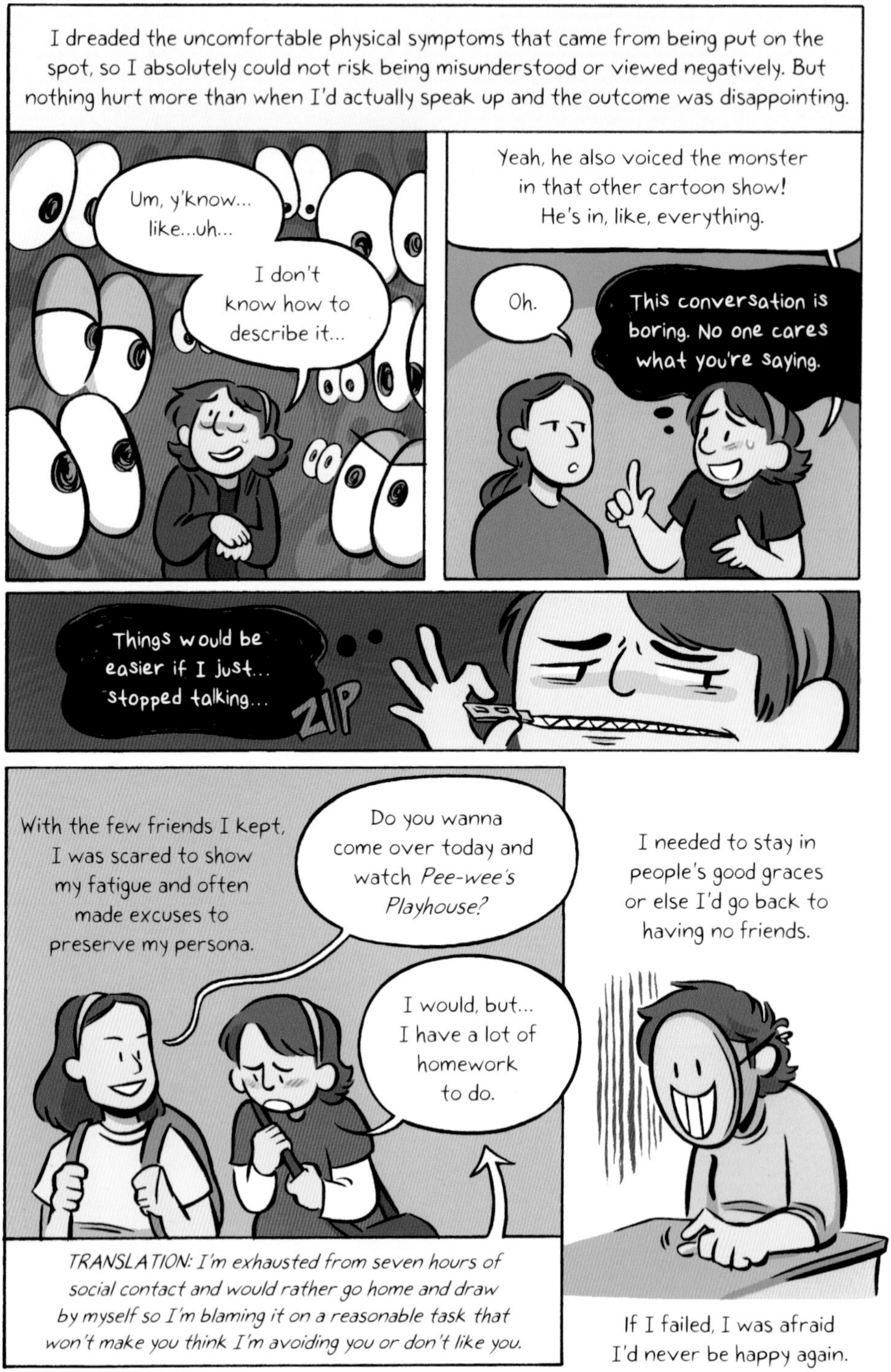
I dreaded the uncomfortable physical symptoms that came from being put on the spot, so I absolutely could not risk being misunderstood or viewed negatively. But nothing hurt more than when I'd actually speak up and the outcome was disappointing.
Um, y'know... like...uh...
I don't know how to describe it...
Yeah, he also voiced the monster in that other cartoon show! He's in, like, everything.
Oh.
This conversation is boring. No one cares what you're saying.
Things would be easier if I just... stopped talking...
ZIP
With the few friends I kept, I was scared to show my fatigue and often made excuses to preserve my persona.
Do you wanna come over today and watch *Pee-wee's Playhouse?*
I would, but... I have a lot of homework to do.
TRANSLATION: I'm exhausted from seven hours of social contact and would rather go home and draw by myself so I'm blaming it on a reasonable task that won't make you think I'm avoiding you or don't like you.
I needed to stay in people's good graces or else I'd go back to having no friends.
If I failed, I was afraid I'd never be happy again.

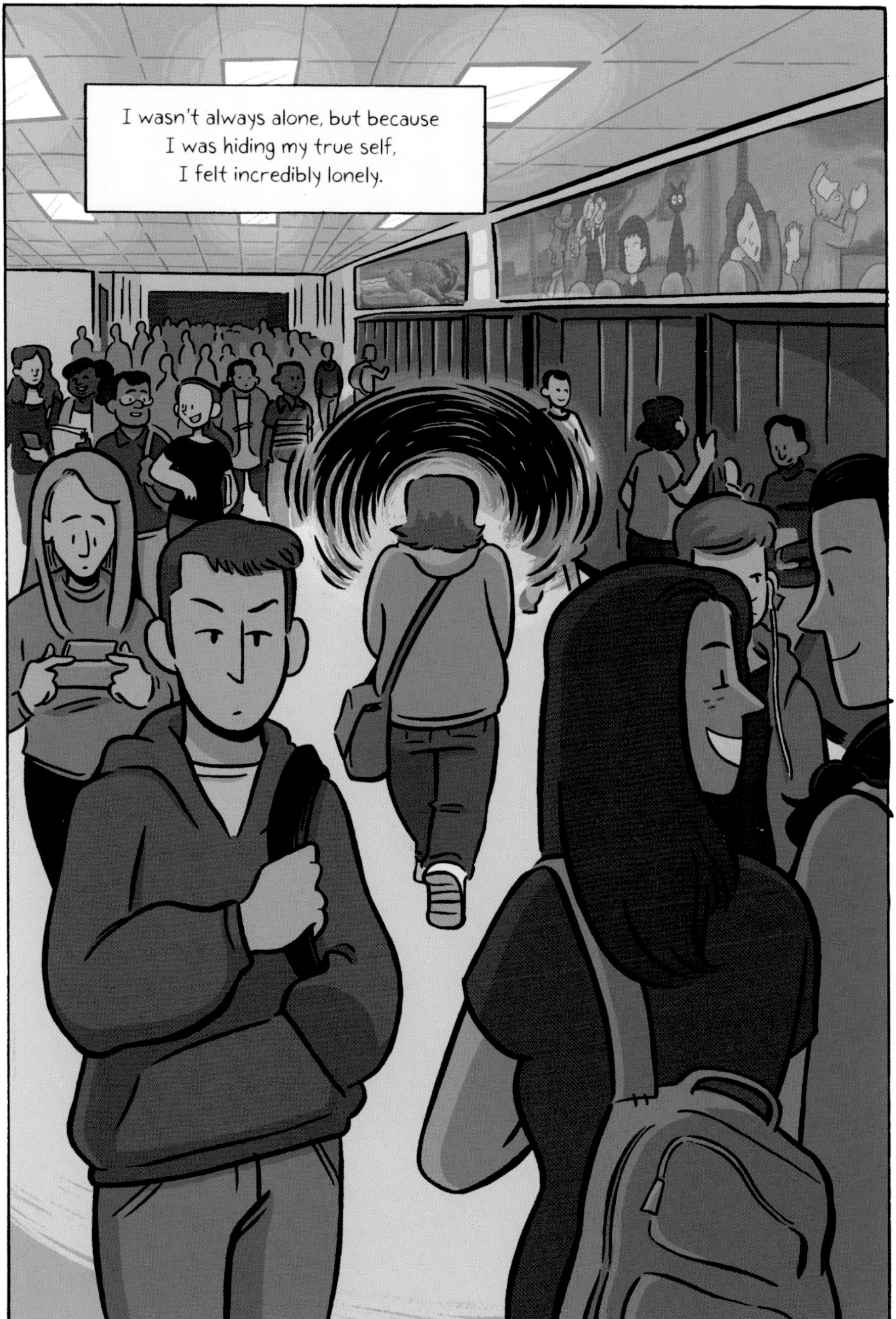
I wasn't always alone, but because
I was hiding my true self,
I felt incredibly lonely.

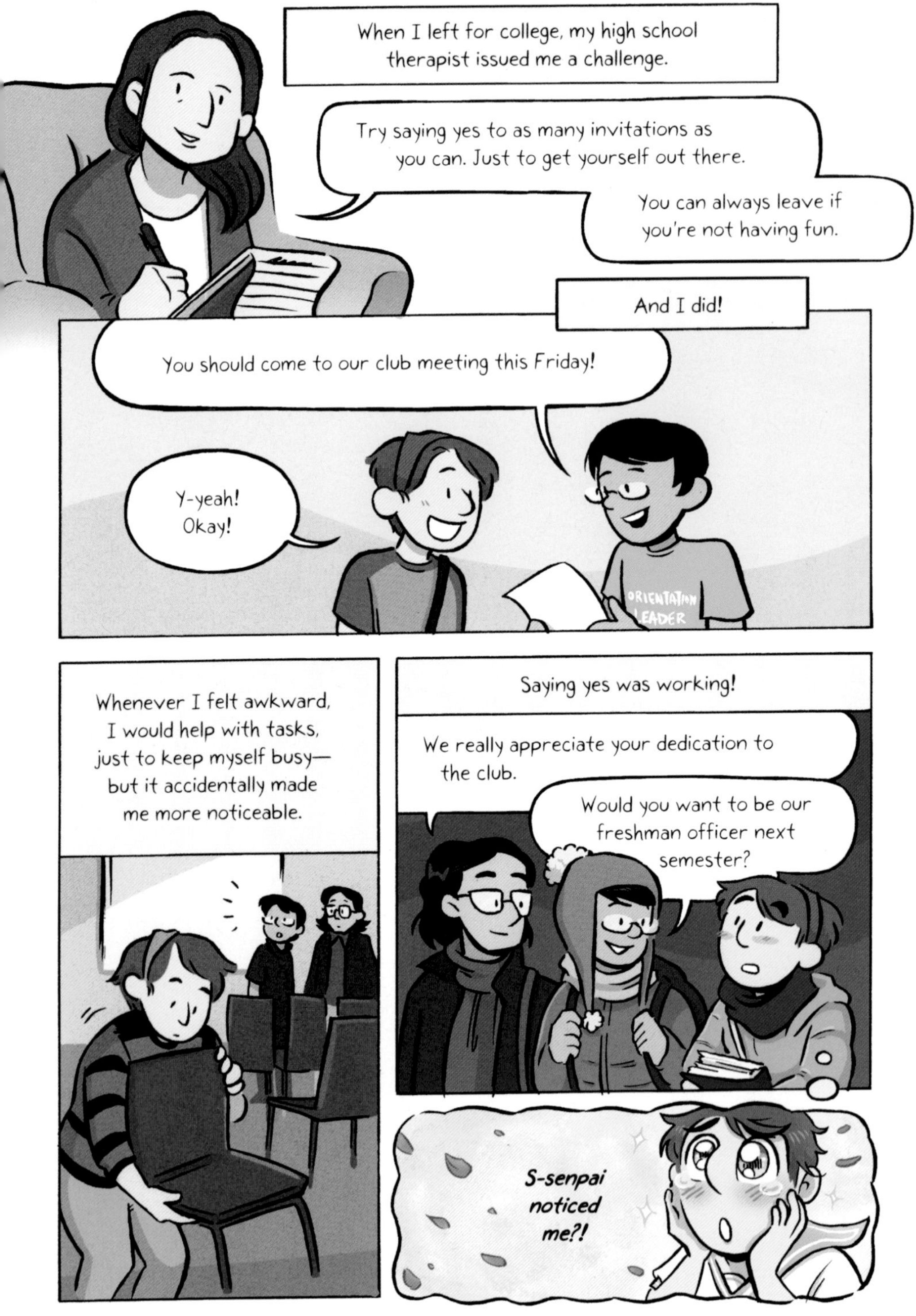
When I left for college, my high school therapist issued me a challenge.
Try saying yes to as many invitations as you can. Just to get yourself out there.
You can always leave if you're not having fun.
And I did!
You should come to our club meeting this Friday!
Y-yeah! Okay!
ORIENTATION LEADER
Whenever I felt awkward, I would help with tasks, just to keep myself busy—but it accidentally made me more noticeable.
Saying yes was working!
We really appreciate your dedication to the club.
Would you want to be our freshman officer next semester?
S-senpai noticed me?!

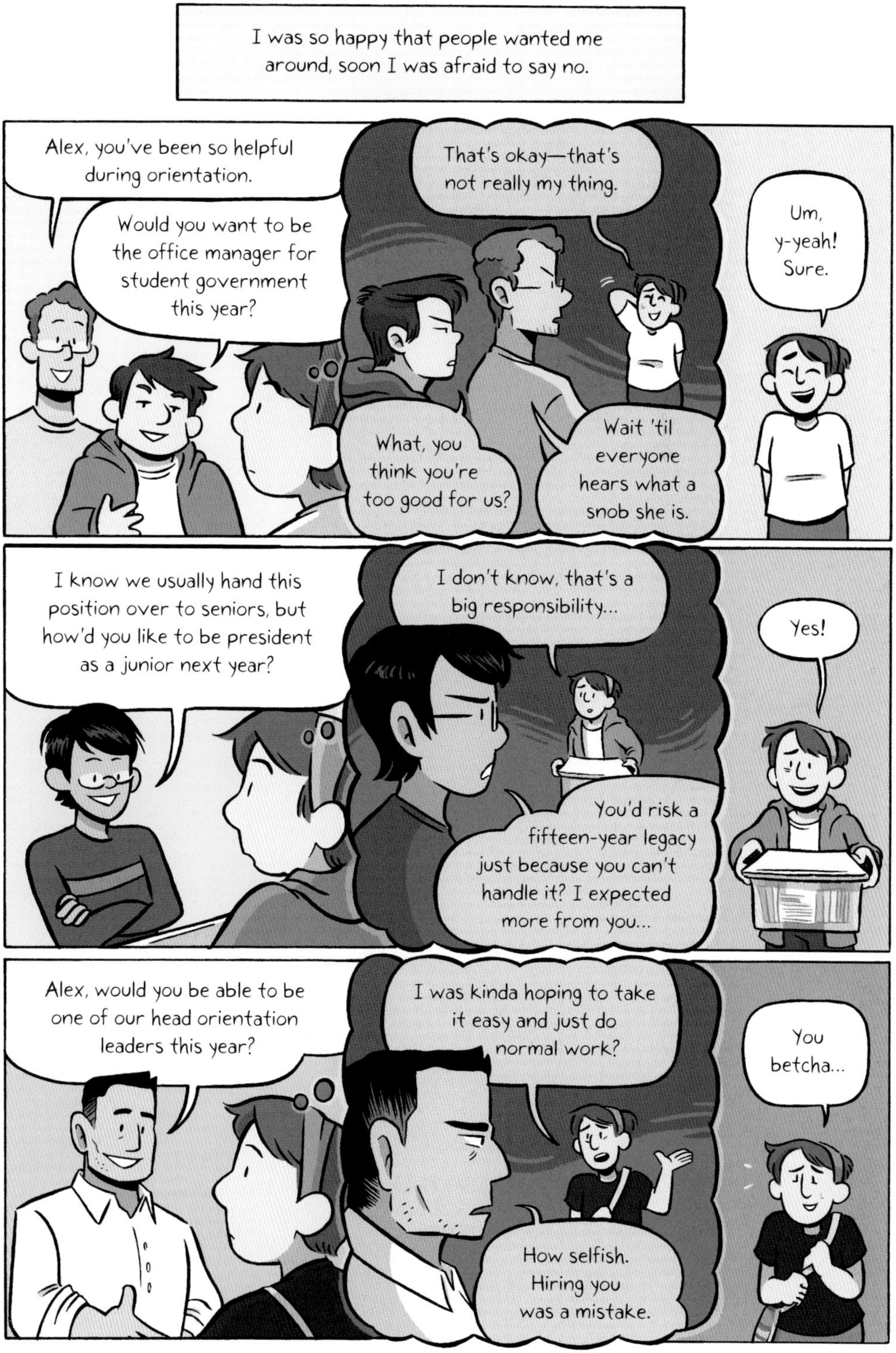
I was so happy that people wanted me around, soon I was afraid to say no.
Alex, you've been so helpful during orientation.
Would you want to be the office manager for student government this year?
That's okay—that's not really my thing.
What, you think you're too good for us?
Wait 'til everyone hears what a snob she is.
Um, y-yeah! Sure.
I know we usually hand this position over to seniors, but how'd you like to be president as a junior next year?
I don't know, that's a big responsibility...
You'd risk a fifteen-year legacy just because you can't handle it? I expected more from you...
Yes!
Alex, would you be able to be one of our head orientation leaders this year?
I was kinda hoping to take it easy and just do normal work?
How selfish. Hiring you was a mistake.
You betcha...

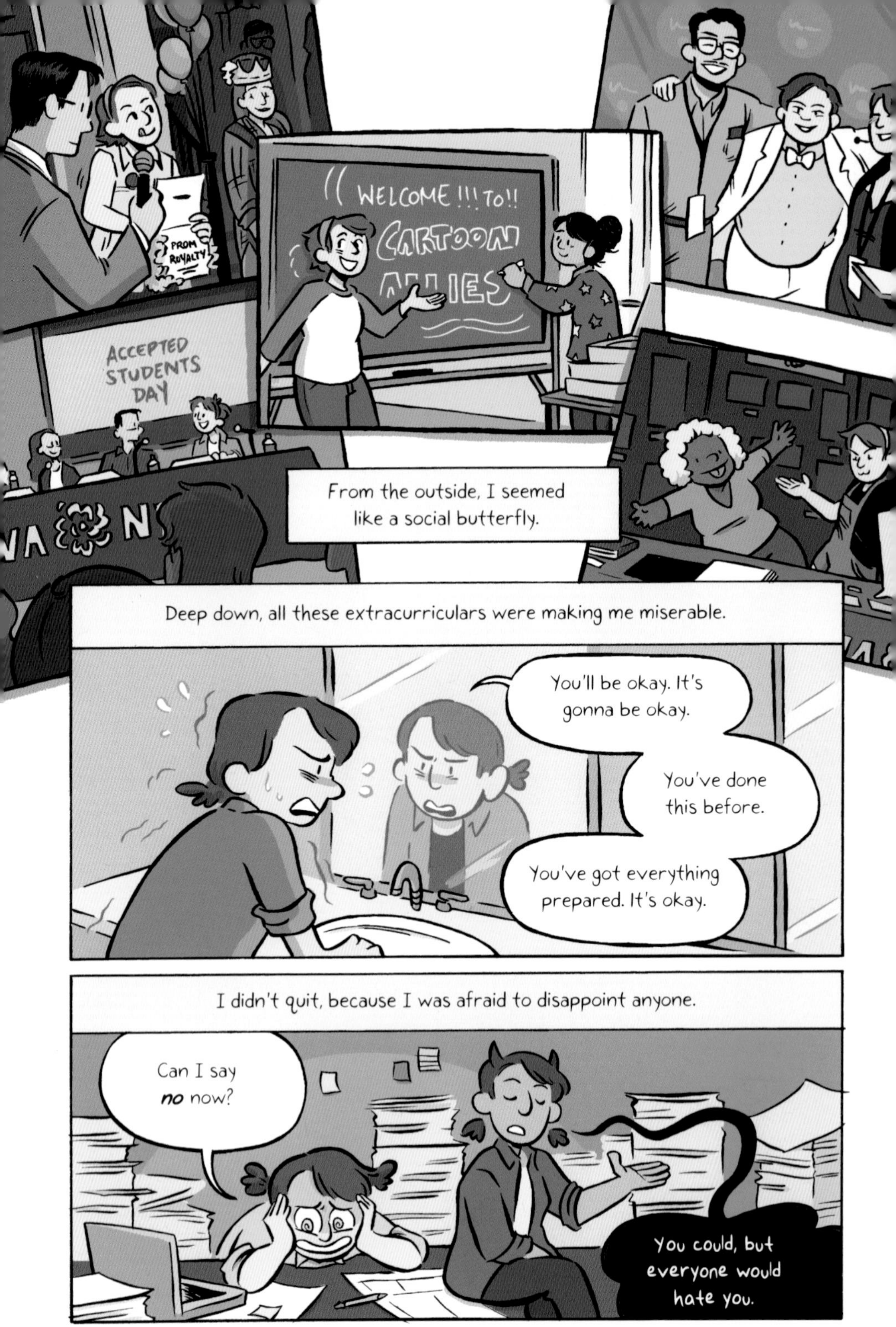
PROM ROYALTY
WELCOME!!! TO!! CARTOON ALLIES
ACCEPTED STUDENTS DAY
From the outside, I seemed like a social butterfly.
Deep down, all these extracurriculars were making me miserable.
You'll be okay. It's gonna be okay.
You've done this before.
You've got everything prepared. It's okay.
I didn't quit, because I was afraid to disappoint anyone.
Can I say *no* now?
You could, but everyone would hate you.

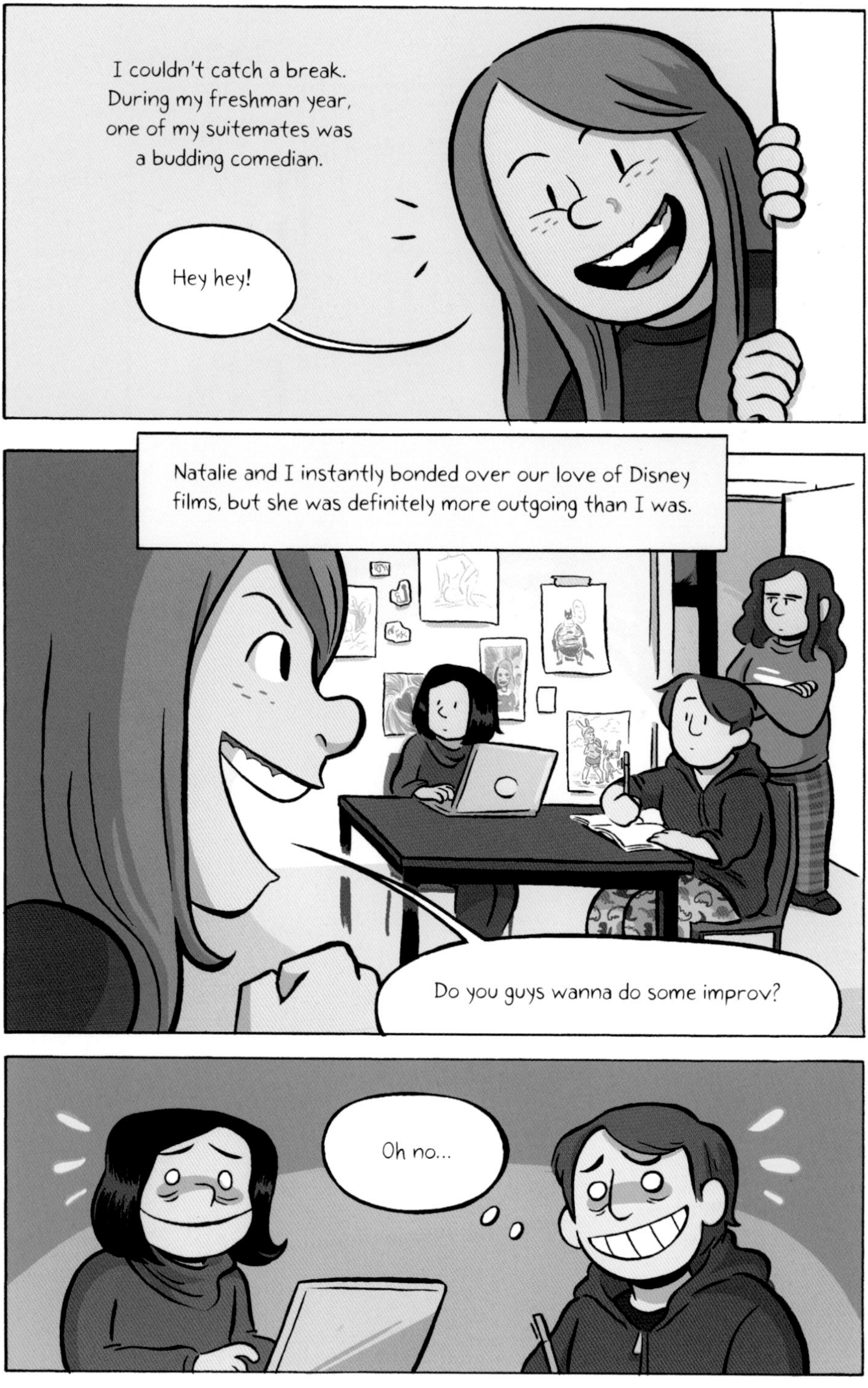
I couldn't catch a break. During my freshman year, one of my suitemates was a budding comedian.
Hey hey!
Natalie and I instantly bonded over our love of Disney films, but she was definitely more outgoing than I was.
Do you guys wanna do some improv?
Oh no...

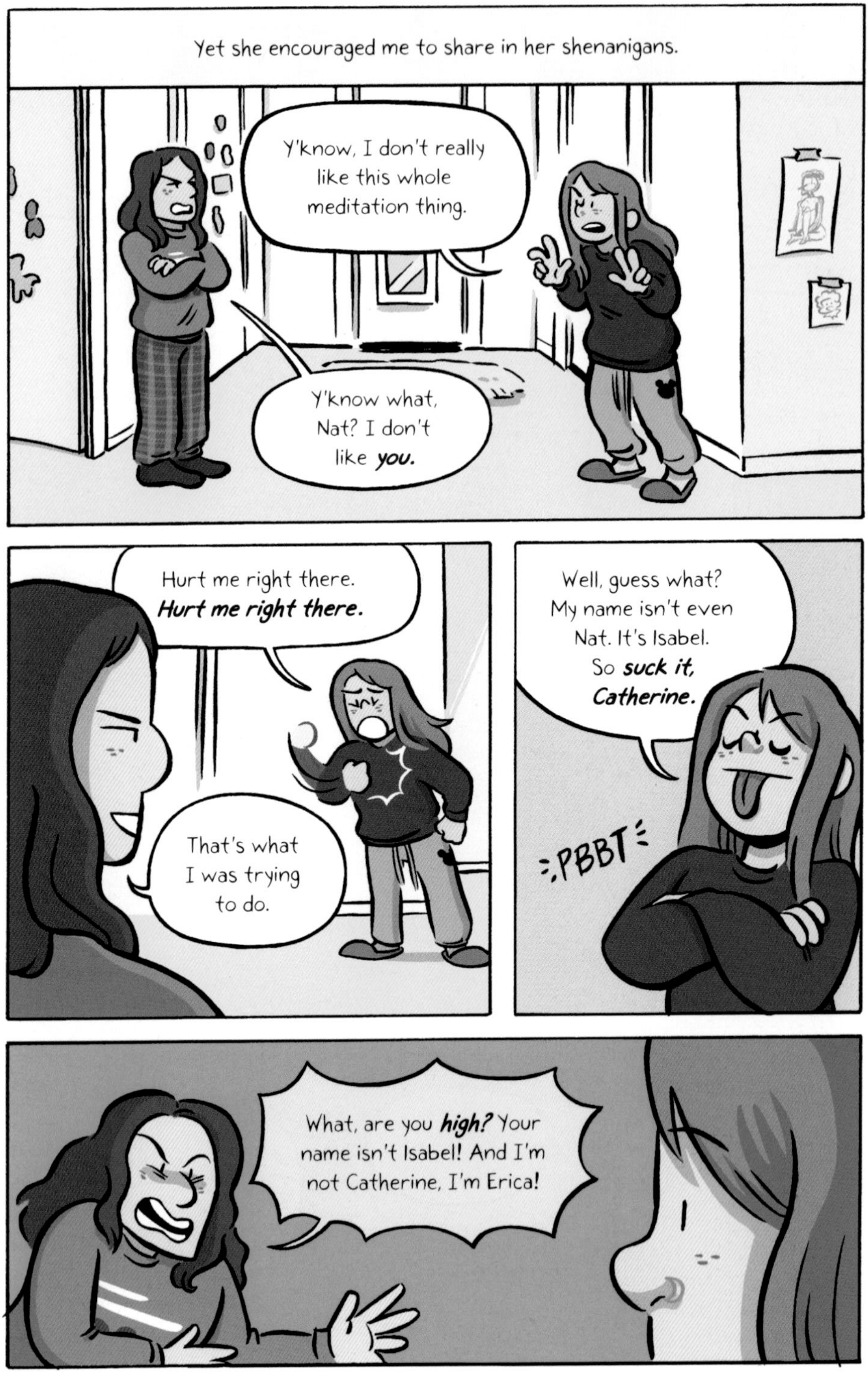
Yet she encouraged me to share in her shenanigans.
Y'know, I don't really like this whole meditation thing.
Y'know what, Nat? I don't like *you.*
Hurt me right there. ***Hurt me right there.***
That's what I was trying to do.
Well, guess what? My name isn't even Nat. It's Isabel. So ***suck it, Catherine.***
PBBT
What, are you ***high?*** Your name isn't Isabel! And I'm not Catherine, I'm Erica!

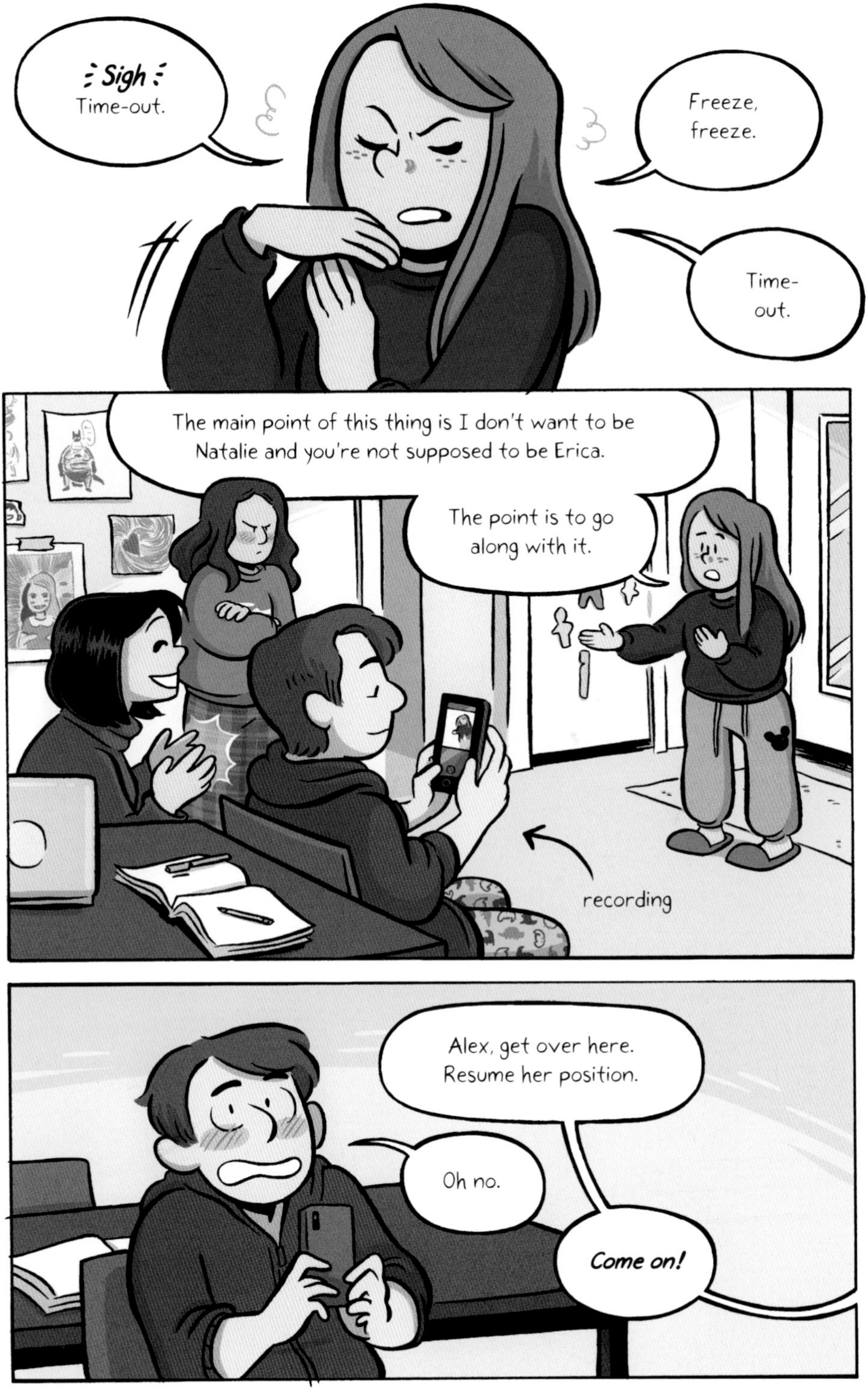

Sigh
Time-out.
Freeze, freeze.
Time-out.
The main point of this thing is I don't want to be Natalie and you're not supposed to be Erica.
The point is to go along with it.
recording
Alex, get over here. Resume her position.
Oh no.
Come on!

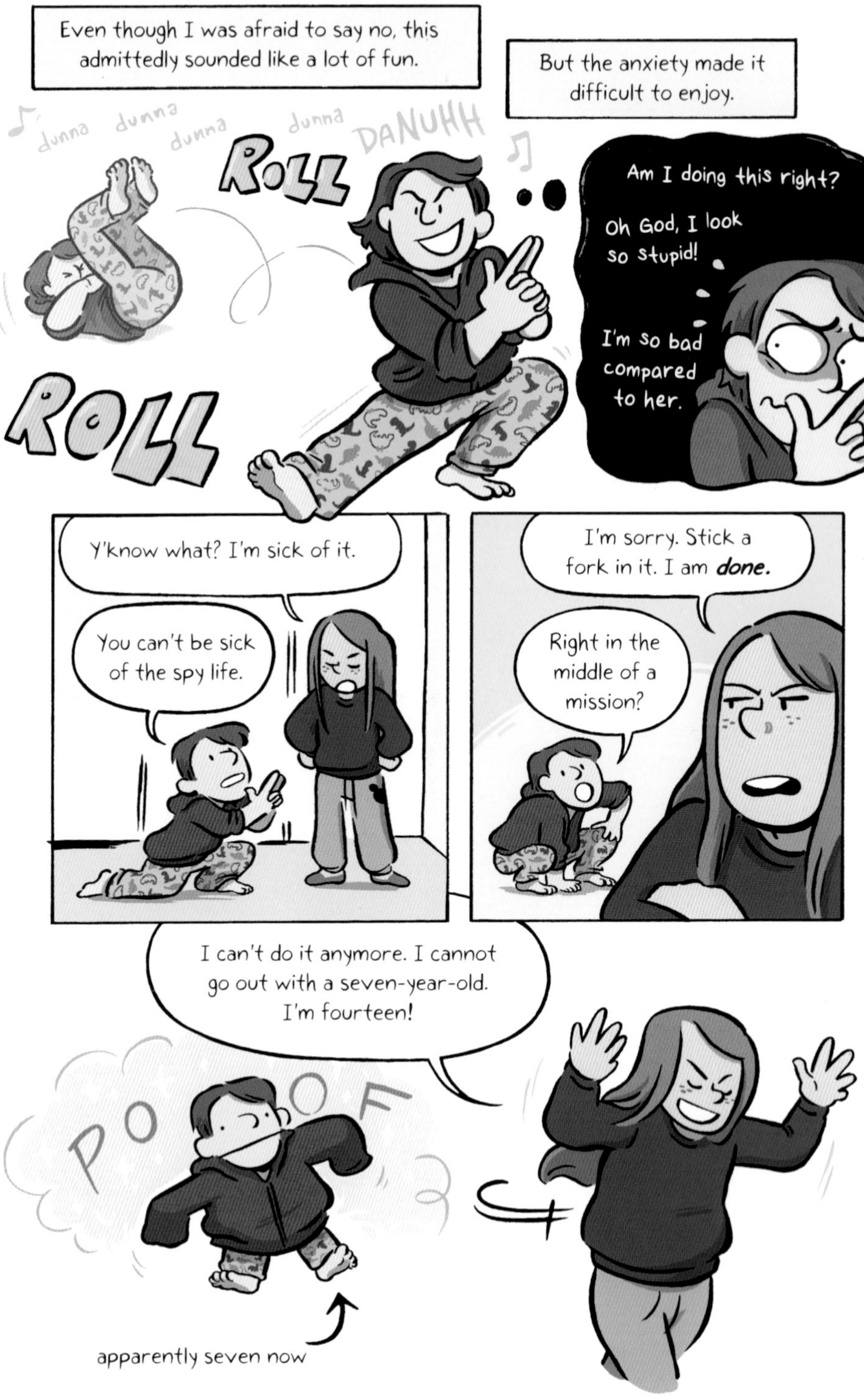
Even though I was afraid to say no, this admittedly sounded like a lot of fun.
dunna dunna dunna dunna DANUHH
ROLL
ROLL
But the anxiety made it difficult to enjoy.
Am I doing this right?
Oh God, I look so stupid!
I'm so bad compared to her.
Y'know what? I'm sick of it.
You can't be sick of the spy life.
I'm sorry. Stick a fork in it. I am **done.**
Right in the middle of a mission?
I can't do it anymore. I cannot go out with a seven-year-old. I'm fourteen!
POOF
apparently seven now

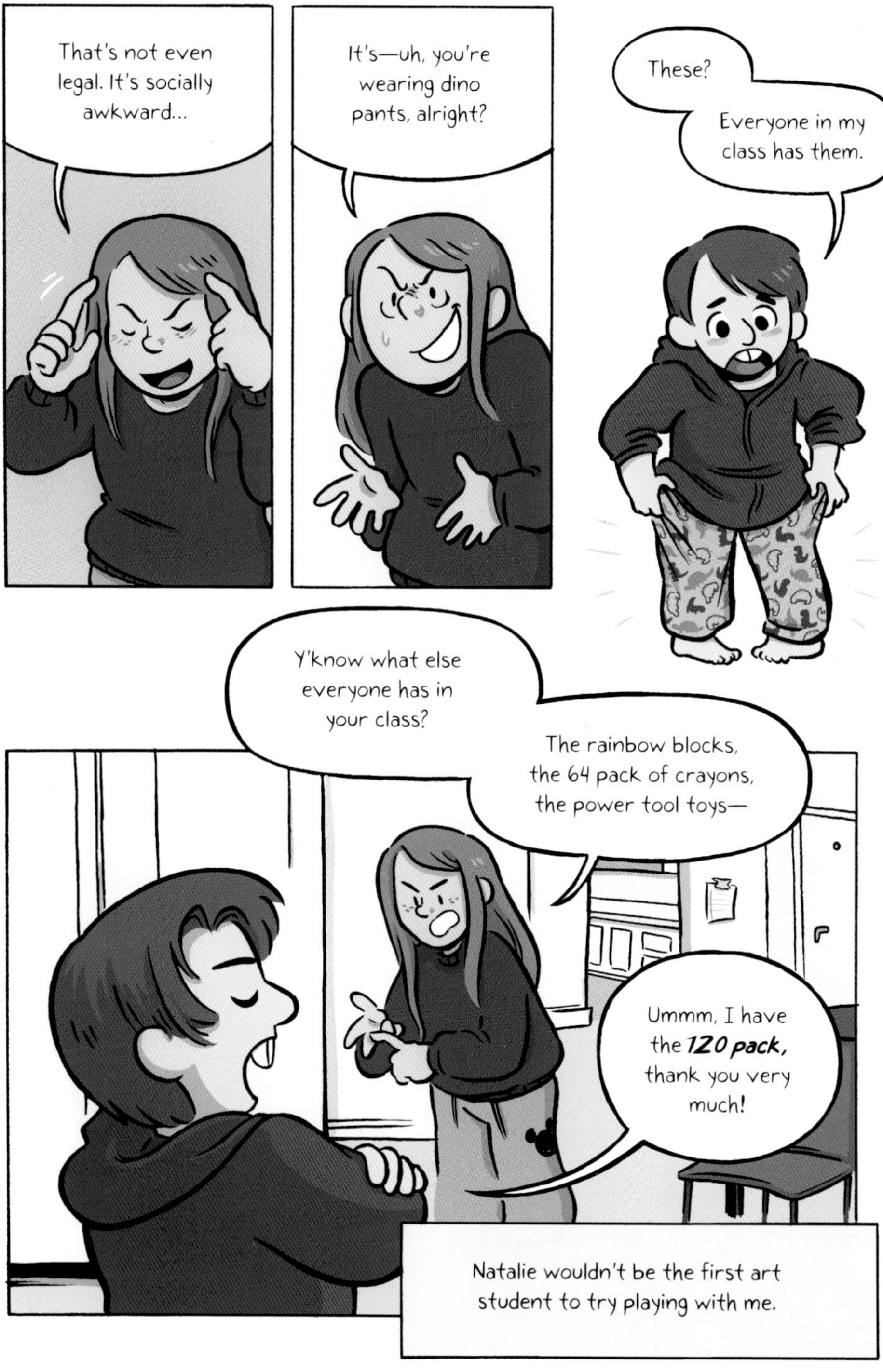

That's not even legal. It's socially awkward...
It's—uh, you're wearing dino pants, alright?
These?
Everyone in my class has them.
Y'know what else everyone has in your class?
The rainbow blocks, the 64 pack of crayons, the power tool toys—
Ummm, I have the **120 pack,** thank you very much!
Natalie wouldn't be the first art student to try playing with me.

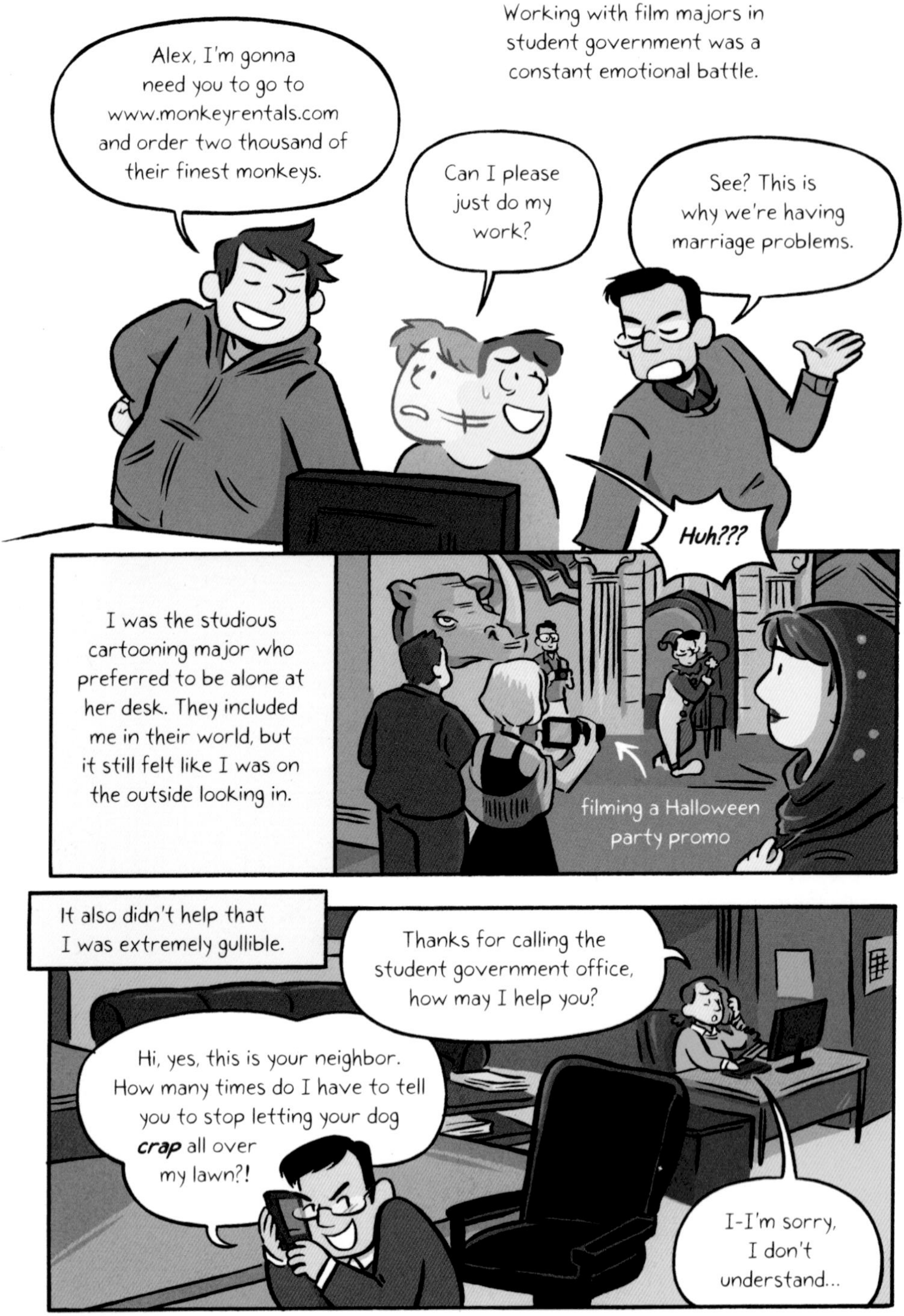
Working with film majors in student government was a constant emotional battle.
Alex, I'm gonna need you to go to www.monkeyrentals.com and order two thousand of their finest monkeys.
Can I please just do my work?
See? This is why we're having marriage problems.
Huh???
I was the studious cartooning major who preferred to be alone at her desk. They included me in their world, but it still felt like I was on the outside looking in.
filming a Halloween party promo
It also didn't help that I was extremely gullible.
Thanks for calling the student government office, how may I help you?
Hi, yes, this is your neighbor. How many times do I have to tell you to stop letting your dog ***crap*** all over my lawn?!
I-I'm sorry, I don't understand...

The pressure to perform even followed me home, where my dad and sister often riffed over dinner.

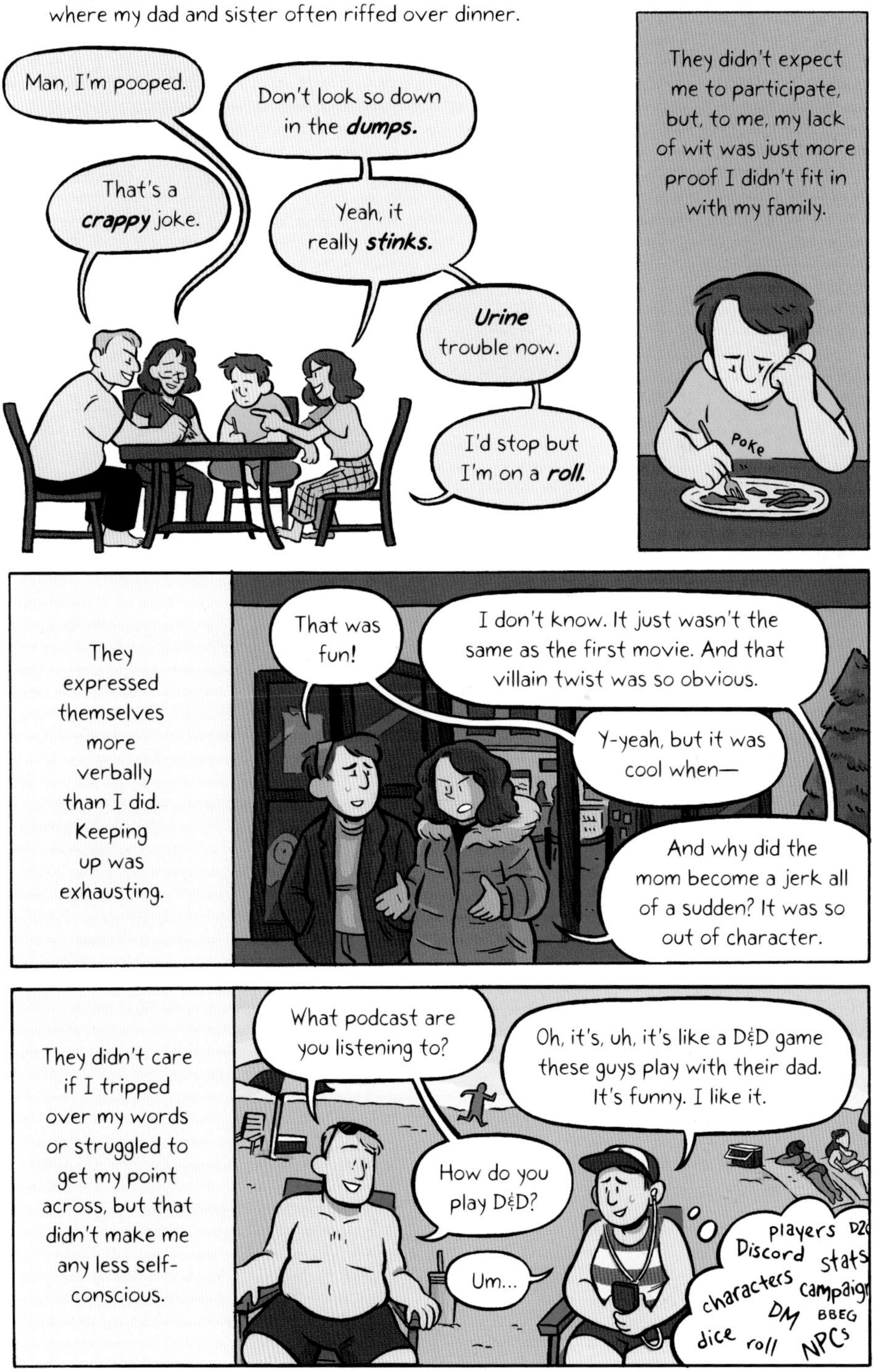
Man, I'm pooped.
That's a *crappy* joke.
Don't look so down in the *dumps.*
Yeah, it really *stinks.*
Urine trouble now.
I'd stop but I'm on a *roll.*
They didn't expect me to participate, but, to me, my lack of wit was just more proof I didn't fit in with my family.
Poke
They expressed themselves more verbally than I did. Keeping up was exhausting.
That was fun!
I don't know. It just wasn't the same as the first movie. And that villain twist was so obvious.
Y-yeah, but it was cool when—
And why did the mom become a jerk all of a sudden? It was so out of character.
They didn't care if I tripped over my words or struggled to get my point across, but that didn't make me any less self-conscious.
What podcast are you listening to?
Oh, it's, uh, it's like a D&D game these guys play with their dad. It's funny. I like it.
How do you play D&D?
Um...
players
Discord
stats
characters
DM
BBEG
dice
roll
NPCs

When Natalie started taking improv classes at the Upright Citizens Brigade, I kept telling myself I couldn't do what she did.

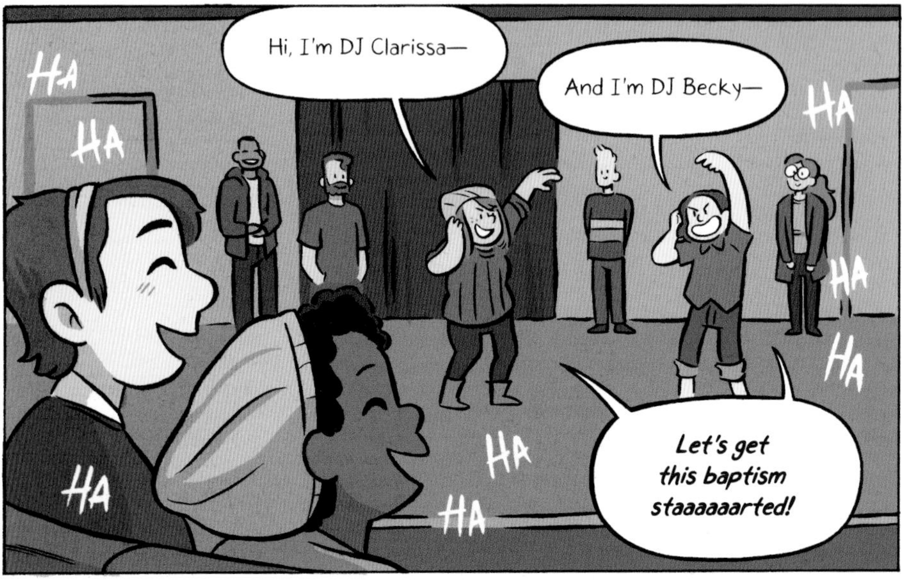

Hi, I'm DJ Clarissa—
And I'm DJ Becky—
Let's get this baptism staaaaaarted!
HA
HA
HA
HA
HA
HA
HA
HA
HA

To put myself out there, on the spot, and make people laugh with the first thing that popped into my mind seemed impossible. My anxiety would never let me do that.

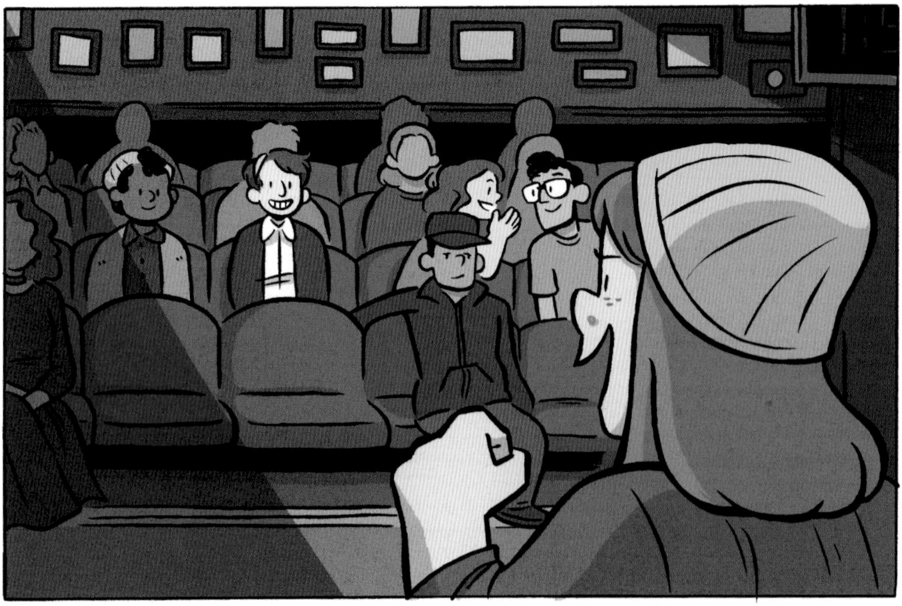

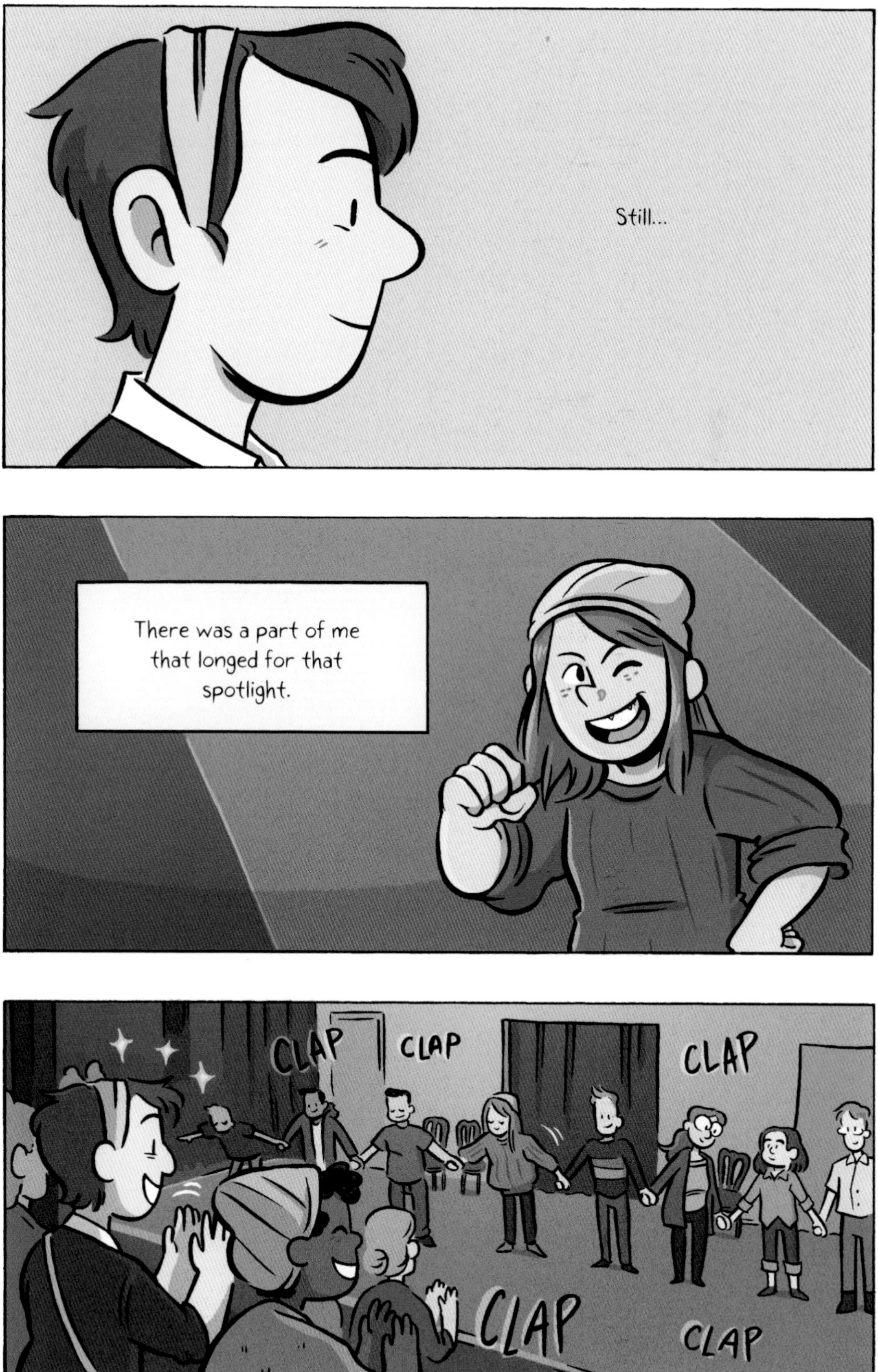

Still...
There was a part of me that longed for that spotlight.
CLAP
CLAP
CLAP
CLAP
CLAP

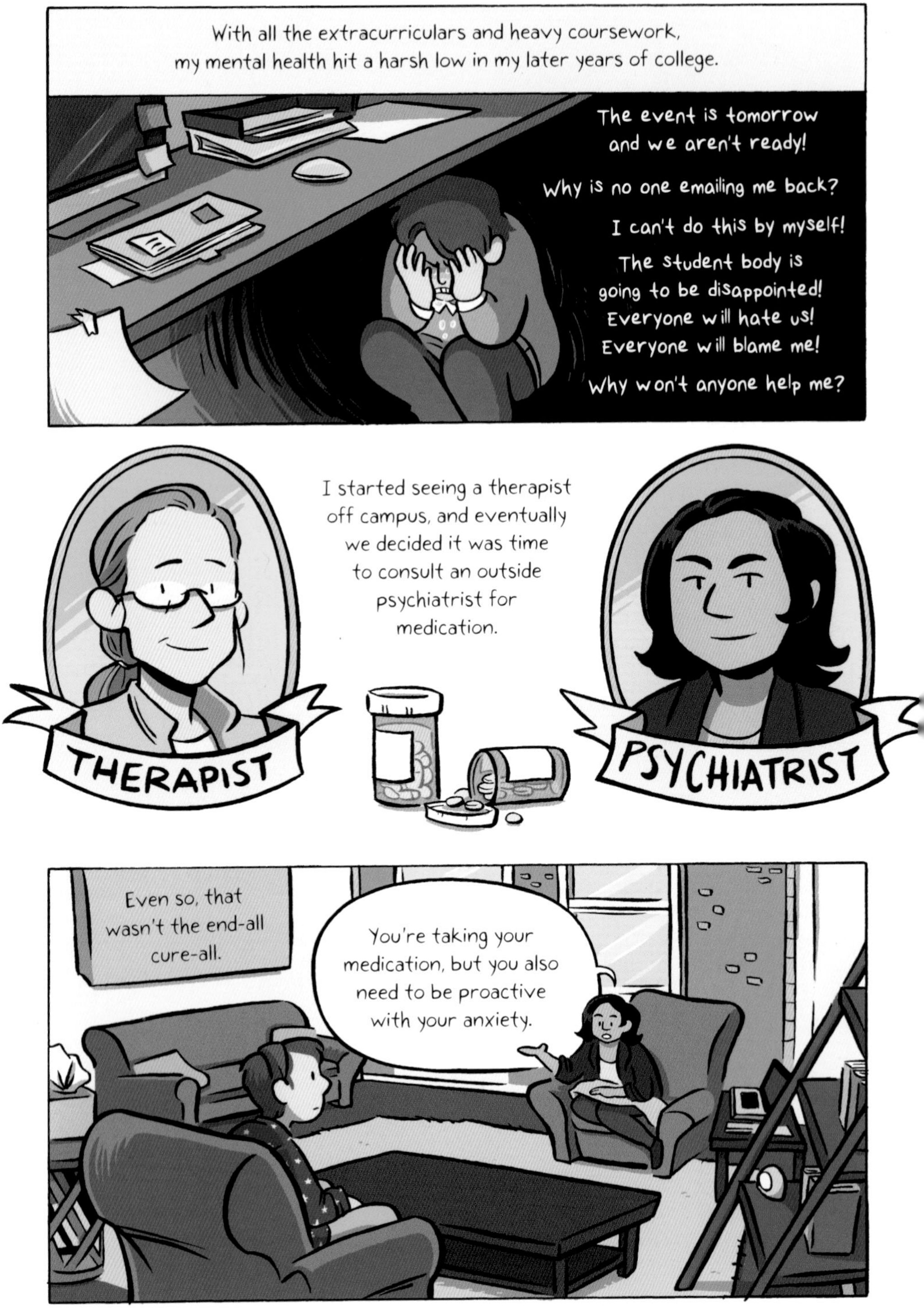
With all the extracurriculars and heavy coursework, my mental health hit a harsh low in my later years of college.
The event is tomorrow and we aren't ready!
Why is no one emailing me back?
I can't do this by myself!
The student body is going to be disappointed!
Everyone will hate us!
Everyone will blame me!
Why won't anyone help me?
I started seeing a therapist off campus, and eventually we decided it was time to consult an outside psychiatrist for medication.
THERAPIST
PSYCHIATRIST
Even so, that wasn't the end-all cure-all.
You're taking your medication, but you also need to be proactive with your anxiety.

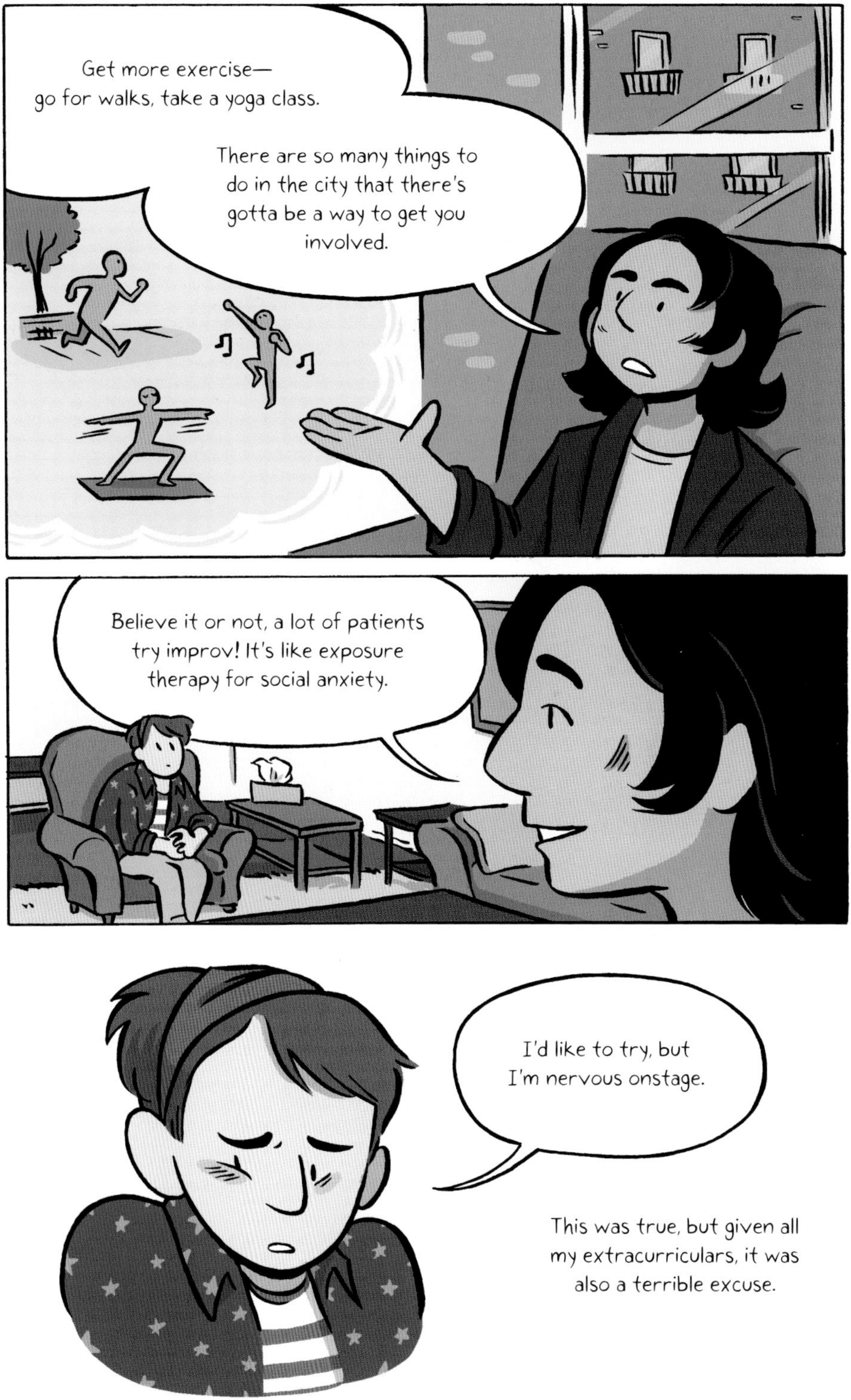
Get more exercise—go for walks, take a yoga class.
There are so many things to do in the city that there's gotta be a way to get you involved.
Believe it or not, a lot of patients try improv! It's like exposure therapy for social anxiety.
I'd like to try, but I'm nervous onstage.
This was true, but given all my extracurriculars, it was also a terrible excuse.

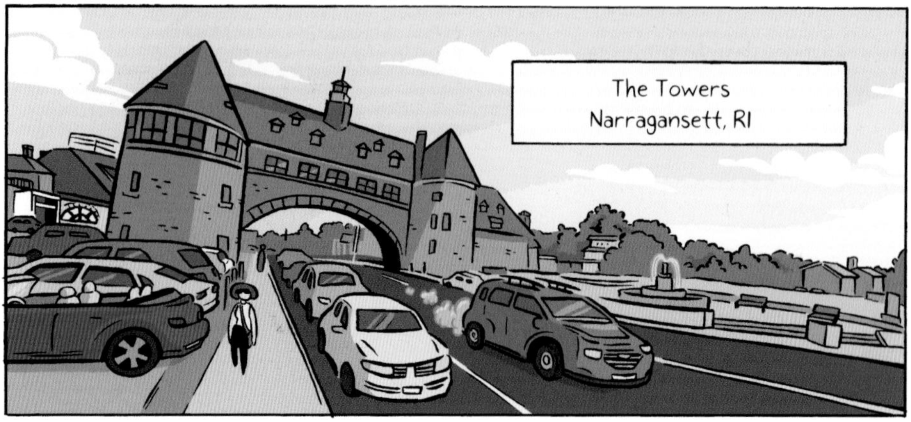
The Towers
Narragansett, RI

Around this time, my parents were trading in my childhood home
for a place near the beaches of southern Rhode Island.

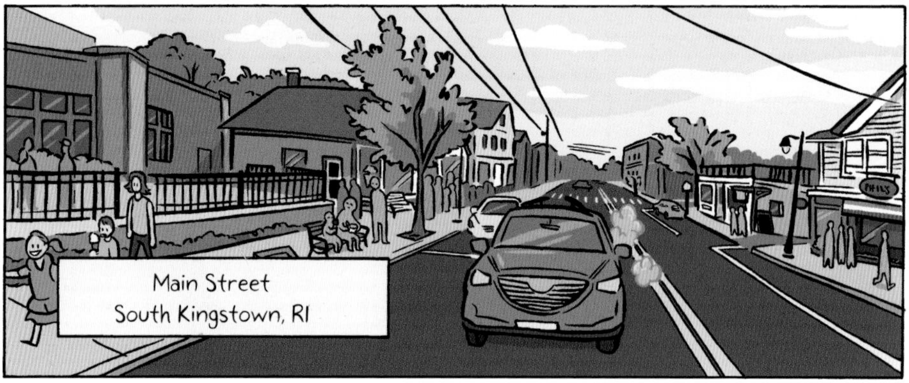
Main Street
South Kingstown, RI

My family had spent a few summers in the area, but
my grumpy teenage self never thought of it highly.

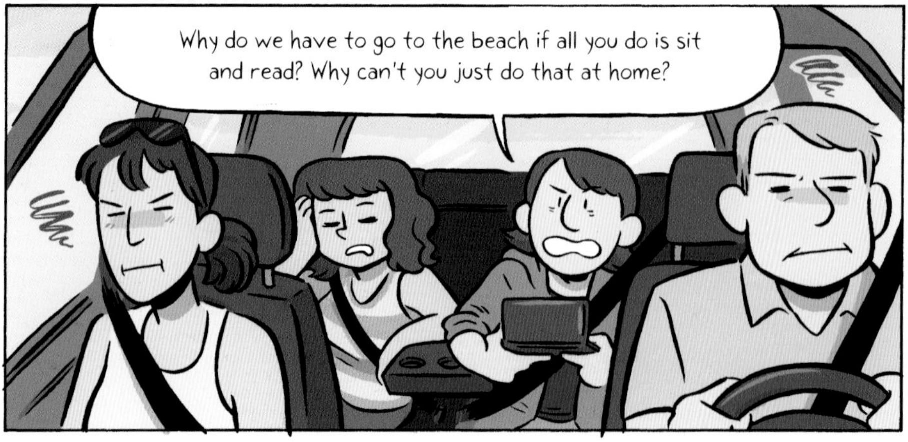
Why do we have to go to the beach if all you do is sit and read? Why can't you just do that at home?

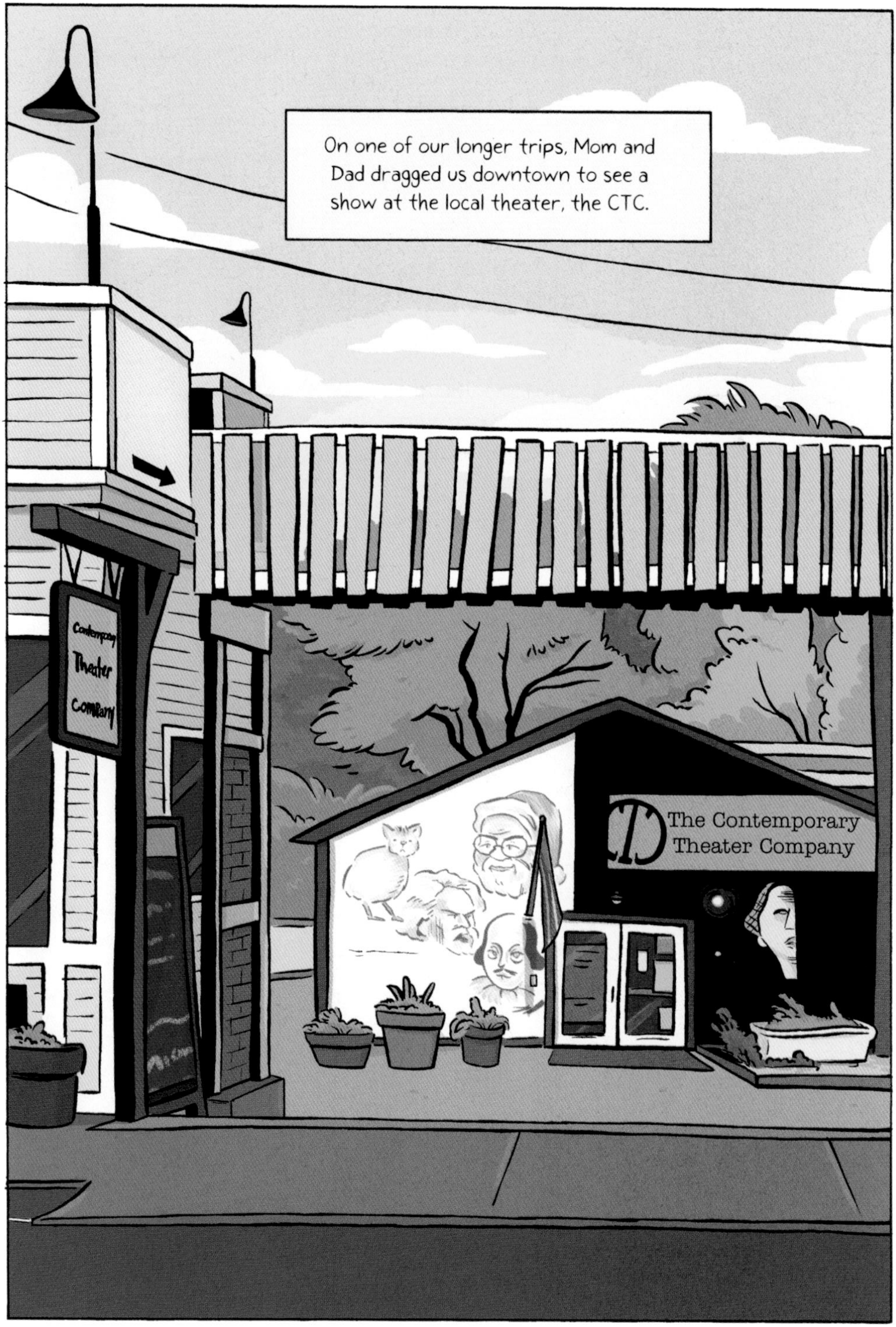
On one of our longer trips, Mom and Dad dragged us downtown to see a show at the local theater, the CTC.
Contemporary Theater Company
The Contemporary Theater Company

We never had a local theater space growing up, but it was still a lot smaller than I expected.

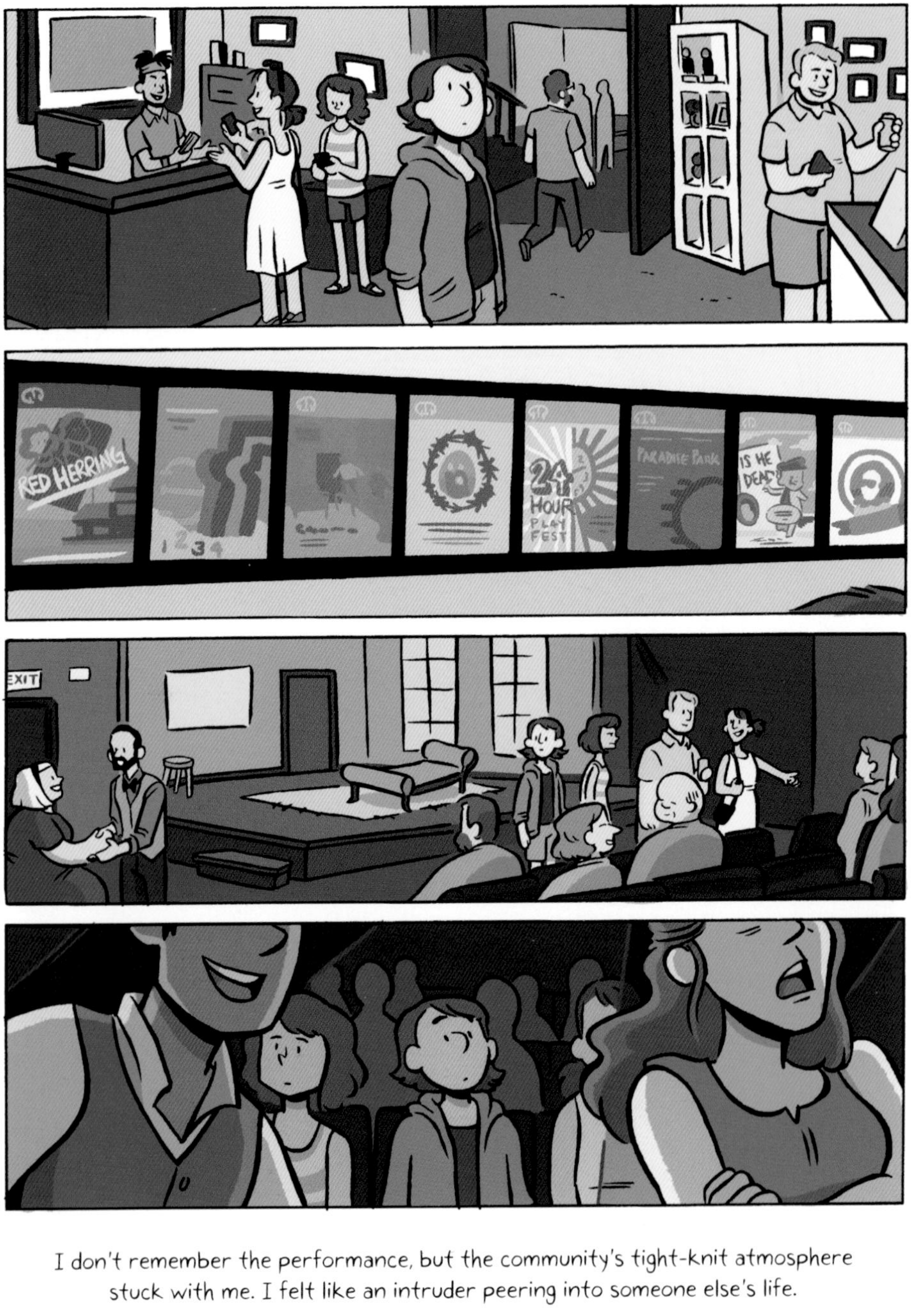
RED HERRING
1 2 3 4
24 HOUR PLAY FEST
PARADISE PARK

I don't remember the performance, but the community's tight-knit atmosphere stuck with me. I felt like an intruder peering into someone else's life.

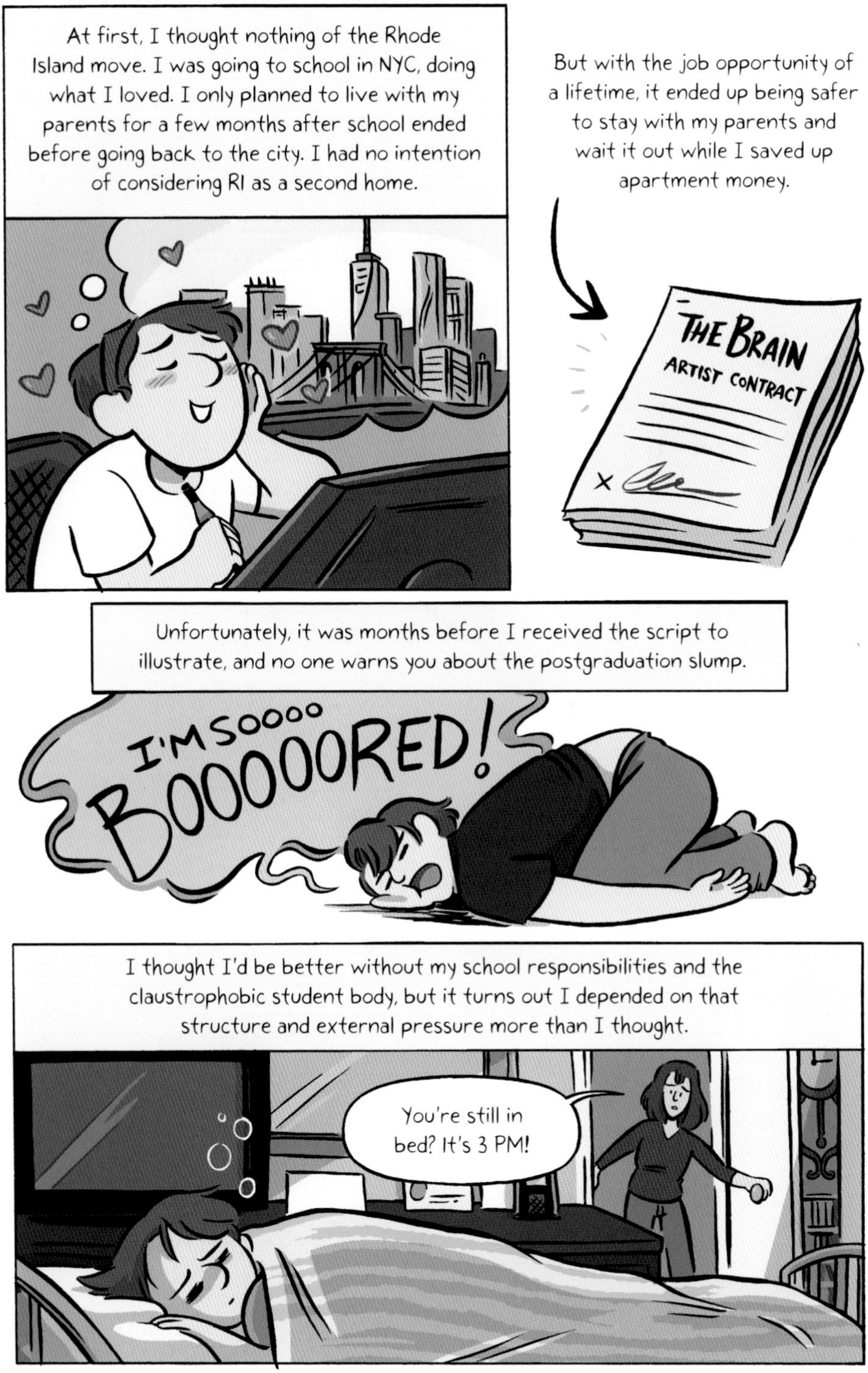
At first, I thought nothing of the Rhode Island move. I was going to school in NYC, doing what I loved. I only planned to live with my parents for a few months after school ended before going back to the city. I had no intention of considering RI as a second home.
But with the job opportunity of a lifetime, it ended up being safer to stay with my parents and wait it out while I saved up apartment money.
THE BRAIN
ARTIST CONTRACT
Unfortunately, it was months before I received the script to illustrate, and no one warns you about the postgraduation slump.
I'M SOOOO BOOOOORED!
I thought I'd be better without my school responsibilities and the claustrophobic student body, but it turns out I depended on that structure and external pressure more than I thought.
You're still in bed? It's 3 PM!

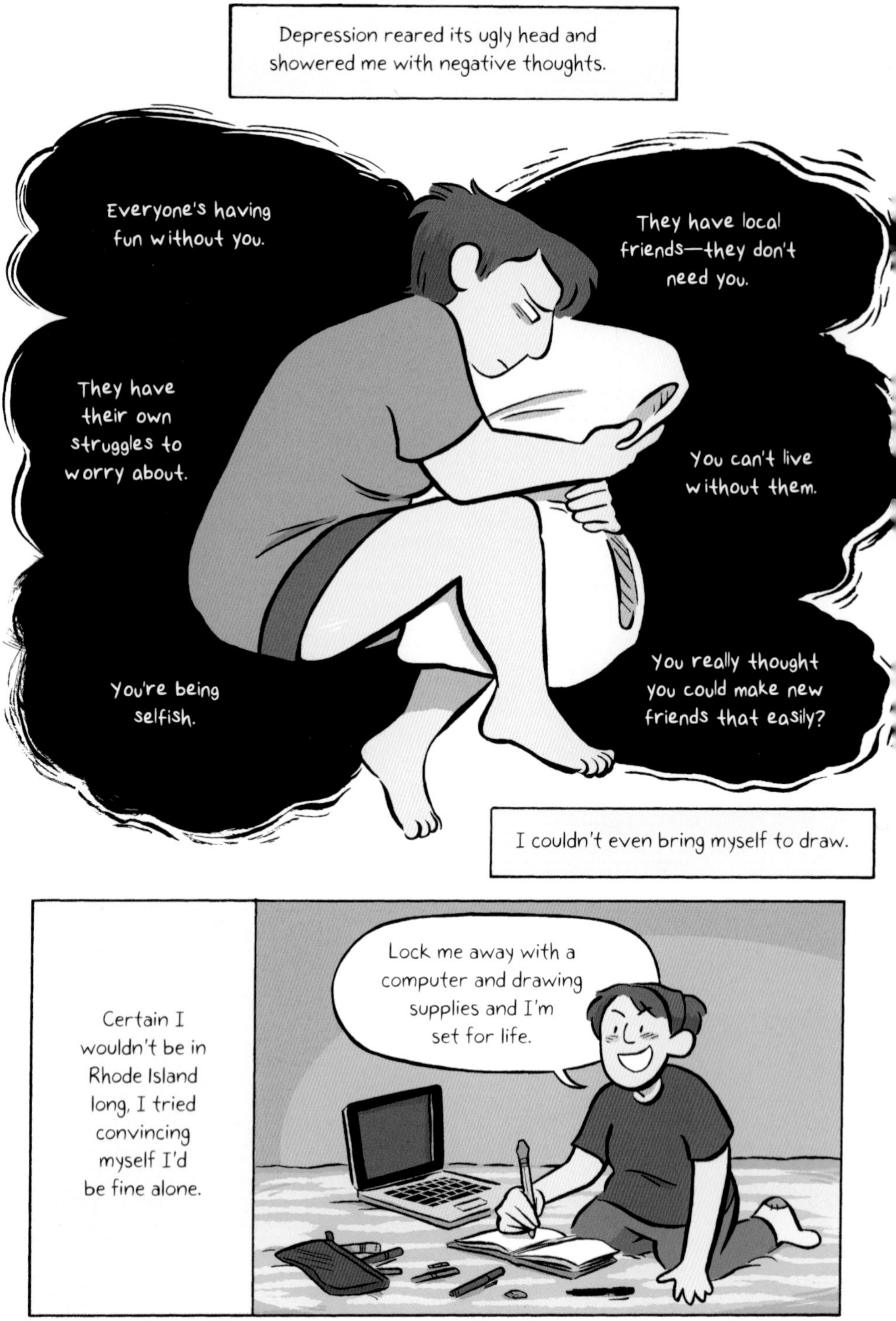
Depression reared its ugly head and showered me with negative thoughts.
Everyone's having fun without you.
They have local friends—they don't need you.
They have their own struggles to worry about.
You can't live without them.
You're being selfish.
You really thought you could make new friends that easily?
I couldn't even bring myself to draw.
Certain I wouldn't be in Rhode Island long, I tried convincing myself I'd be fine alone.
Lock me away with a computer and drawing supplies and I'm set for life.

But being alone and being lonely
are two very different things.

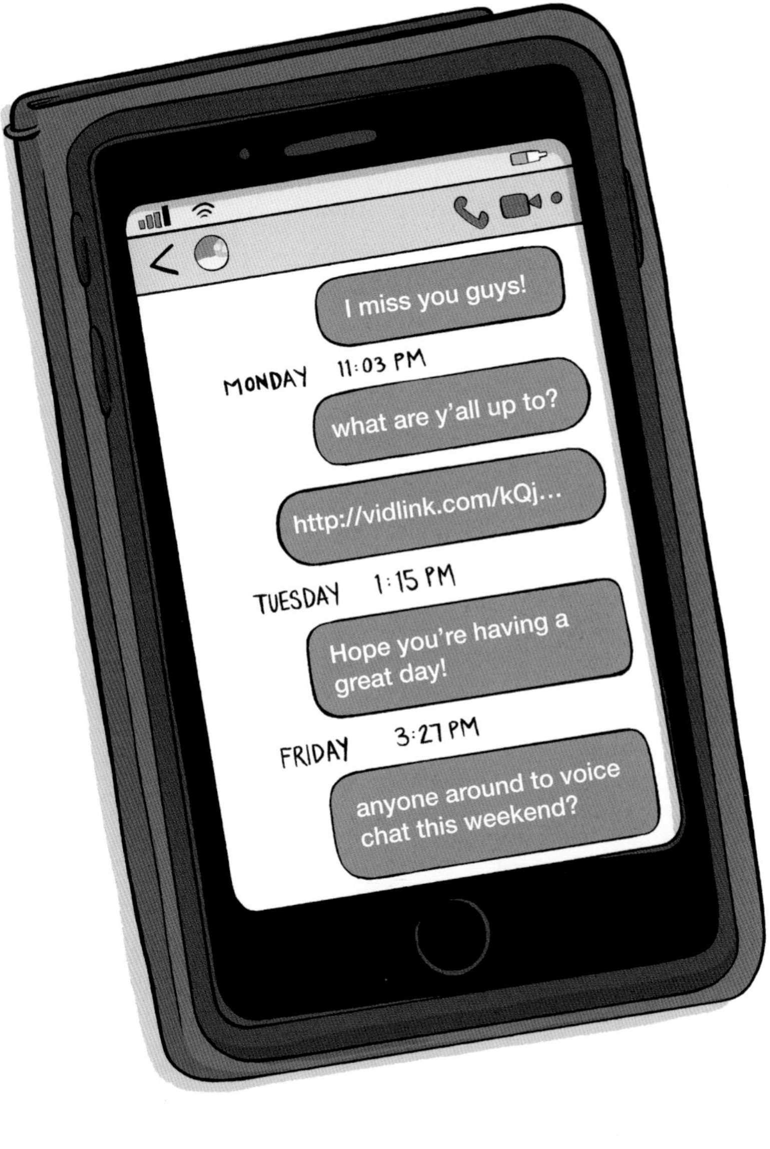
I miss you guys!
MONDAY 11:03 PM
what are y'all up to?
http://vidlink.com/kQj...
TUESDAY 1:15 PM
Hope you're having a great day!
FRIDAY 3:27 PM
anyone around to voice chat this weekend?

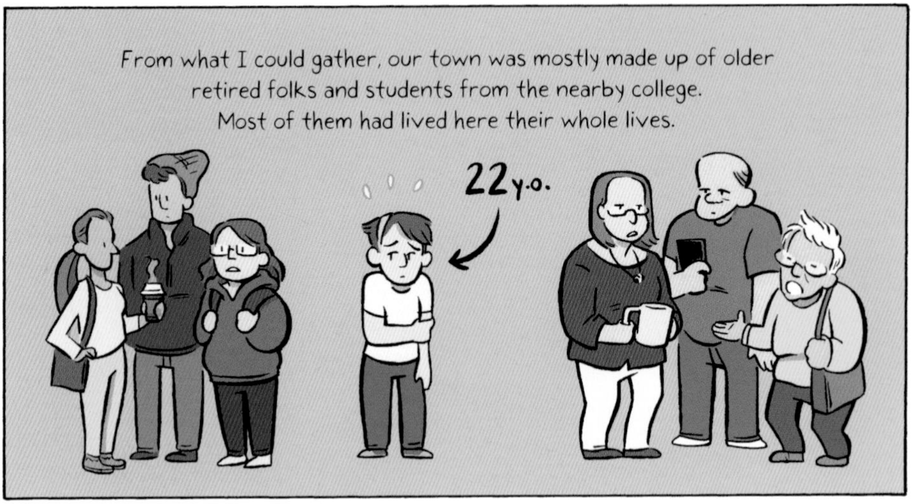
From what I could gather, our town was mostly made up of older retired folks and students from the nearby college. Most of them had lived here their whole lives.
22 y.o.

Miles away from my closest friends, in a new town where I was a stranger, I felt more isolated than ever.

The only people I hung out with were my parents, and that dependence opened up a whole other can of insecurities.

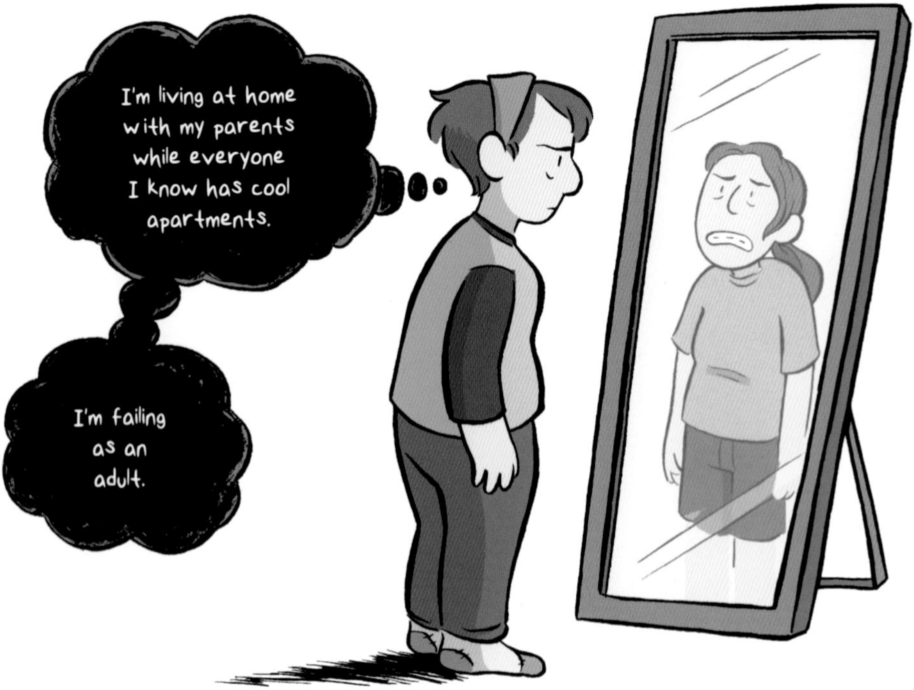
I'm living at home with my parents while everyone I know has cool apartments.
I'm failing as an adult.

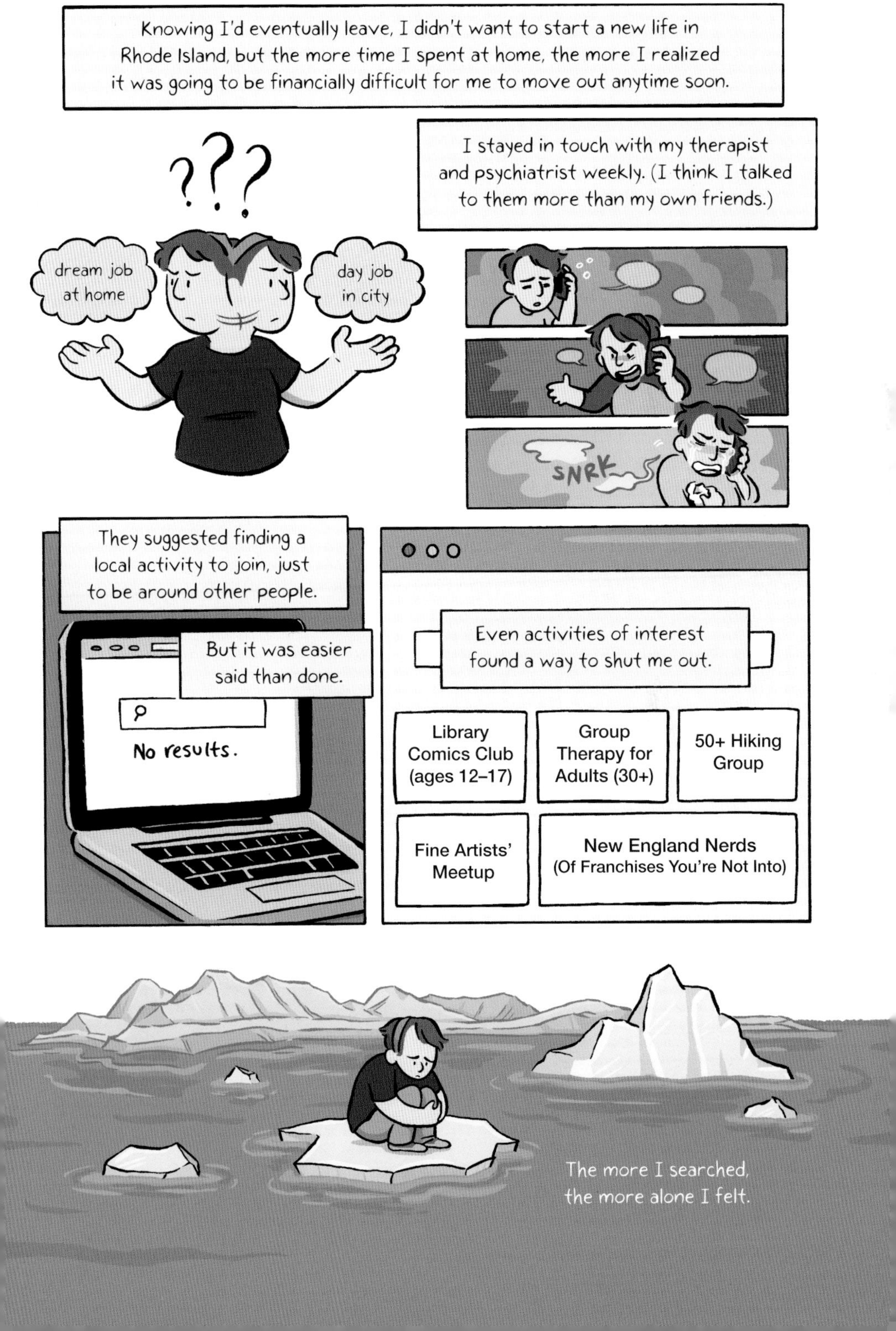
Knowing I'd eventually leave, I didn't want to start a new life in Rhode Island, but the more time I spent at home, the more I realized it was going to be financially difficult for me to move out anytime soon.
???
dream job at home
day job in city
I stayed in touch with my therapist and psychiatrist weekly. (I think I talked to them more than my own friends.)
SNRK
They suggested finding a local activity to join, just to be around other people.
But it was easier said than done.
No results.
Even activities of interest found a way to shut me out.
Library Comics Club (ages 12–17)
Group Therapy for Adults (30+)
50+ Hiking Group
Fine Artists' Meetup
New England Nerds (Of Franchises You're Not Into)
The more I searched, the more alone I felt.

The CTC held an improv show every Friday night called Micetro— a "competition" that resulted in a winner each week.

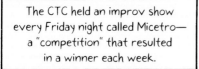

the format is spelled *Micetro* because *Maestro* looked too pretentious

...I don't know why this is their logo

Mom and I would go some nights just as an excuse to get out of the house.

Round one, begin!

Hoo!

Often when I sat in the audience, I tried to predict what came next or imagined how I would have responded in the same situation. Never as more than a daydream.

There's only one way to stop those Norwegians from reaching the mountaintop...

Set a trap?

Ask them to be our friends!

But it started following me.

IMPROV COMEDY

Every Friday and Saturday

IMPROV

MICETRO
Every Friday at 9:30

CLASSES
improv 101
improv 303
kids Club

Like it was destiny.

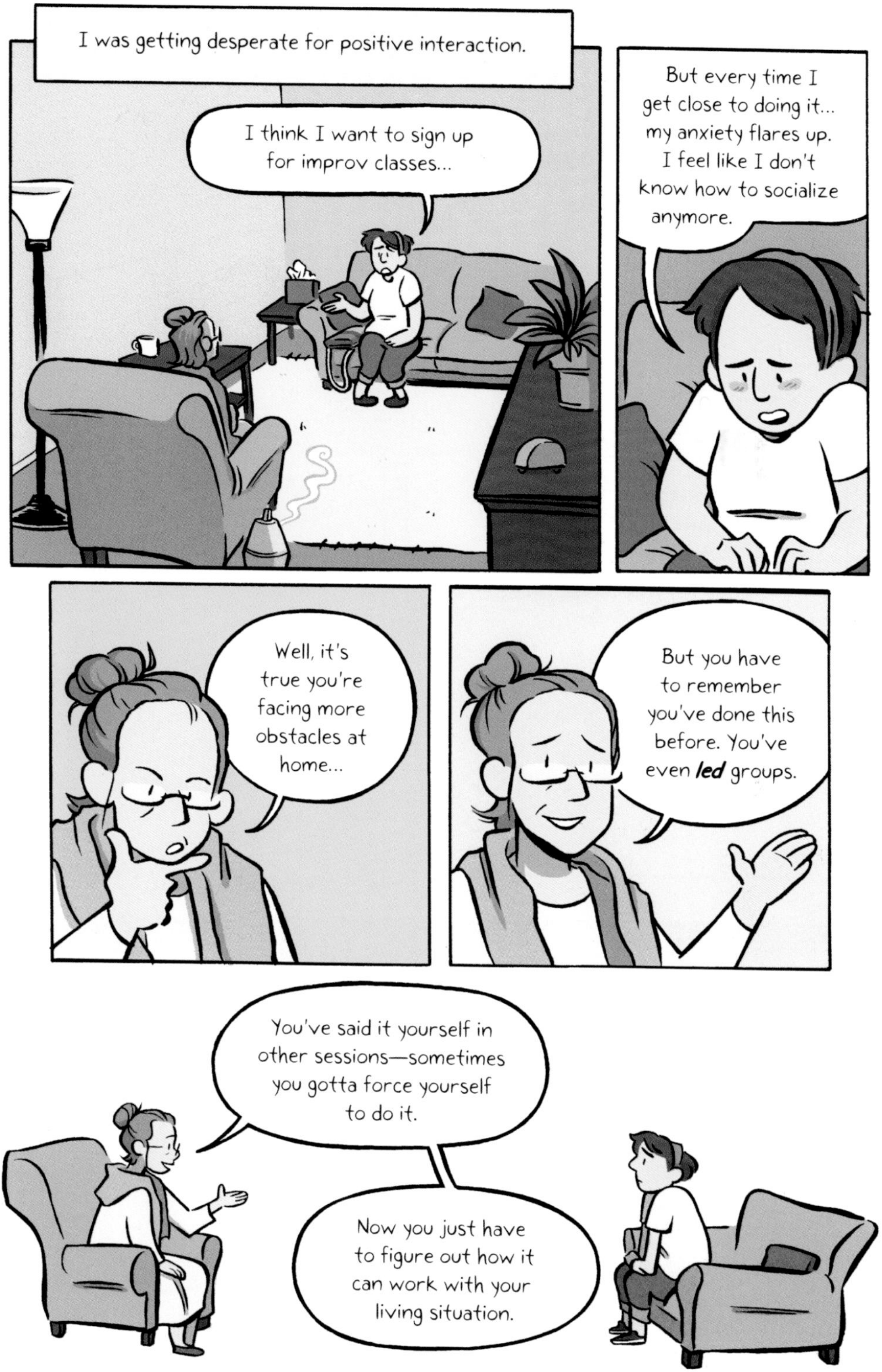
I was getting desperate for positive interaction.
I think I want to sign up for improv classes...
But every time I get close to doing it... my anxiety flares up. I feel like I don't know how to socialize anymore.
Well, it's true you're facing more obstacles at home...
But you have to remember you've done this before. You've even *led* groups.
You've said it yourself in other sessions—sometimes you gotta force yourself to do it.
Now you just have to figure out how it can work with your living situation.

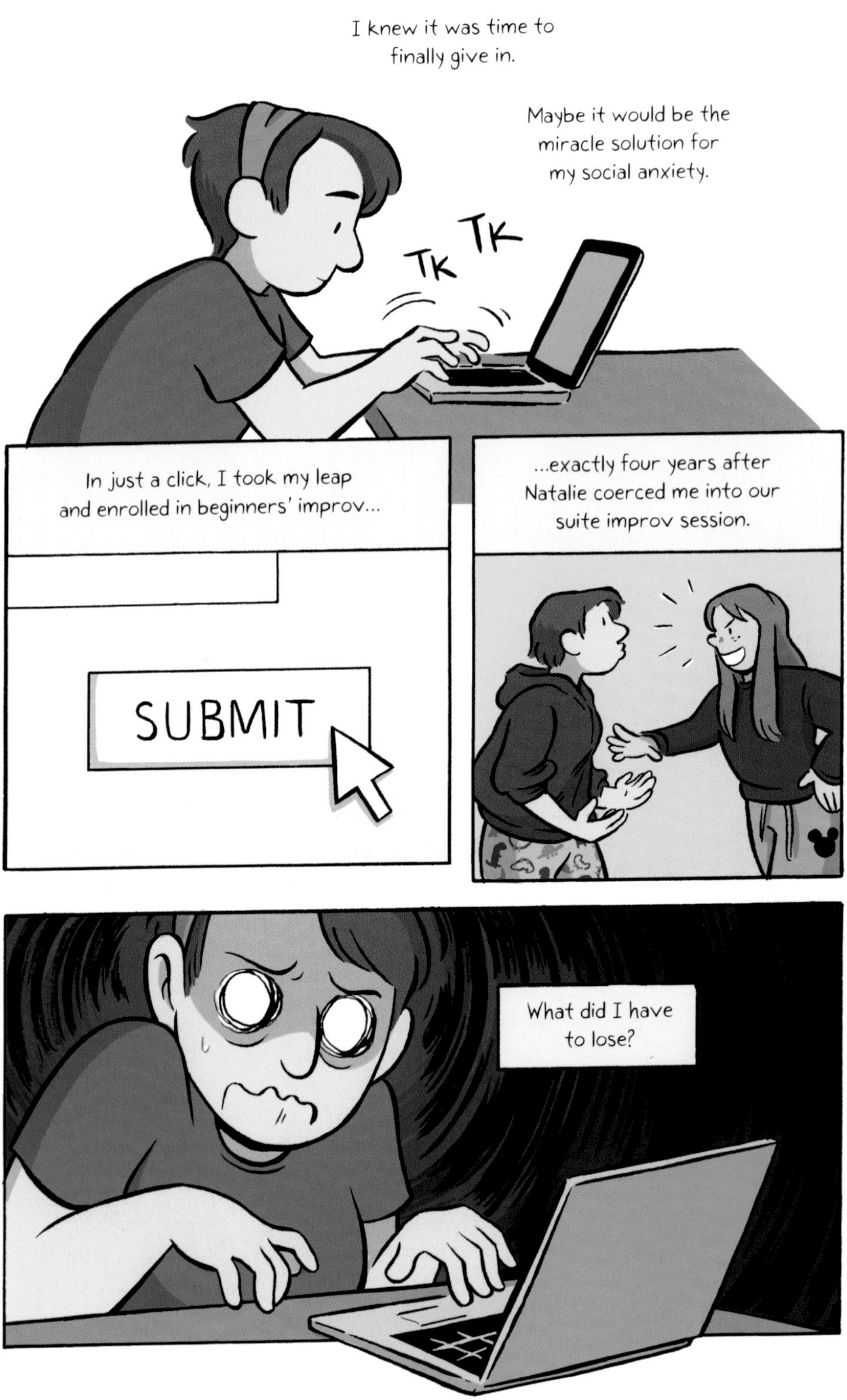
I knew it was time to finally give in.
Maybe it would be the miracle solution for my social anxiety.
TK
TK
In just a click, I took my leap and enrolled in beginners' improv...
SUBMIT
...exactly four years after Natalie coerced me into our suite improv session.
What did I have to lose?

PART 2

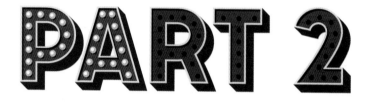

Listen, I know improv gets a lot of flak...

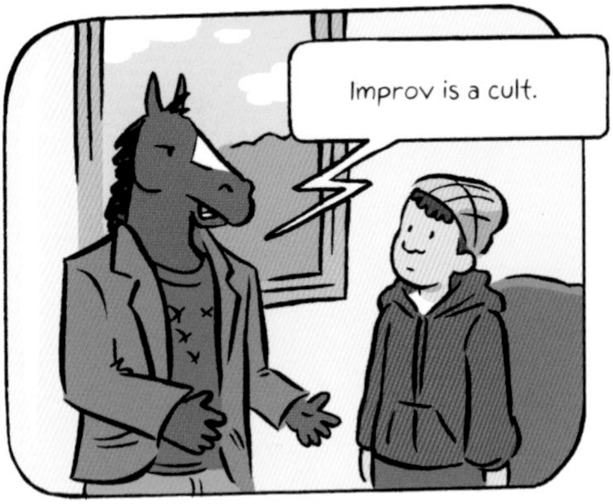
Improv is a cult.

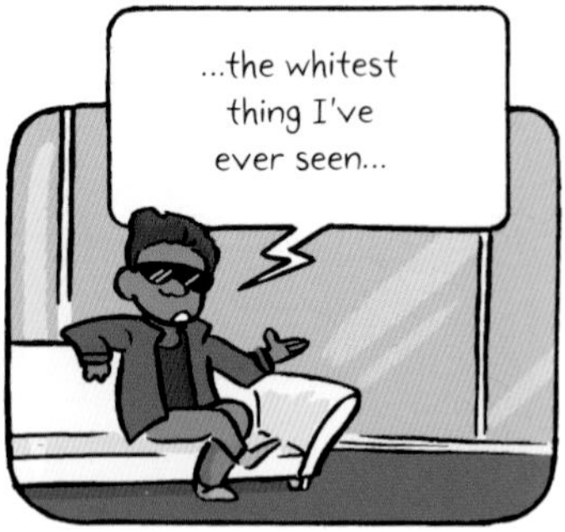
...the whitest thing I've ever seen...

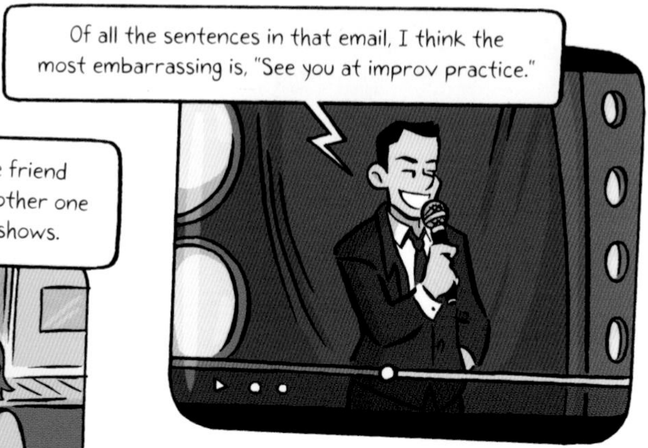
Of all the sentences in that email, I think the most embarrassing is, "See you at improv practice."

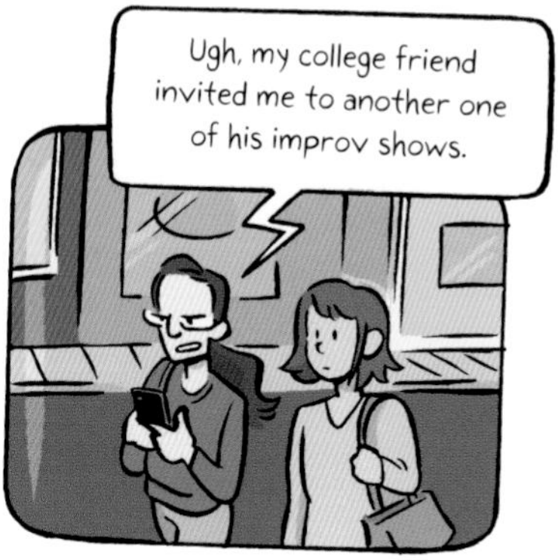
Ugh, my college friend invited me to another one of his improv shows.

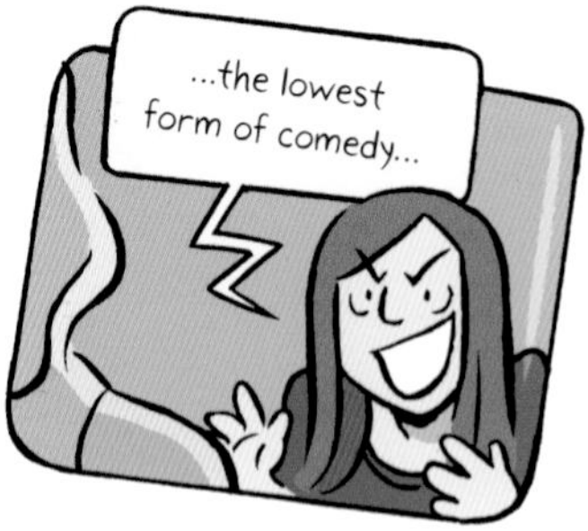
...the lowest form of comedy...

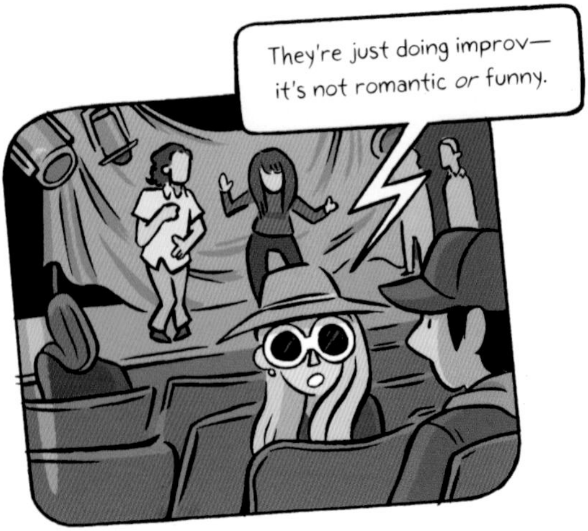
They're just doing improv—it's not romantic *or* funny.

This isn't a book-length ad to persuade you into trying it.

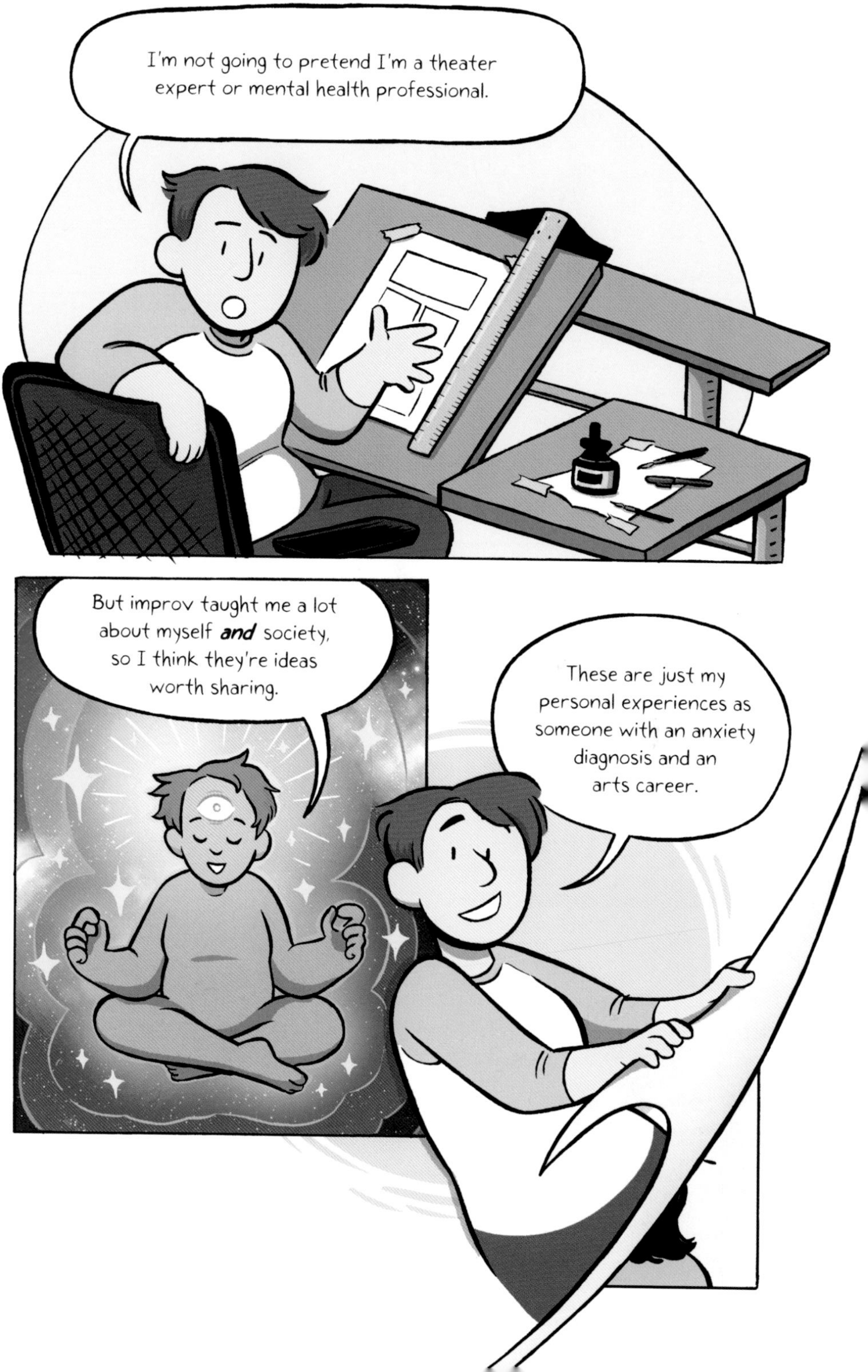
I'm not going to pretend I'm a theater expert or mental health professional.
But improv taught me a lot about myself **and** society, so I think they're ideas worth sharing.
These are just my personal experiences as someone with an anxiety diagnosis and an arts career.

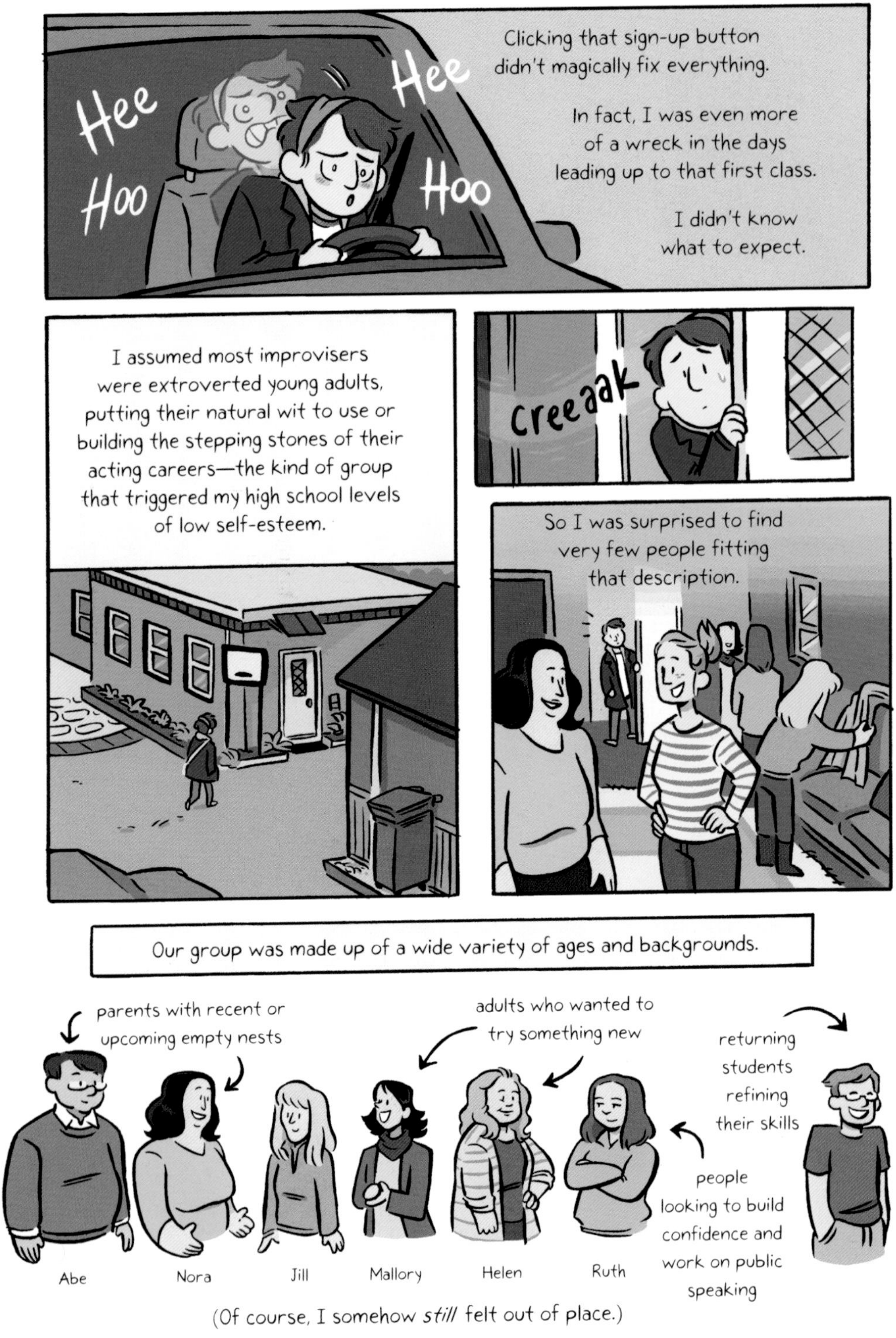

Clicking that sign-up button didn't magically fix everything.
In fact, I was even more of a wreck in the days leading up to that first class.
I didn't know what to expect.
Hee Hoo
Hee Hoo
I assumed most improvisers were extroverted young adults, putting their natural wit to use or building the stepping stones of their acting careers—the kind of group that triggered my high school levels of low self-esteem.
creeaak
So I was surprised to find very few people fitting that description.
Our group was made up of a wide variety of ages and backgrounds.
parents with recent or upcoming empty nests
adults who wanted to try something new
returning students refining their skills
people looking to build confidence and work on public speaking
Abe
Nora
Jill
Mallory
Helen
Ruth
(Of course, I somehow *still* felt out of place.)

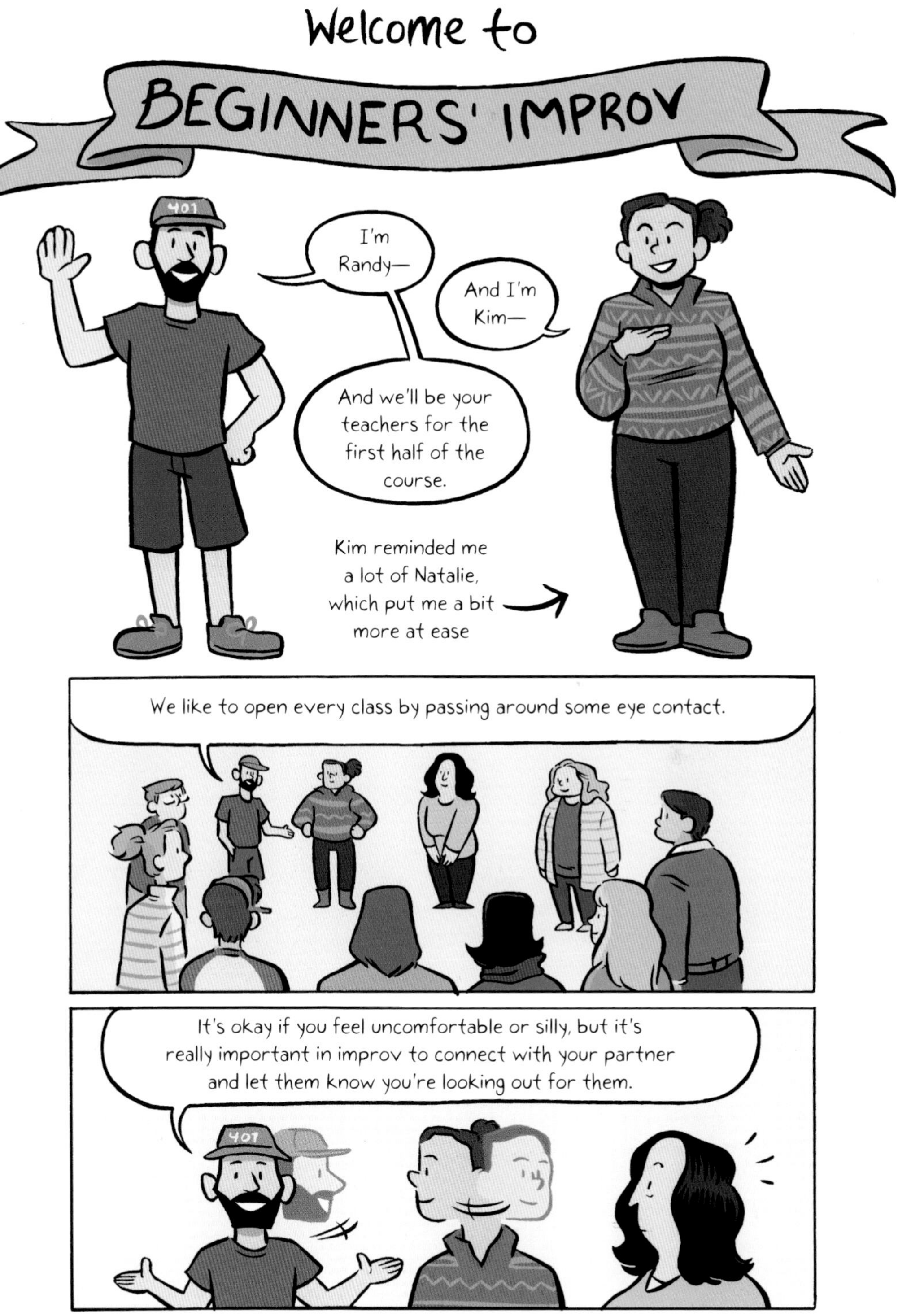
Welcome to
BEGINNERS' IMPROV
401
I'm Randy—
And I'm Kim—
And we'll be your teachers for the first half of the course.
Kim reminded me a lot of Natalie, which put me a bit more at ease
We like to open every class by passing around some eye contact.
It's okay if you feel uncomfortable or silly, but it's really important in improv to connect with your partner and let them know you're looking out for them.
401

Eye contact has always been a struggle for me.

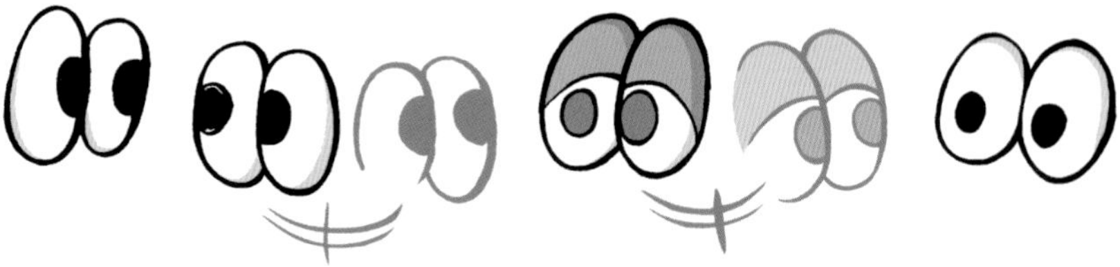

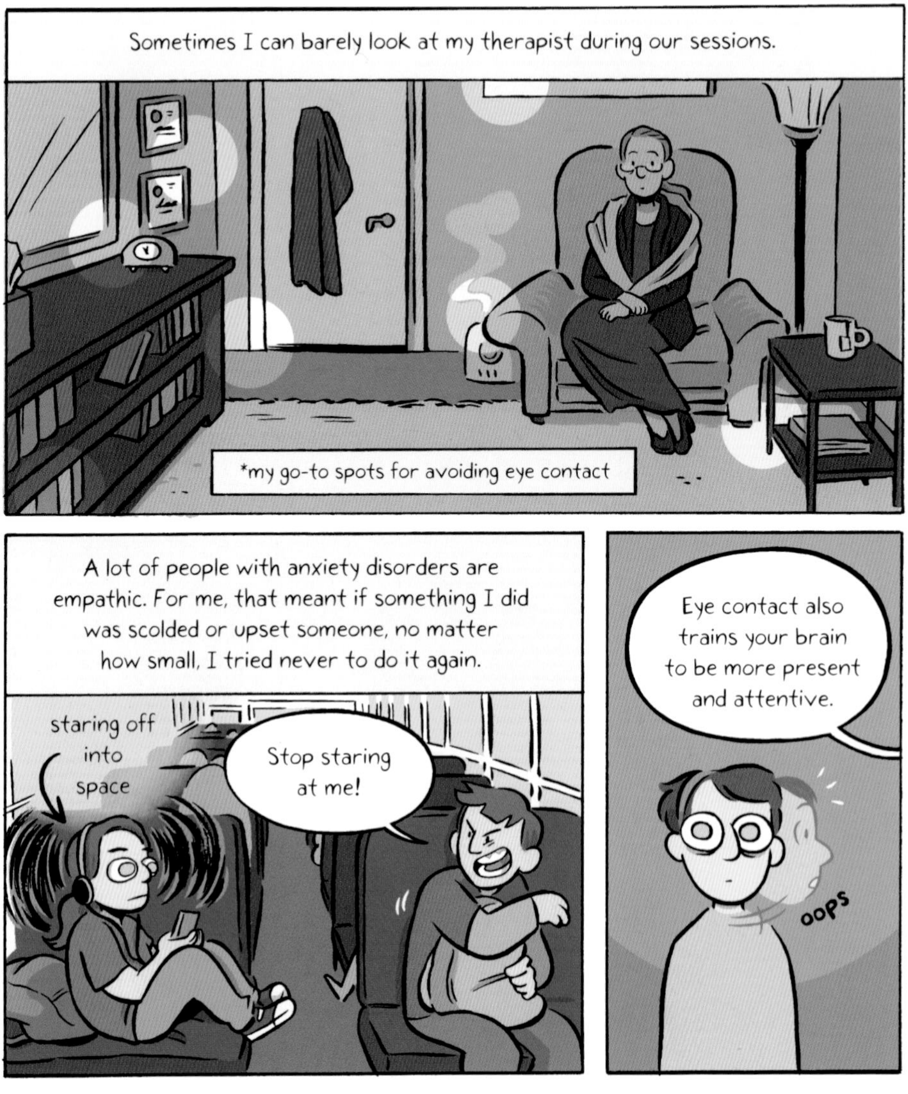
Sometimes I can barely look at my therapist during our sessions.
*my go-to spots for avoiding eye contact
A lot of people with anxiety disorders are empathic. For me, that meant if something I did was scolded or upset someone, no matter how small, I tried never to do it again.
staring off into space
Stop staring at me!
Eye contact also trains your brain to be more present and attentive.
OOPS

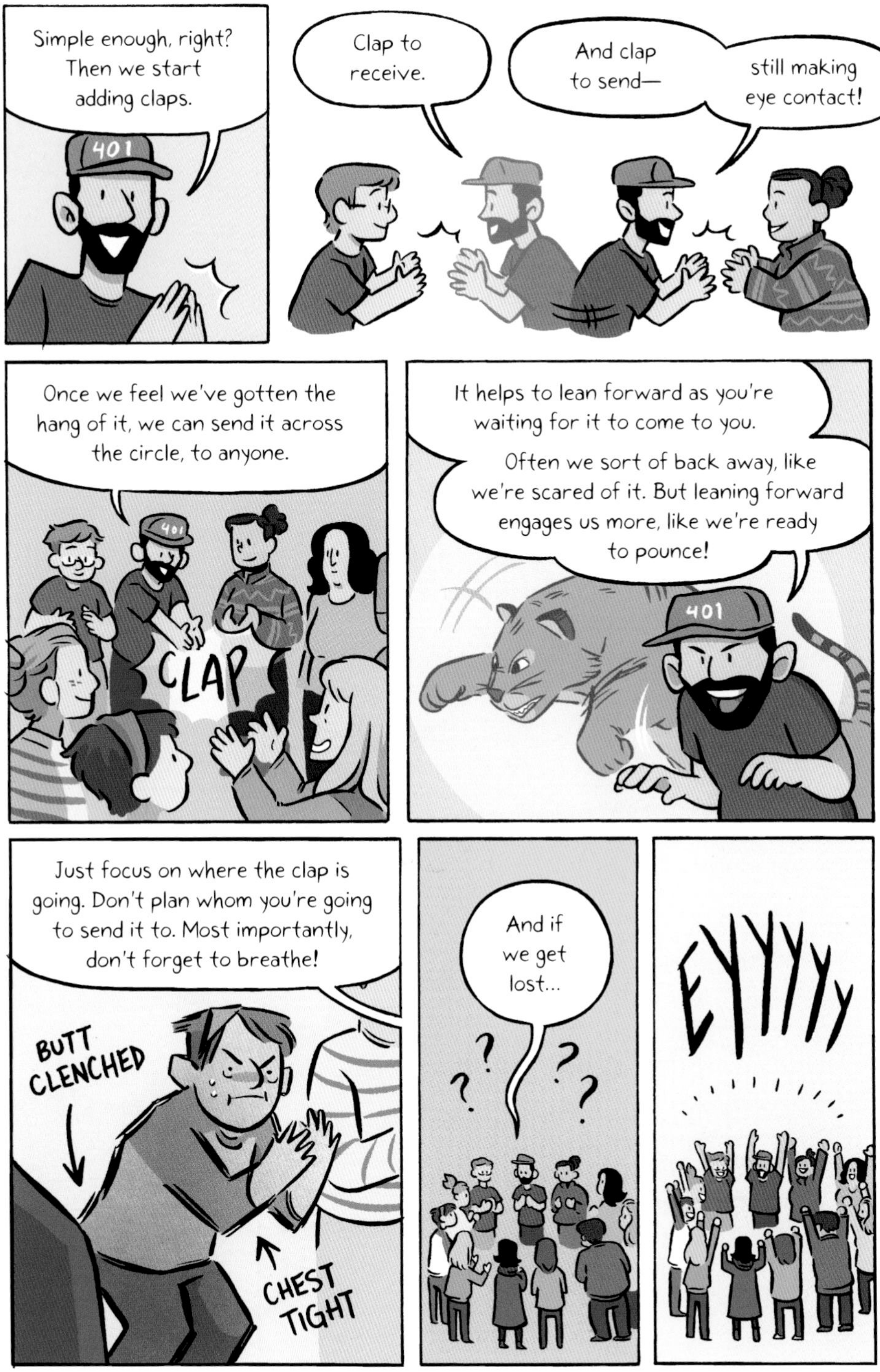

Simple enough, right? Then we start adding claps.
Clap to receive.
And clap to send—
still making eye contact!
401
Once we feel we've gotten the hang of it, we can send it across the circle, to anyone.
401
CLAP
It helps to lean forward as you're waiting for it to come to you.
Often we sort of back away, like we're scared of it. But leaning forward engages us more, like we're ready to pounce!
401
Just focus on where the clap is going. Don't plan whom you're going to send it to. Most importantly, don't forget to breathe!
BUTT CLENCHED
CHEST TIGHT
And if we get lost...
? ? ? ?
EYYYYy

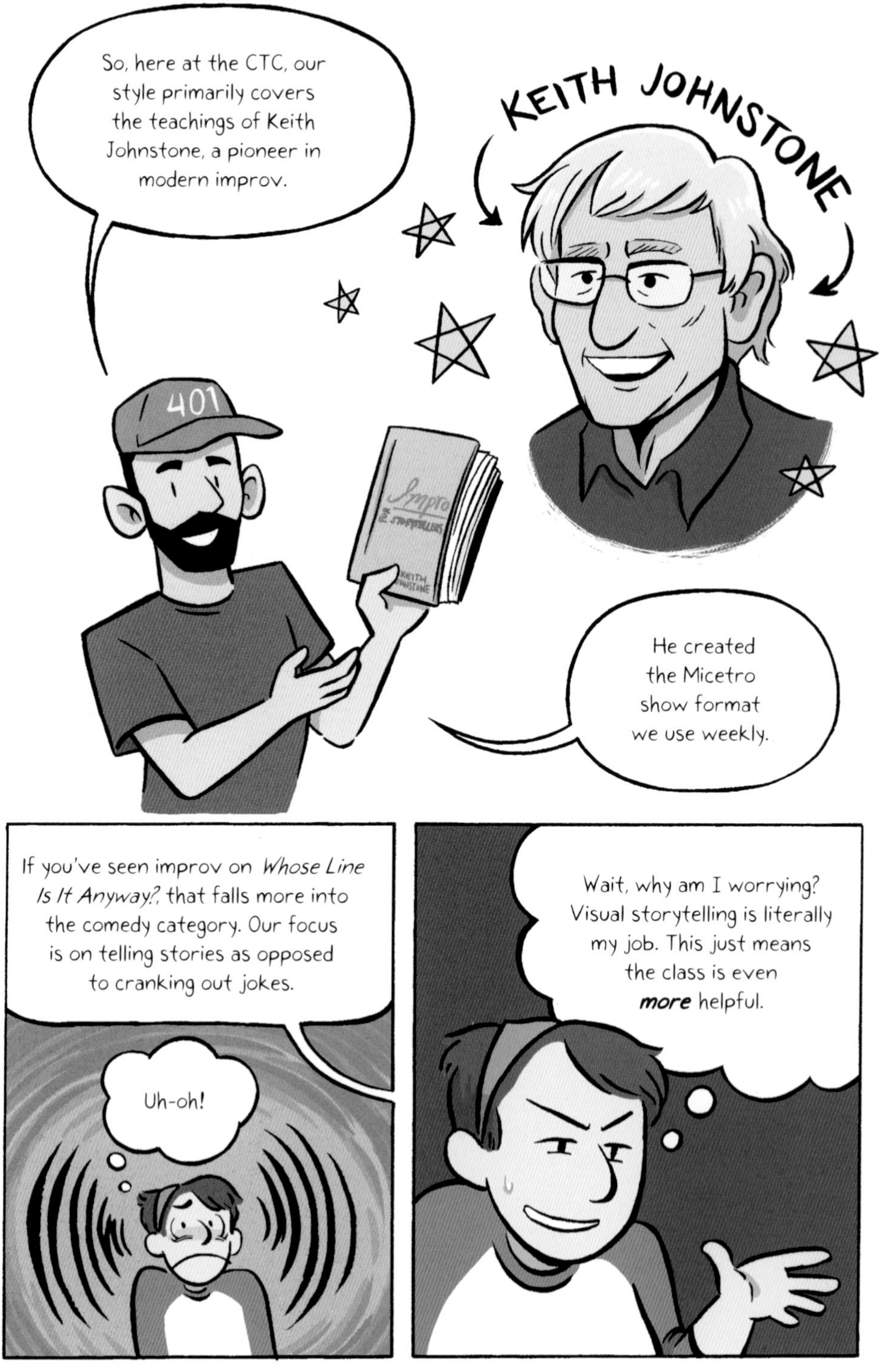
So, here at the CTC, our style primarily covers the teachings of Keith Johnstone, a pioneer in modern improv.
KEITH JOHNSTONE
401
Impro for Storytellers
KEITH JOHNSTONE
He created the Micetro show format we use weekly.
If you've seen improv on *Whose Line Is It Anyway?*, that falls more into the comedy category. Our focus is on telling stories as opposed to cranking out jokes.
Uh-oh!
Wait, why am I worrying? Visual storytelling is literally my job. This just means the class is even ***more*** helpful.

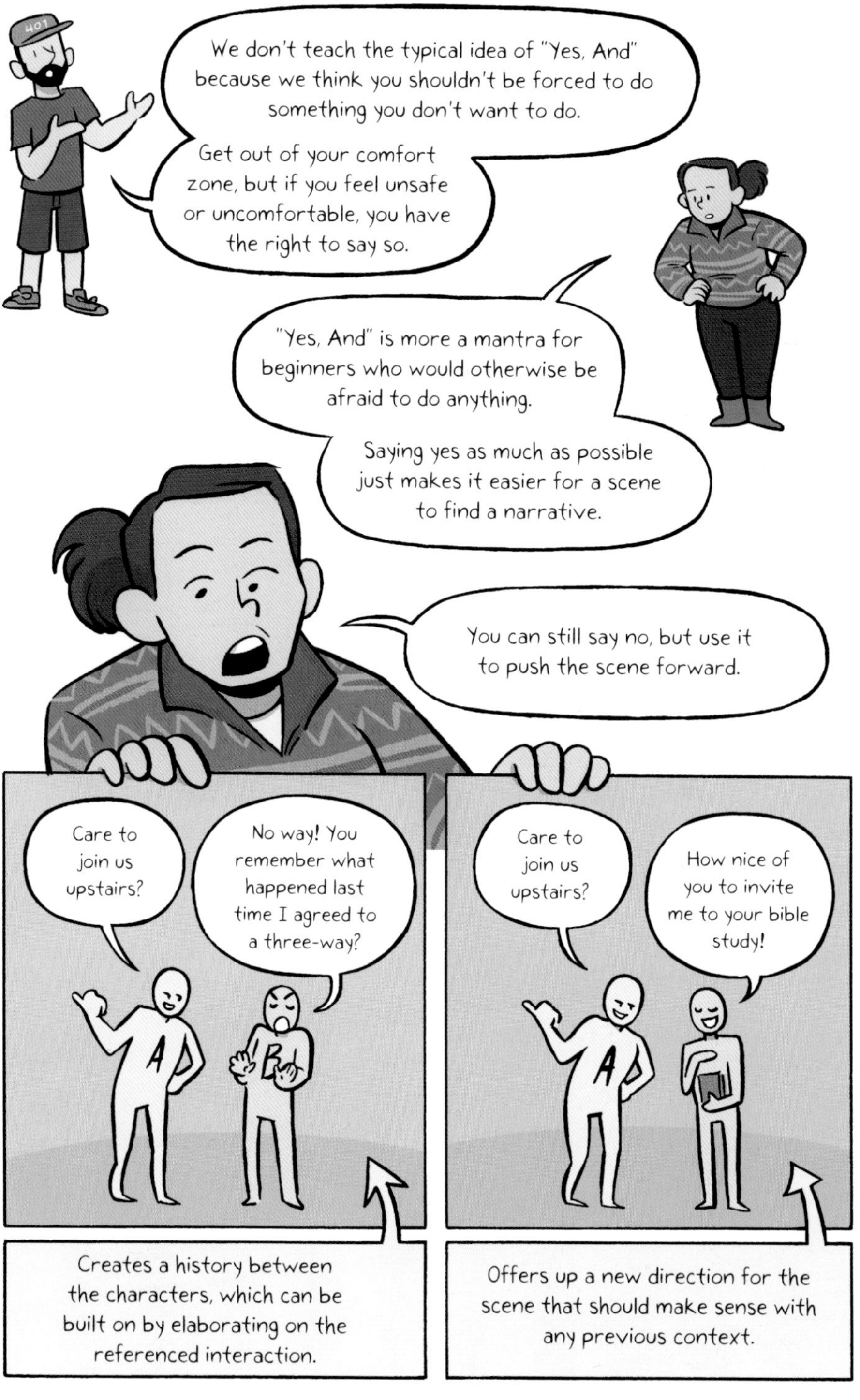

We don't teach the typical idea of "Yes, And" because we think you shouldn't be forced to do something you don't want to do.
Get out of your comfort zone, but if you feel unsafe or uncomfortable, you have the right to say so.
"Yes, And" is more a mantra for beginners who would otherwise be afraid to do anything.
Saying yes as much as possible just makes it easier for a scene to find a narrative.
You can still say no, but use it to push the scene forward.
Care to join us upstairs?
No way! You remember what happened last time I agreed to a three-way?
Care to join us upstairs?
How nice of you to invite me to your bible study!
Creates a history between the characters, which can be built on by elaborating on the referenced interaction.
Offers up a new direction for the scene that should make sense with any previous context.

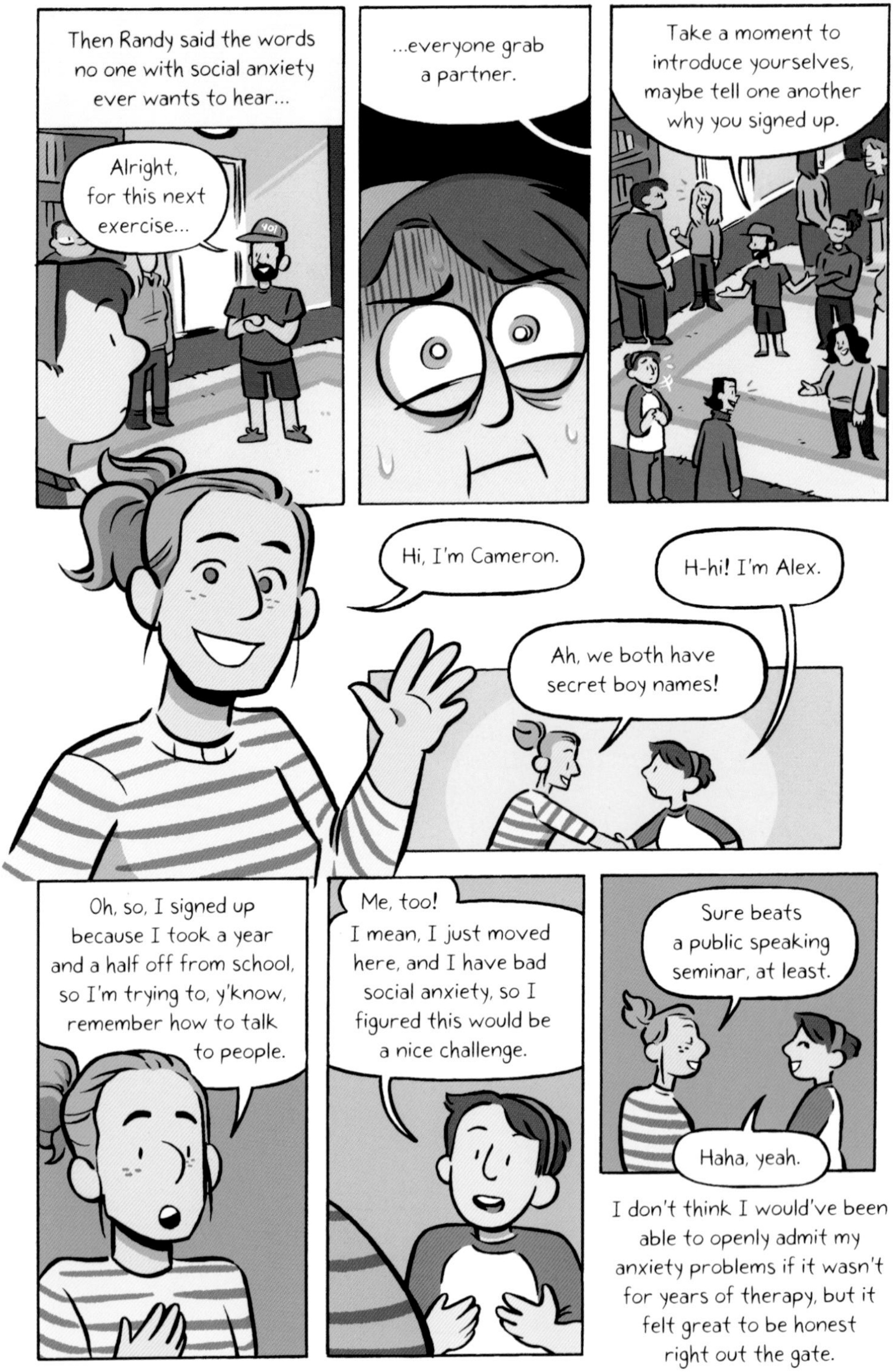

Then Randy said the words no one with social anxiety ever wants to hear...
Alright, for this next exercise...
...everyone grab a partner.
Take a moment to introduce yourselves, maybe tell one another why you signed up.
Hi, I'm Cameron.
H-hi! I'm Alex.
Ah, we both have secret boy names!
Oh, so, I signed up because I took a year and a half off from school, so I'm trying to, y'know, remember how to talk to people.
Me, too!
I mean, I just moved here, and I have bad social anxiety, so I figured this would be a nice challenge.
Sure beats a public speaking seminar, at least.
Haha, yeah.
I don't think I would've been able to openly admit my anxiety problems if it wasn't for years of therapy, but it felt great to be honest right out the gate.

FORK & KNIFE

It's what we call a "freeze game."

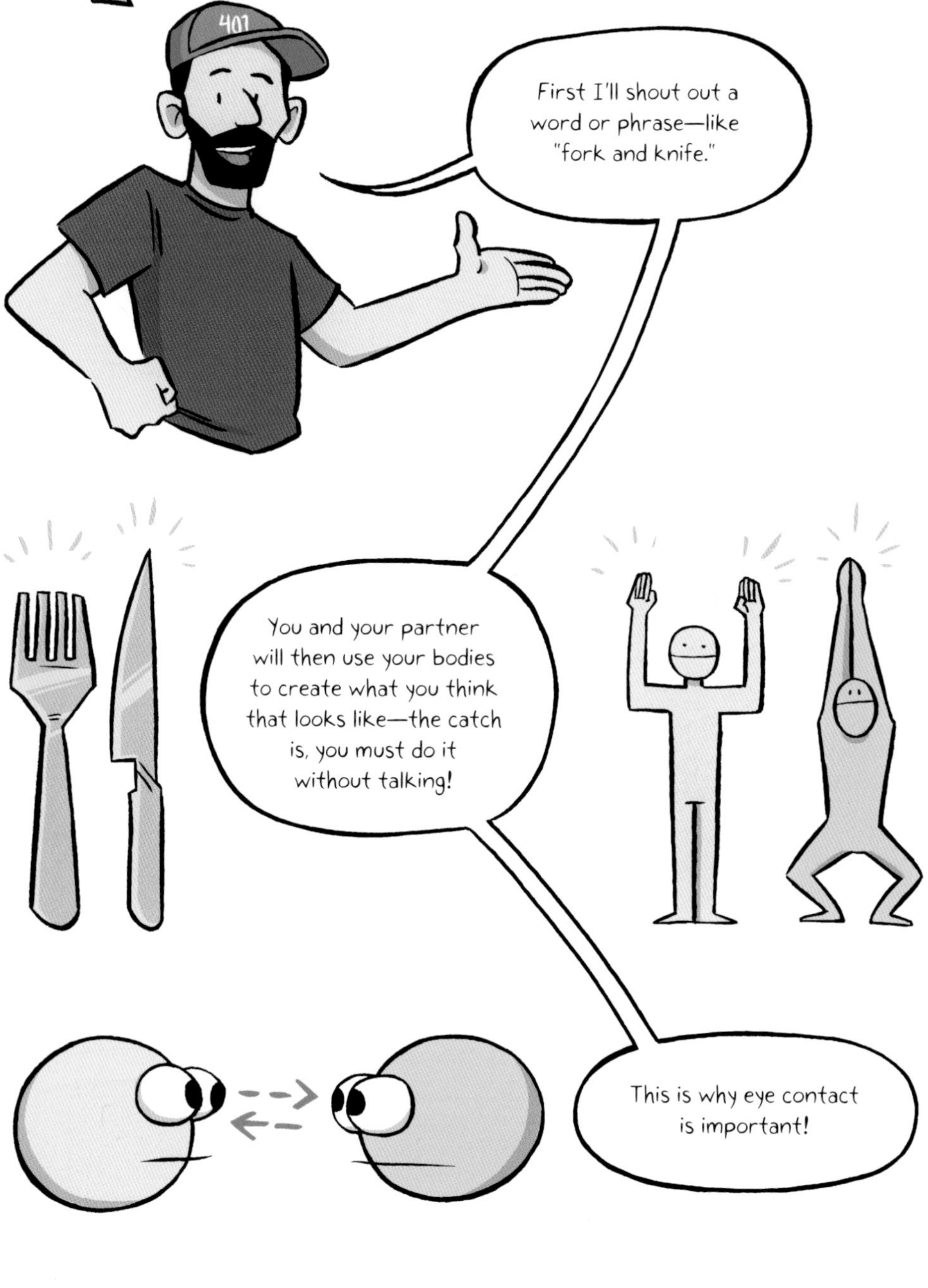
407
First I'll shout out a word or phrase—like "fork and knife."
You and your partner will then use your bodies to create what you think that looks like—the catch is, you must do it without talking!
This is why eye contact is important!

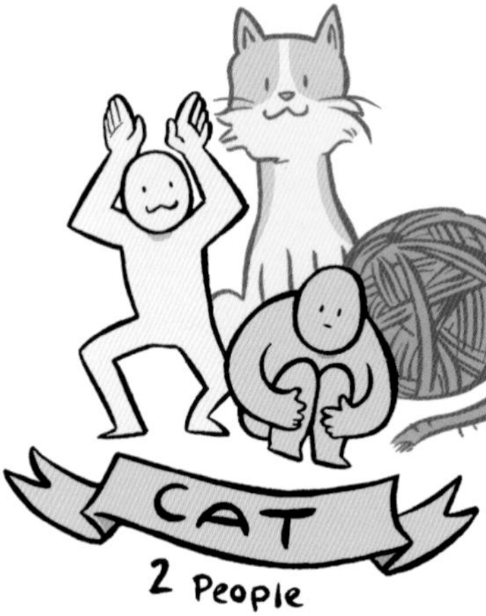
CAT
2 People

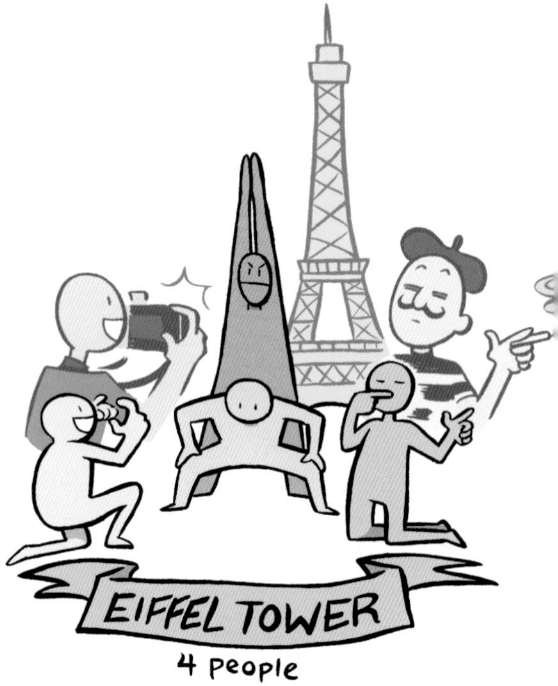
EIFFEL TOWER
4 people

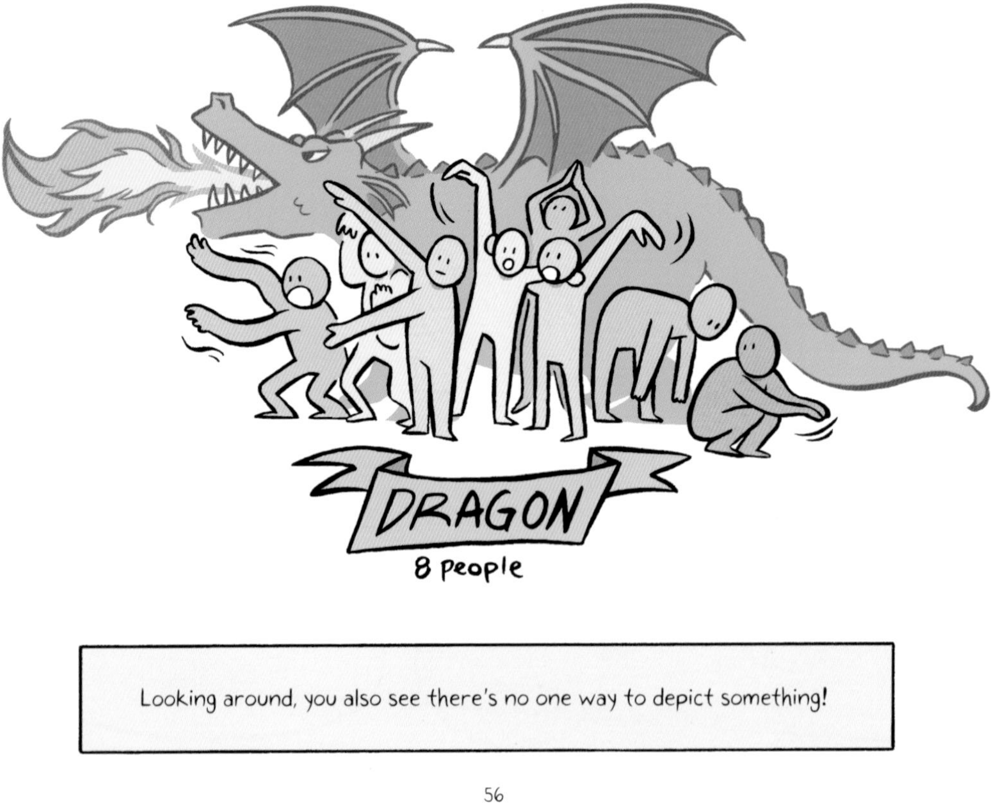
DRAGON
8 people

Looking around, you also see there's no one way to depict something!

is a similar theater freeze game.

One player starts in the center and poses like an activity they have in mind.

Another player can then hop in and "complete the image" with how they interpret the activity.

Thank you.

The original player thanks their partner and leaves to start the cycle again, creating another unrelated scene using the last pair's remaining pose.

Thank you.

*Since we were newbies, we just focused on physicality, but other versions involve acting out the whole scene.

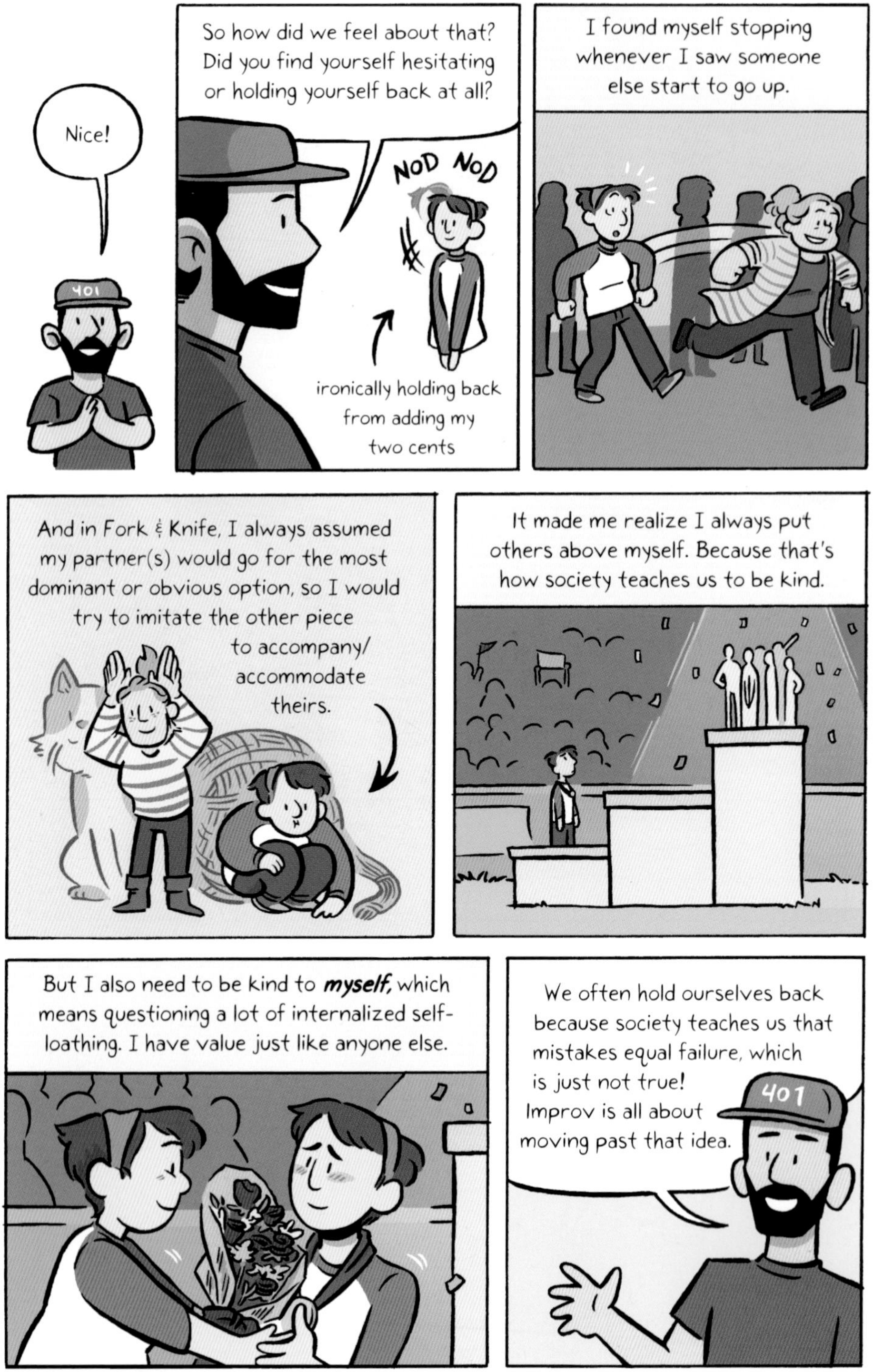

Nice!
So how did we feel about that? Did you find yourself hesitating or holding yourself back at all?
NOD NOD
ironically holding back from adding my two cents
I found myself stopping whenever I saw someone else start to go up.
And in Fork & Knife, I always assumed my partner(s) would go for the most dominant or obvious option, so I would try to imitate the other piece to accompany/ accommodate theirs.
It made me realize I always put others above myself. Because that's how society teaches us to be kind.
But I also need to be kind to ***myself,*** which means questioning a lot of internalized self-loathing. I have value just like anyone else.
We often hold ourselves back because society teaches us that mistakes equal failure, which is just not true! Improv is all about moving past that idea.

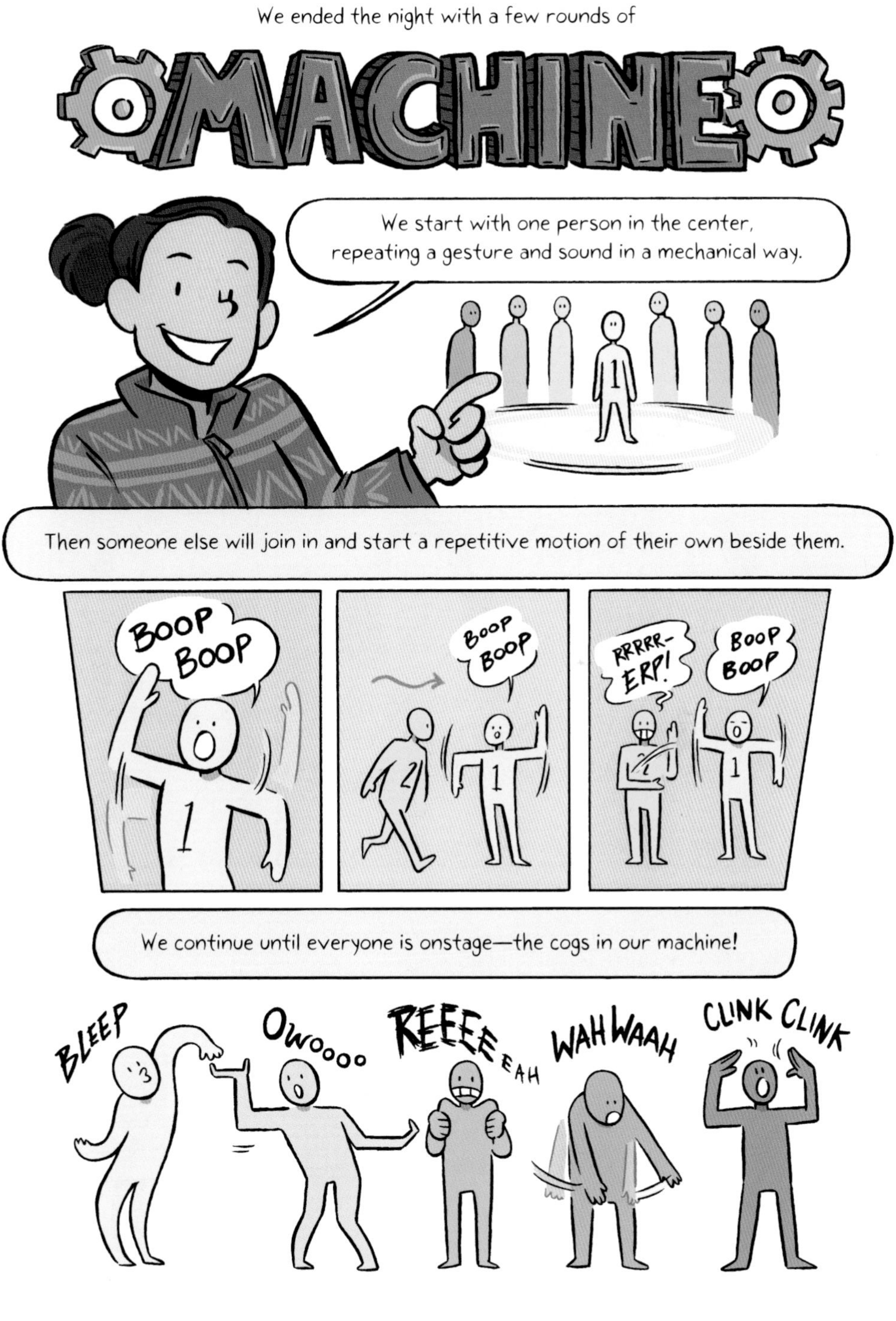
We ended the night with a few rounds of
MACHINE
We start with one person in the center, repeating a gesture and sound in a mechanical way.
1
Then someone else will join in and start a repetitive motion of their own beside them.
BOOP BOOP
1
BOOP BOOP
2
1
RRRRR-ERP!
BOOP BOOP
2
1
We continue until everyone is onstage—the cogs in our machine!
BLEEP
Owoooo
REEEE EAH
WAH WAAH
CLINK CLINK

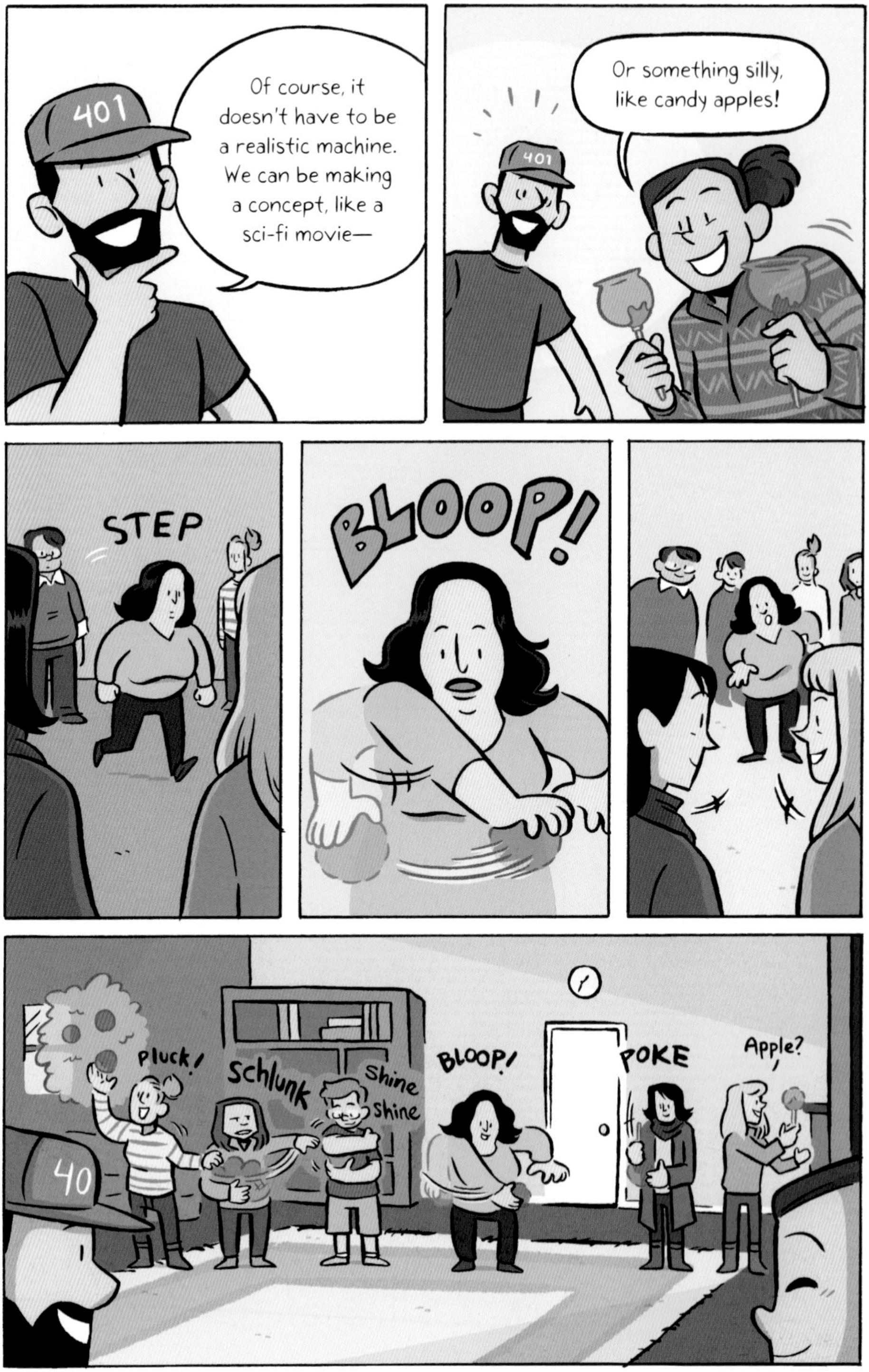

Of course, it doesn't have to be a realistic machine. We can be making a concept, like a sci-fi movie—
Or something silly, like candy apples!
STEP
BLOOP!
PLUCK!
SCHLUNK
Shine shine
BLOOP!
POKE
Apple?

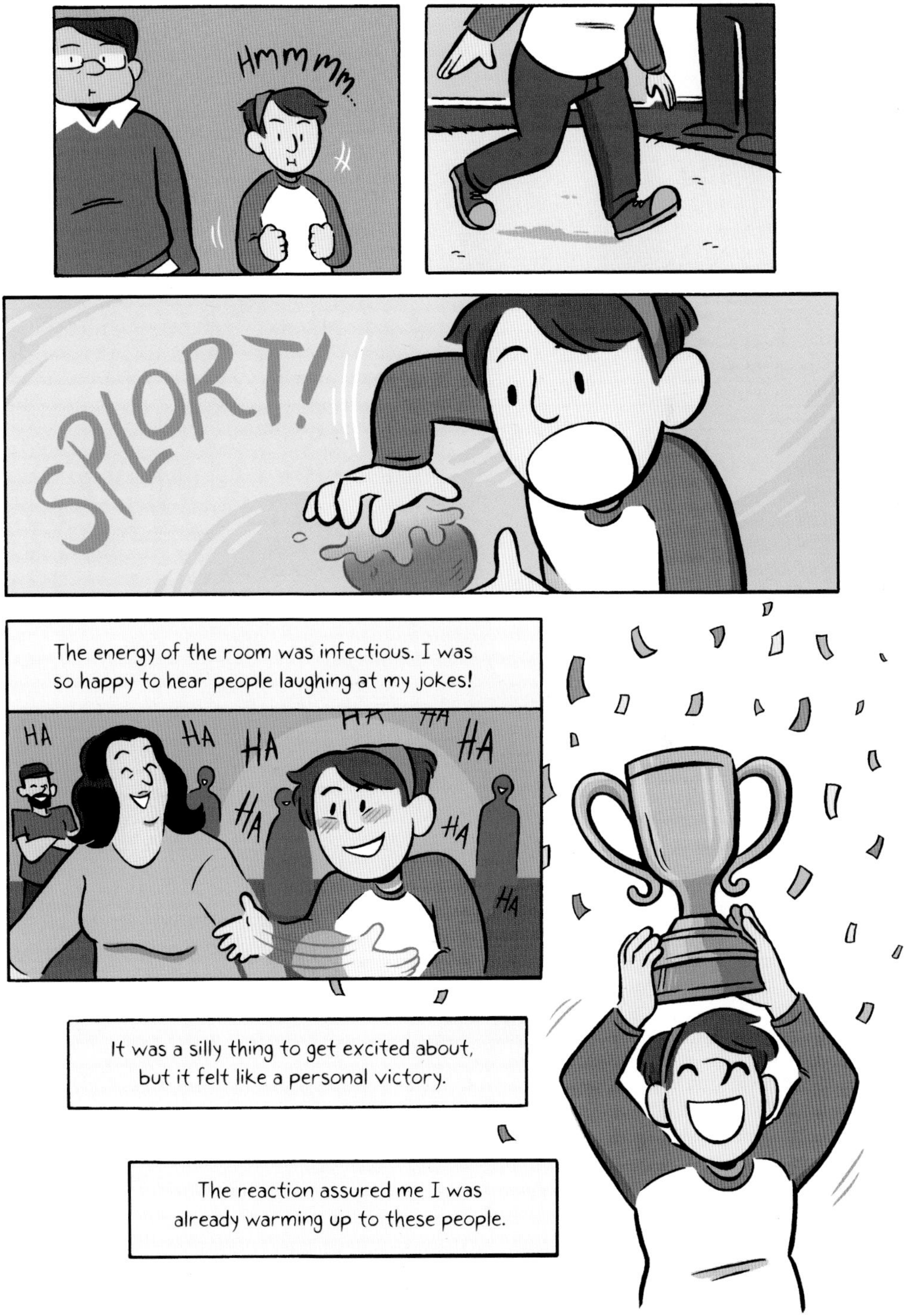
Hmmmmm...
SPLORT!
The energy of the room was infectious. I was so happy to hear people laughing at my jokes!
HA HA HA HA HA HA HA HA HA HA
It was a silly thing to get excited about, but it felt like a personal victory.
The reaction assured me I was already warming up to these people.

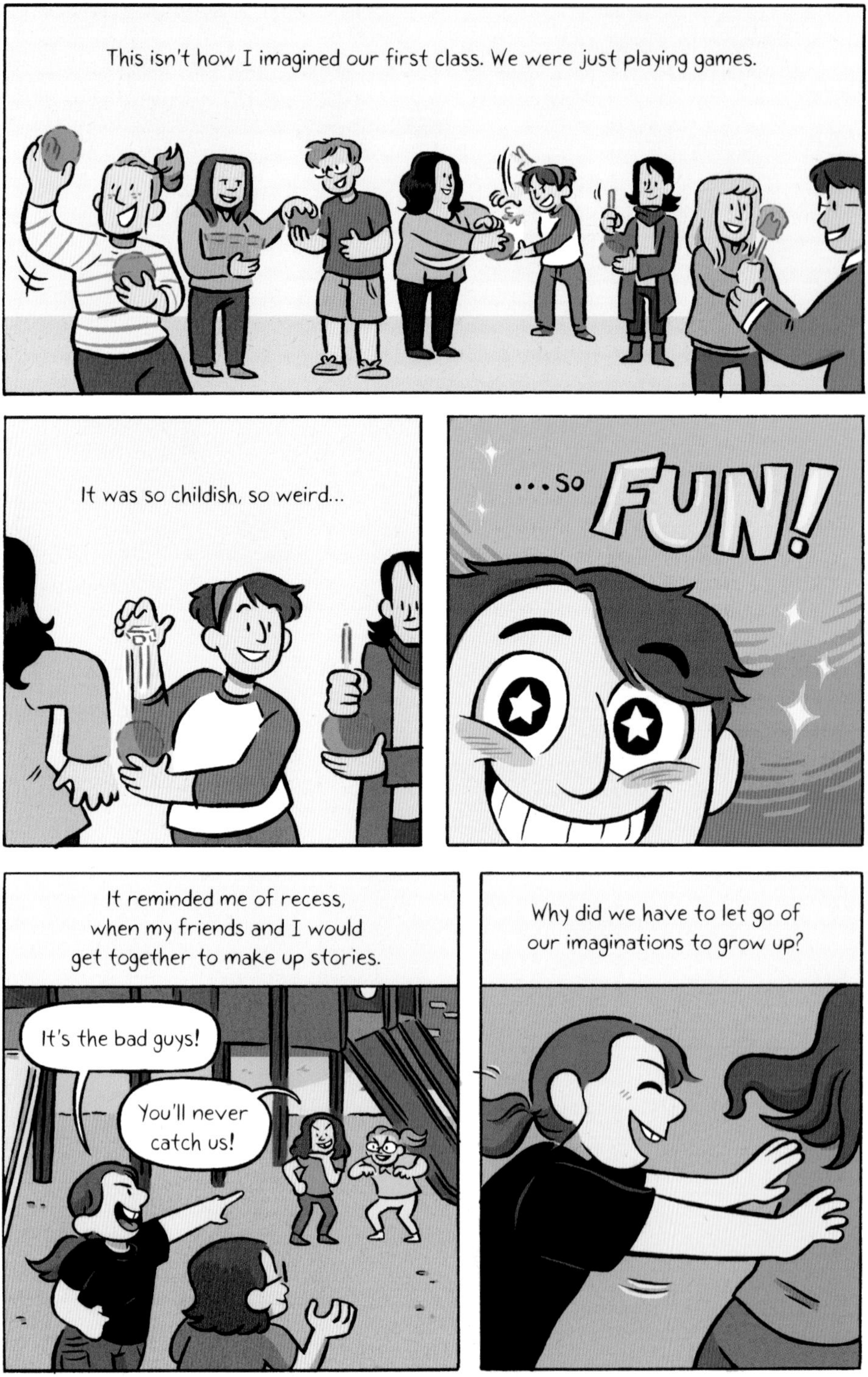
This isn't how I imagined our first class. We were just playing games.
It was so childish, so weird...
...so
FUN!
It reminded me of recess, when my friends and I would get together to make up stories.
It's the bad guys!
You'll never catch us!
Why did we have to let go of our imaginations to grow up?

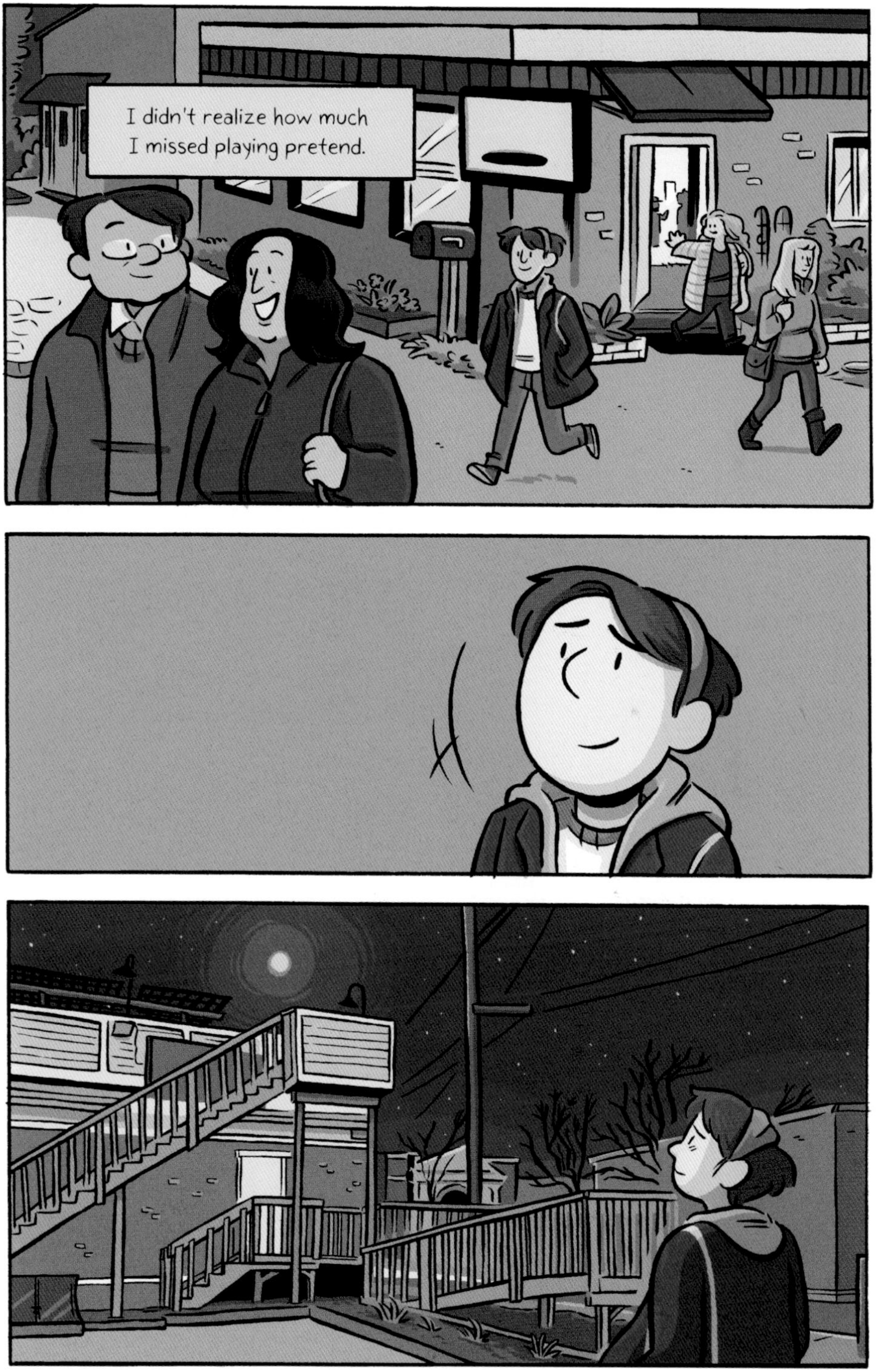
I didn't realize how much
I missed playing pretend.

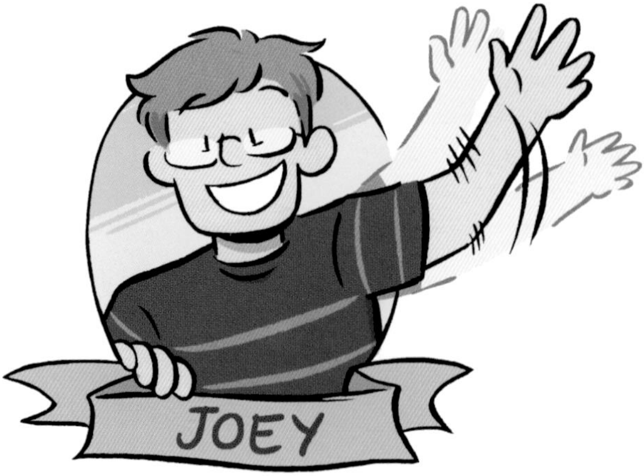
JOEY

I met Joey during our second class. He was a regular performer who was using the course to refresh his skills.

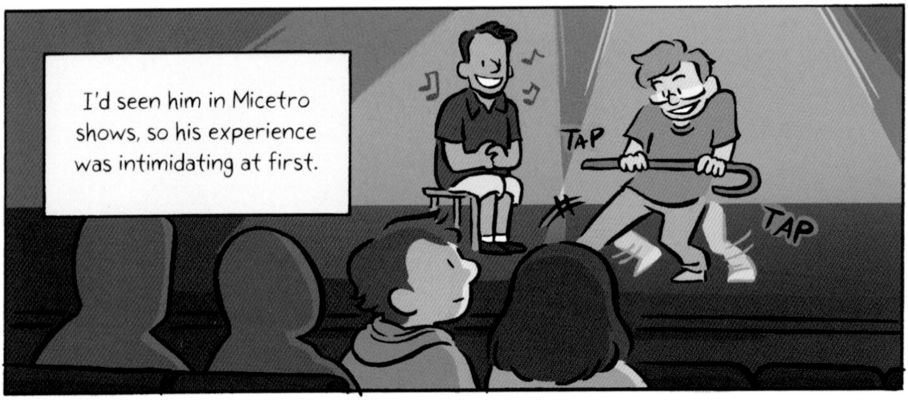
I'd seen him in Micetro shows, so his experience was intimidating at first.
TAP
TAP

He was always excited to play. Energetic. Like a happy li'l puppy.

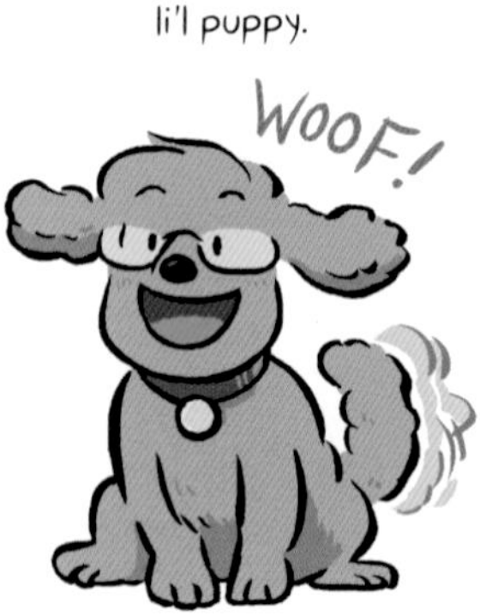
WOOF!

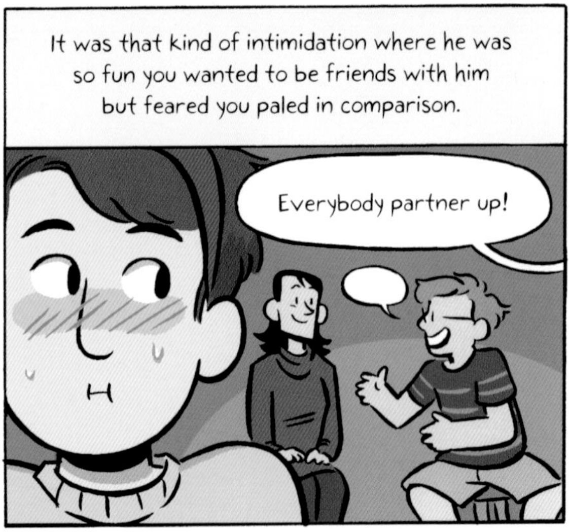
It was that kind of intimidation where he was so fun you wanted to be friends with him but feared you paled in comparison.
Everybody partner up!

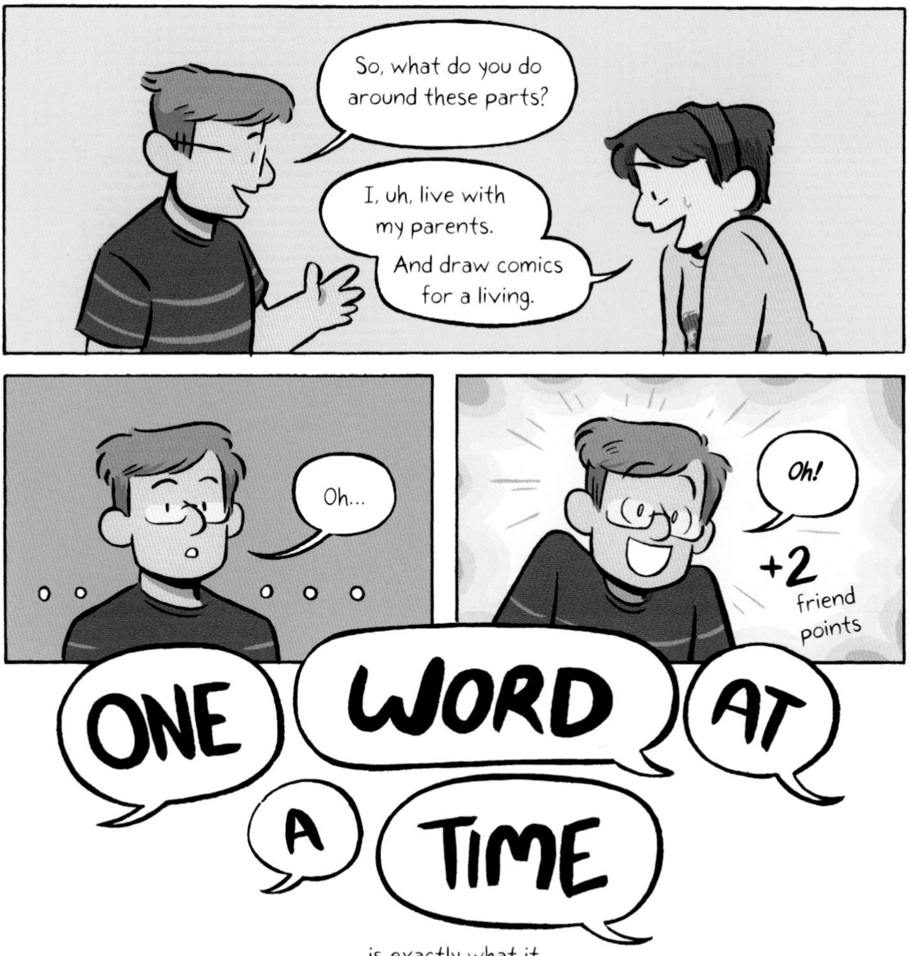
So, what do you do around these parts?
I, uh, live with my parents.
And draw comics for a living.
Oh...
Oh!
+2 friend points

ONE WORD AT A TIME

is exactly what it sounds like.

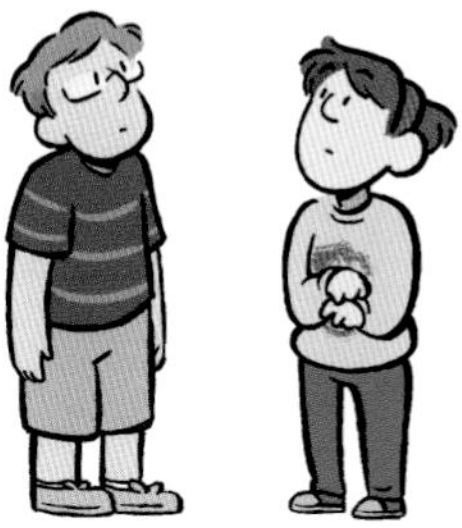

You and a partner work together to tell a story, alternating turns with each word. It's surprisingly difficult!

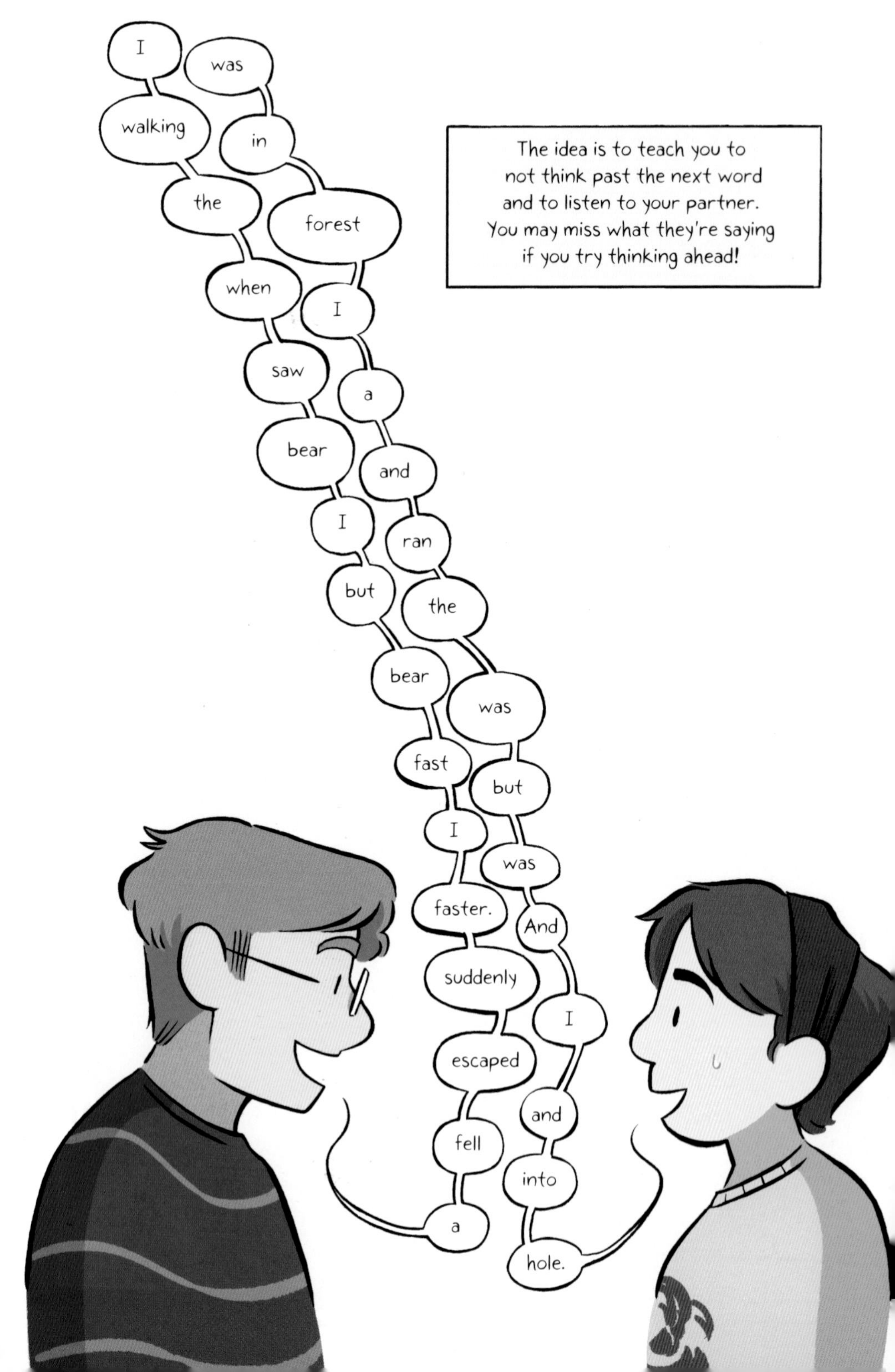

The idea is to teach you to not think past the next word and to listen to your partner. You may miss what they're saying if you try thinking ahead!
I
was
walking
in
the
forest
when
I
saw
a
bear
and
I
ran
but
the
bear
was
fast
but
I
was
faster.
And
suddenly
I
escaped
and
fell
into
a
hole.

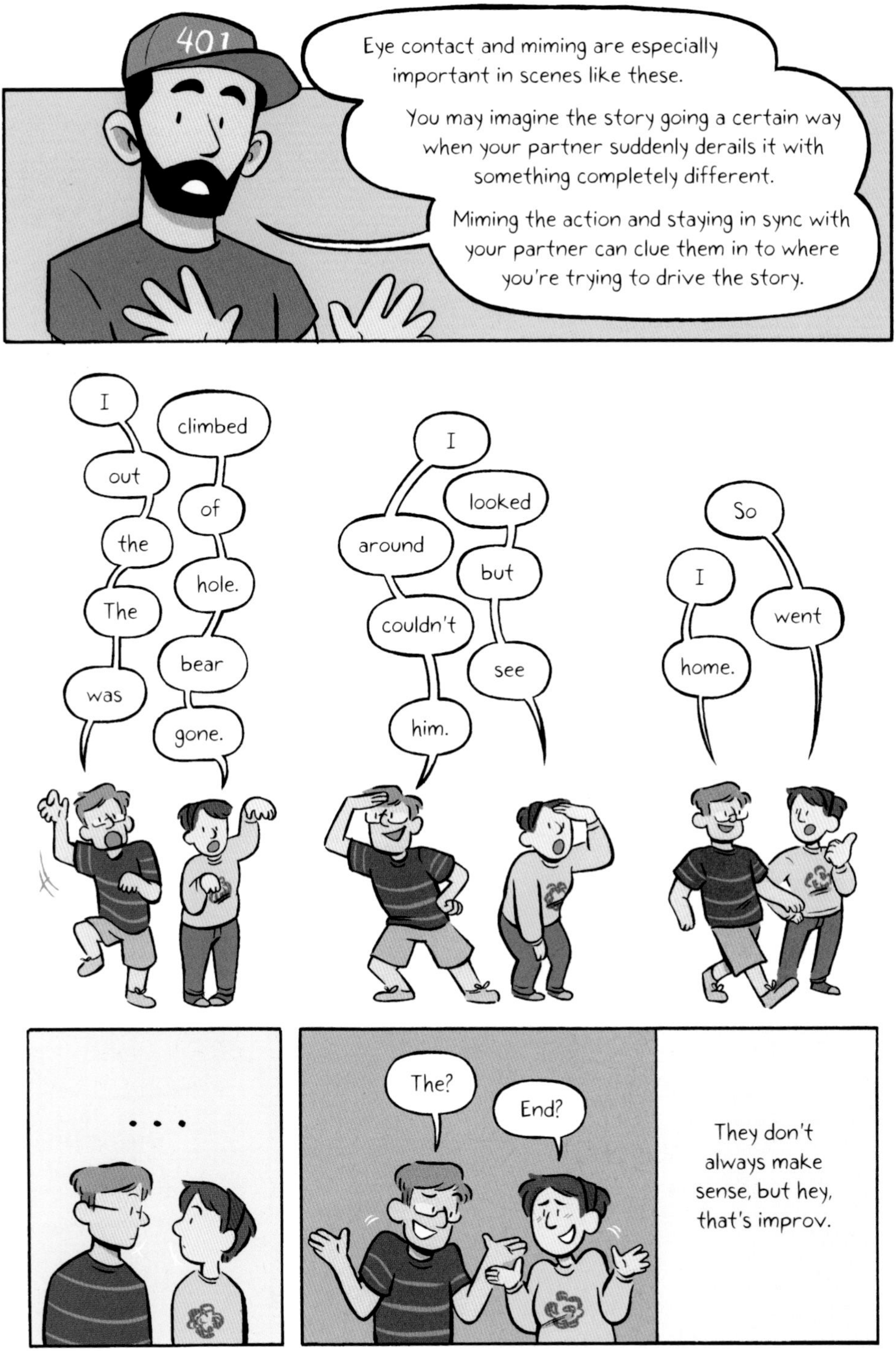
Eye contact and miming are especially important in scenes like these.
You may imagine the story going a certain way when your partner suddenly derails it with something completely different.
Miming the action and staying in sync with your partner can clue them in to where you're trying to drive the story.
401
I
climbed
out
of
the
hole.
The
bear
was
gone.
I
looked
around
but
couldn't
see
him.
So
I
went
home.
. . .
The?
End?
They don't always make sense, but hey, that's improv.

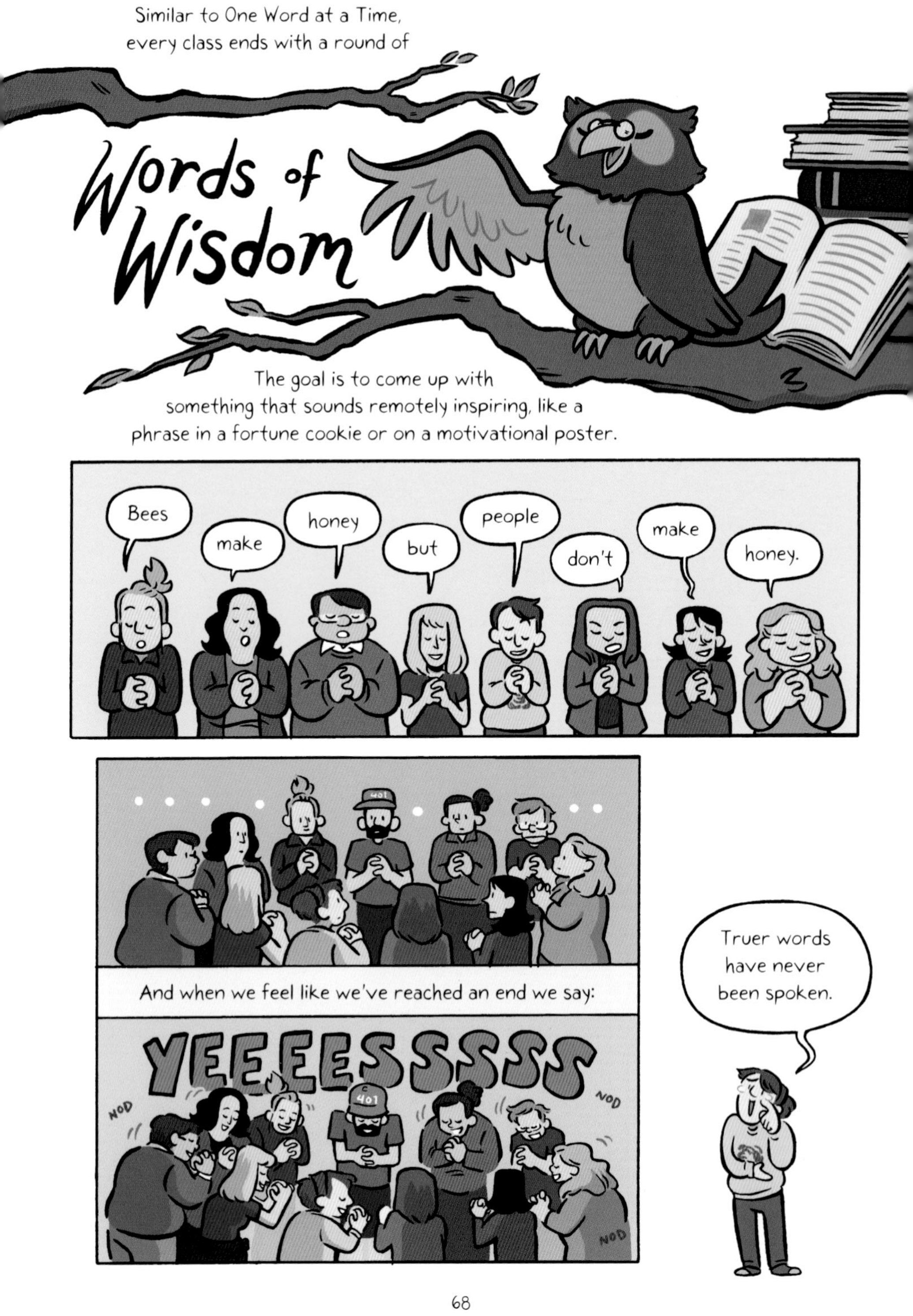

Similar to One Word at a Time,
every class ends with a round of
Words of Wisdom
The goal is to come up with
something that sounds remotely inspiring, like a
phrase in a fortune cookie or on a motivational poster.
Bees
make
honey
but
people
don't
make
honey.
401
And when we feel like we've reached an end we say:
YEEEESSSSS
401
NOD
NOD
NOD
Truer words
have never
been spoken.

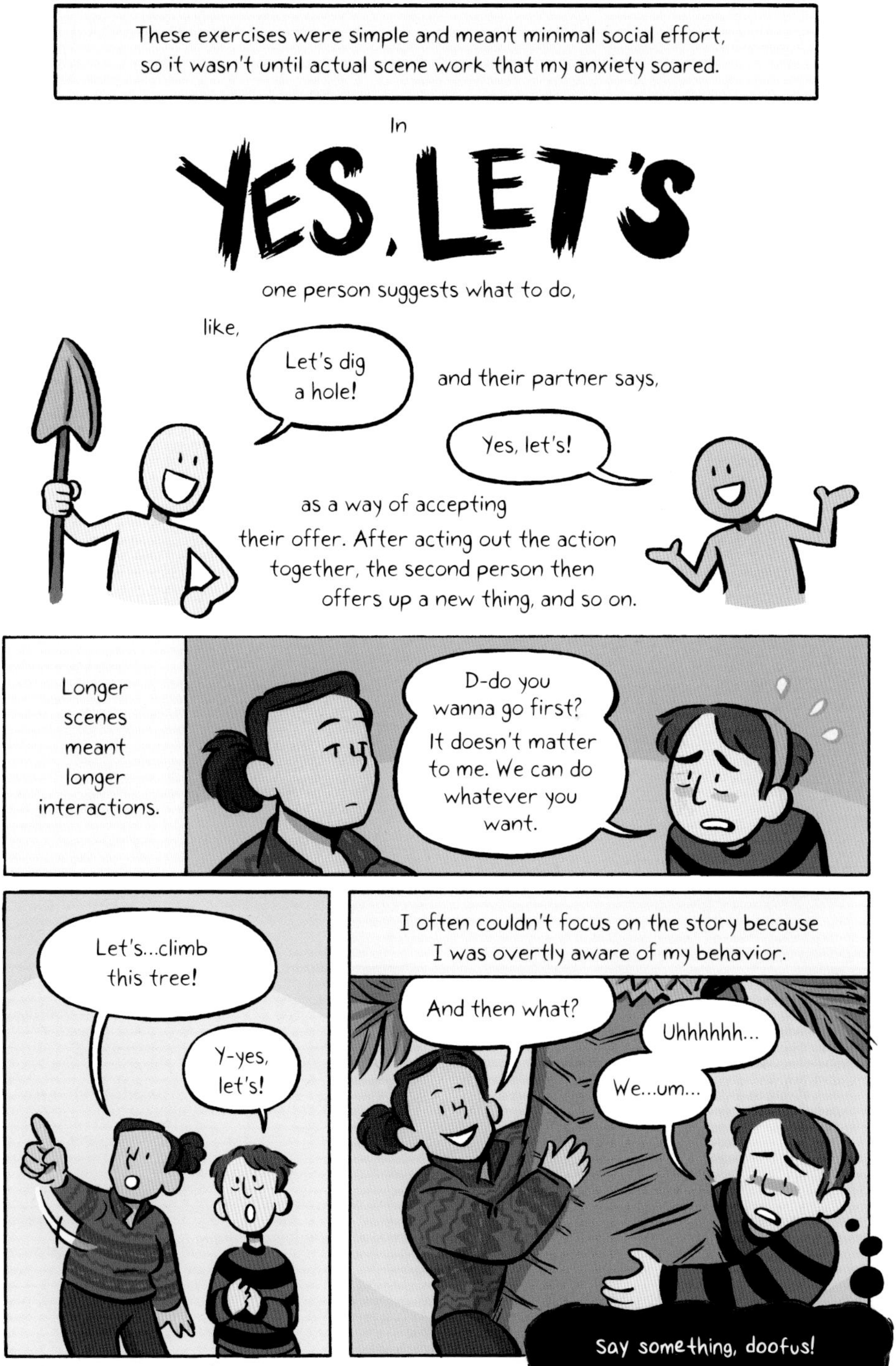
These exercises were simple and meant minimal social effort, so it wasn't until actual scene work that my anxiety soared.
In
YES, LET'S
one person suggests what to do,
like,
Let's dig a hole!
and their partner says,
Yes, let's!
as a way of accepting their offer. After acting out the action together, the second person then offers up a new thing, and so on.
Longer scenes meant longer interactions.
D-do you wanna go first? It doesn't matter to me. We can do whatever you want.
Let's...climb this tree!
Y-yes, let's!
I often couldn't focus on the story because I was overtly aware of my behavior.
And then what?
Uhhhhhh...
We...um...
Say something, doofus!

*Later on, we learned if we were uninspired, we could say "Nope!" (cheerfully) and offer up a new suggestion.

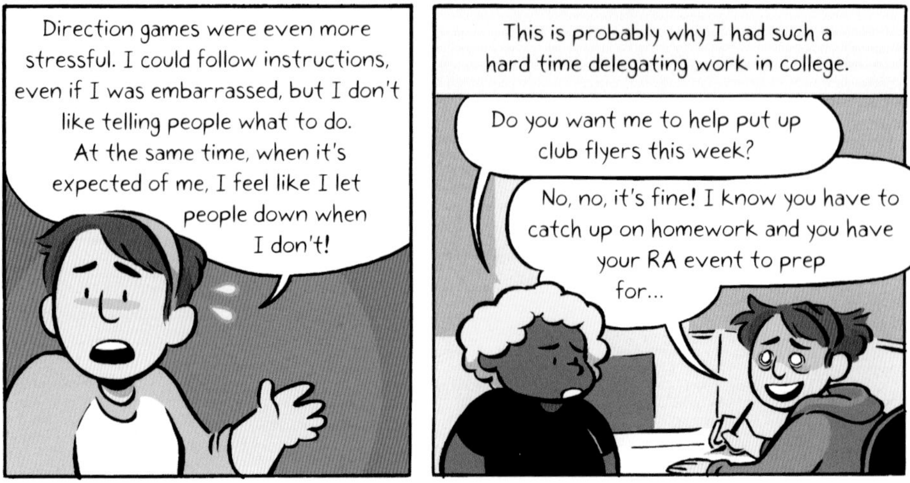
Direction games were even more stressful. I could follow instructions, even if I was embarrassed, but I don't like telling people what to do. At the same time, when it's expected of me, I feel like I let people down when I don't!
This is probably why I had such a hard time delegating work in college.
Do you want me to help put up club flyers this week?
No, no, it's fine! I know you have to catch up on homework and you have your RA event to prep for...

What Comes Next...?

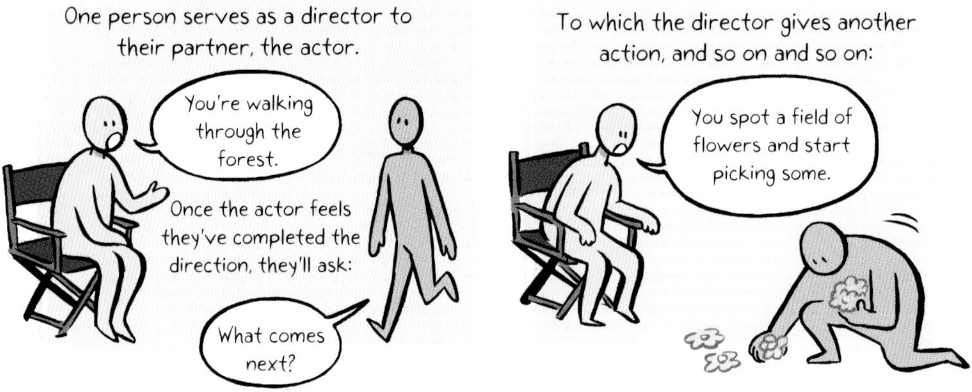
One person serves as a director to their partner, the actor.
You're walking through the forest.
Once the actor feels they've completed the direction, they'll ask:
What comes next?
To which the director gives another action, and so on and so on:
You spot a field of flowers and start picking some.

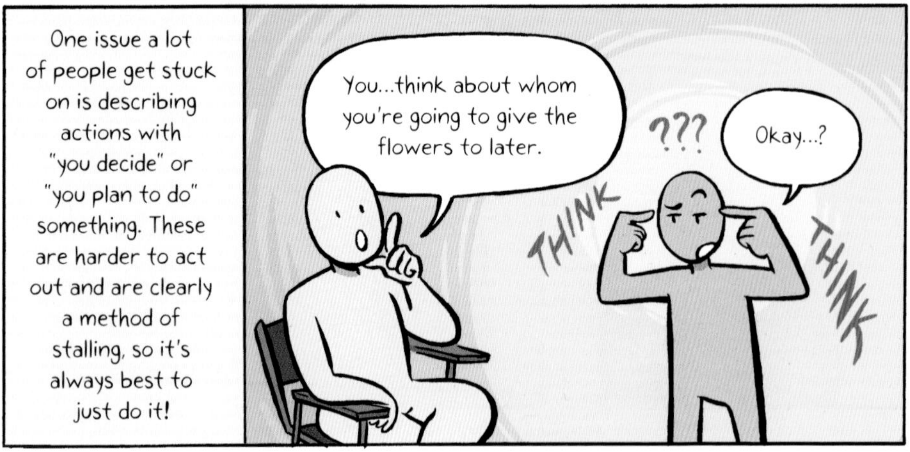
One issue a lot of people get stuck on is describing actions with "you decide" or "you plan to do" something. These are harder to act out and are clearly a method of stalling, so it's always best to just do it!
You...think about whom you're going to give the flowers to later.
???
Okay...?
THINK
THINK

Advance & Expand

In this game, the director is more of a support for the actor, who is telling the story. It's the director's job to keep the narrative on track by interrupting with **advance** or **expand**.

Advance means "move the story along," like we've been in one place too long and we want to see what happens next.

Expand means "stop the story"—or more specifically, spend more time on the action just mentioned. Give us more detail. What do you see? What do you smell? How are you feeling?

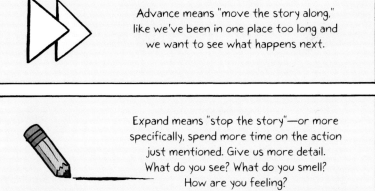

The constant switching forces you to stop worrying about the future and tend to what you're doing in the moment.

So the game's more into the idea of "You go ahead and I'll help you out," as opposed to "I'm gonna tell you what to do and you're gonna follow."

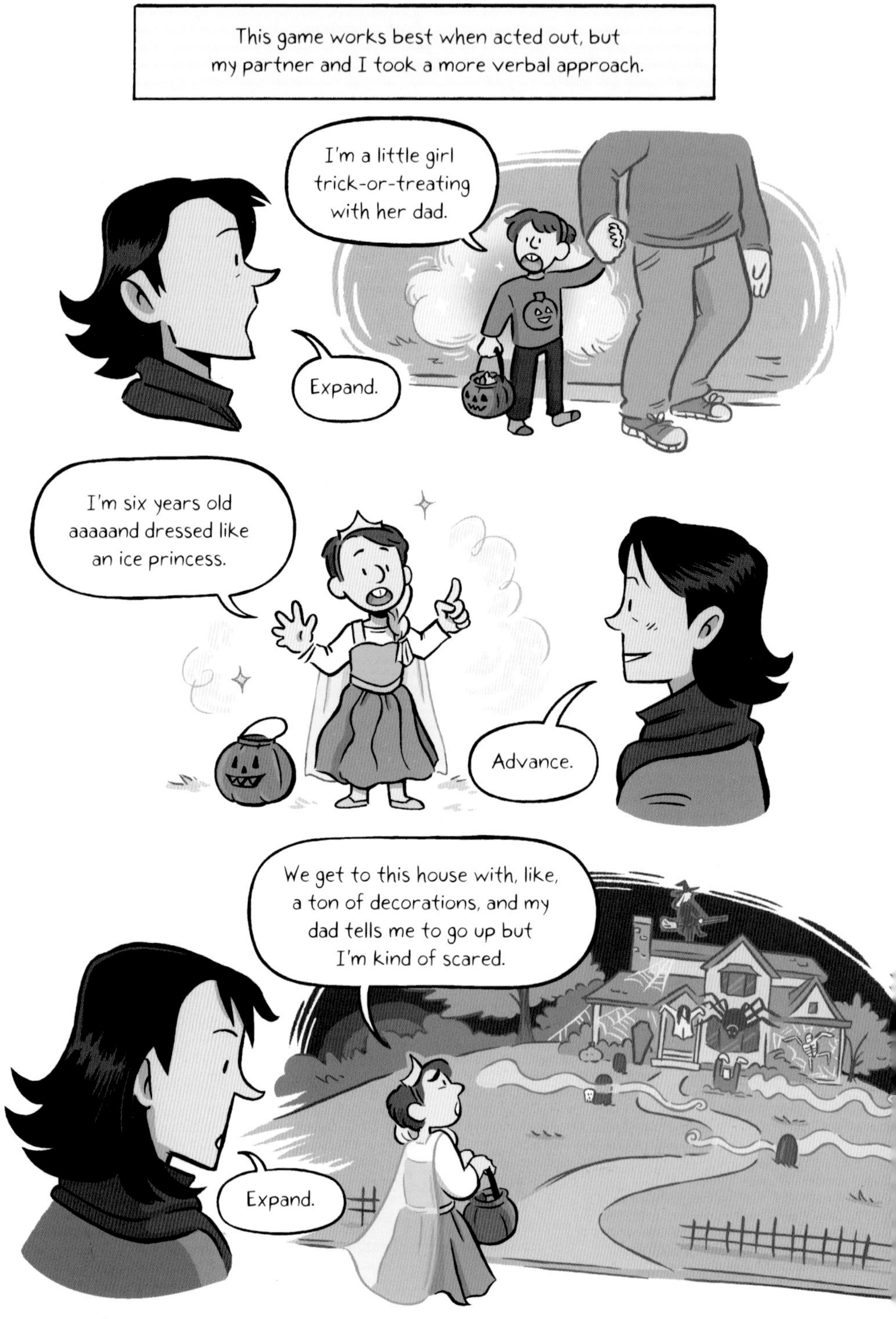
This game works best when acted out, but my partner and I took a more verbal approach.
I'm a little girl trick-or-treating with her dad.
Expand.
I'm six years old aaaaand dressed like an ice princess.
Advance.
We get to this house with, like, a ton of decorations, and my dad tells me to go up but I'm kind of scared.
Expand.

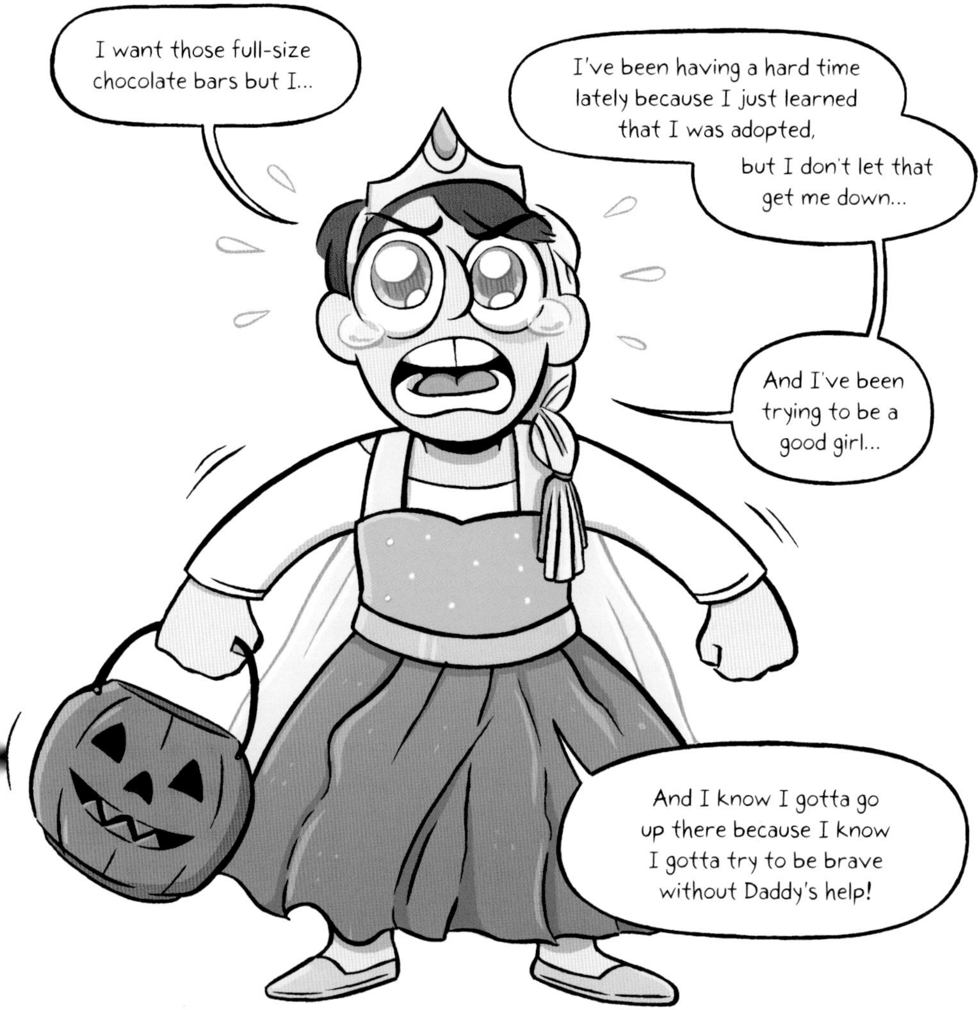
I want those full-size chocolate bars but I...
I've been having a hard time lately because I just learned that I was adopted,
but I don't let that get me down...
And I've been trying to be a good girl...
And I know I gotta go up there because I know I gotta try to be brave without Daddy's help!

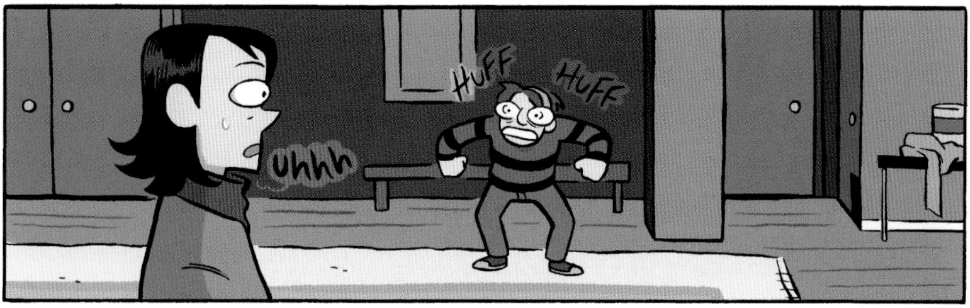
HUFF
HUFF
Uhhh

The idea of these exercises is to learn to relinquish control and accept that you won't always be driving the scene.

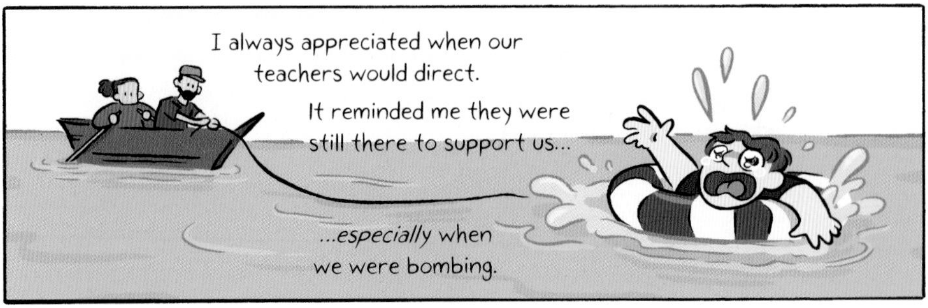
I always appreciated when our teachers would direct.
It reminded me they were still there to support us...
...*especially* when we were bombing.

COULD'VE SAID clearly demonstrates this.

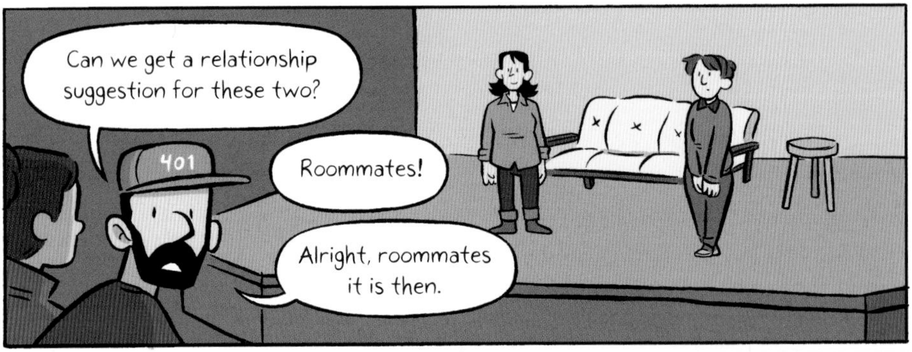
Can we get a relationship suggestion for these two?
401
Roommates!
Alright, roommates it is then.

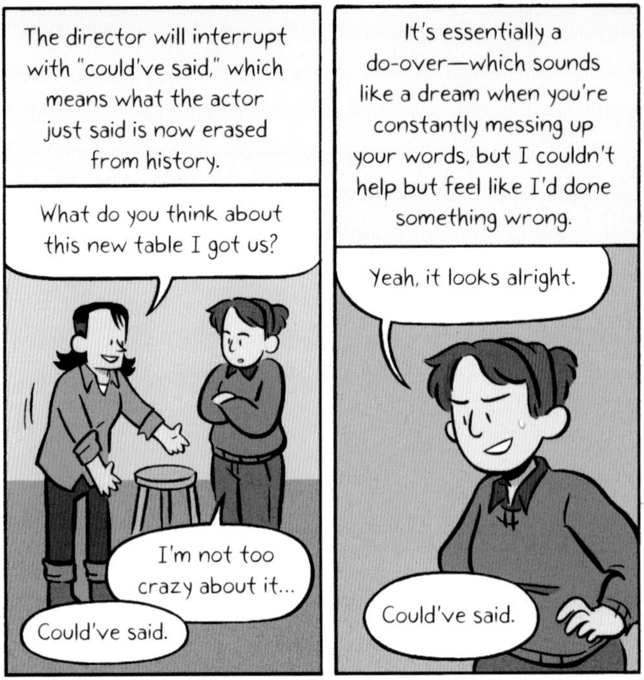
The director will interrupt with "could've said," which means what the actor just said is now erased from history.
What do you think about this new table I got us?
I'm not too crazy about it...
Could've said.
It's essentially a do-over—which sounds like a dream when you're constantly messing up your words, but I couldn't help but feel like I'd done something wrong.
Yeah, it looks alright.
Could've said.

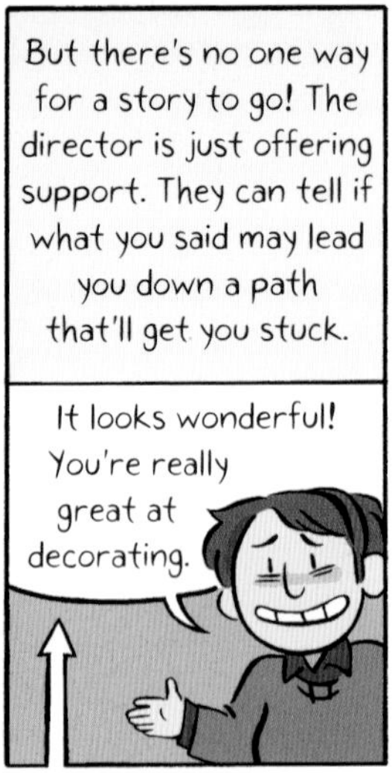
But there's no one way for a story to go! The director is just offering support. They can tell if what you said may lead you down a path that'll get you stuck.
It looks wonderful! You're really great at decorating.

Positive, but also gives us more character background: Mallory is a great decorator, and Alex admires her for it.

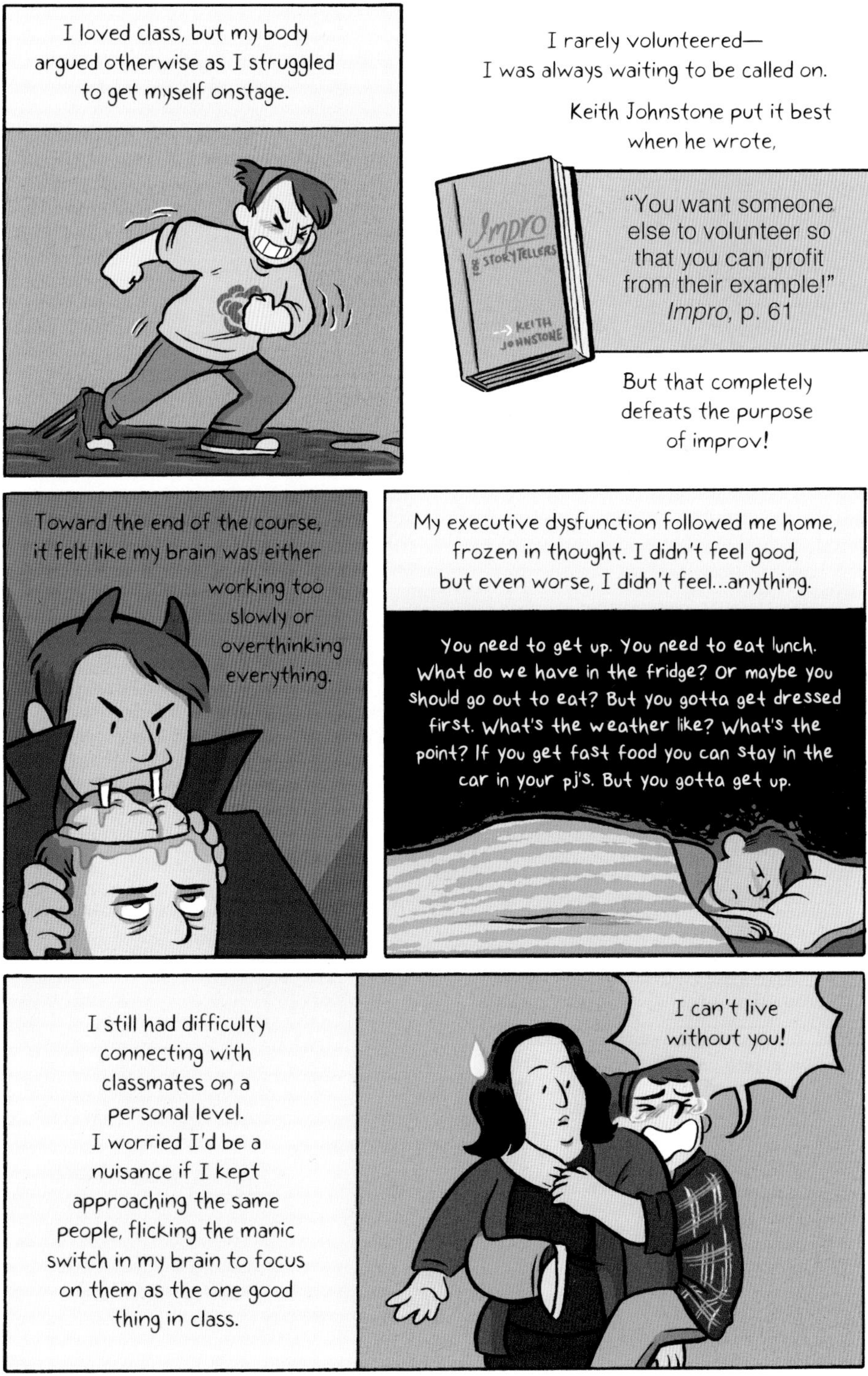
I loved class, but my body argued otherwise as I struggled to get myself onstage.
I rarely volunteered— I was always waiting to be called on.
Keith Johnstone put it best when he wrote,
Impro
for Storytellers
Keith Johnstone
"You want someone else to volunteer so that you can profit from their example!" *Impro*, p. 61
But that completely defeats the purpose of improv!
Toward the end of the course, it felt like my brain was either
working too slowly or overthinking everything.
My executive dysfunction followed me home, frozen in thought. I didn't feel good, but even worse, I didn't feel...anything.
You need to get up. You need to eat lunch. What do we have in the fridge? Or maybe you should go out to eat? But you gotta get dressed first. What's the weather like? What's the point? If you get fast food you can stay in the car in your pj's. But you gotta get up.
I still had difficulty connecting with classmates on a personal level. I worried I'd be a nuisance if I kept approaching the same people, flicking the manic switch in my brain to focus on them as the one good thing in class.
I can't live without you!

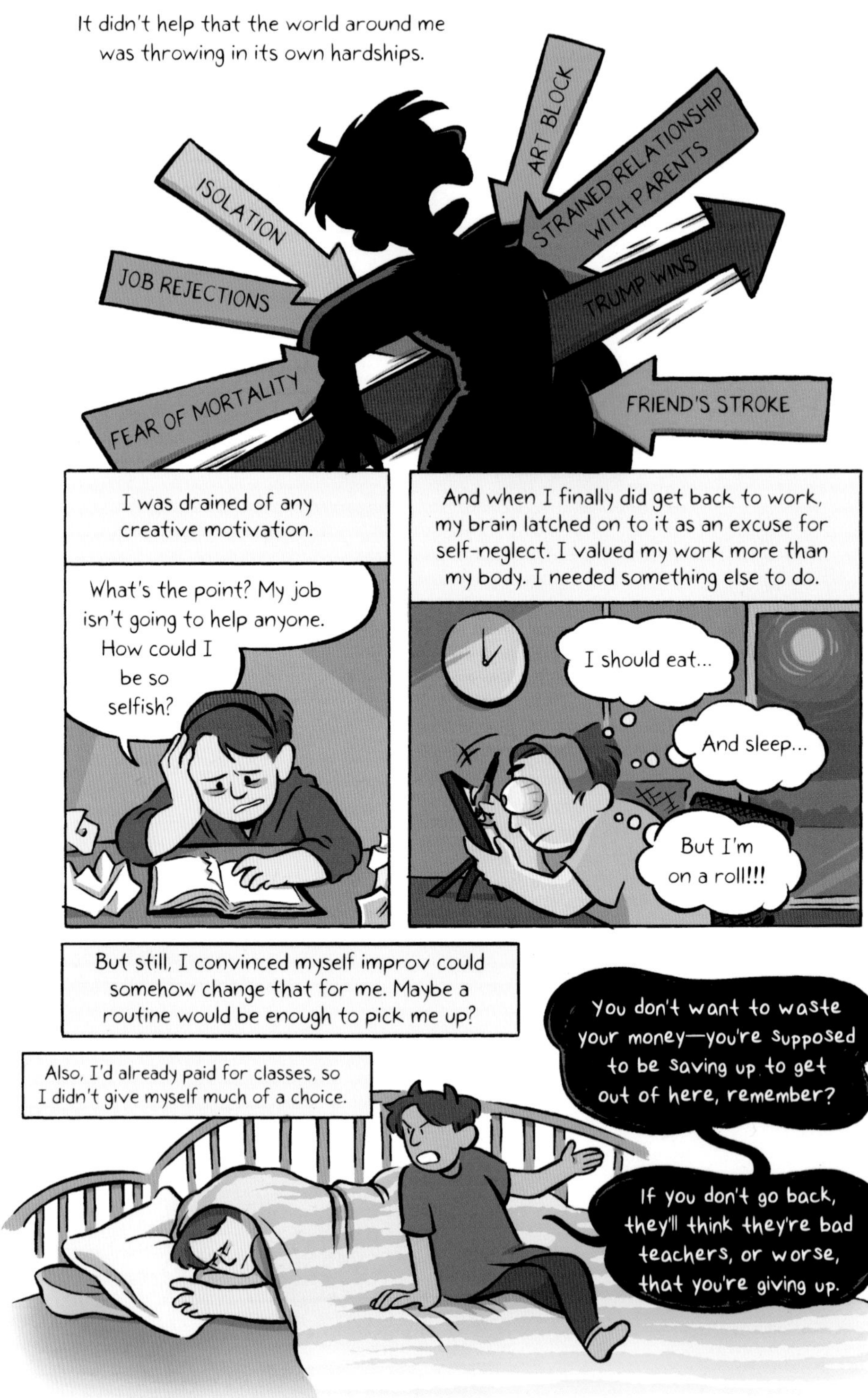
It didn't help that the world around me was throwing in its own hardships.
ISOLATION
ART BLOCK
STRAINED RELATIONSHIP WITH PARENTS
JOB REJECTIONS
TRUMP WINS
FEAR OF MORTALITY
FRIEND'S STROKE
I was drained of any creative motivation.
What's the point? My job isn't going to help anyone. How could I be so selfish?
And when I finally did get back to work, my brain latched on to it as an excuse for self-neglect. I valued my work more than my body. I needed something else to do.
I should eat...
And sleep...
But I'm on a roll!!!
But still, I convinced myself improv could somehow change that for me. Maybe a routine would be enough to pick me up?
Also, I'd already paid for classes, so I didn't give myself much of a choice.
You don't want to waste your money—you're supposed to be saving up to get out of here, remember?
If you don't go back, they'll think they're bad teachers, or worse, that you're giving up.

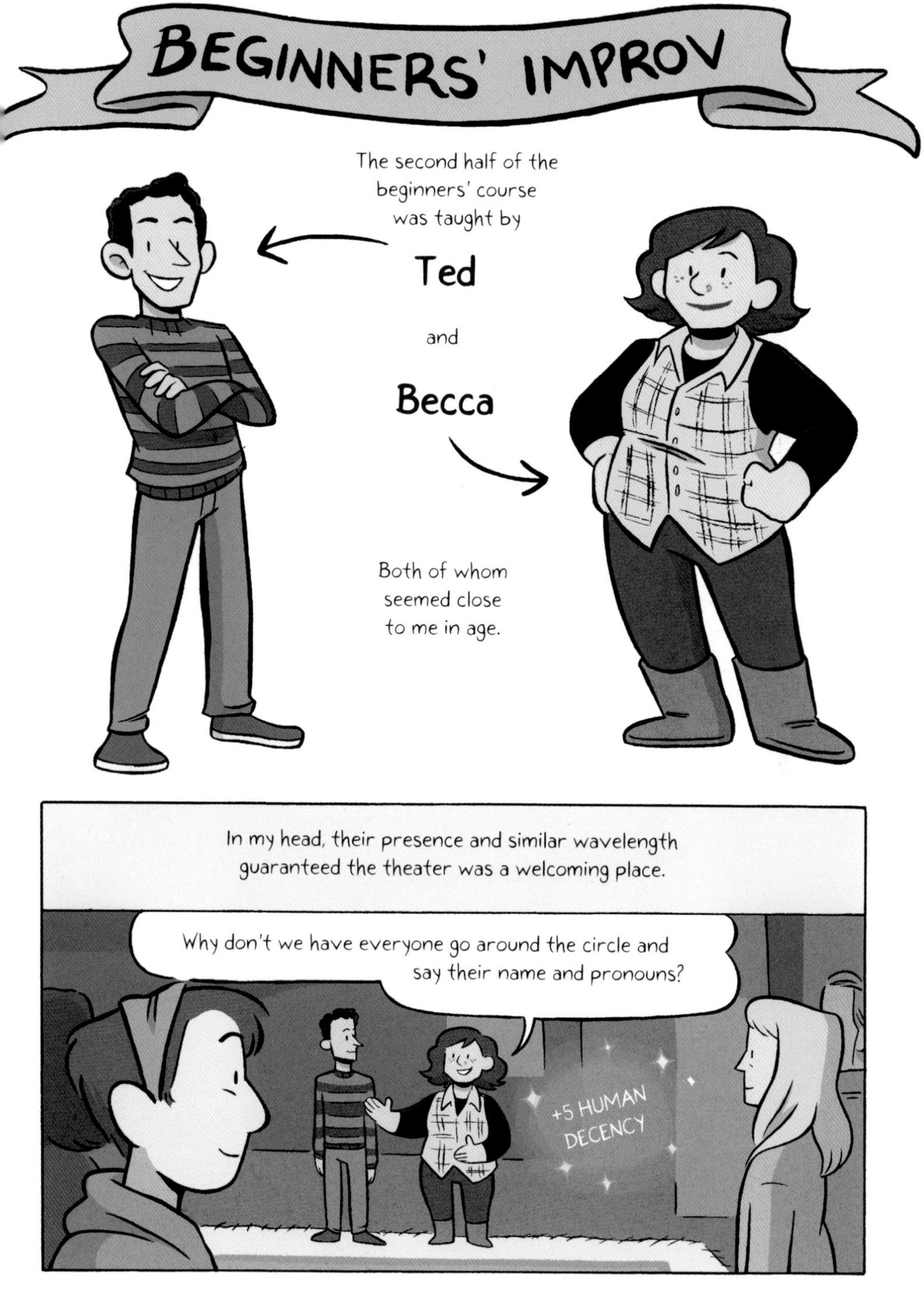
BEGINNERS' IMPROV
The second half of the beginners' course was taught by
Ted
and
Becca
Both of whom seemed close to me in age.
In my head, their presence and similar wavelength guaranteed the theater was a welcoming place.
Why don't we have everyone go around the circle and say their name and pronouns?
+5 HUMAN DECENCY

Ted ran us through some breathing exercises to start, but it seemed like eye contact and clapping games were universal warm-ups throughout CTC classes.

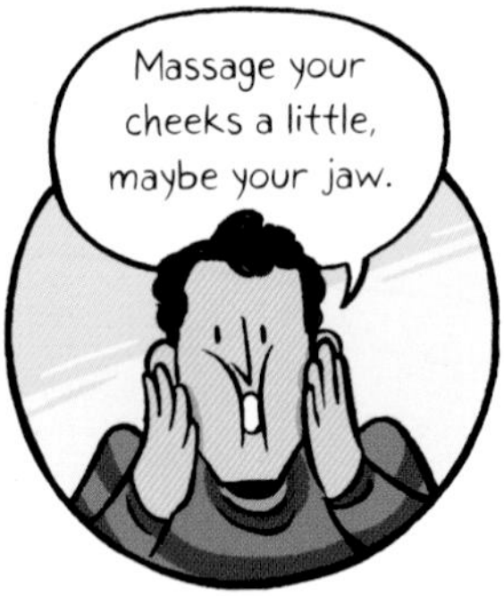
Massage your cheeks a little, maybe your jaw.

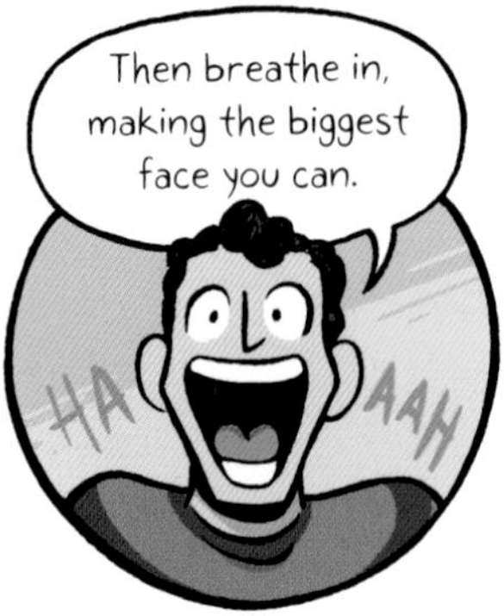
Then breathe in, making the biggest face you can.
HA
AAH

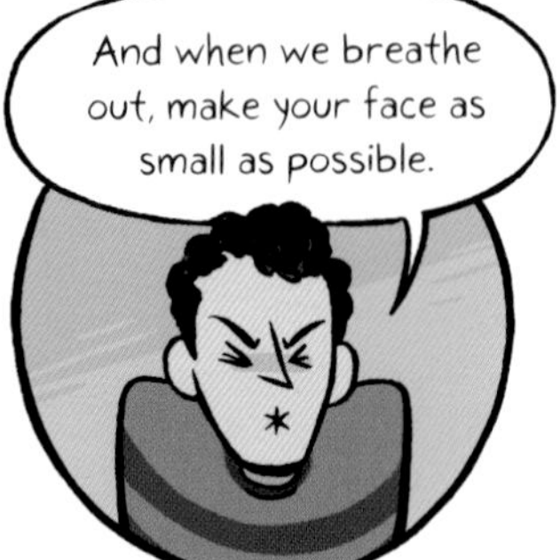
And when we breathe out, make your face as small as possible.

The Clapping Game is an introductory icebreaker and a good brainteaser.

ROUND 1.

In the first round, you clap to a person, much like you would during an eye contact circle, and say your name.

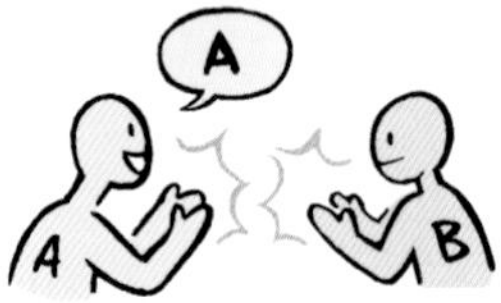
A
A
B

ROUND 2.

Then, to practice learning everyone's names, the next round has you clap to a person and say their name. (It's okay to ask if you don't remember!)

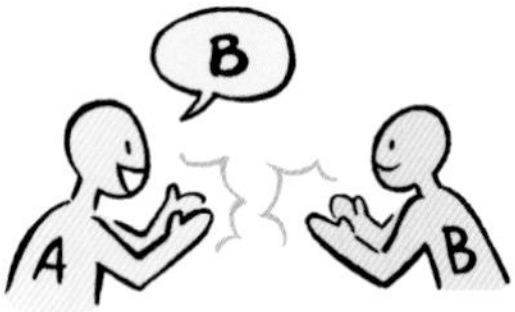
B
A
B

ROUND 3.

Now is where it gets tricky. Clap to a person and say the name of the person you want them to clap to. It sounds simple but it's easy to get your wires crossed.

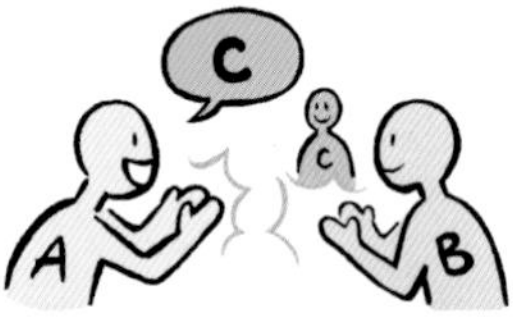
C
A
C
B

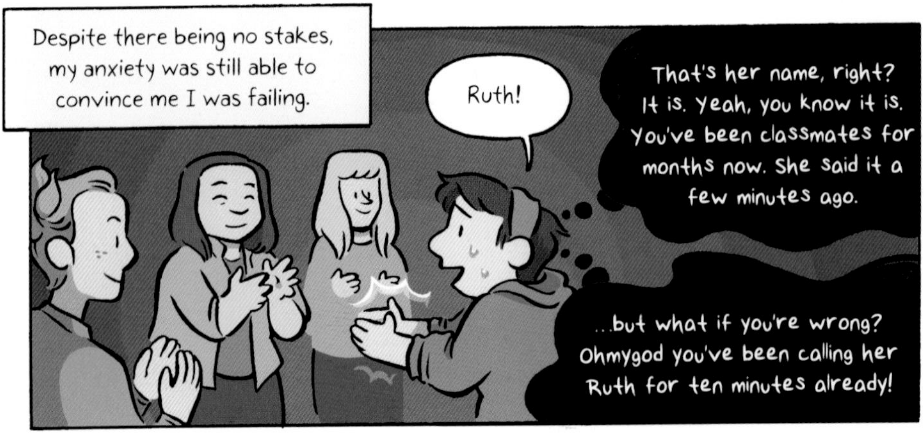
Despite there being no stakes, my anxiety was still able to convince me I was failing.
Ruth!
That's her name, right? It is. Yeah, you know it is. You've been classmates for months now. She said it a few minutes ago.
...but what if you're wrong? Ohmygod you've been calling her Ruth for ten minutes already!

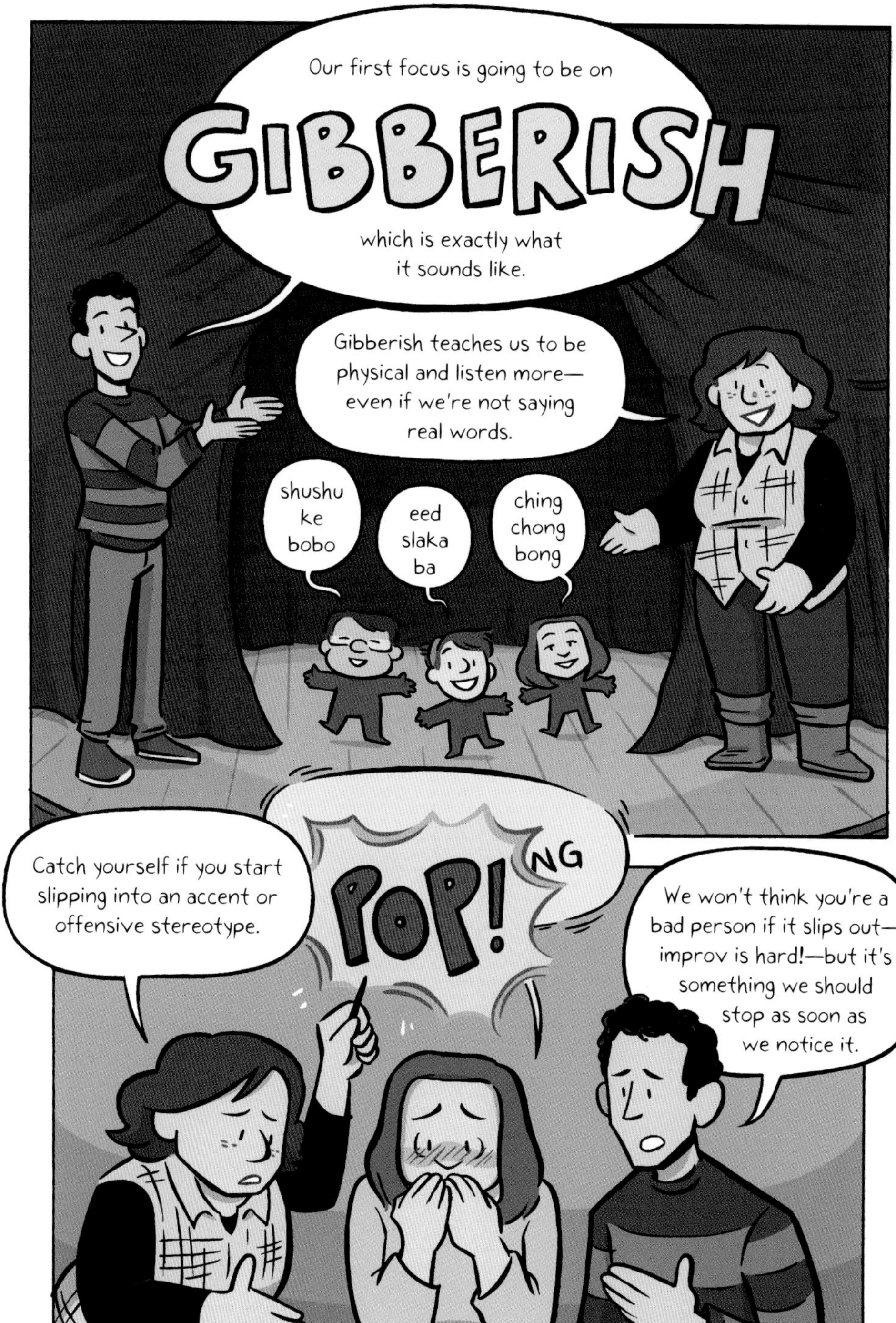

Our first focus is going to be on
GIBBERISH
which is exactly what it sounds like.
Gibberish teaches us to be physical and listen more—even if we're not saying real words.
shushu ke bobo
eed slaka ba
ching chong bong
Catch yourself if you start slipping into an accent or offensive stereotype.
POP!
NG
We won't think you're a bad person if it slips out—improv is hard!—but it's something we should stop as soon as we notice it.

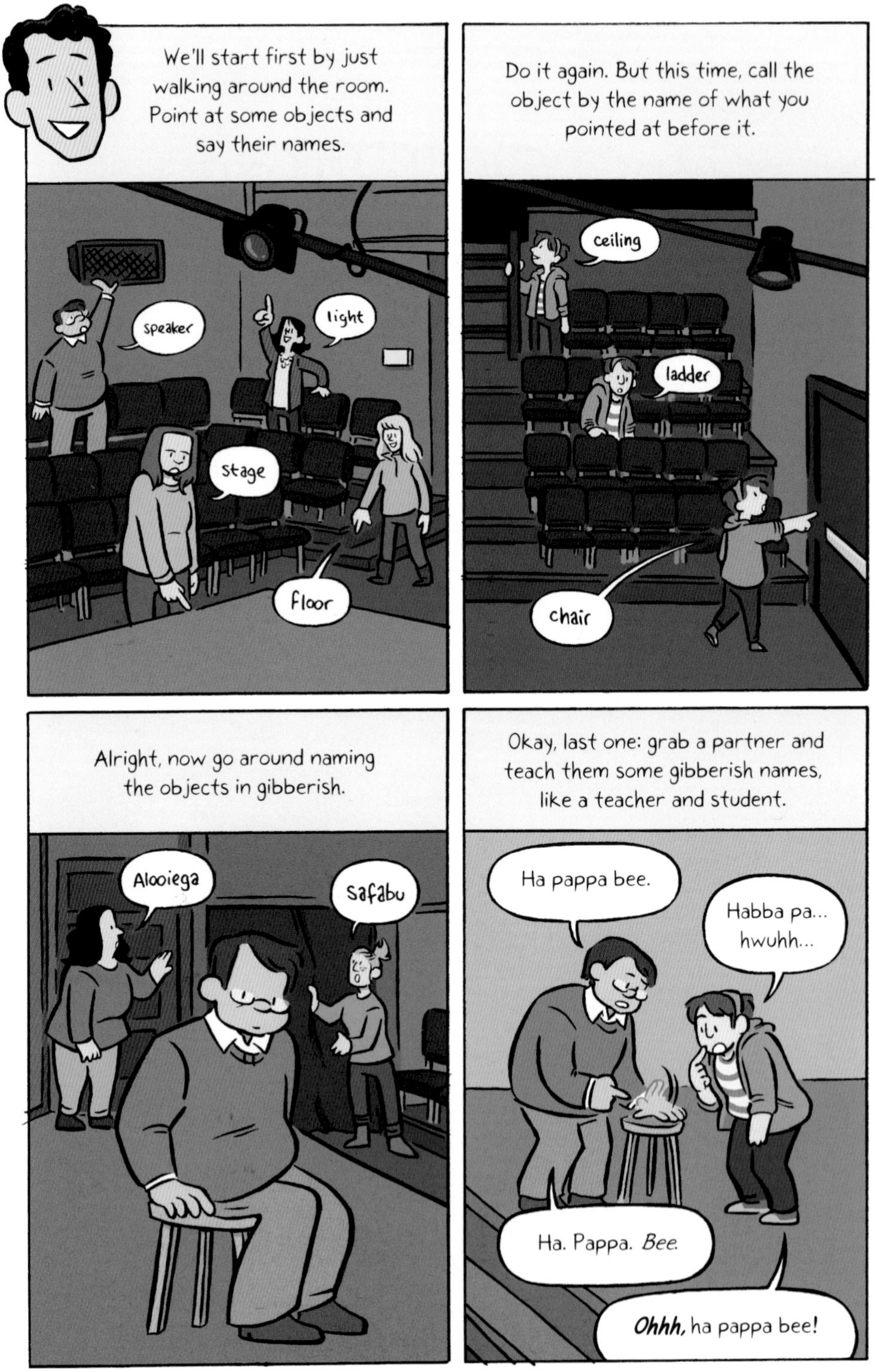
We'll start first by just walking around the room. Point at some objects and say their names.
speaker
light
stage
floor
Do it again. But this time, call the object by the name of what you pointed at before it.
ceiling
ladder
chair
Alright, now go around naming the objects in gibberish.
Alooiega
safabu
Okay, last one: grab a partner and teach them some gibberish names, like a teacher and student.
Ha pappa bee.
Habba pa... hwuhh...
Ha. Pappa. *Bee.*
Ohhh, ha pappa bee!

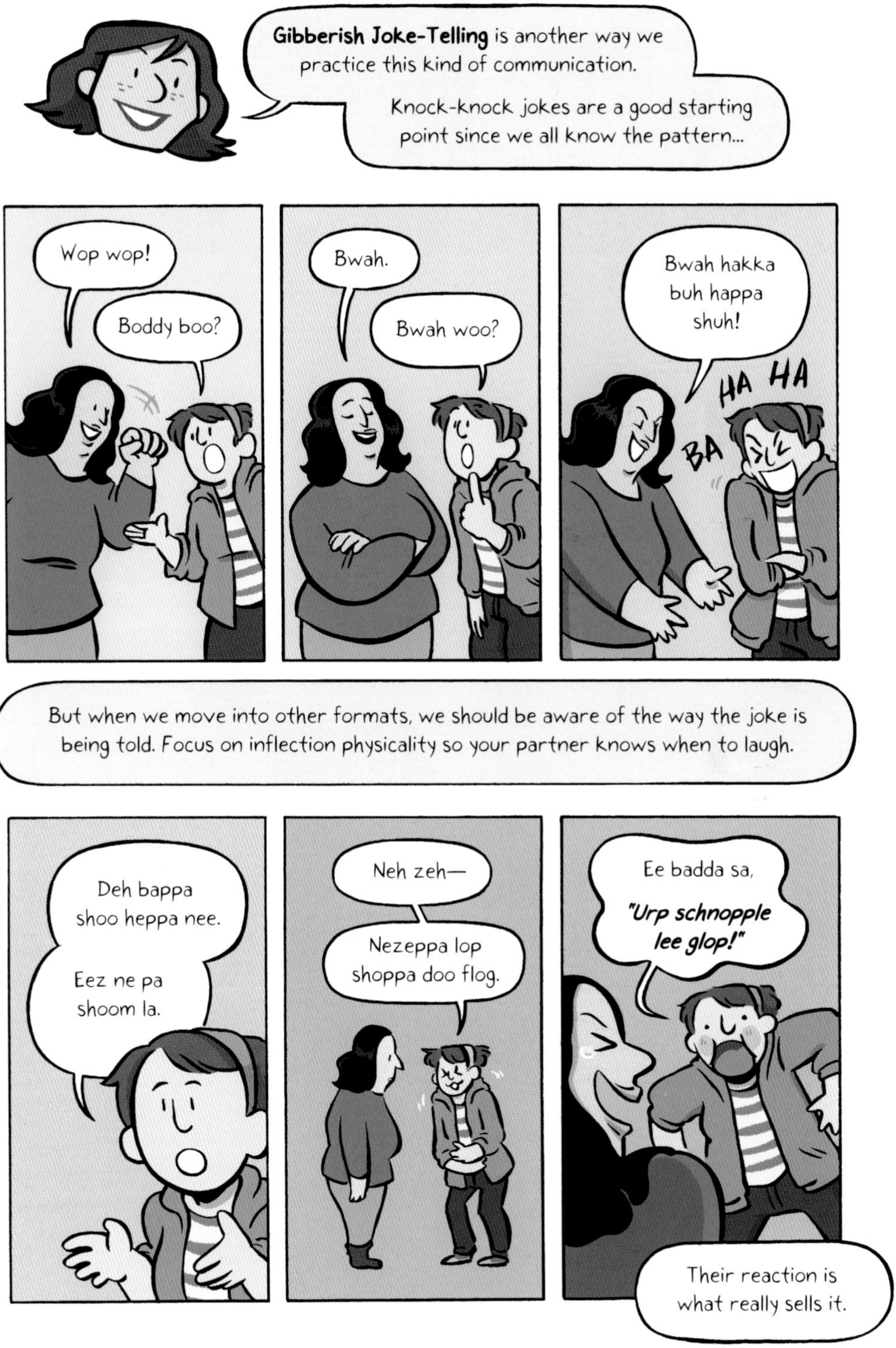

Gibberish Joke-Telling is another way we practice this kind of communication.
Knock-knock jokes are a good starting point since we all know the pattern...
Wop wop!
Boddy boo?
Bwah.
Bwah woo?
Bwah hakka buh happa shuh!
HA HA
BA
But when we move into other formats, we should be aware of the way the joke is being told. Focus on inflection physicality so your partner knows when to laugh.
Deh bappa shoo heppa nee.
Eez ne pa shoom la.
Neh zeh—
Nezeppa lop shoppa doo flog.
Ee badda sa,
"Urp schnopple lee glop!"
Their reaction is what really sells it.

EPIC POEM & INTERPRETIVE DANCE

WHAT YOU'LL NEED:

One gibberish poet   Three backup dancers   One translator

After getting a fake poem title from the audience, the poet speaks in gibberish, pausing after each verse. Simultaneously, the dancers move in accordance with their tone and the title's implications.

A lot of pressure is put on the translator in this game. They need to pay attention to both the poet's diction and the dancers' miming to string together a narrative.

But after the first verse or two, the poet knows how to guide the poem, the dancers have a better idea of what to act out, and the translator has more ideas to work with. It's actually kind of beautiful.

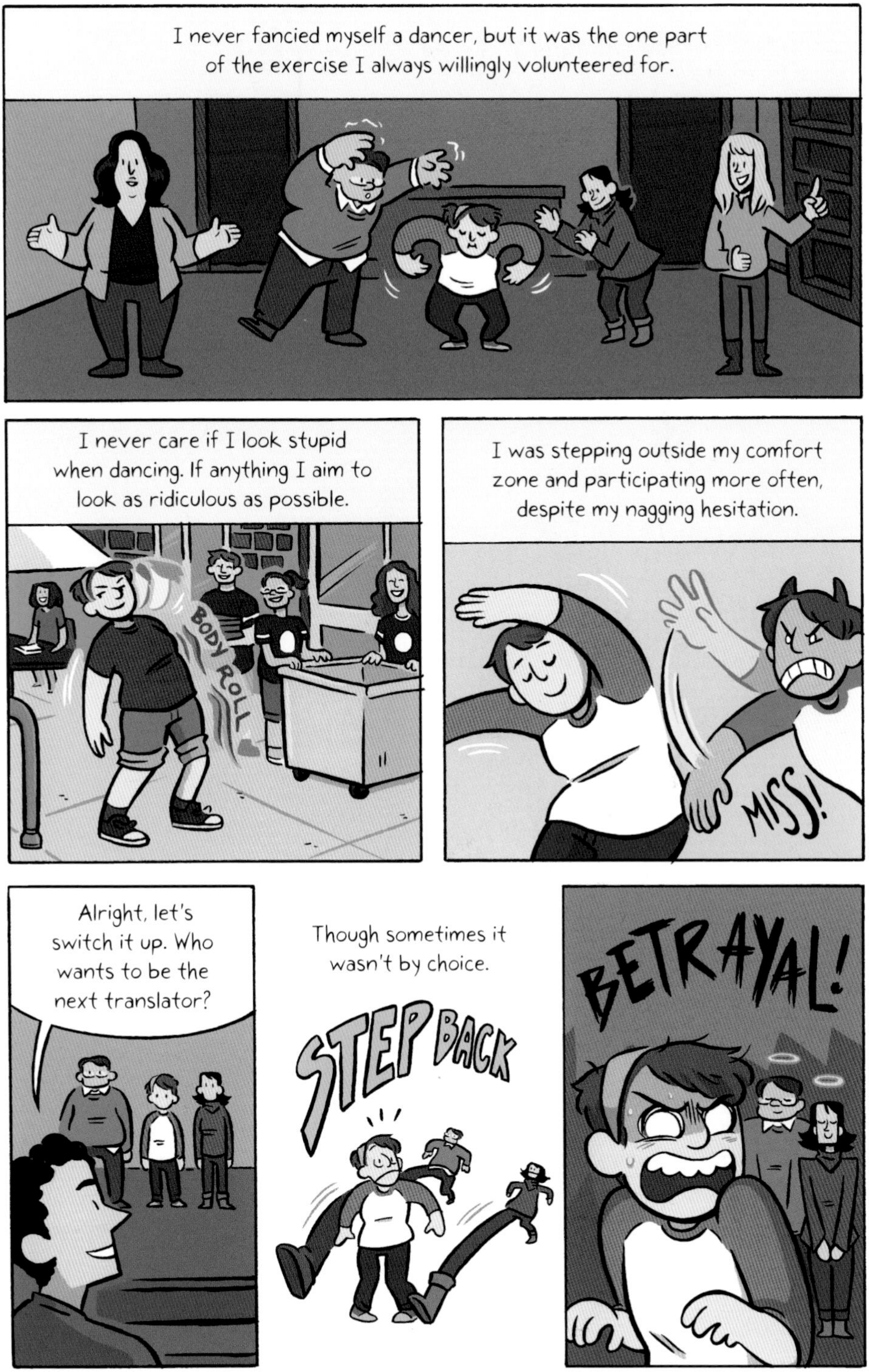
I never fancied myself a dancer, but it was the one part of the exercise I always willingly volunteered for.
I never care if I look stupid when dancing. If anything I aim to look as ridiculous as possible.
BODY ROLL
I was stepping outside my comfort zone and participating more often, despite my nagging hesitation.
MISS!
Alright, let's switch it up. Who wants to be the next translator?
Though sometimes it wasn't by choice.
STEP BACK
BETRAYAL!

BEGINNERS' IMPROV PRESENTS Our Ship Sank

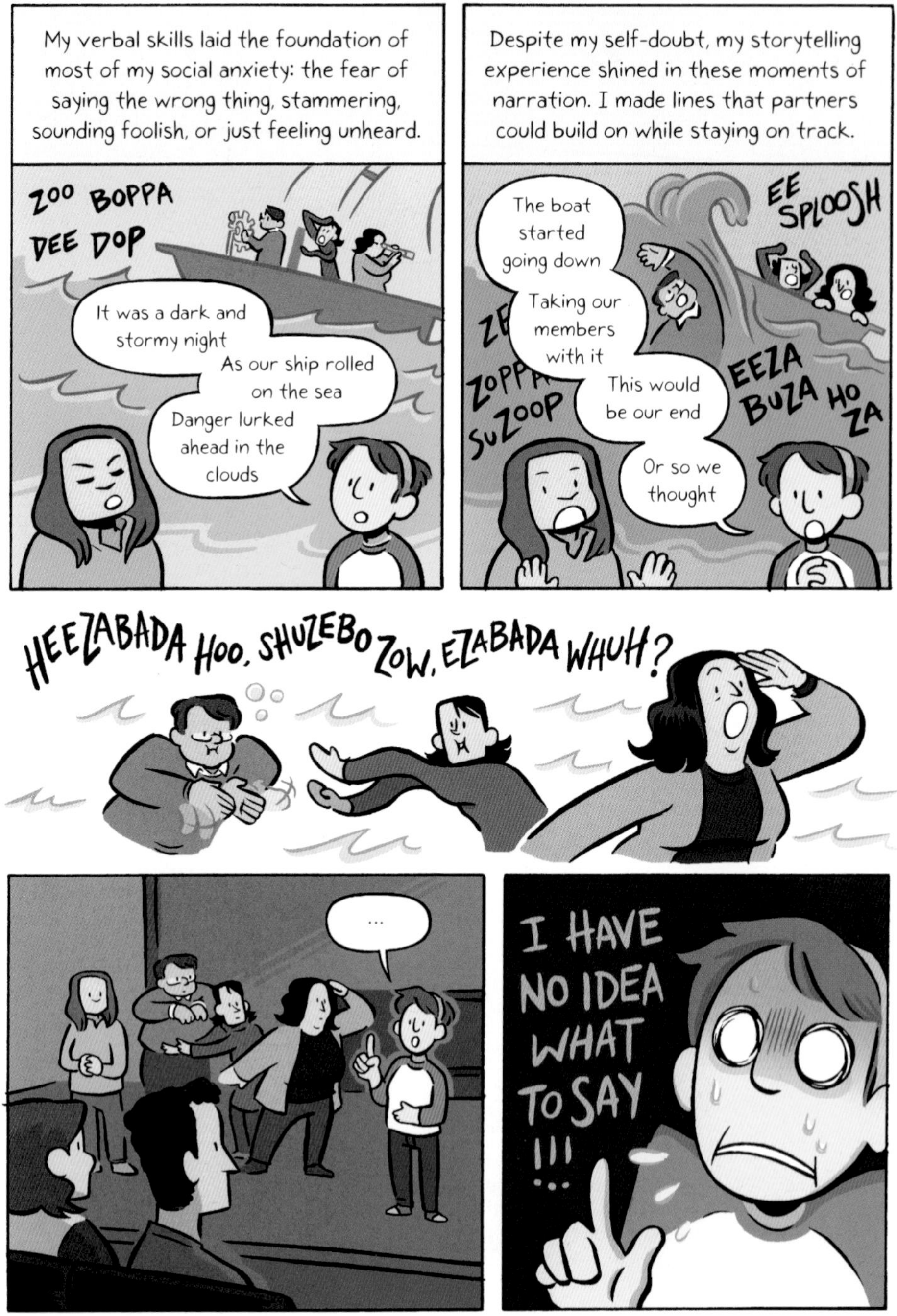

My verbal skills laid the foundation of most of my social anxiety: the fear of saying the wrong thing, stammering, sounding foolish, or just feeling unheard.
ZOO BOPPA DEE DOP
It was a dark and stormy night
As our ship rolled on the sea
Danger lurked ahead in the clouds
Despite my self-doubt, my storytelling experience shined in these moments of narration. I made lines that partners could build on while staying on track.
EE SPLOOSH
The boat started going down
Taking our members with it
ZOPPA SUZOOP
This would be our end
EEZA BUZA HO ZA
Or so we thought
HEEZABADA HOO, SHUZEBO ZOW, EZABADA WHUH?
...
I HAVE NO IDEA WHAT TO SAY !!!

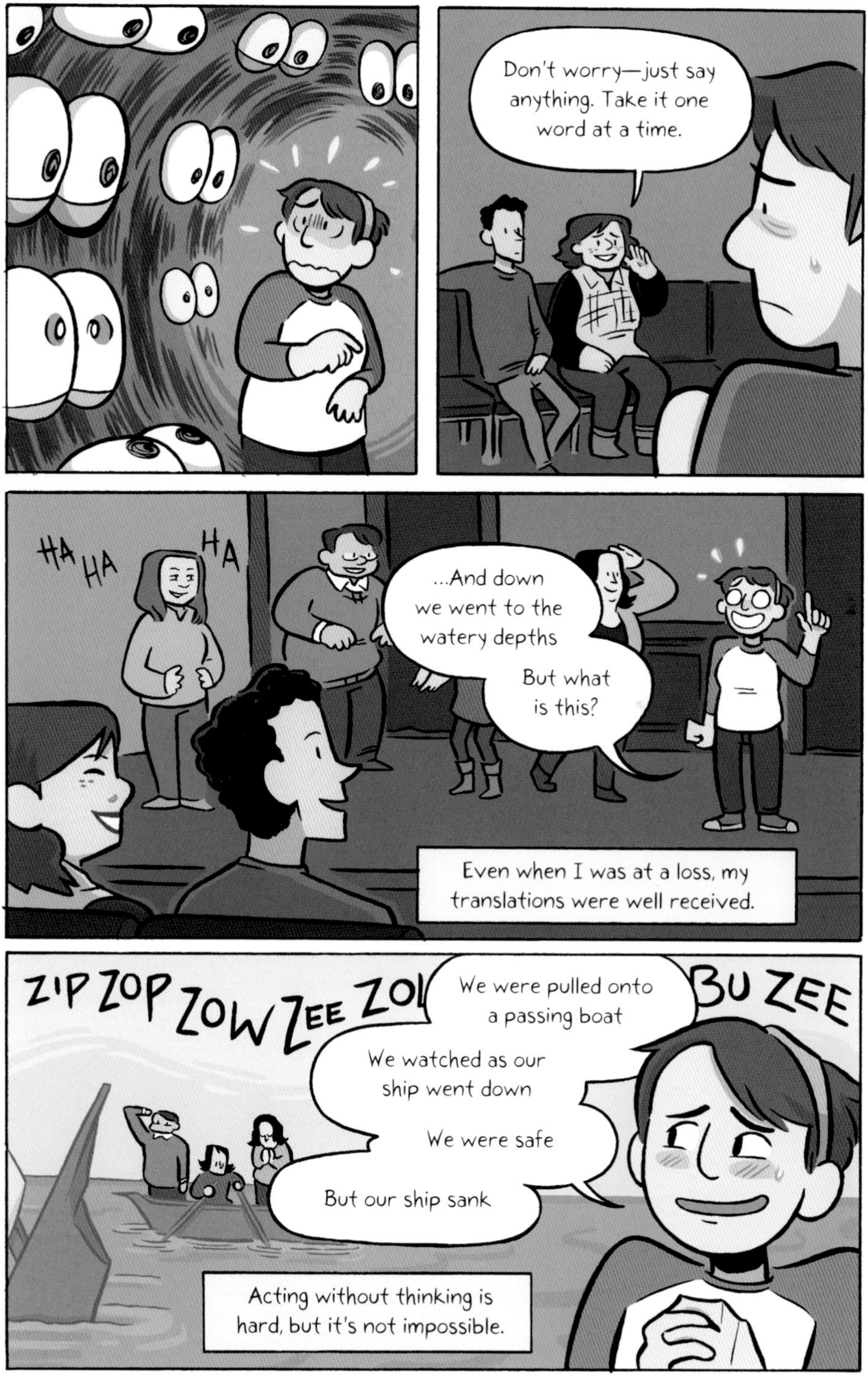
Don't worry—just say anything. Take it one word at a time.
HA HA HA
...And down we went to the watery depths
But what is this?
Even when I was at a loss, my translations were well received.
ZIP ZOP ZOW ZEE ZOI
BU ZEE
We were pulled onto a passing boat
We watched as our ship went down
We were safe
But our ship sank
Acting without thinking is hard, but it's not impossible.

We moved on to

GENRE

with some rounds of **Genre Circle,** where we each took turns going around and listing off our associations with the presented topic. It's a great example of how improv relies on the obvious.

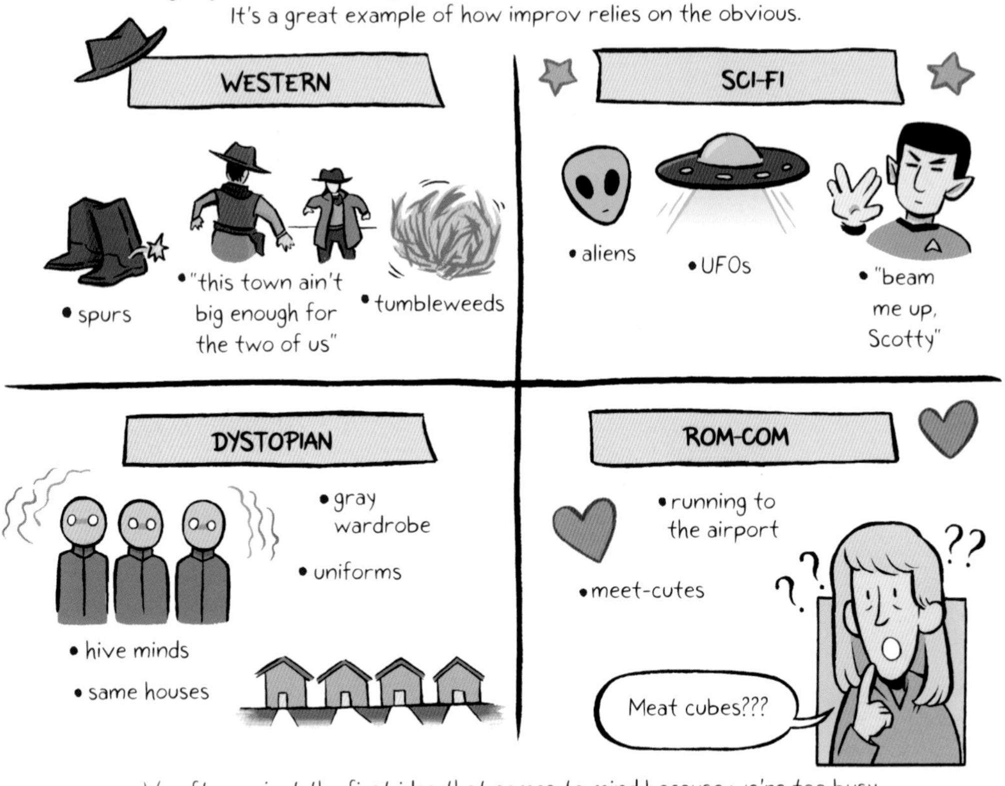
WESTERN
• spurs
• "this town ain't big enough for the two of us"
• tumbleweeds
SCI-FI
• aliens
• UFOs
• "beam me up, Scotty"
DYSTOPIAN
• gray wardrobe
• uniforms
• hive minds
• same houses
ROM-COM
• running to the airport
• meet-cutes
??
?
?
Meat cubes???

We often reject the first idea that comes to mind because we're too busy policing our thoughts, looking for one that's "interesting" or "original."

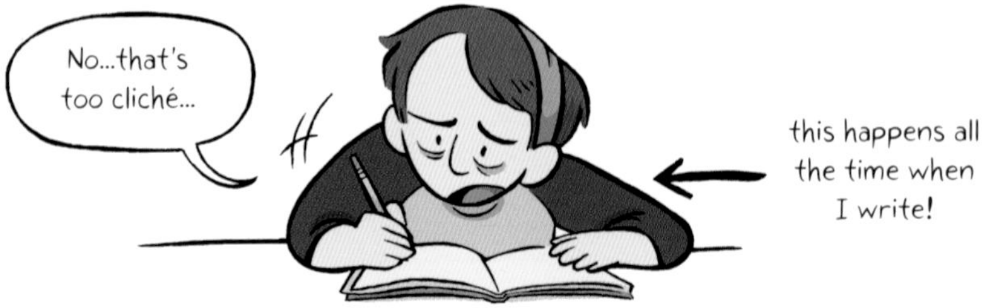
No...that's too cliché...
this happens all the time when I write!

By allowing ourselves to be average, we unearth ideas that would otherwise be overlooked. What's obvious to you might not be obvious to someone else.

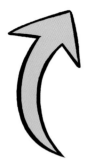

To exemplify how genre can change a scene, we played

GENRE REPLAY

performing a small scene and then repeating it in the style of a suggested genre.

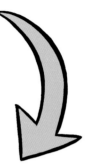

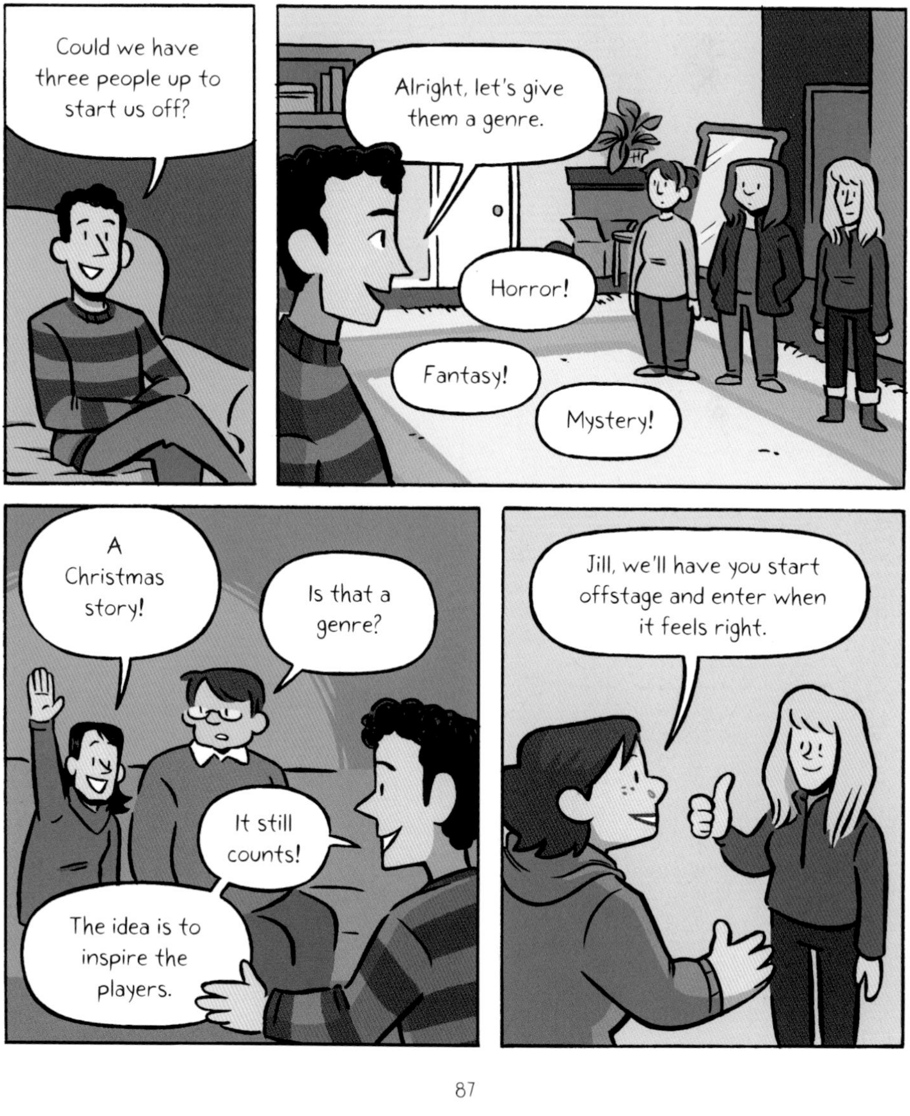
Could we have three people up to start us off?
Alright, let's give them a genre.
Horror!
Fantasy!
Mystery!
A Christmas story!
Is that a genre?
It still counts!
The idea is to inspire the players.
Jill, we'll have you start offstage and enter when it feels right.

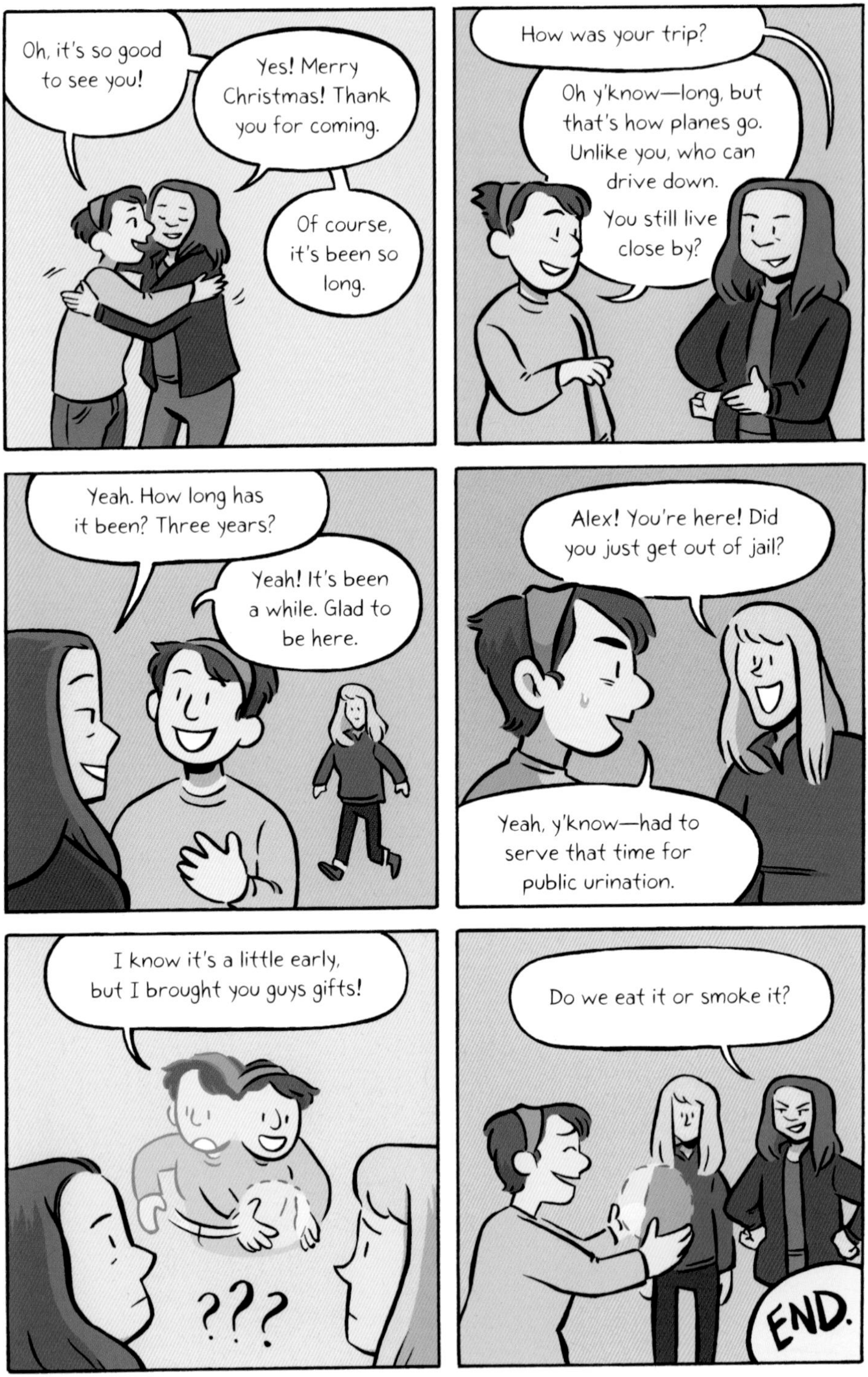
Oh, it's so good to see you!
Yes! Merry Christmas! Thank you for coming.
Of course, it's been so long.
How was your trip?
Oh y'know—long, but that's how planes go. Unlike you, who can drive down.
You still live close by?
Yeah. How long has it been? Three years?
Yeah! It's been a while. Glad to be here.
Alex! You're here! Did you just get out of jail?
Yeah, y'know—had to serve that time for public urination.
I know it's a little early, but I brought you guys gifts!
???
Do we eat it or smoke it?
END.

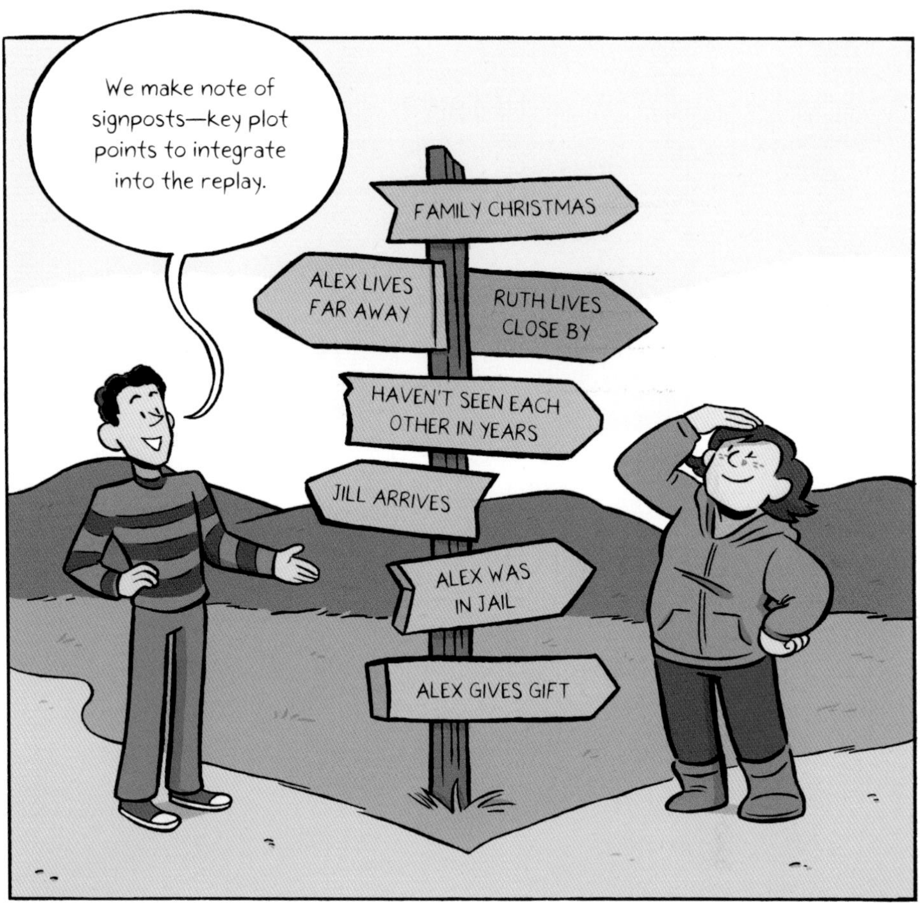
We make note of signposts—key plot points to integrate into the replay.
FAMILY CHRISTMAS
ALEX LIVES FAR AWAY
RUTH LIVES CLOSE BY
HAVEN'T SEEN EACH OTHER IN YEARS
JILL ARRIVES
ALEX WAS IN JAIL
ALEX GIVES GIFT

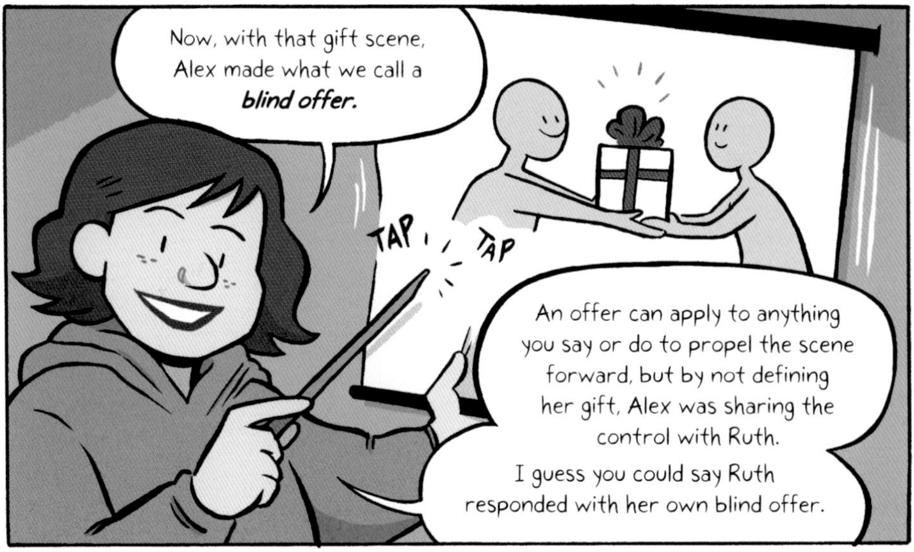
Now, with that gift scene, Alex made what we call a ***blind offer.***
TAP
TAP
An offer can apply to anything you say or do to propel the scene forward, but by not defining her gift, Alex was sharing the control with Ruth.
I guess you could say Ruth responded with her own blind offer.

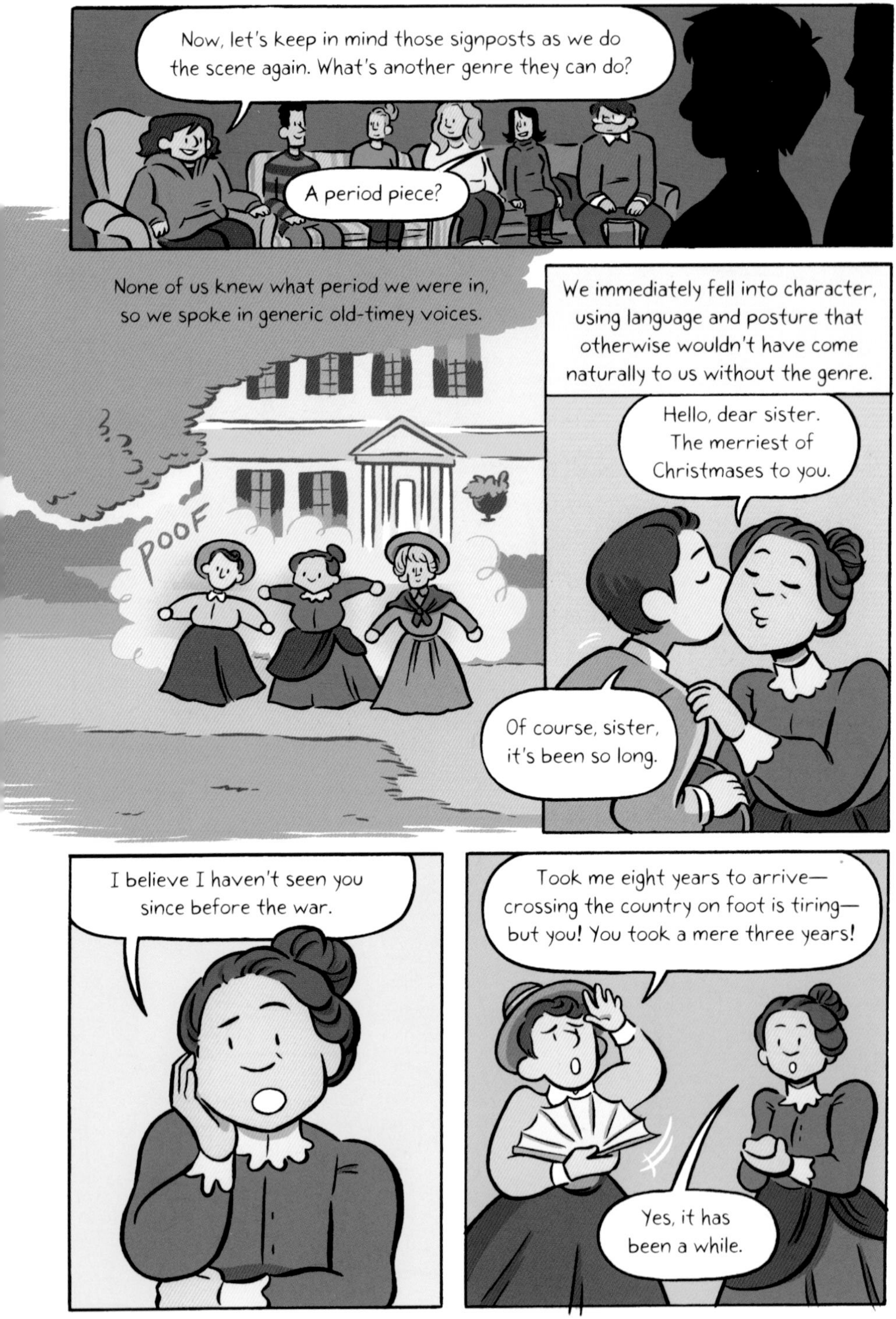
Now, let's keep in mind those signposts as we do the scene again. What's another genre they can do?
A period piece?
None of us knew what period we were in, so we spoke in generic old-timey voices.
POOF
We immediately fell into character, using language and posture that otherwise wouldn't have come naturally to us without the genre.
Hello, dear sister. The merriest of Christmases to you.
Of course, sister, it's been so long.
I believe I haven't seen you since before the war.
Took me eight years to arrive—crossing the country on foot is tiring—but you! You took a mere three years!
Yes, it has been a while.

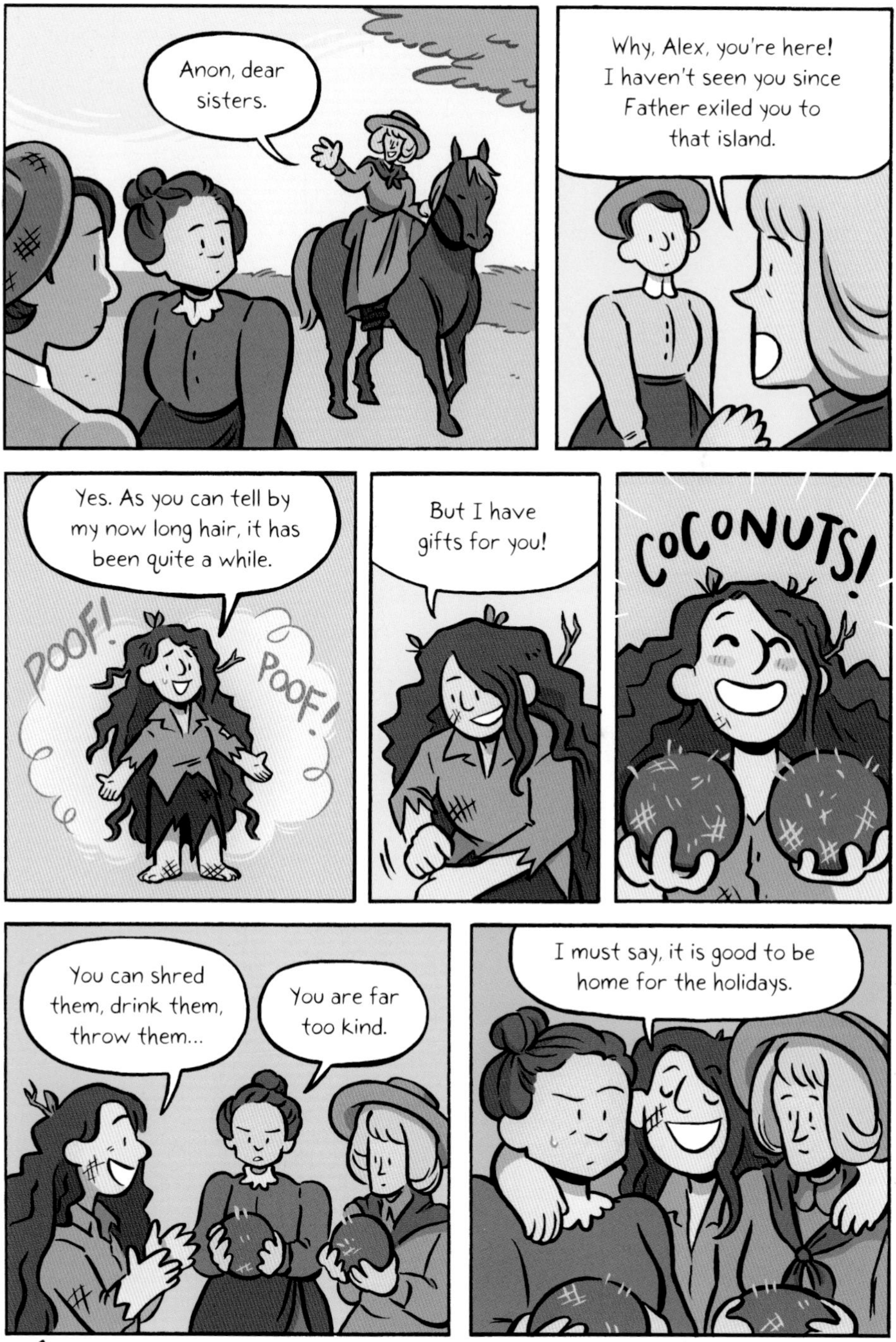
Anon, dear sisters.
Why, Alex, you're here! I haven't seen you since Father exiled you to that island.
Yes. As you can tell by my now long hair, it has been quite a while.
POOF!
POOF!
But I have gifts for you!
COCONUTS!
You can shred them, drink them, throw them...
You are far too kind.
I must say, it is good to be home for the holidays.

↑ *In this replay, I instead made a* ***controlling offer,*** *where I specified the mimed object, mostly out of fear that I had confused Ruth in the last round! More advanced improvisers tend to leave their offers more open-ended.*

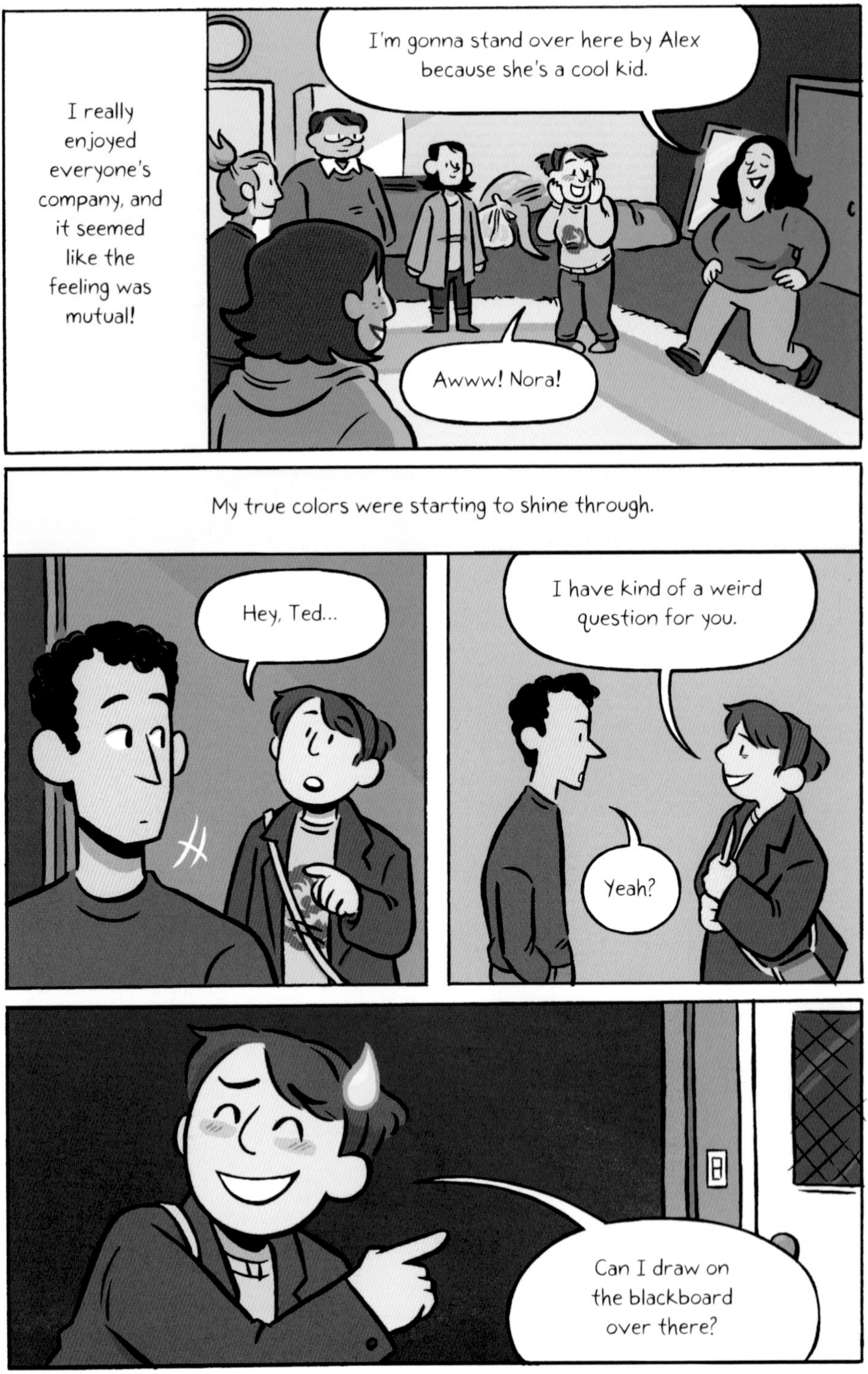
I really enjoyed everyone's company, and it seemed like the feeling was mutual!
I'm gonna stand over here by Alex because she's a cool kid.
Awww! Nora!
My true colors were starting to shine through.
Hey, Ted...
I have kind of a weird question for you.
Yeah?
Can I draw on the blackboard over there?

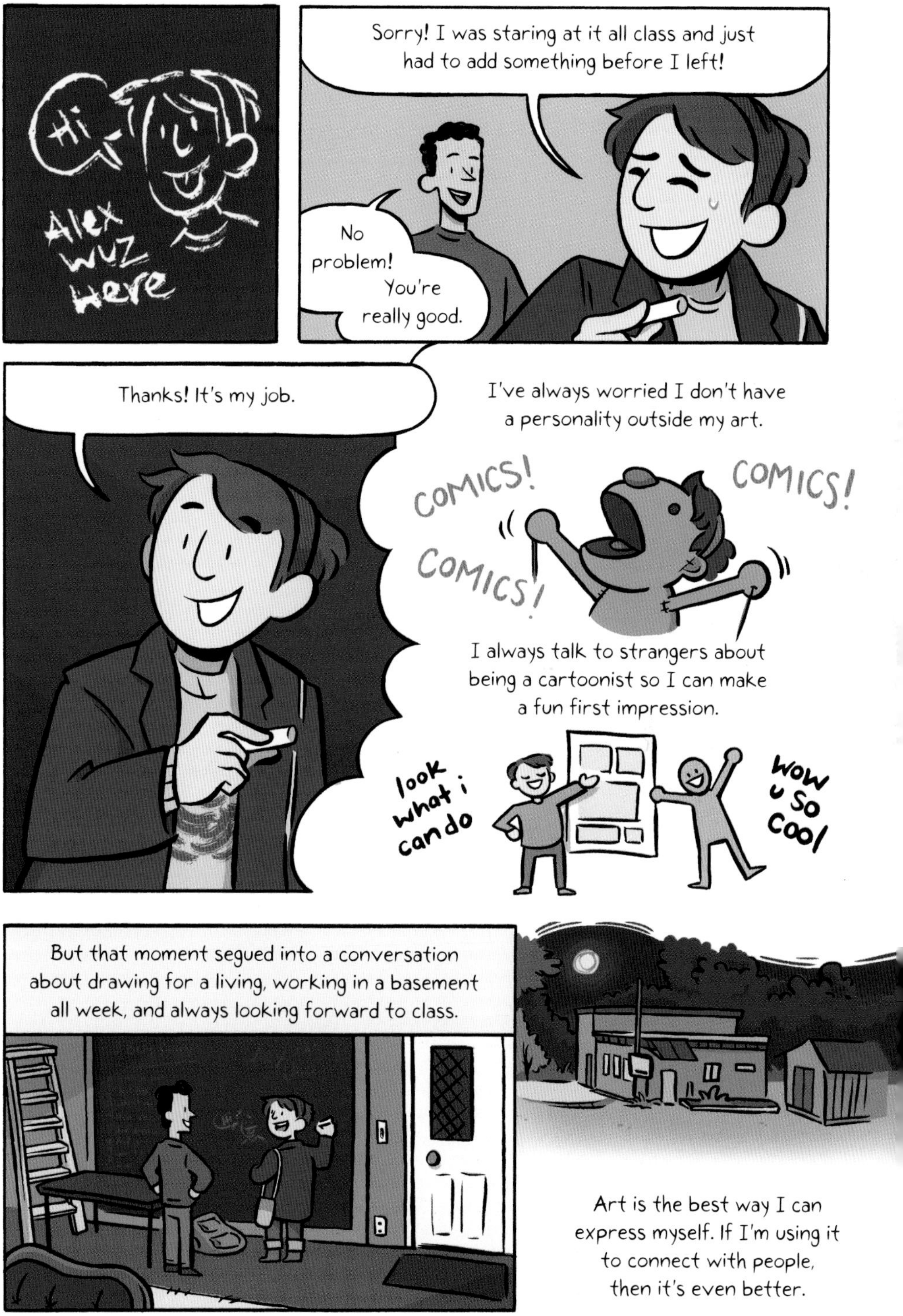
Hi
Alex wuz here
Sorry! I was staring at it all class and just had to add something before I left!
No problem! You're really good.
Thanks! It's my job.
I've always worried I don't have a personality outside my art.
COMICS!
COMICS!
COMICS!
I always talk to strangers about being a cartoonist so I can make a fun first impression.
look what i can do
wow u so cool
But that moment segued into a conversation about drawing for a living, working in a basement all week, and always looking forward to class.
Art is the best way I can express myself. If I'm using it to connect with people, then it's even better.

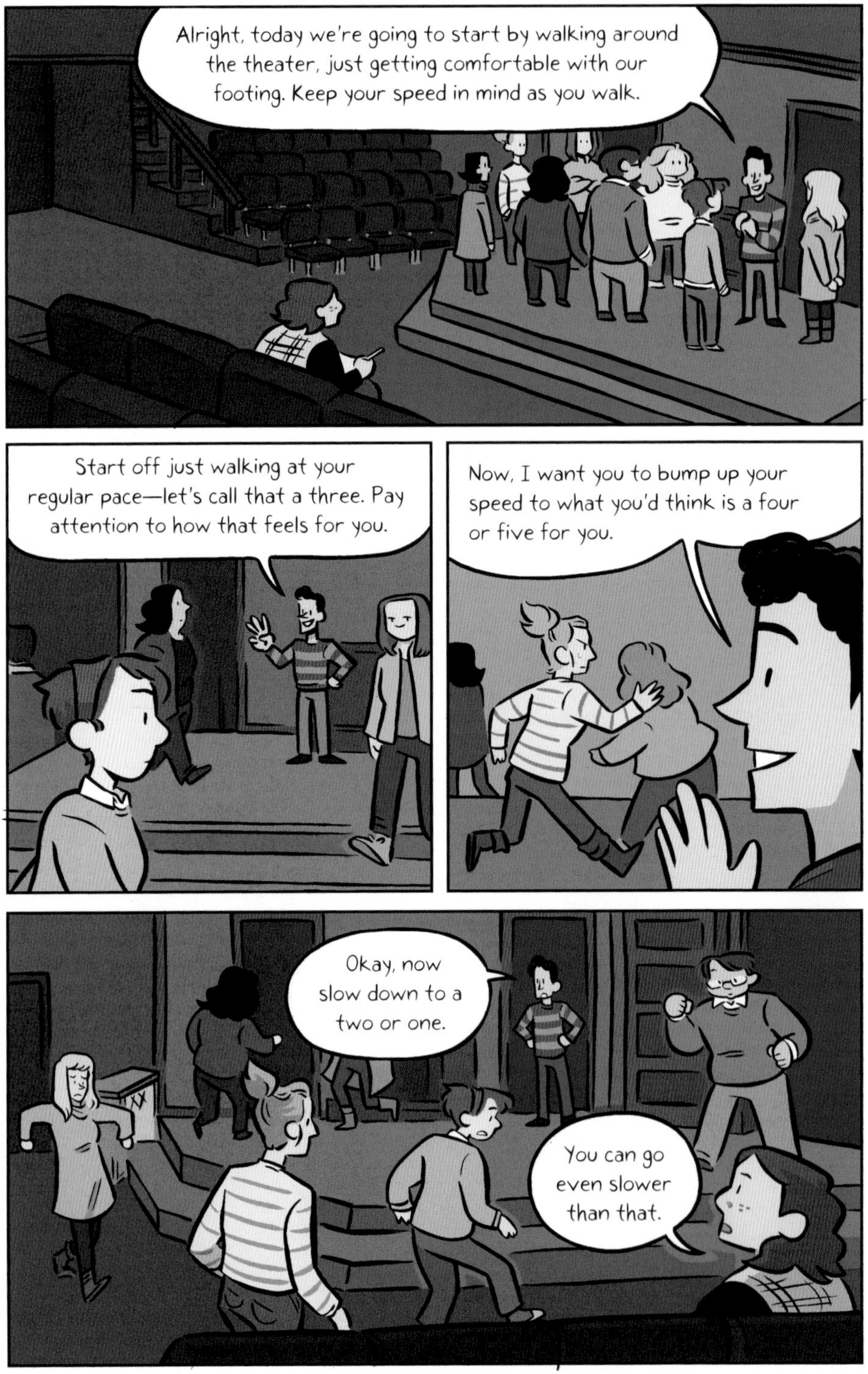
Alright, today we're going to start by walking around the theater, just getting comfortable with our footing. Keep your speed in mind as you walk.
Start off just walking at your regular pace—let's call that a three. Pay attention to how that feels for you.
Now, I want you to bump up your speed to what you'd think is a four or five for you.
Okay, now slow down to a two or one.
You can go even slower than that.

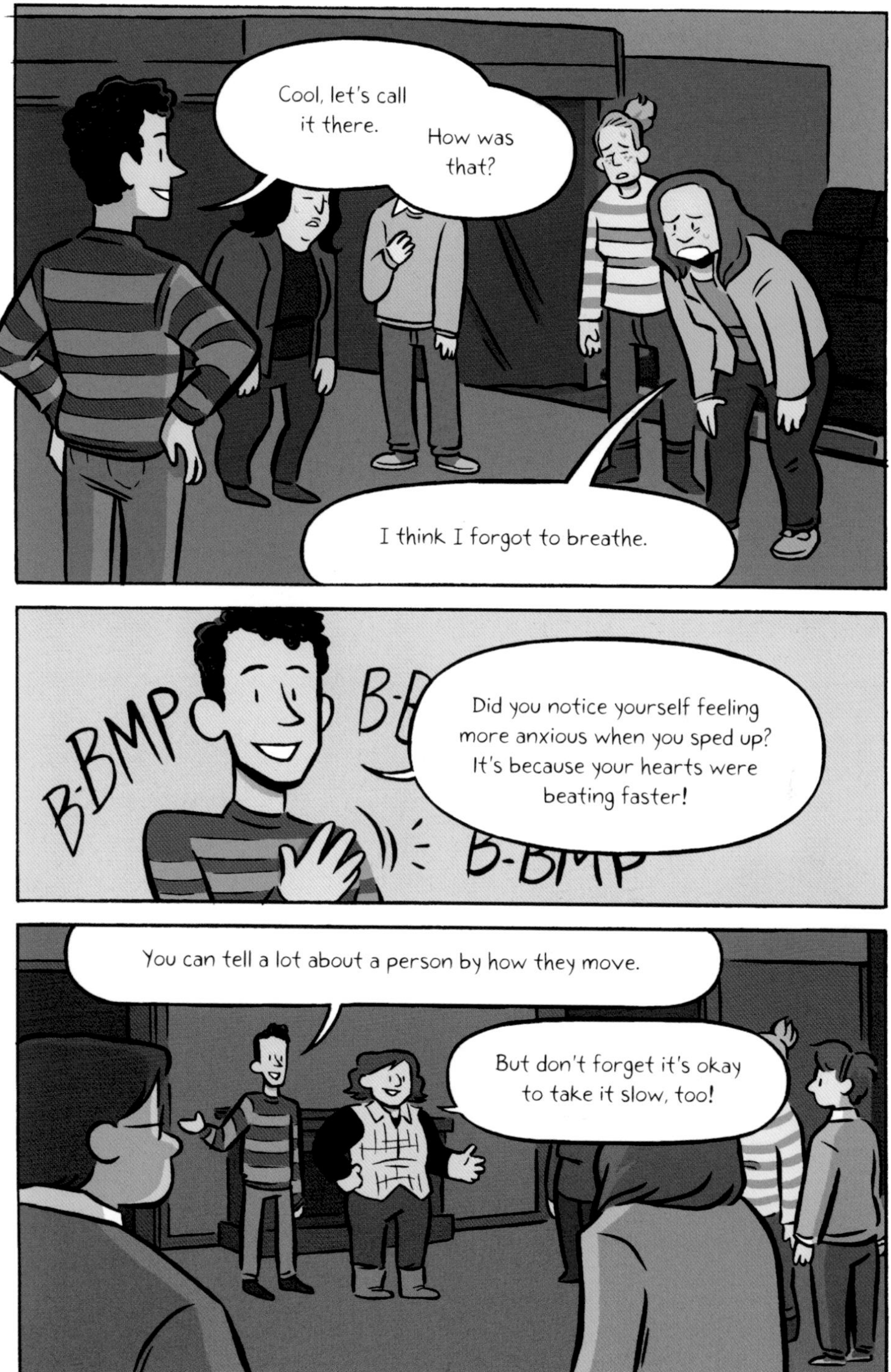
Cool, let's call it there.
How was that?
I think I forgot to breathe.
B-BMP
Did you notice yourself feeling more anxious when you sped up? It's because your hearts were beating faster!
B-BMP
You can tell a lot about a person by how they move.
But don't forget it's okay to take it slow, too!

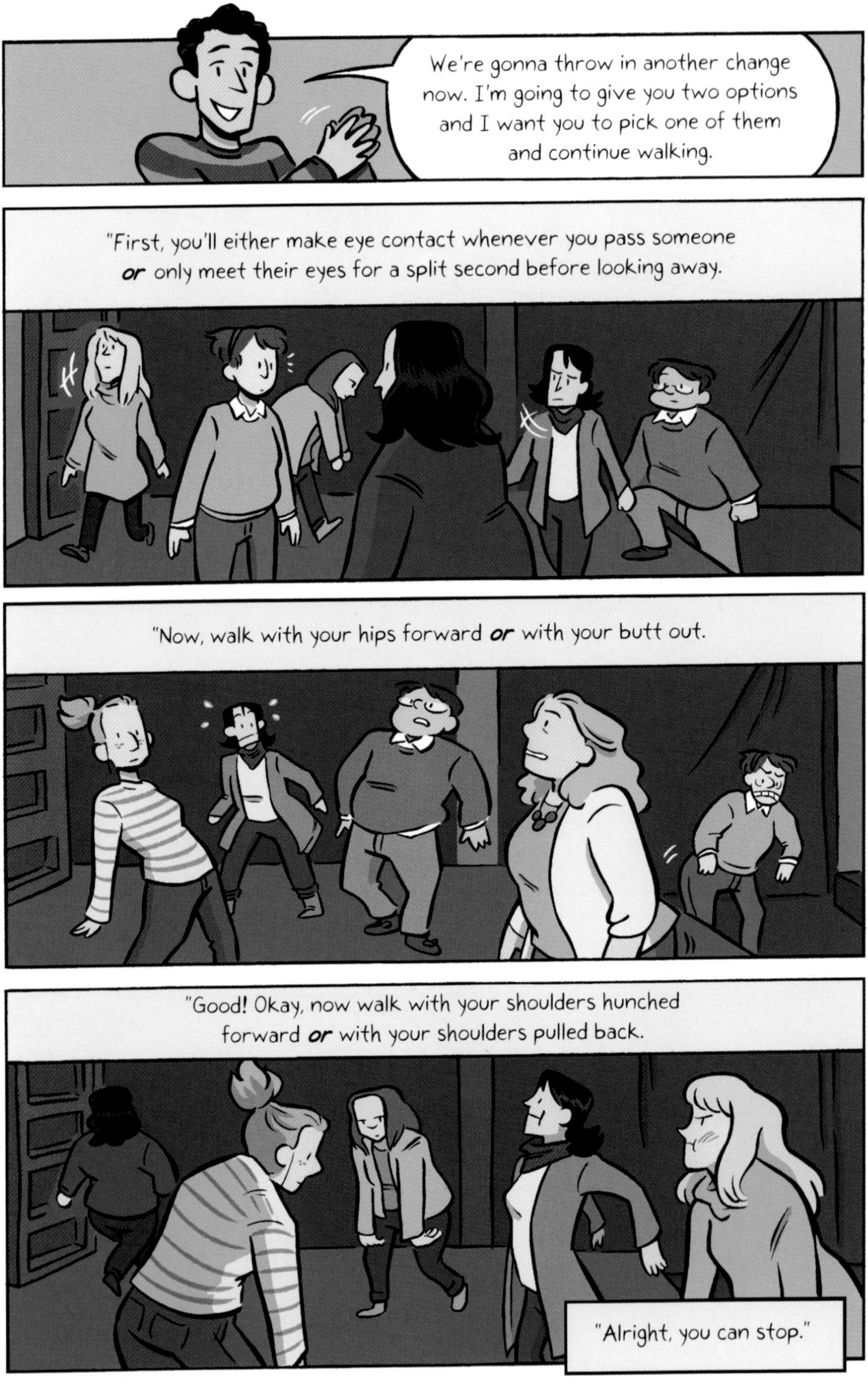
We're gonna throw in another change now. I'm going to give you two options and I want you to pick one of them and continue walking.
"First, you'll either make eye contact whenever you pass someone ***or*** only meet their eyes for a split second before looking away.
"Now, walk with your hips forward ***or*** with your butt out.
"Good! Okay, now walk with your shoulders hunched forward ***or*** with your shoulders pulled back.
"Alright, you can stop."

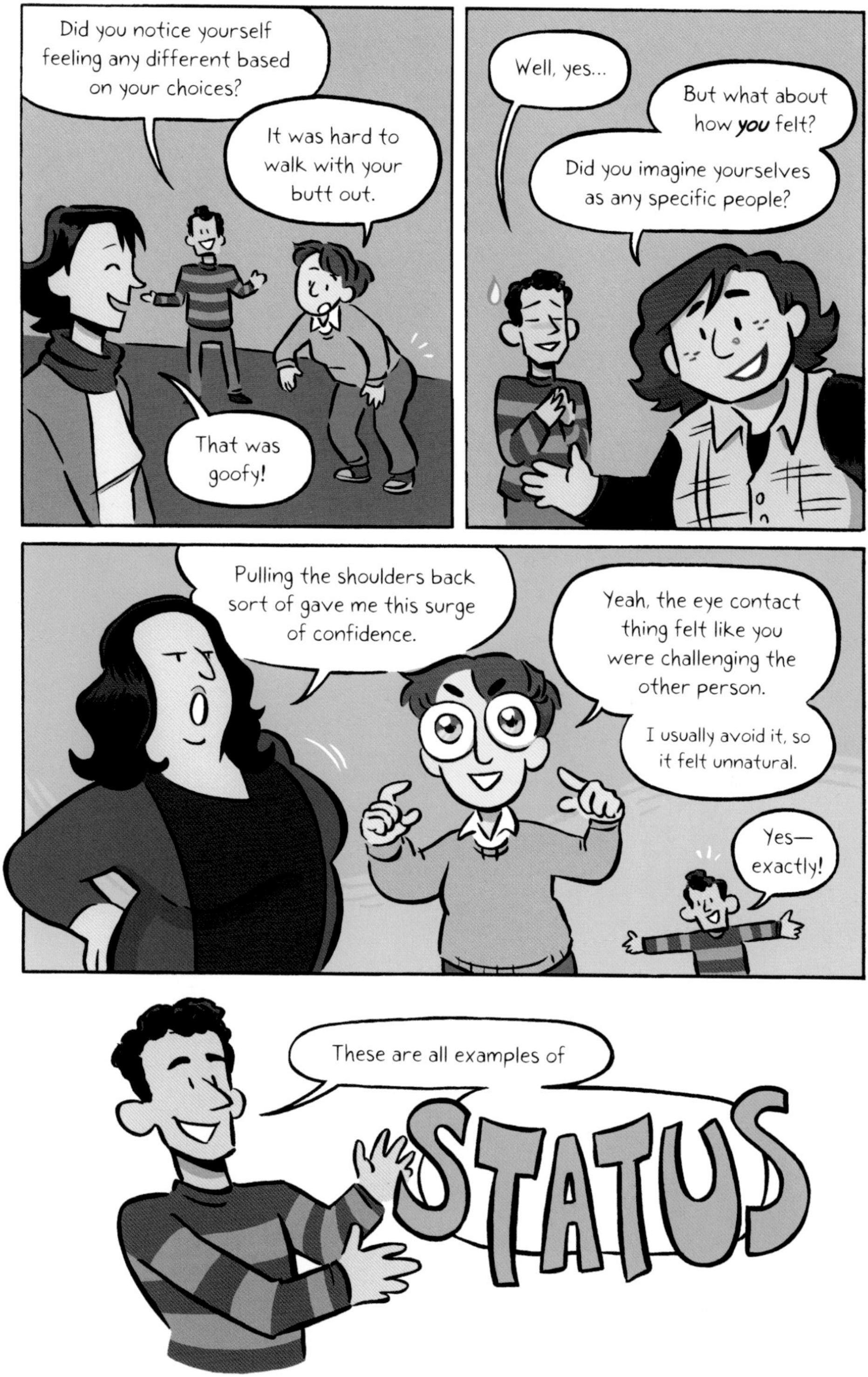
Did you notice yourself feeling any different based on your choices?
It was hard to walk with your butt out.
That was goofy!
Well, yes...
But what about how **you** felt?
Did you imagine yourselves as any specific people?
Pulling the shoulders back sort of gave me this surge of confidence.
Yeah, the eye contact thing felt like you were challenging the other person.
I usually avoid it, so it felt unnatural.
Yes—exactly!
These are all examples of
STATUS

Keith Johnstone describes status as:

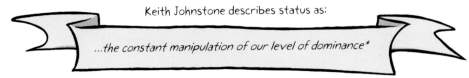

...*the constant manipulation of our level of dominance**

We usually describe things as **high** or **low** status,
but it doesn't refer to your class status or morals.

Rather, it's all about how you carry yourself—your body language,
the amount of space you take up, how you talk about yourself, etc.

Oh! Like how some people
say power poses raise
your confidence?

Kind of!

You'd be surprised how much you can convey
just by switching the direction of your legs!

open and
involved

sharing more
space

crossed arms
indicate more
closed off

twisting away,
like doesn't
want to engage

focused on
the other
person

Impro for Storytellers, p. 219

98

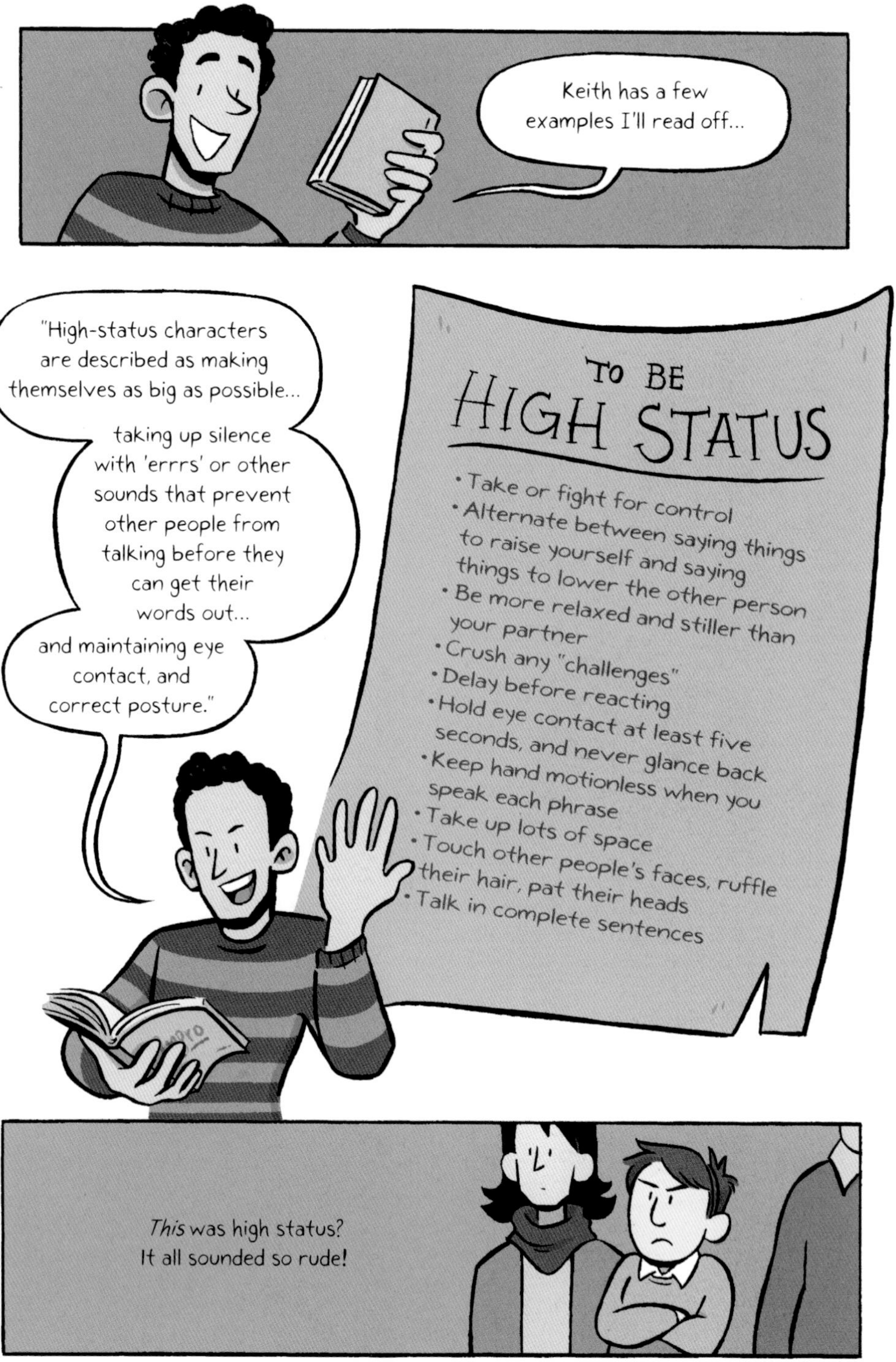

Keith has a few examples I'll read off...
"High-status characters are described as making themselves as big as possible...
taking up silence with 'errrs' or other sounds that prevent other people from talking before they can get their words out...
and maintaining eye contact, and correct posture."
TO BE HIGH STATUS
• Take or fight for control
• Alternate between saying things to raise yourself and saying things to lower the other person
• Be more relaxed and stiller than your partner
• Crush any "challenges"
• Delay before reacting
• Hold eye contact at least five seconds, and never glance back
• Keep hand motionless when you speak each phrase
• Take up lots of space
• Touch other people's faces, ruffle their hair, pat their heads
• Talk in complete sentences
This was high status? It all sounded so rude!

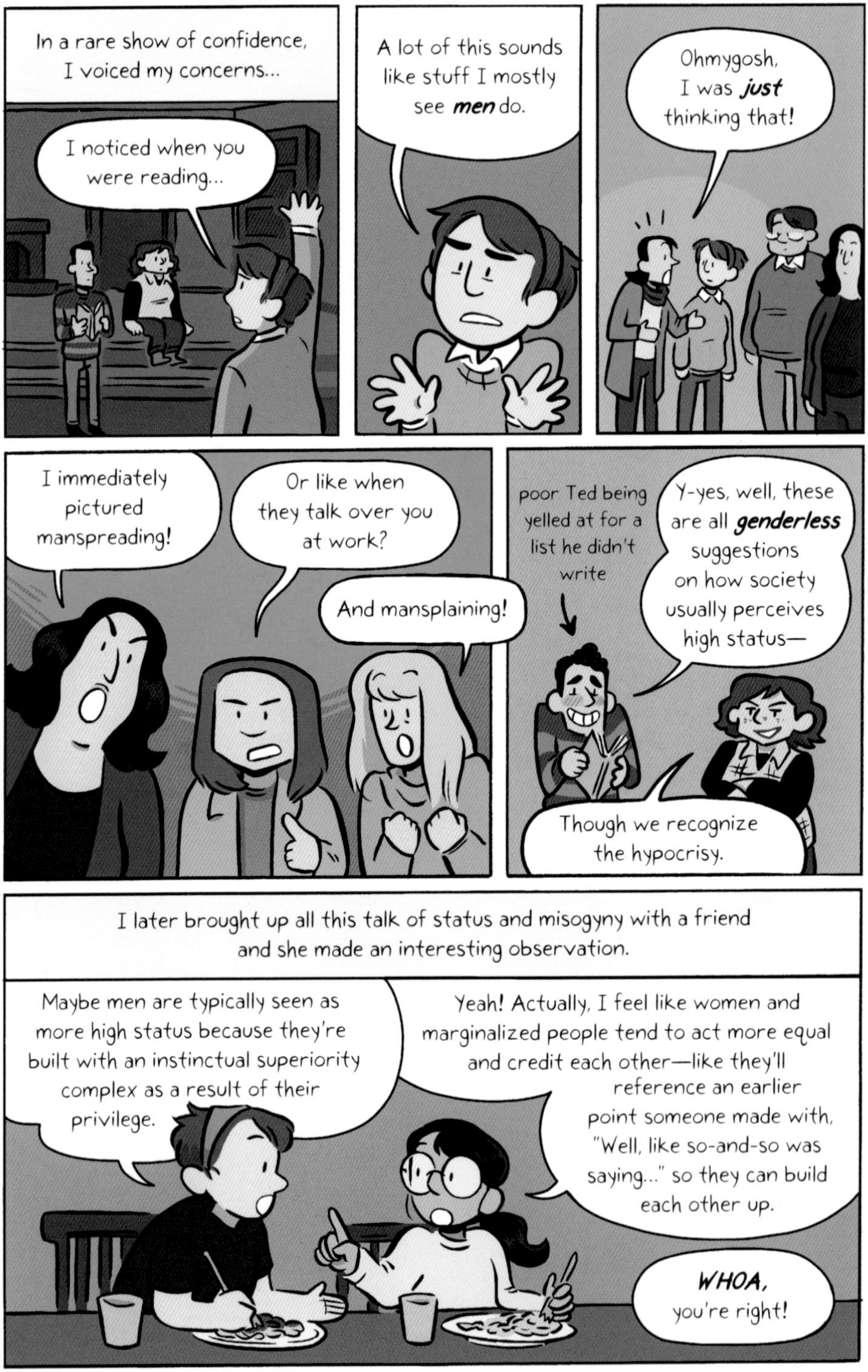
In a rare show of confidence, I voiced my concerns...
I noticed when you were reading...
A lot of this sounds like stuff I mostly see *men* do.
Ohmygosh, I was *just* thinking that!
I immediately pictured manspreading!
Or like when they talk over you at work?
And mansplaining!
poor Ted being yelled at for a list he didn't write
Y-yes, well, these are all *genderless* suggestions on how society usually perceives high status—
Though we recognize the hypocrisy.
I later brought up all this talk of status and misogyny with a friend and she made an interesting observation.
Maybe men are typically seen as more high status because they're built with an instinctual superiority complex as a result of their privilege.
Yeah! Actually, I feel like women and marginalized people tend to act more equal and credit each other—like they'll reference an earlier point someone made with, "Well, like so-and-so was saying..." so they can build each other up.
WHOA, you're right!

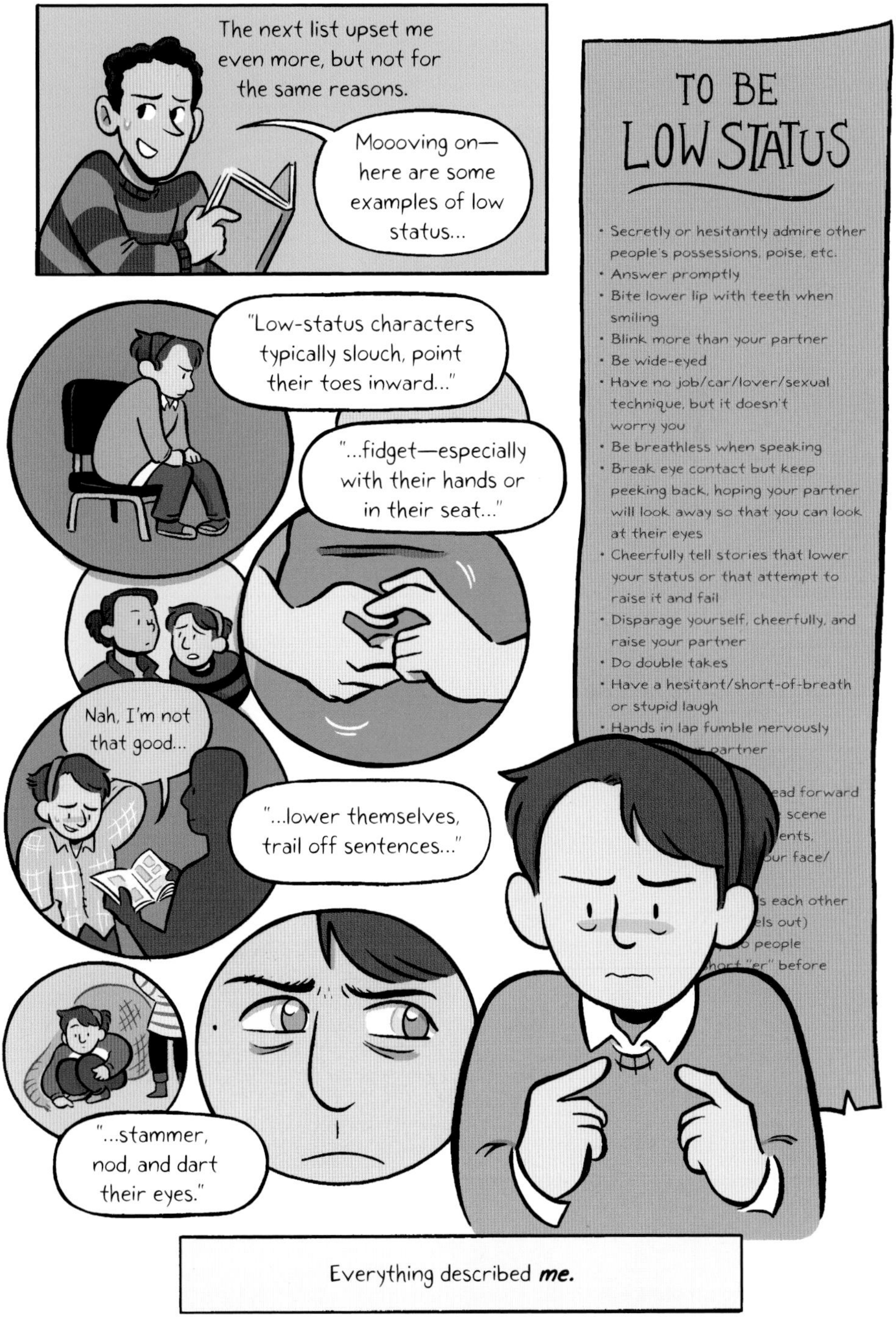
The next list upset me even more, but not for the same reasons.
Moooving on— here are some examples of low status...
TO BE LOW STATUS
• Secretly or hesitantly admire other people's possessions, poise, etc.
• Answer promptly
• Bite lower lip with teeth when smiling
• Blink more than your partner
• Be wide-eyed
• Have no job/car/lover/sexual technique, but it doesn't worry you
• Be breathless when speaking
• Break eye contact but keep peeking back, hoping your partner will look away so that you can look at their eyes
• Cheerfully tell stories that lower your status or that attempt to raise it and fail
• Disparage yourself, cheerfully, and raise your partner
• Do double takes
• Have a hesitant/short-of-breath or stupid laugh
• Hands in lap fumble nervously
"Low-status characters typically slouch, point their toes inward..."
"...fidget—especially with their hands or in their seat..."
Nah, I'm not that good...
"...lower themselves, trail off sentences..."
"...stammer, nod, and dart their eyes."
Everything described *me.*

Is this how people saw me? Could everyone see my anxieties in my body language all this time?

It felt like I'd been given a failing grade—a thoroughly checked-off list on how not to behave.

LIFE REPORT CA[RD]

F	NORMALCY
D	COHERENCE
F	EYE CONTACT
D	LIKABILITY
	RELAT

I'm sure no one really noticed, but now my self-loathing had new reasons to rear its ugly head.

Don't look away!

Stand up straight!

Everyone knows how weak you are.

You're closing yourself off to them!

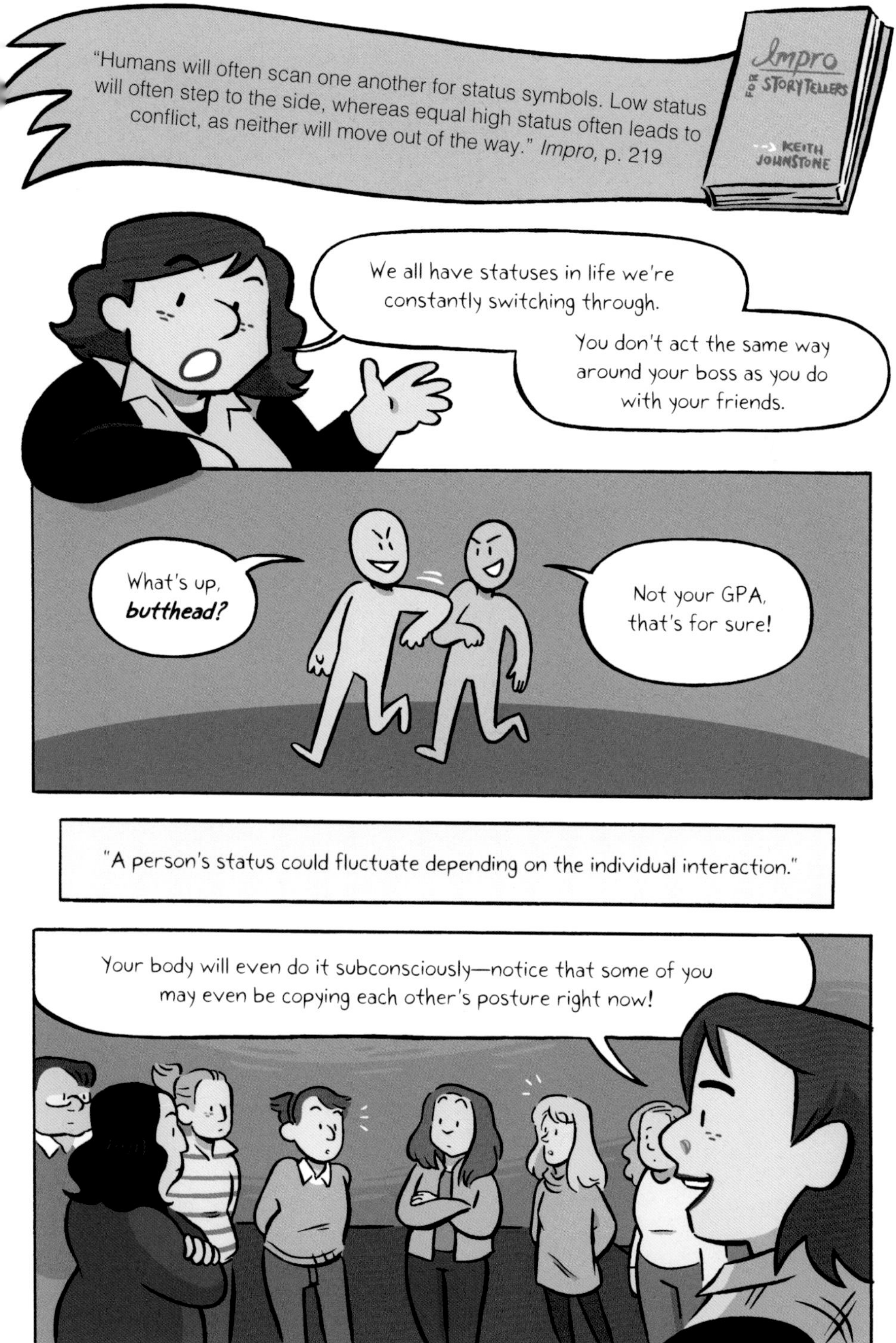
"Humans will often scan one another for status symbols. Low status will often step to the side, whereas equal high status often leads to conflict, as neither will move out of the way." *Impro*, p. 219
Impro FOR STORYTELLERS
KEITH JOHNSTONE
We all have statuses in life we're constantly switching through.
You don't act the same way around your boss as you do with your friends.
What's up, *butthead?*
Not your GPA, that's for sure!
"A person's status could fluctuate depending on the individual interaction."
Your body will even do it subconsciously—notice that some of you may even be copying each other's posture right now!

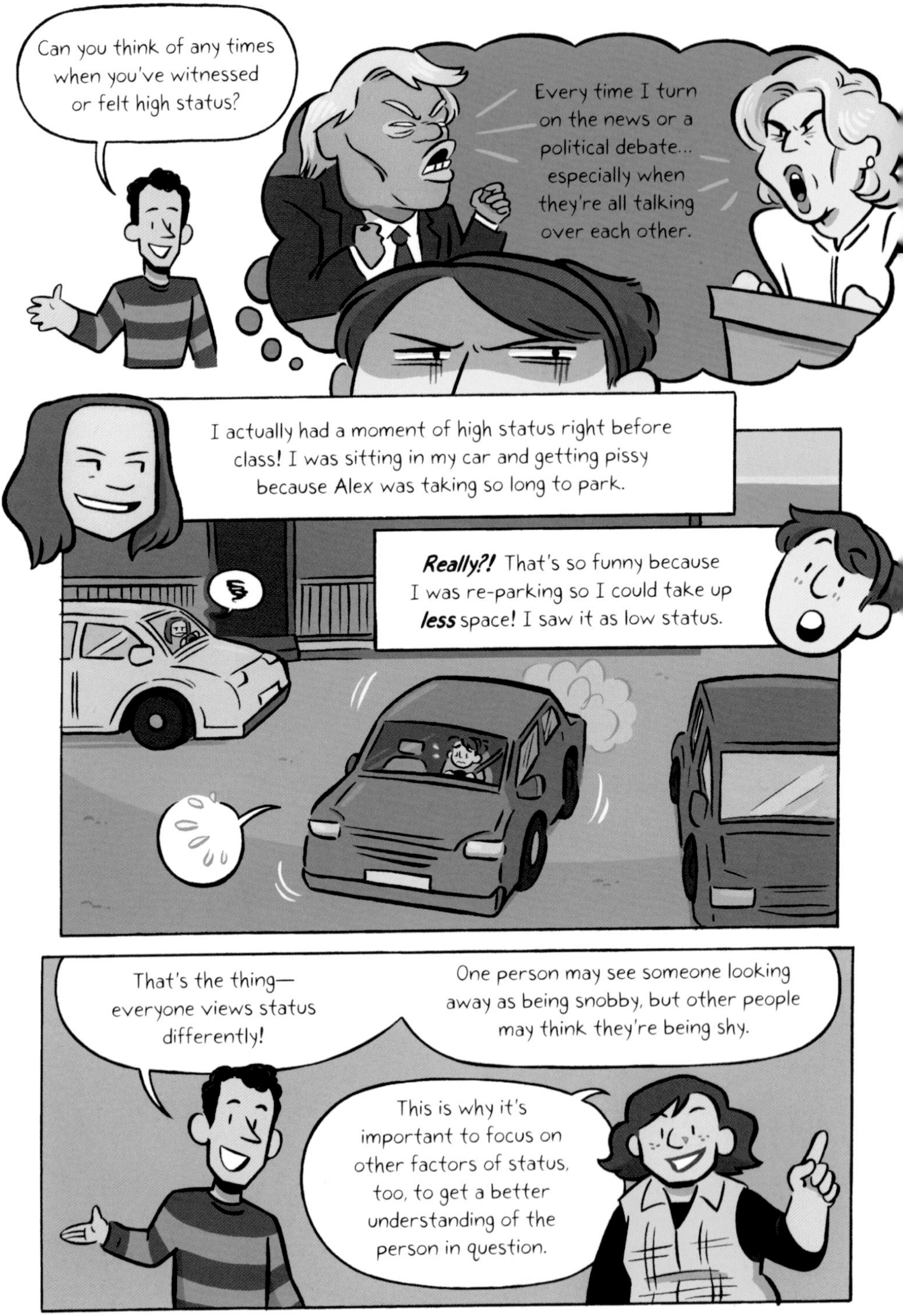
Can you think of any times when you've witnessed or felt high status?
Every time I turn on the news or a political debate... especially when they're all talking over each other.
I actually had a moment of high status right before class! I was sitting in my car and getting pissy because Alex was taking so long to park.
Really?! That's so funny because I was re-parking so I could take up ***less*** space! I saw it as low status.
That's the thing— everyone views status differently!
One person may see someone looking away as being snobby, but other people may think they're being shy.
This is why it's important to focus on other factors of status, too, to get a better understanding of the person in question.

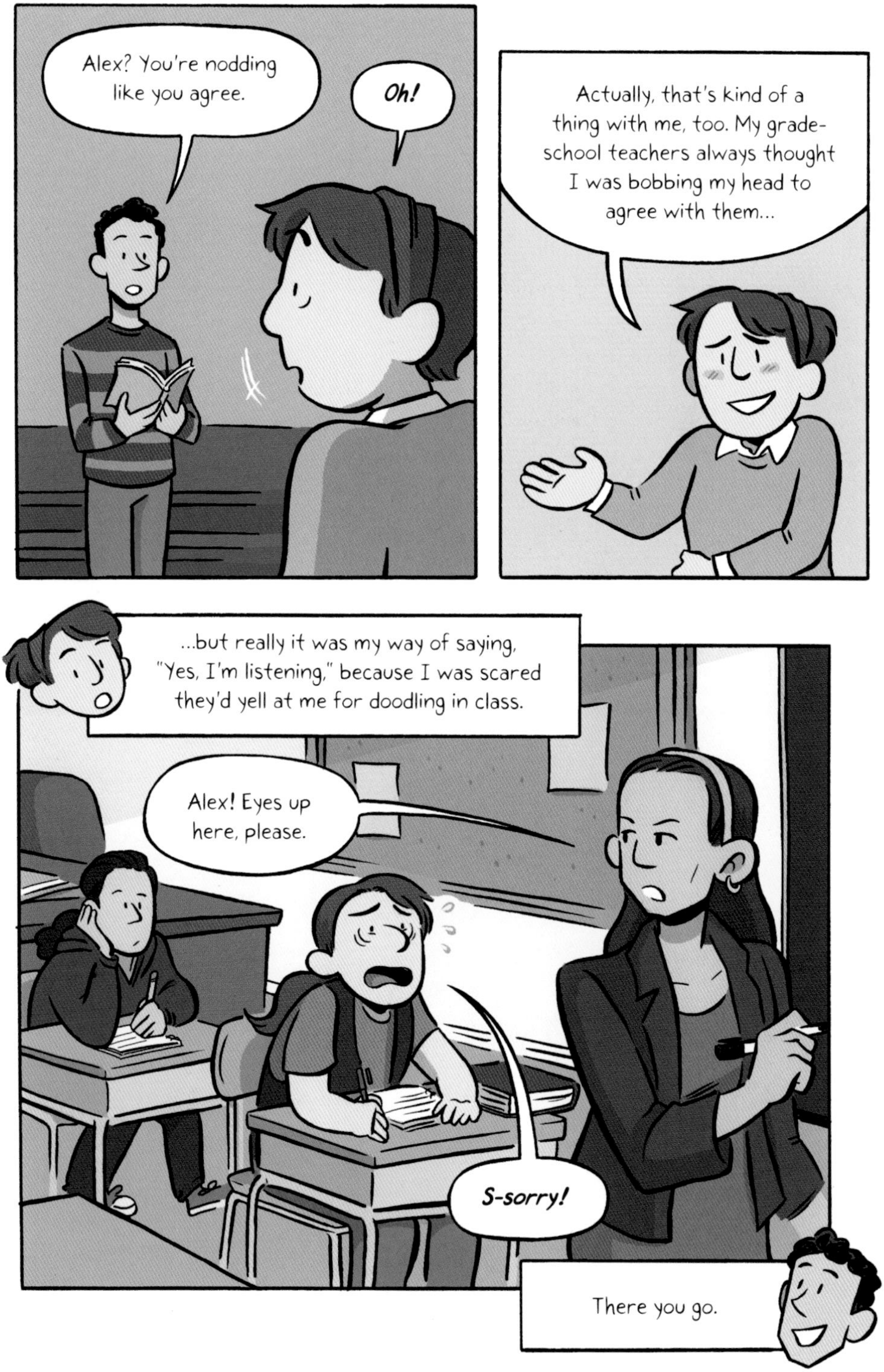

Alex? You're nodding like you agree.
Oh!
Actually, that's kind of a thing with me, too. My grade-school teachers always thought I was bobbing my head to agree with them...
...but really it was my way of saying, "Yes, I'm listening," because I was scared they'd yell at me for doodling in class.
Alex! Eyes up here, please.
S-sorry!
There you go.

Status scenes can go any number of ways...

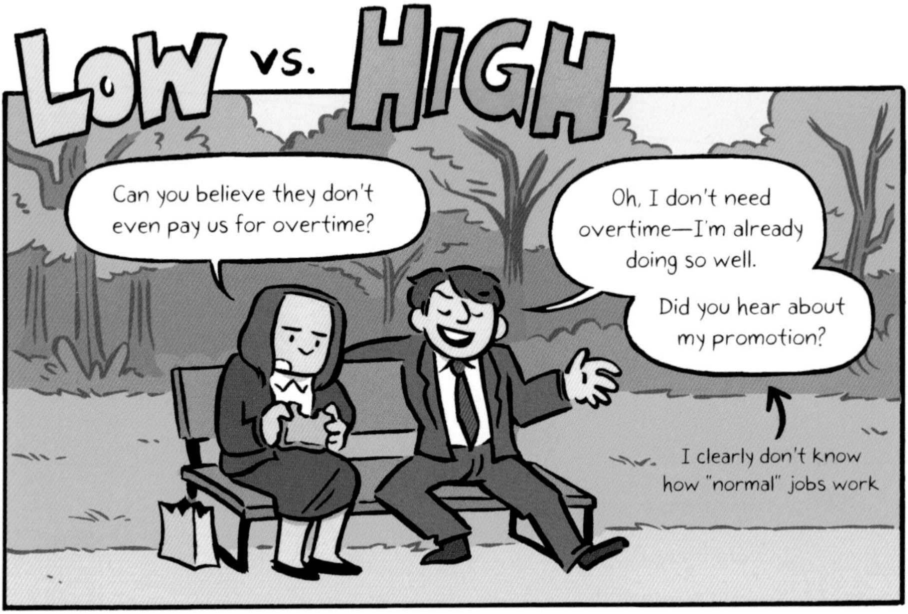
LOW vs. HIGH
Can you believe they don't even pay us for overtime?
Oh, I don't need overtime—I'm already doing so well.
Did you hear about my promotion?
I clearly don't know how "normal" jobs work

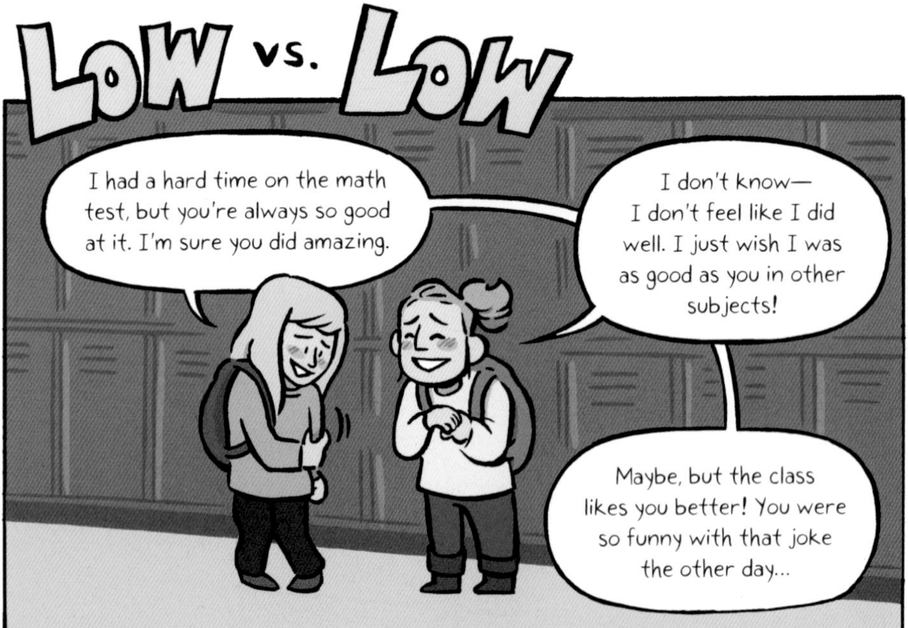
LOW vs. LOW
I had a hard time on the math test, but you're always so good at it. I'm sure you did amazing.
I don't know— I don't feel like I did well. I just wish I was as good as you in other subjects!
Maybe, but the class likes you better! You were so funny with that joke the other day...

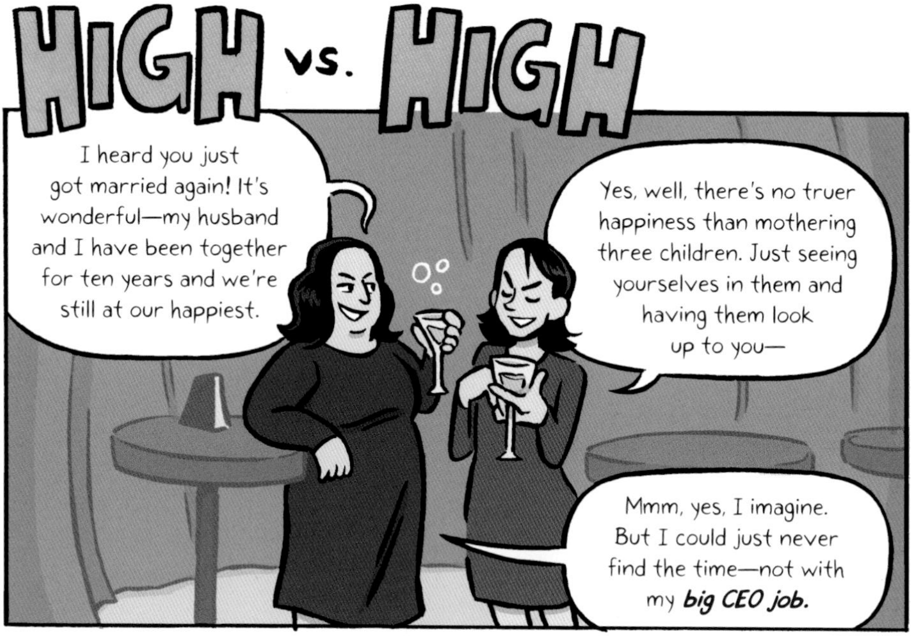
HIGH vs. HIGH
I heard you just got married again! It's wonderful—my husband and I have been together for ten years and we're still at our happiest.
Yes, well, there's no truer happiness than mothering three children. Just seeing yourselves in them and having them look up to you—
Mmm, yes, I imagine. But I could just never find the time—not with my ***big CEO job.***

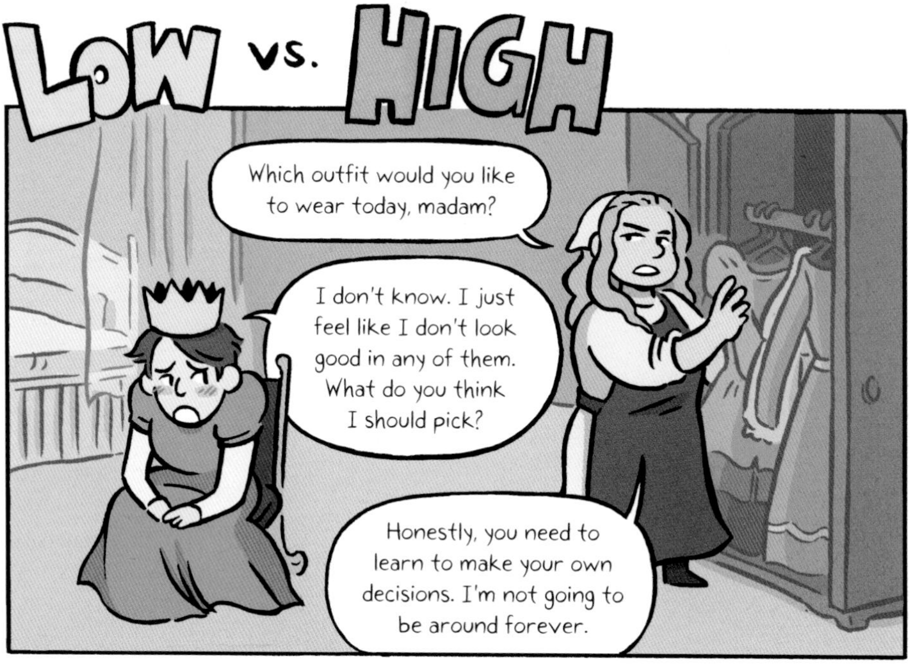
LOW vs. HIGH
Which outfit would you like to wear today, madam?
I don't know. I just feel like I don't look good in any of them. What do you think I should pick?
Honestly, you need to learn to make your own decisions. I'm not going to be around forever.

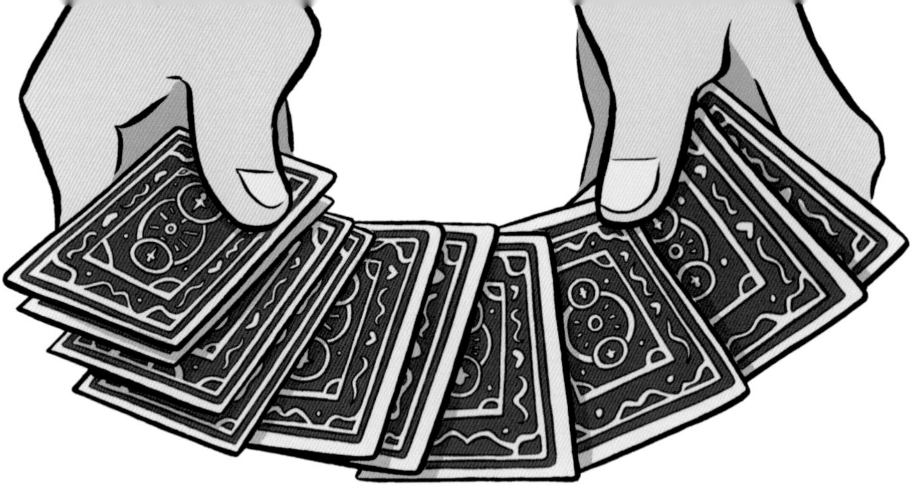

We tried our hand at status on a party scene, with a twist—our status would be determined by playing cards, taped to our foreheads. We would have to guess our number based on other peoples' cards and how they treated us.

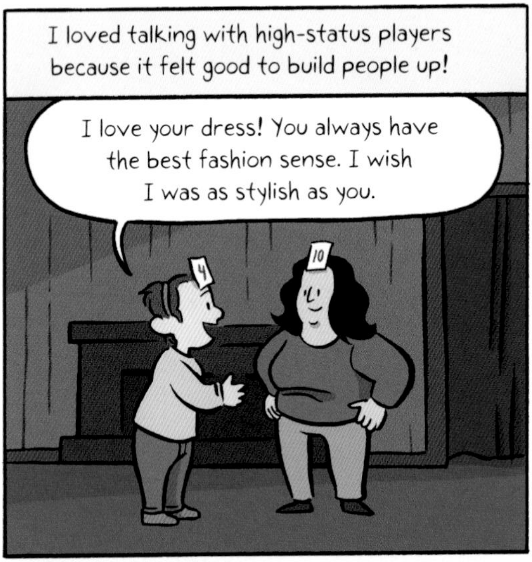

I loved talking with high-status players because it felt good to build people up!
I love your dress! You always have the best fashion sense. I wish I was as stylish as you.
4
10

Plus it was easier to slip in puns.

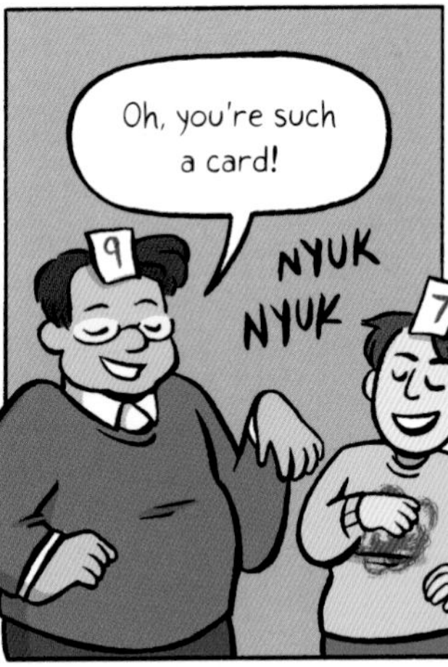

Oh, you're such a card!
9
NYUK NYUK
7

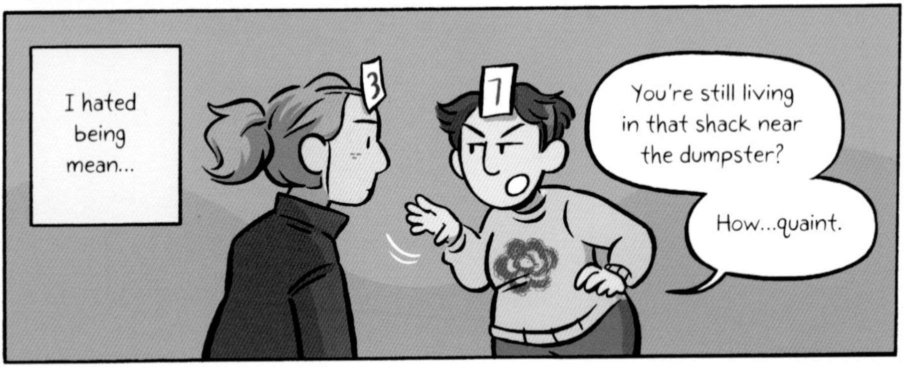

I hated being mean...
3
7
You're still living in that shack near the dumpster?
How...quaint.

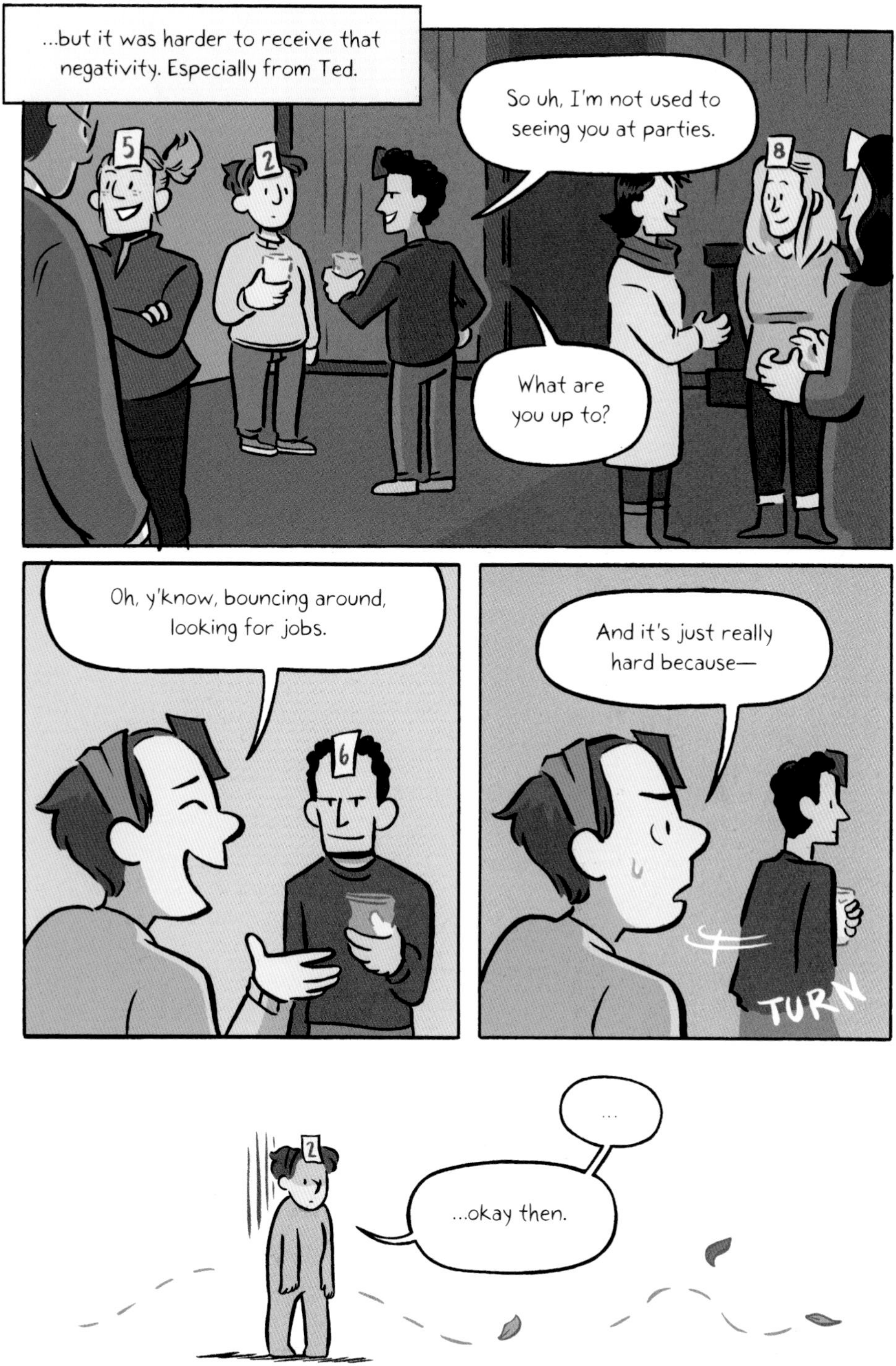
...but it was harder to receive that negativity. Especially from Ted.
So uh, I'm not used to seeing you at parties.
What are you up to?
5
2
8
Oh, y'know, bouncing around, looking for jobs.
6
And it's just really hard because—
TURN
...
...okay then.
2

I was thrilled when we could put status on hold and finally get into

MUSIC!

We played games like:

ELECTRIC COMPANY

In a circle, alternating two people at a time, each player says a syllable or makes a sound and then the whole circle repeats the combined word or sound in unison.

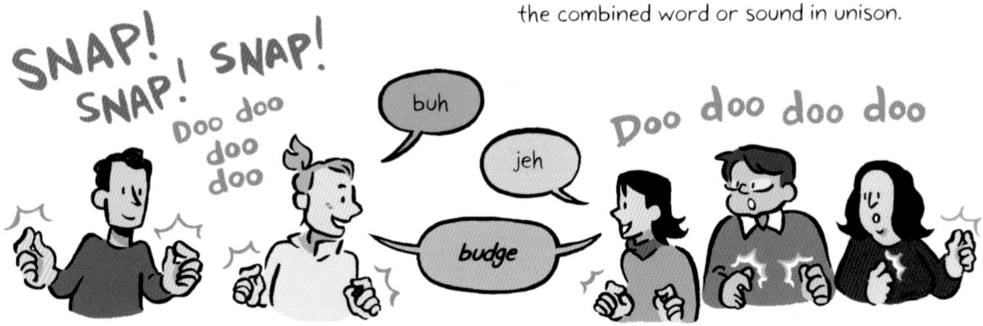
SNAP!
SNAP! SNAP!
Doo doo doo doo
buh
jeh
budge
Doo doo doo doo

We're not aiming to make actual words, but sometimes it happens by stream of consciousness!

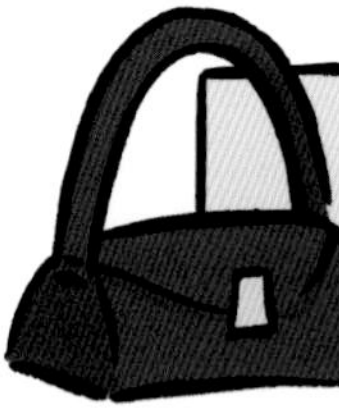

PURSE

A rhyming game where you list items in your purse, with the chorus:

*"PURSE, PURSE, IN MY PURSE
I'M GONNA PUT IT IN MY PURSE"*

I've got a **CAT** IN MY PURSE!

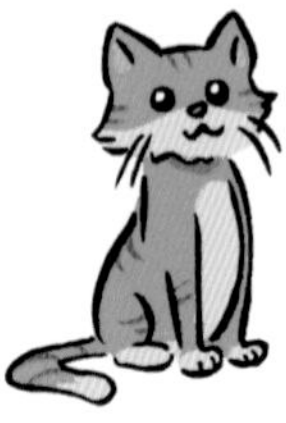

I've got a **BAT** IN MY PURSE!

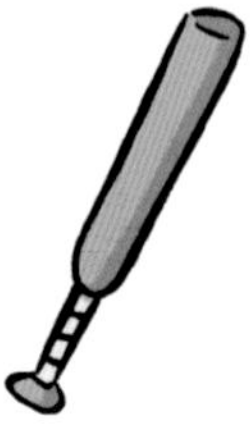

I've got a **RAT** IN MY PURSE!

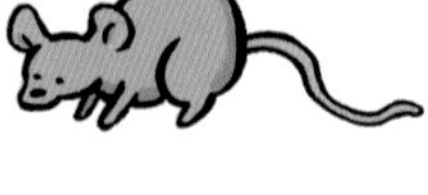

I'm gonna **SCAT** IN MY PURSE!

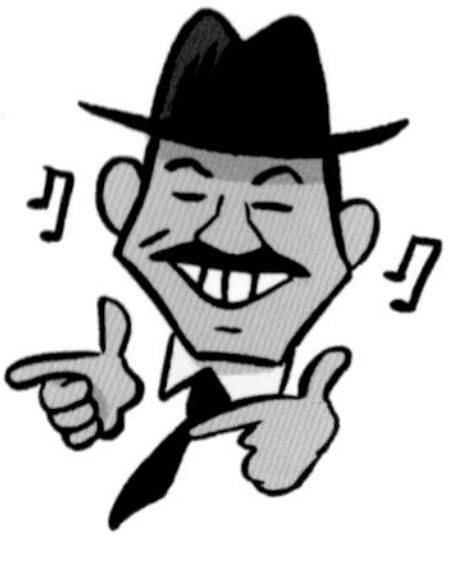

(I know reading about music isn't as effective as hearing it, but bear with me!)

BEASTIE RAP

Similar to Purse's focus on rhyme, and named after the Beastie Boys for its rhythm, you want the audience and other players to expect the word and say it with you, so you lead up to it with context clues.

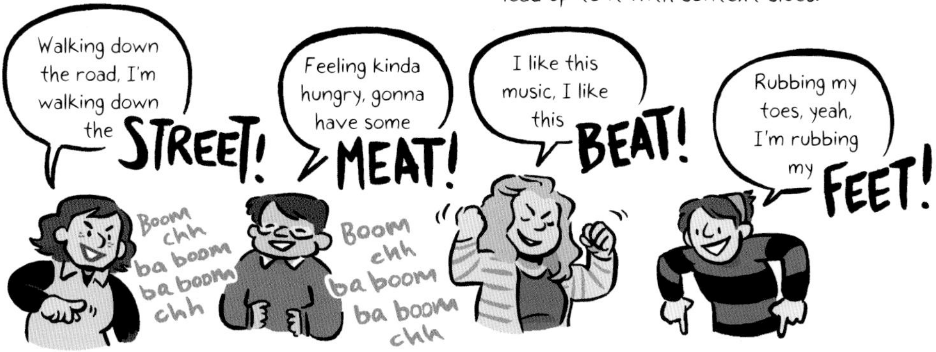
Walking down the road, I'm walking down the STREET!
Boom chh ba boom ba boom chh
Feeling kinda hungry, gonna have some MEAT!
Boom chh ba boom ba boom chh
I like this music, I like this BEAT!
Rubbing my toes, yeah, I'm rubbing my FEET!

DOO-RUN

Like One Word at a Time, but in this game a single player adds a stanza or line before passing it off to the next person, now following a specific tune.

It's easiest for each line to rhyme in an AABBB pattern, but not necessary.

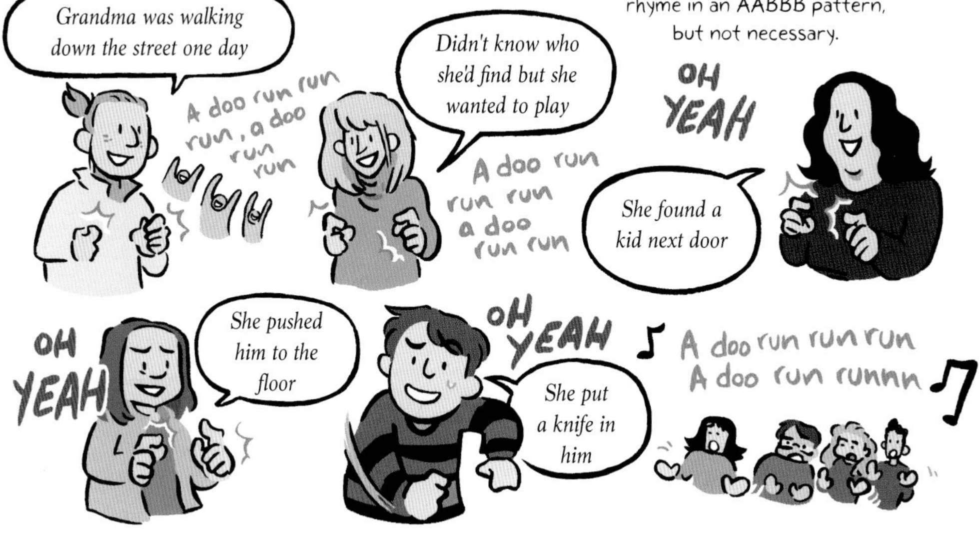
Grandma was walking down the street one day
A doo run run, a doo run run
Didn't know who she'd find but she wanted to play
A doo run run run a doo run run
OH YEAH
She found a kid next door
OH YEAH
She pushed him to the floor
OH YEAH
She put a knife in him
A doo run run run run
A doo run runnn

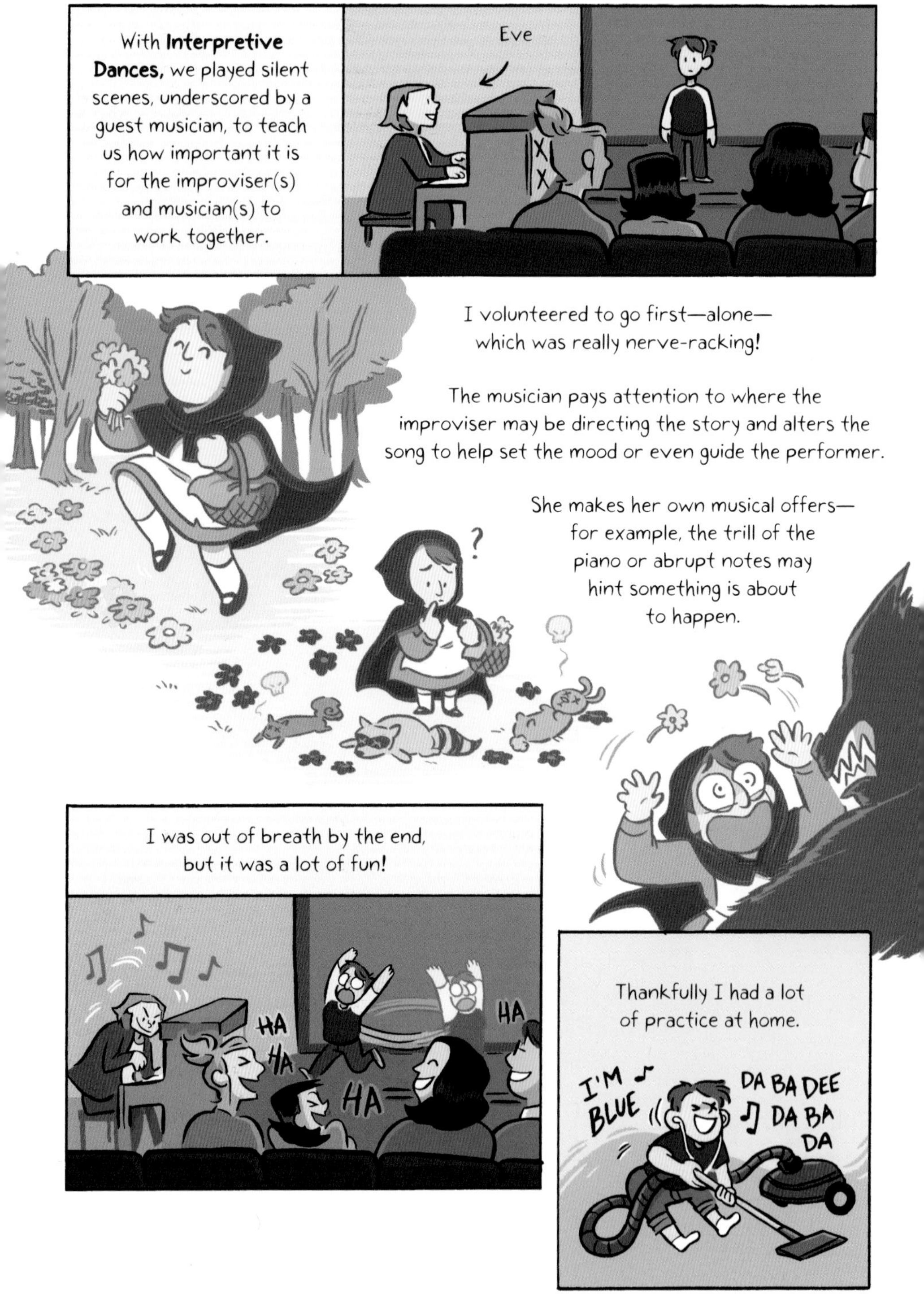
With **Interpretive Dances,** we played silent scenes, underscored by a guest musician, to teach us how important it is for the improviser(s) and musician(s) to work together.
Eve
I volunteered to go first—alone—which was really nerve-racking!
The musician pays attention to where the improviser may be directing the story and alters the song to help set the mood or even guide the performer.
She makes her own musical offers—for example, the trill of the piano or abrupt notes may hint something is about to happen.
?
I was out of breath by the end, but it was a lot of fun!
HA
HA
HA
HA
Thankfully I had a lot of practice at home.
I'M BLUE
DA BA DEE DA BA DA

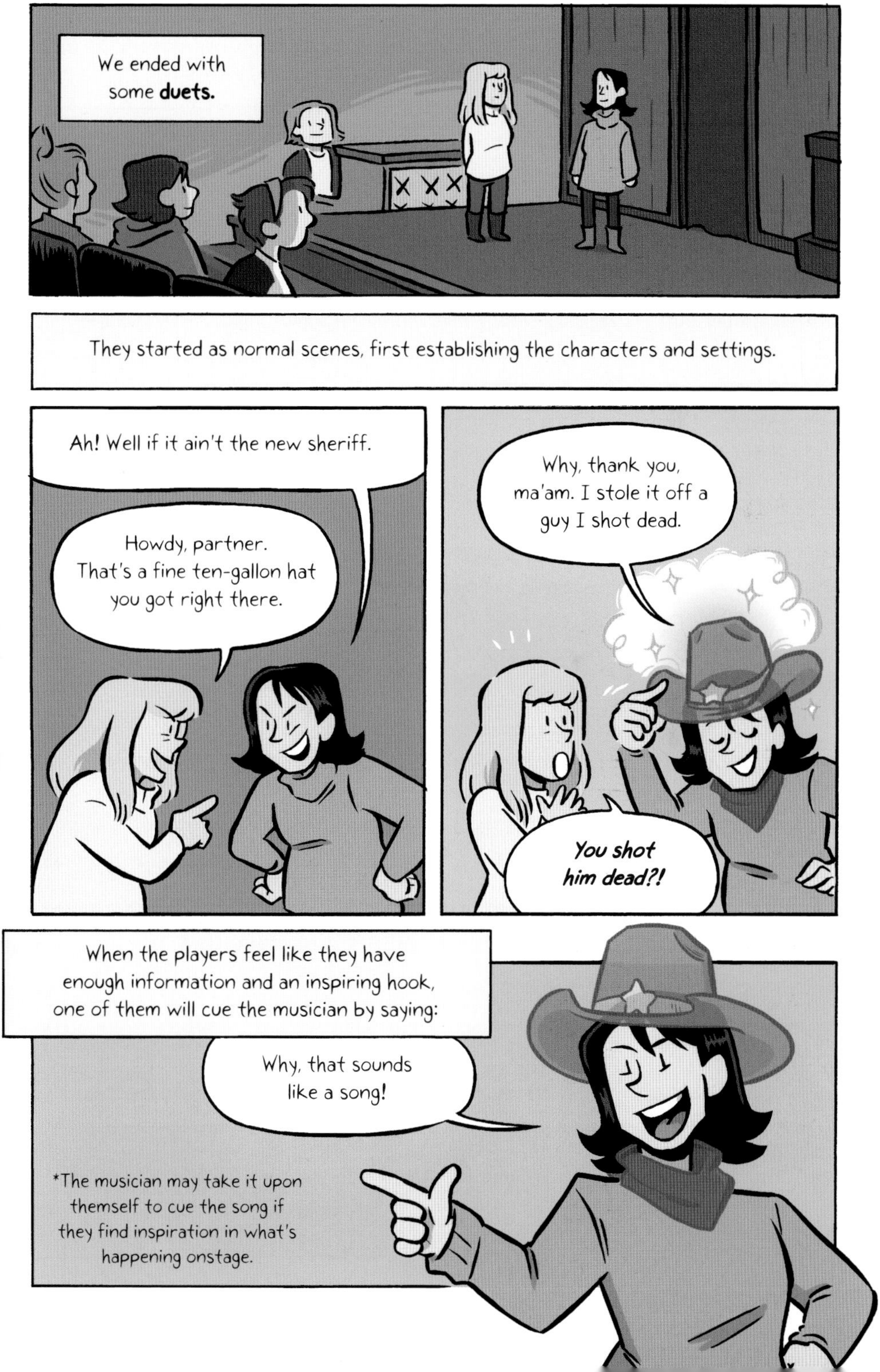
We ended with some **duets.**
They started as normal scenes, first establishing the characters and settings.
Ah! Well if it ain't the new sheriff.
Howdy, partner. That's a fine ten-gallon hat you got right there.
Why, thank you, ma'am. I stole it off a guy I shot dead.
You shot him dead?!
When the players feel like they have enough information and an inspiring hook, one of them will cue the musician by saying:
Why, that sounds like a song!
*The musician may take it upon themself to cue the song if they find inspiration in what's happening onstage.

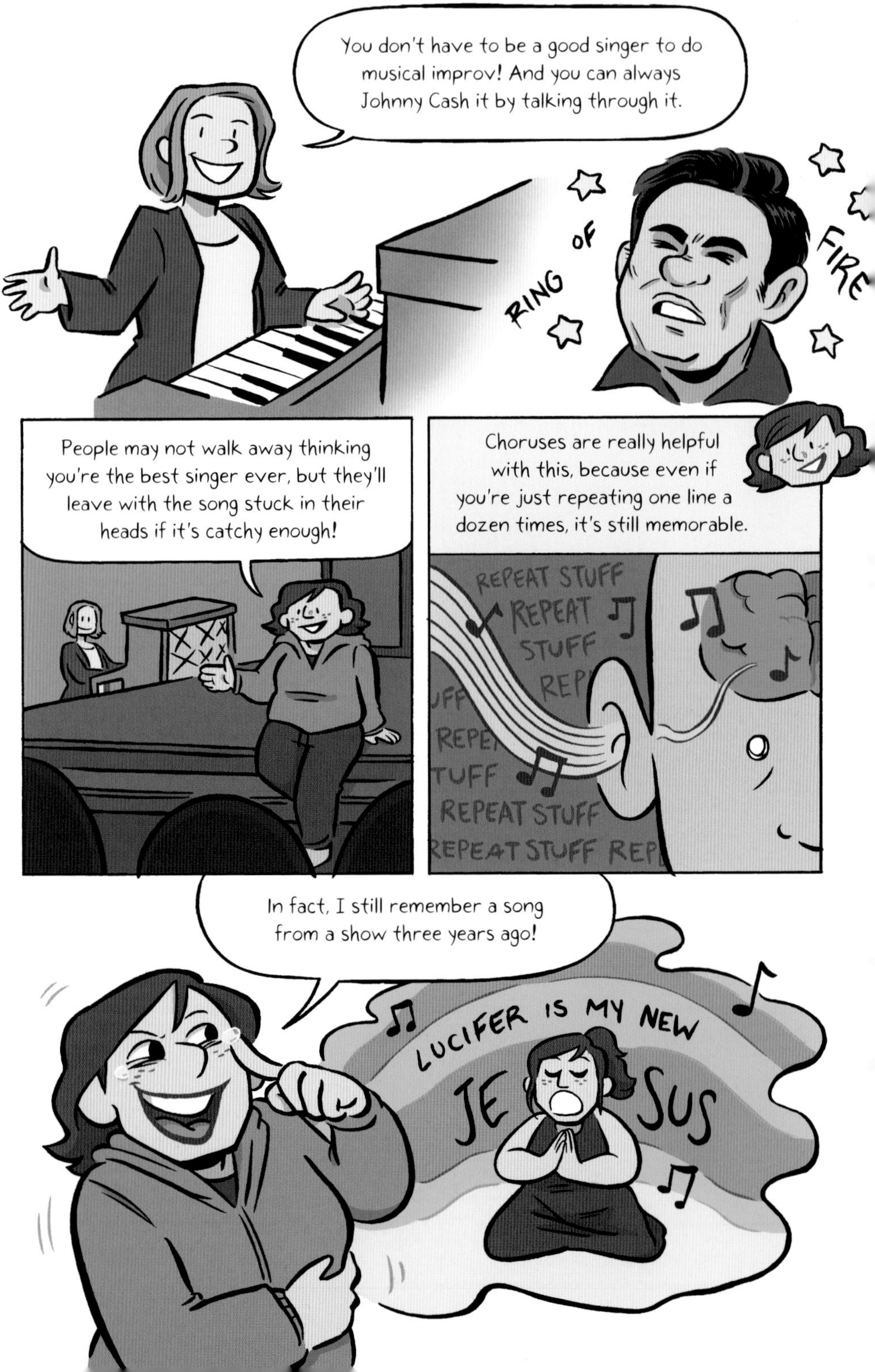

You don't have to be a good singer to do musical improv! And you can always Johnny Cash it by talking through it.
RING OF FIRE
People may not walk away thinking you're the best singer ever, but they'll leave with the song stuck in their heads if it's catchy enough!
Choruses are really helpful with this, because even if you're just repeating one line a dozen times, it's still memorable.
REPEAT STUFF
REPEAT STUFF
REPEAT STUFF
REPEAT STUFF REP
In fact, I still remember a song from a show three years ago!
LUCIFER IS MY NEW JE SUS

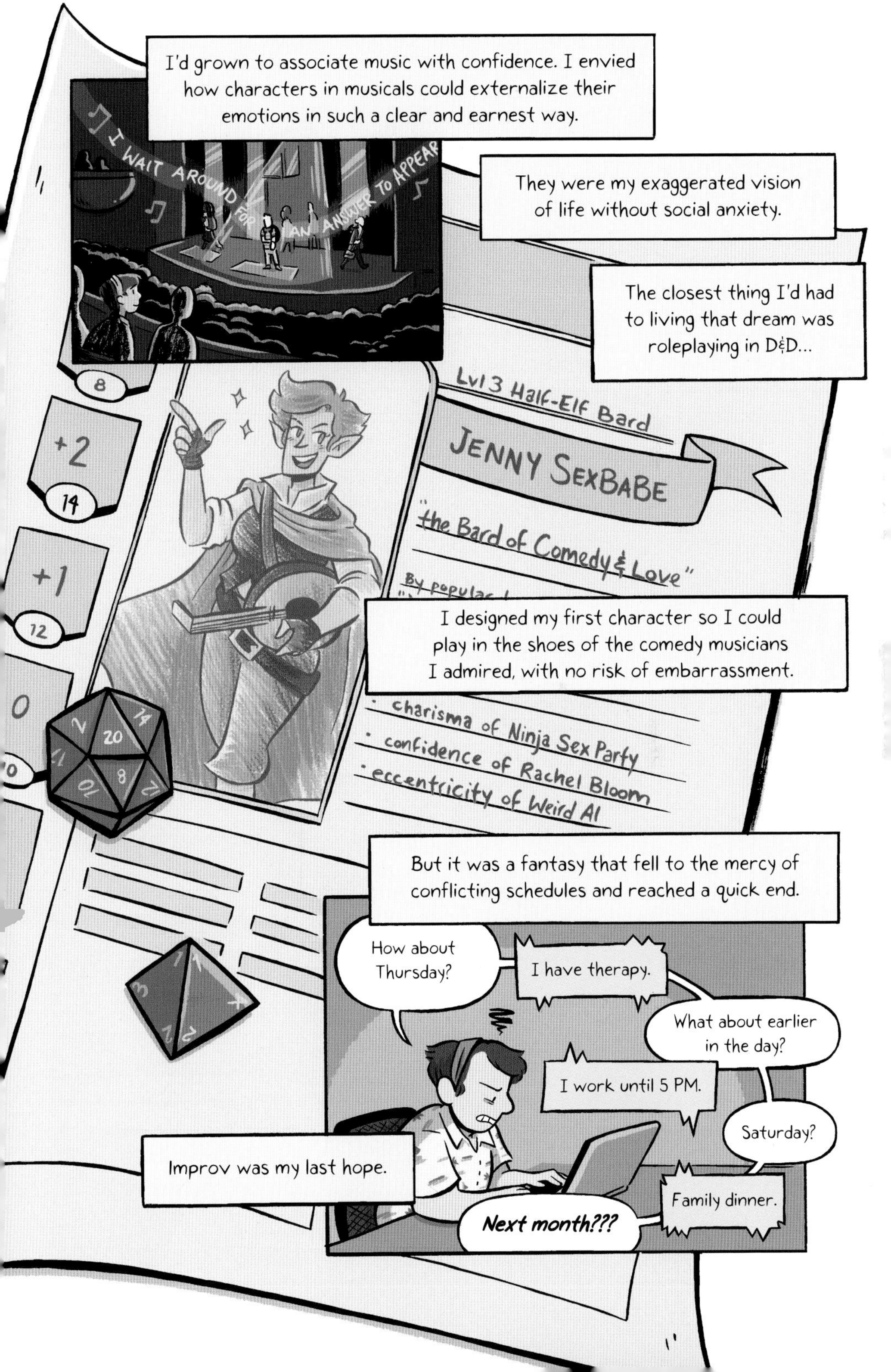
I'd grown to associate music with confidence. I envied how characters in musicals could externalize their emotions in such a clear and earnest way.
♪ I WAIT AROUND FOR AN ANSWER TO APPEAR ♪
They were my exaggerated vision of life without social anxiety.
The closest thing I'd had to living that dream was roleplaying in D&D...
8
+2
14
+1
12
0
20
Lvl 3 Half-Elf Bard
JENNY SEXBABE
"the Bard of Comedy & Love"
I designed my first character so I could play in the shoes of the comedy musicians I admired, with no risk of embarrassment.
· charisma of Ninja Sex Party
· confidence of Rachel Bloom
· eccentricity of Weird Al
But it was a fantasy that fell to the mercy of conflicting schedules and reached a quick end.
How about Thursday?
I have therapy.
What about earlier in the day?
I work until 5 PM.
Saturday?
Family dinner.
Next month???
Improv was my last hope.

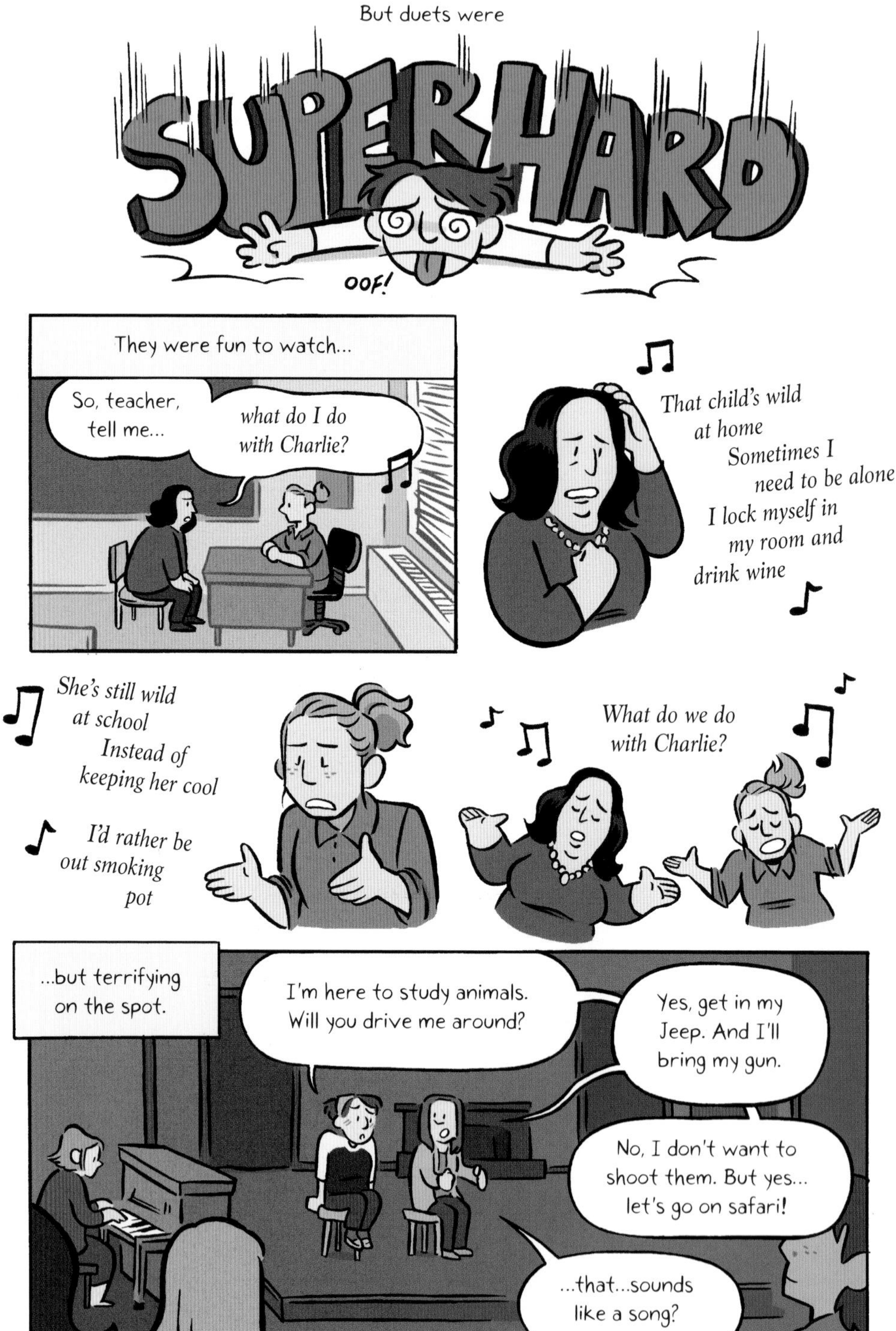
But duets were
SUPERHARD
OOF!
They were fun to watch...
So, teacher, tell me...
what do I do with Charlie?
That child's wild at home Sometimes I need to be alone I lock myself in my room and drink wine
She's still wild at school Instead of keeping her cool
I'd rather be out smoking pot
What do we do with Charlie?
...but terrifying on the spot.
I'm here to study animals. Will you drive me around?
Yes, get in my Jeep. And I'll bring my gun.
No, I don't want to shoot them. But yes... let's go on safari!
...that...sounds like a song?

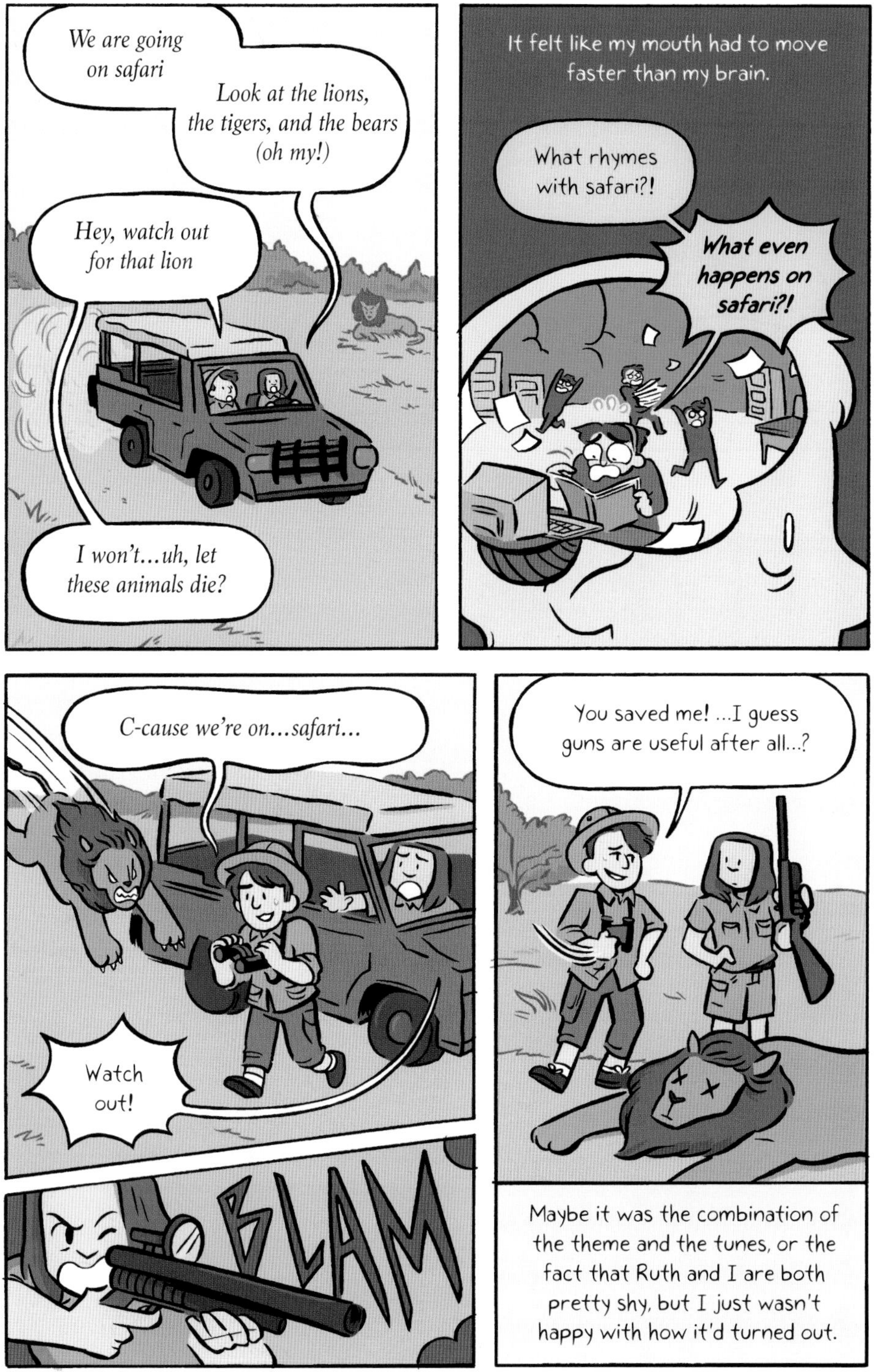
We are going on safari
Look at the lions, the tigers, and the bears (oh my!)
Hey, watch out for that lion
I won't...uh, let these animals die?
It felt like my mouth had to move faster than my brain.
What rhymes with safari?!
What even happens on safari?!
C-cause we're on...safari...
Watch out!
BLAM
You saved me! ...I guess guns are useful after all...?
Maybe it was the combination of the theme and the tunes, or the fact that Ruth and I are both pretty shy, but I just wasn't happy with how it'd turned out.

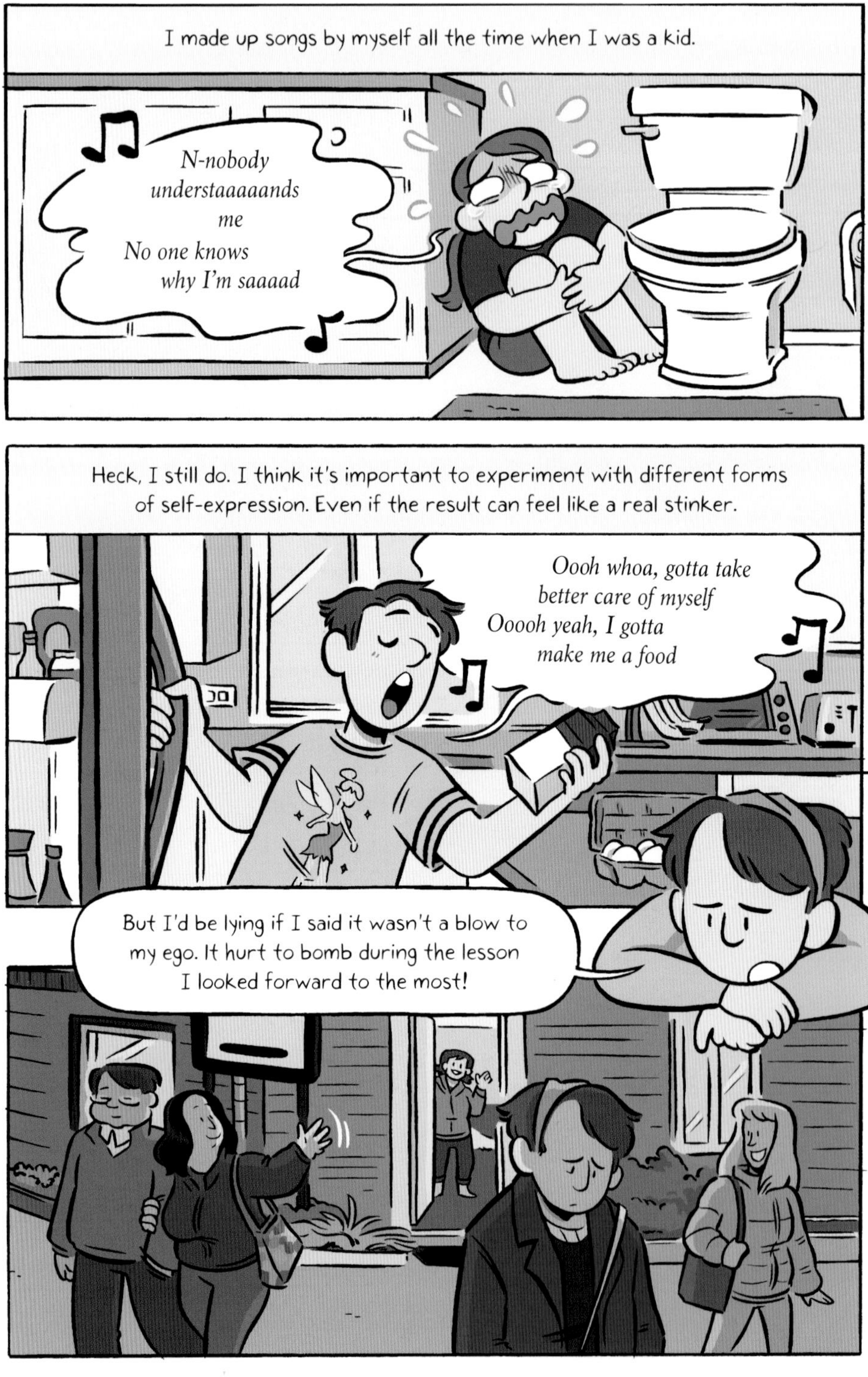
I made up songs by myself all the time when I was a kid.
N-nobody understaaaaands me No one knows why I'm saaaad
Heck, I still do. I think it's important to experiment with different forms of self-expression. Even if the result can feel like a real stinker.
Oooh whoa, gotta take better care of myself Ooooh yeah, I gotta make me a food
But I'd be lying if I said it wasn't a blow to my ego. It hurt to bomb during the lesson I looked forward to the most!

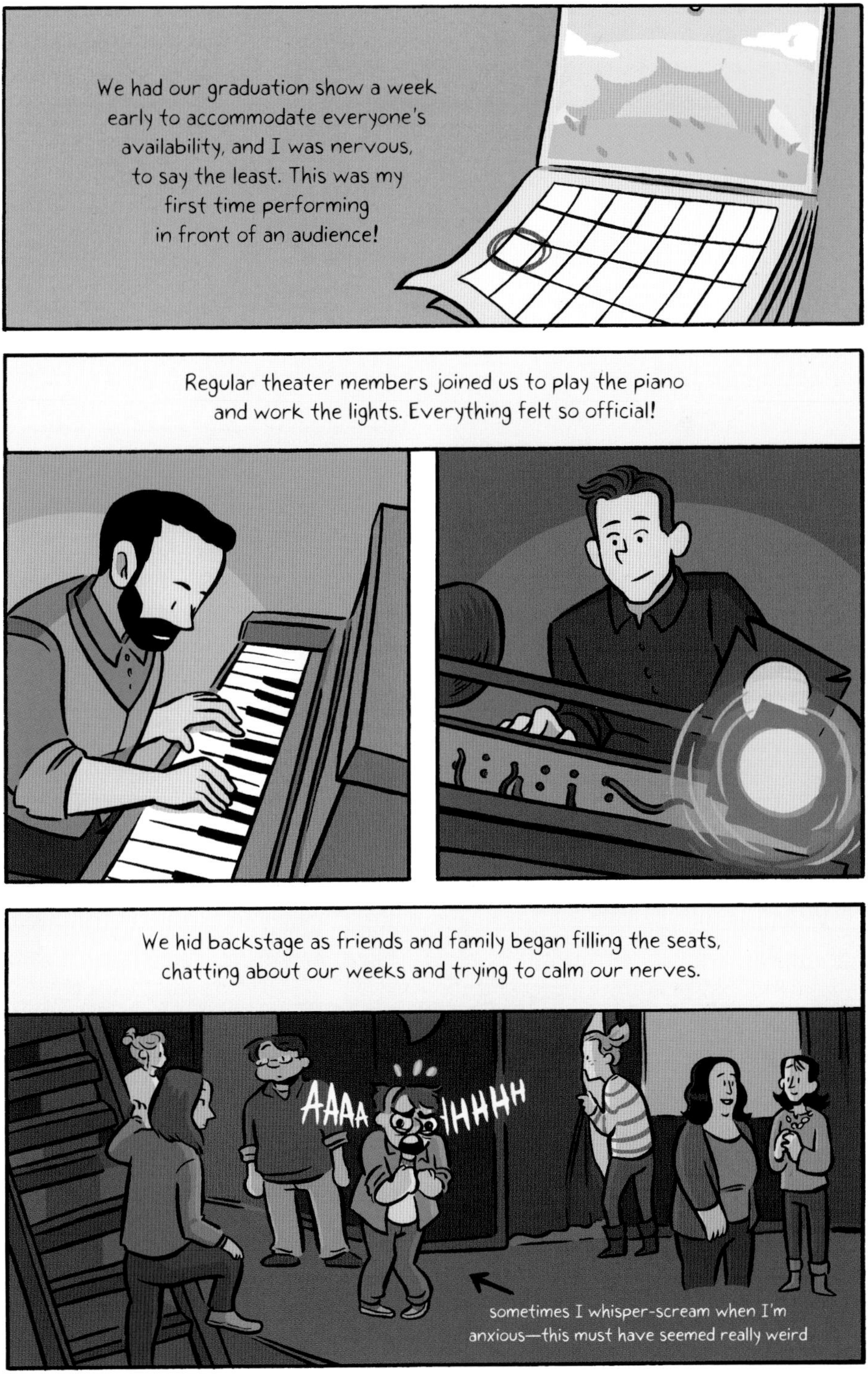
We had our graduation show a week early to accommodate everyone's availability, and I was nervous, to say the least. This was my first time performing in front of an audience!
Regular theater members joined us to play the piano and work the lights. Everything felt so official!
We hid backstage as friends and family began filling the seats, chatting about our weeks and trying to calm our nerves.
AAAAHHHHH
sometimes I whisper-scream when I'm anxious—this must have seemed really weird

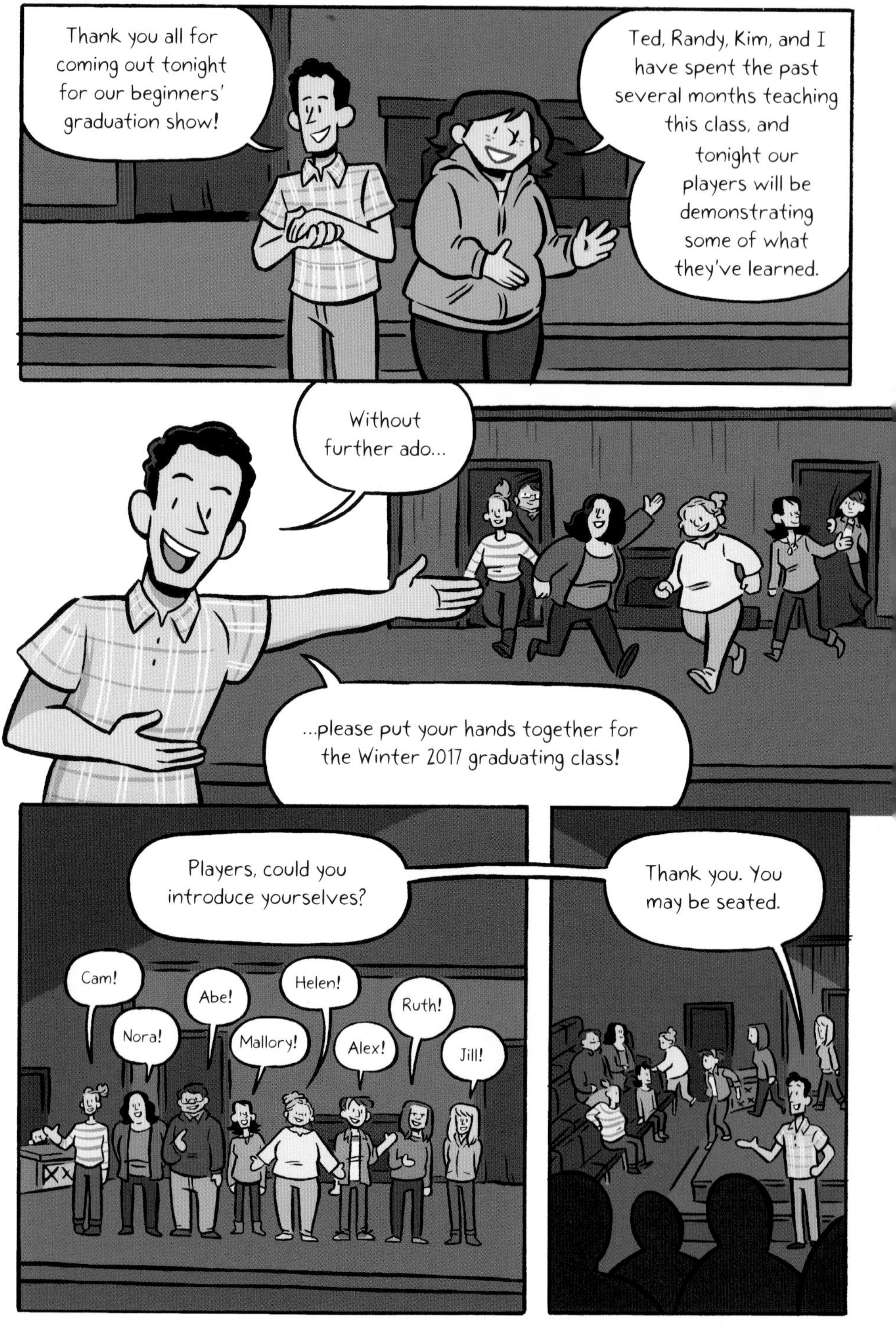
Thank you all for coming out tonight for our beginners' graduation show!
Ted, Randy, Kim, and I have spent the past several months teaching this class, and tonight our players will be demonstrating some of what they've learned.
Without further ado...
...please put your hands together for the Winter 2017 graduating class!
Players, could you introduce yourselves?
Cam!
Nora!
Abe!
Mallory!
Helen!
Alex!
Ruth!
Jill!
Thank you. You may be seated.

The show went on to exemplify the exercises we learned throughout the course.

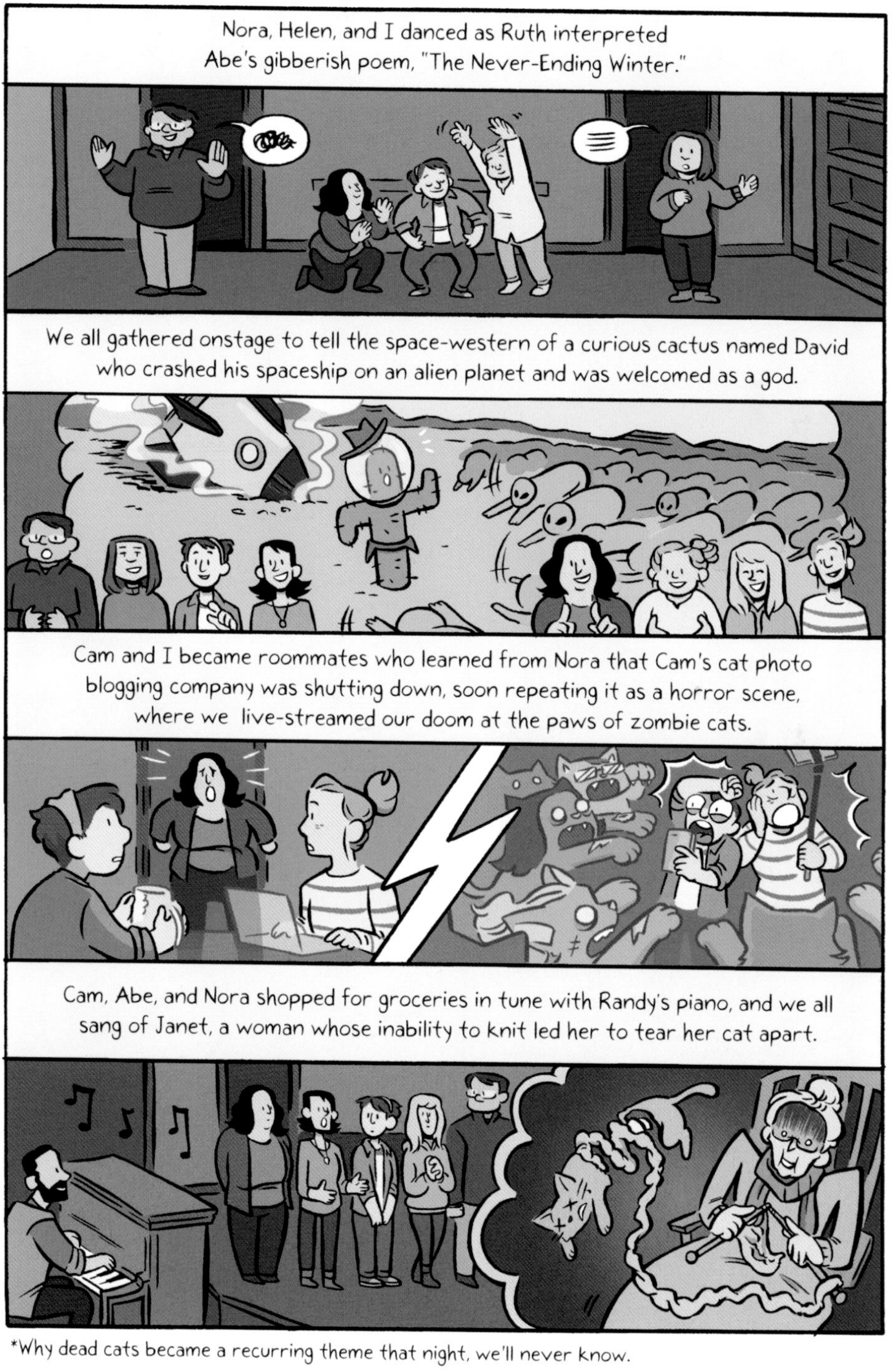
Nora, Helen, and I danced as Ruth interpreted Abe's gibberish poem, "The Never-Ending Winter."
We all gathered onstage to tell the space-western of a curious cactus named David who crashed his spaceship on an alien planet and was welcomed as a god.
Cam and I became roommates who learned from Nora that Cam's cat photo blogging company was shutting down, soon repeating it as a horror scene, where we live-streamed our doom at the paws of zombie cats.
Cam, Abe, and Nora shopped for groceries in tune with Randy's piano, and we all sang of Janet, a woman whose inability to knit led her to tear her cat apart.

*Why dead cats became a recurring theme that night, we'll never know.

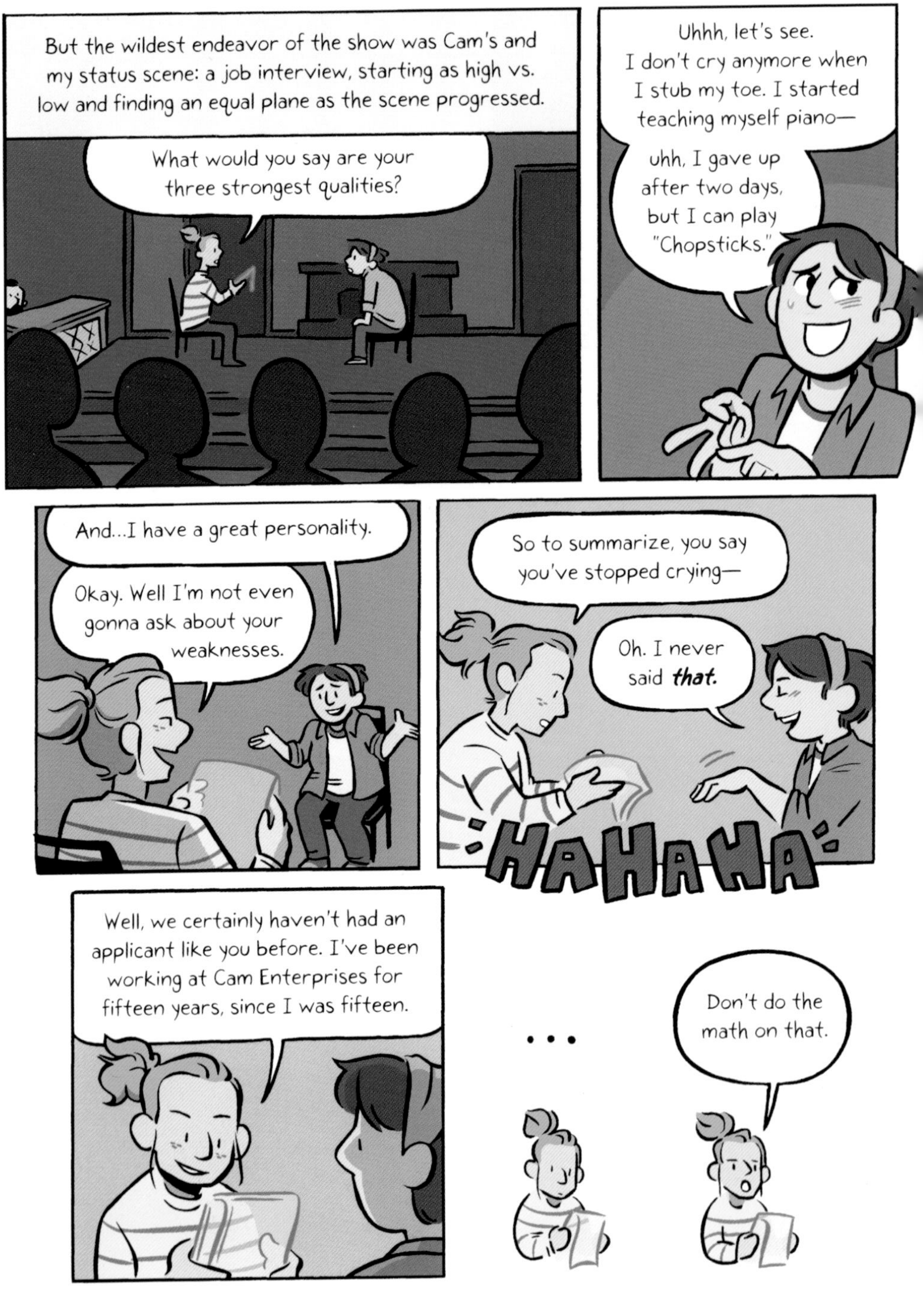
But the wildest endeavor of the show was Cam's and my status scene: a job interview, starting as high vs. low and finding an equal plane as the scene progressed.
What would you say are your three strongest qualities?
Uhhh, let's see. I don't cry anymore when I stub my toe. I started teaching myself piano—
uhh, I gave up after two days, but I can play "Chopsticks."
And...I have a great personality.
Okay. Well I'm not even gonna ask about your weaknesses.
So to summarize, you say you've stopped crying—
Oh. I never said *that.*
HAHAHA
Well, we certainly haven't had an applicant like you before. I've been working at Cam Enterprises for fifteen years, since I was fifteen.
...
Don't do the math on that.

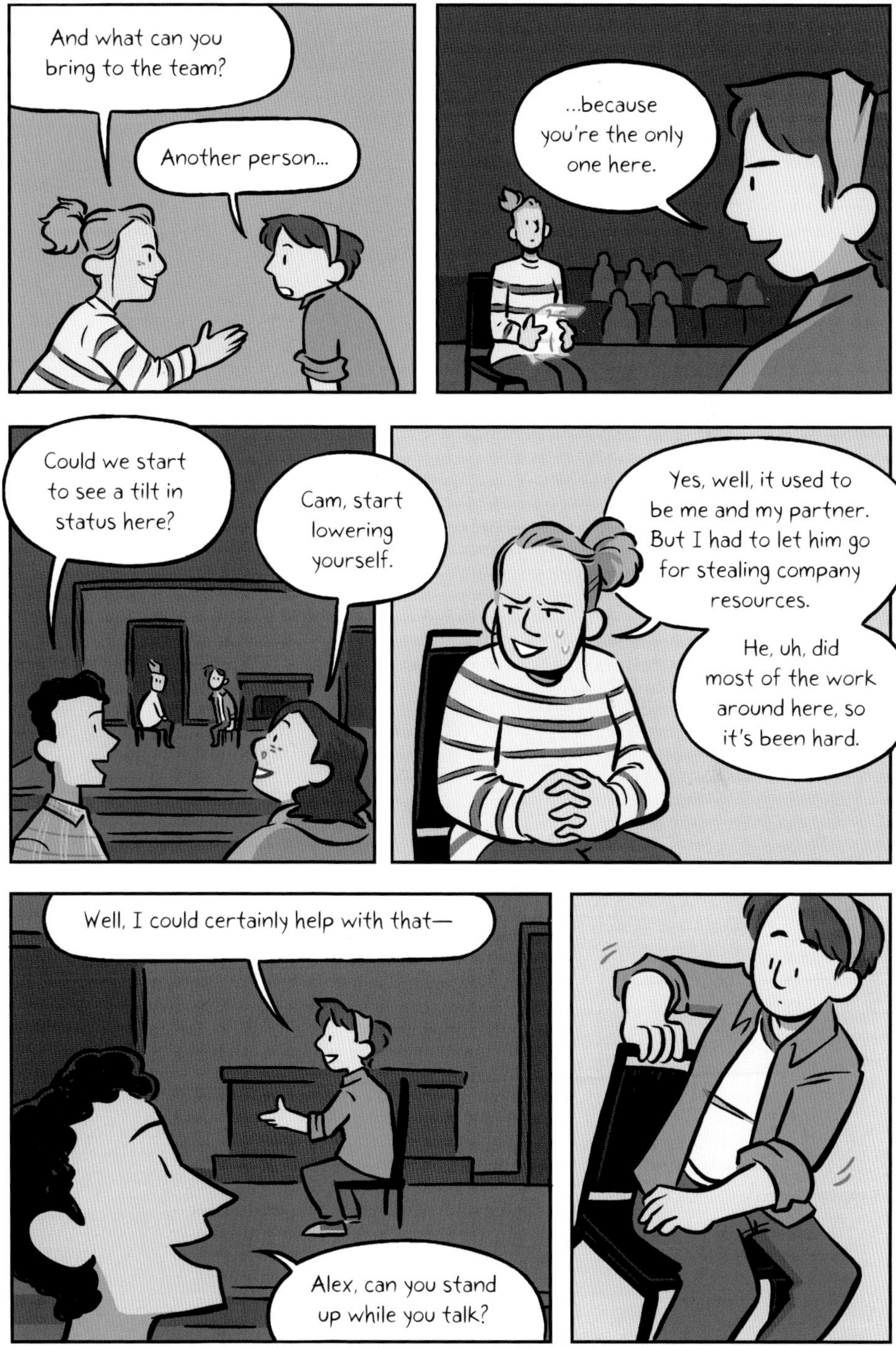
And what can you bring to the team?
Another person...
...because you're the only one here.
Could we start to see a tilt in status here?
Cam, start lowering yourself.
Yes, well, it used to be me and my partner. But I had to let him go for stealing company resources.
He, uh, did most of the work around here, so it's been hard.
Well, I could certainly help with that—
Alex, can you stand up while you talk?

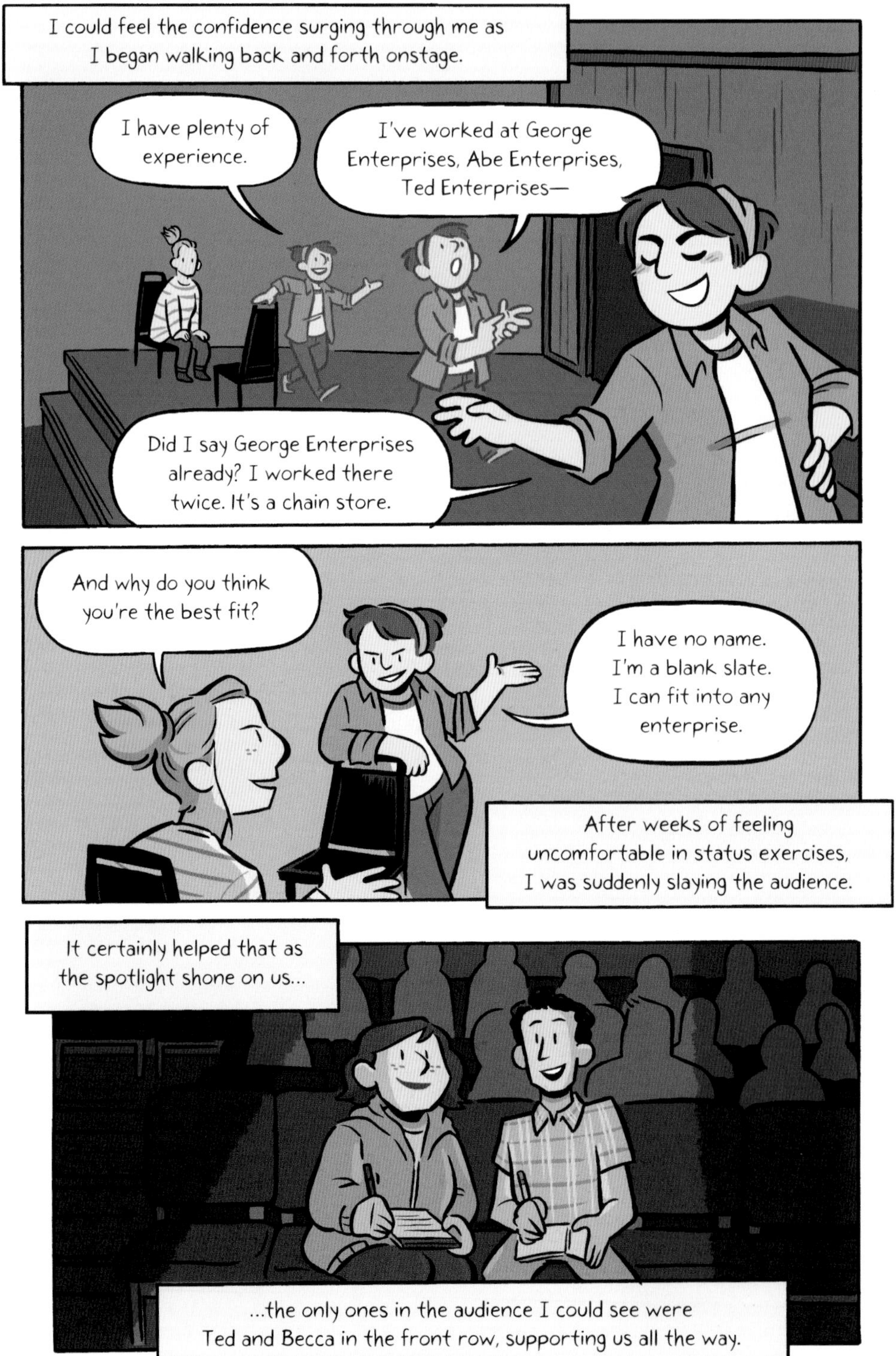
I could feel the confidence surging through me as
I began walking back and forth onstage.
I have plenty of
experience.
I've worked at George
Enterprises, Abe Enterprises,
Ted Enterprises—
Did I say George Enterprises
already? I worked there
twice. It's a chain store.
And why do you think
you're the best fit?
I have no name.
I'm a blank slate.
I can fit into any
enterprise.
After weeks of feeling
uncomfortable in status exercises,
I was suddenly slaying the audience.
It certainly helped that as
the spotlight shone on us...
...the only ones in the audience I could see were
Ted and Becca in the front row, supporting us all the way.

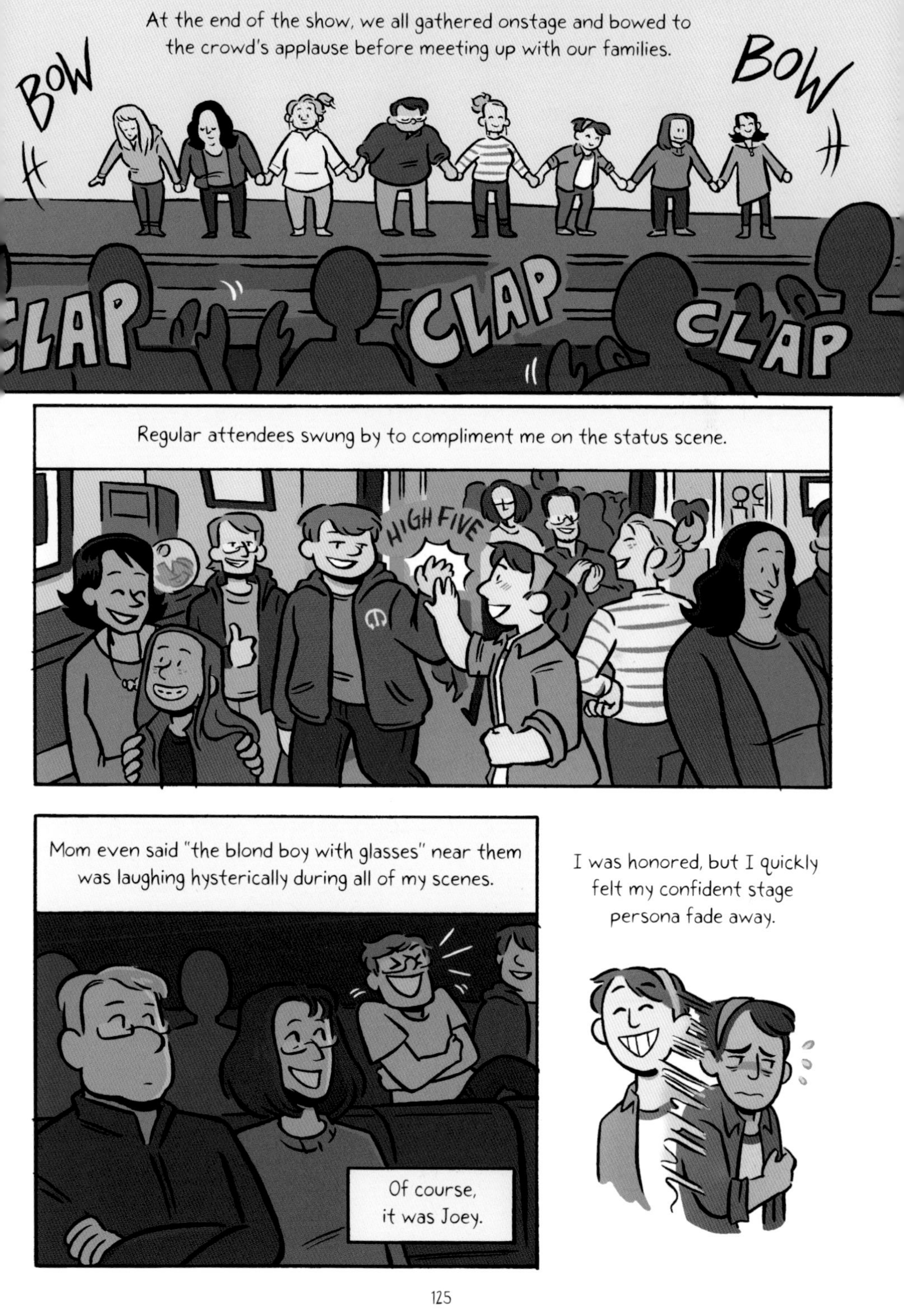
At the end of the show, we all gathered onstage and bowed to the crowd's applause before meeting up with our families.
BOW
BOW
CLAP
CLAP
CLAP
Regular attendees swung by to compliment me on the status scene.
HIGH FIVE
Mom even said "the blond boy with glasses" near them was laughing hysterically during all of my scenes.
Of course, it was Joey.
I was honored, but I quickly felt my confident stage persona fade away.

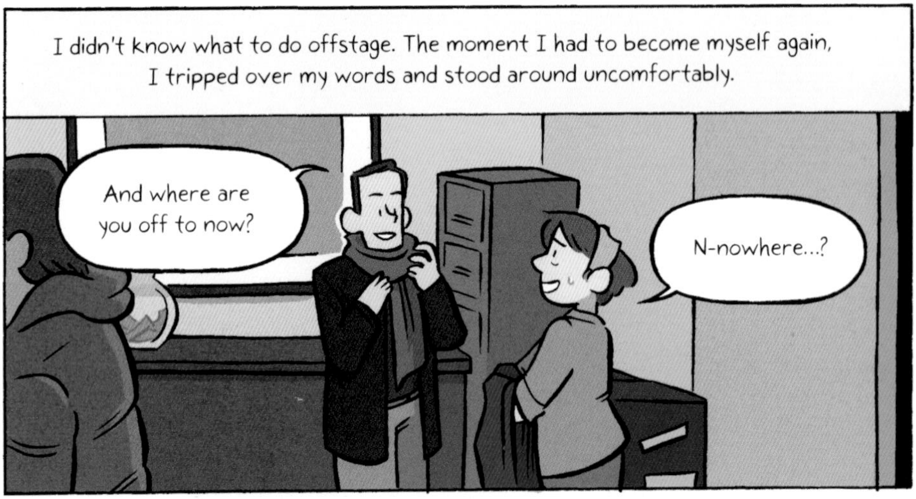
I didn't know what to do offstage. The moment I had to become myself again, I tripped over my words and stood around uncomfortably.
And where are you off to now?
N-nowhere...?

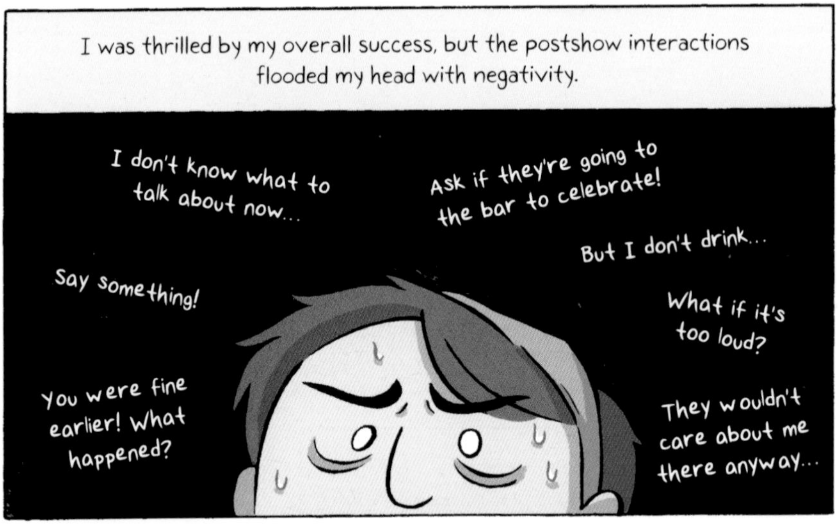
I was thrilled by my overall success, but the postshow interactions flooded my head with negativity.
I don't know what to talk about now...
Ask if they're going to the bar to celebrate!
But I don't drink...
Say something!
What if it's too loud?
You were fine earlier! What happened?
They wouldn't care about me there anyway...

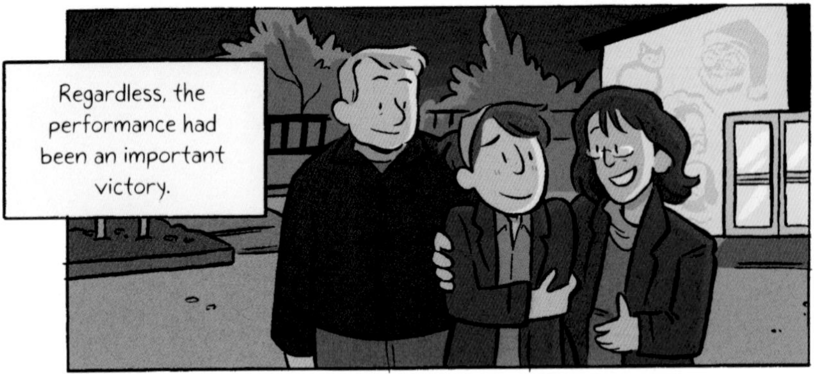
Regardless, the performance had been an important victory.

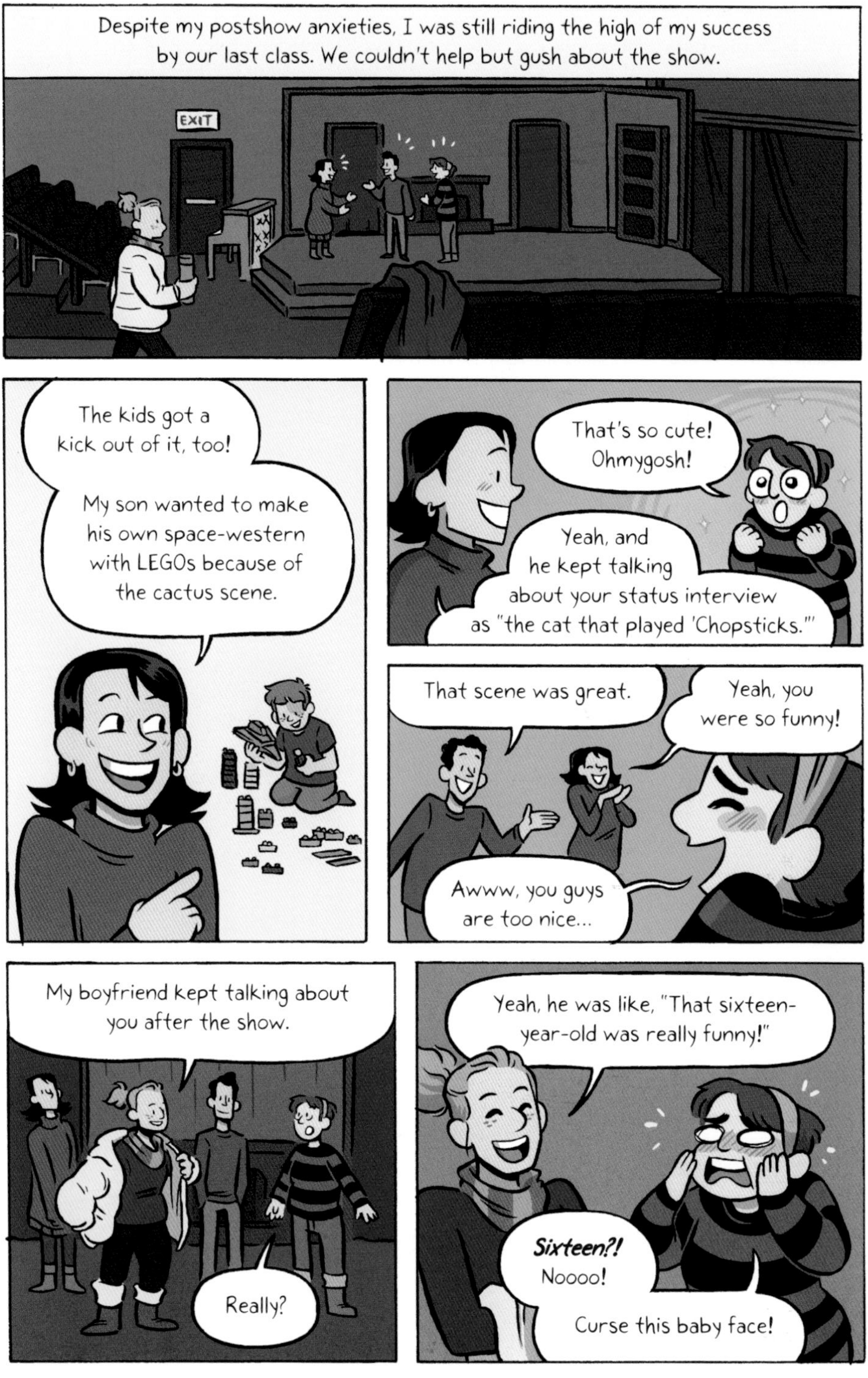
Despite my postshow anxieties, I was still riding the high of my success by our last class. We couldn't help but gush about the show.
EXIT
The kids got a kick out of it, too!
My son wanted to make his own space-western with LEGOs because of the cactus scene.
That's so cute! Ohmygosh!
Yeah, and he kept talking about your status interview as "the cat that played 'Chopsticks.'"
That scene was great.
Yeah, you were so funny!
Awww, you guys are too nice...
My boyfriend kept talking about you after the show.
Really?
Yeah, he was like, "That sixteen-year-old was really funny!"
Sixteen?! Noooo!
Curse this baby face!

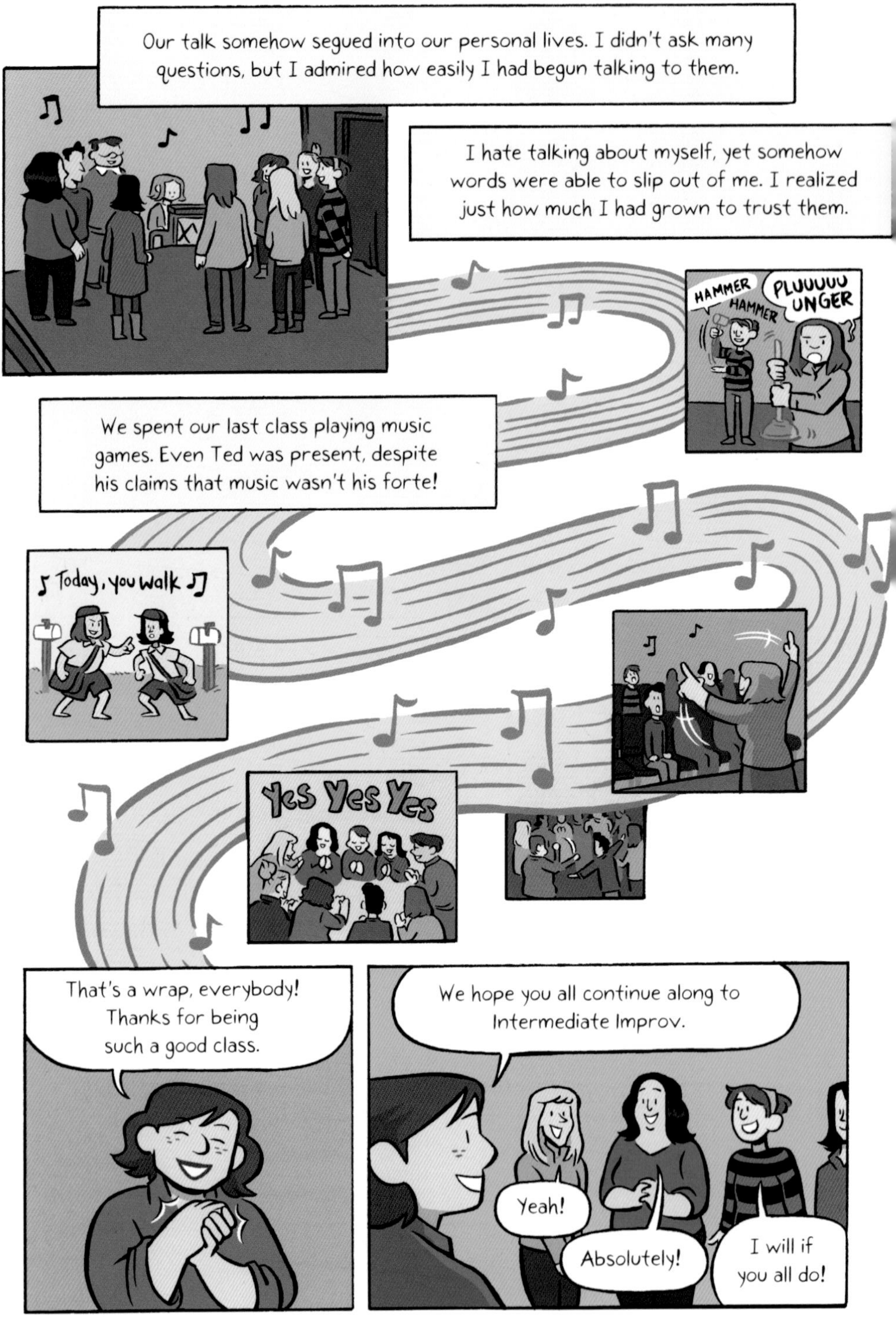
Our talk somehow segued into our personal lives. I didn't ask many questions, but I admired how easily I had begun talking to them.
I hate talking about myself, yet somehow words were able to slip out of me. I realized just how much I had grown to trust them.
HAMMER HAMMER
PLUUUUU UNGER
We spent our last class playing music games. Even Ted was present, despite his claims that music wasn't his forte!
Today, you walk
Yes Yes Yes
That's a wrap, everybody! Thanks for being such a good class.
We hope you all continue along to Intermediate Improv.
Yeah!
Absolutely!
I will if you all do!

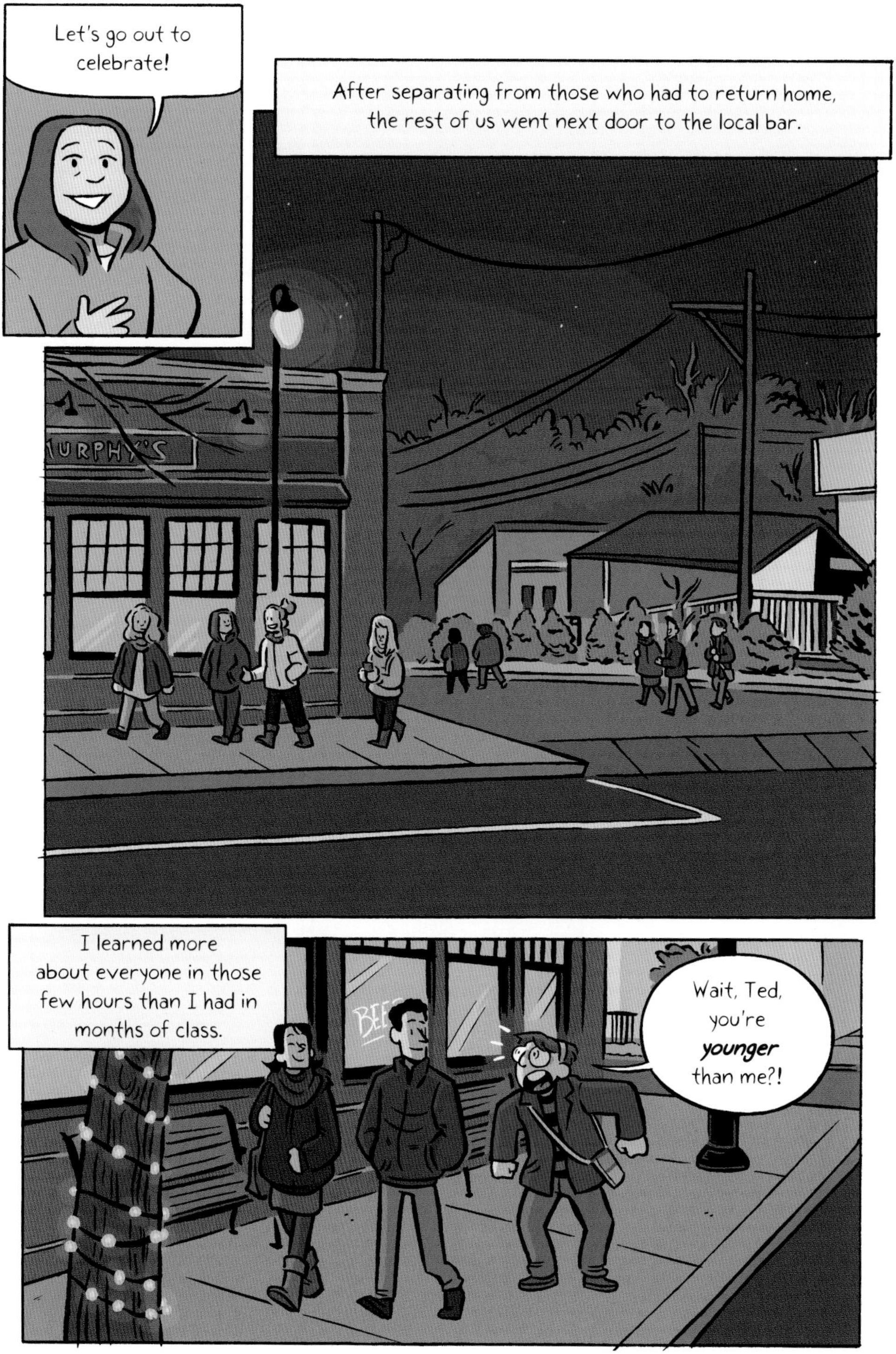
Let's go out to celebrate!
After separating from those who had to return home, the rest of us went next door to the local bar.
MURPHY'S
I learned more about everyone in those few hours than I had in months of class.
Wait, Ted, you're *younger* than me?!

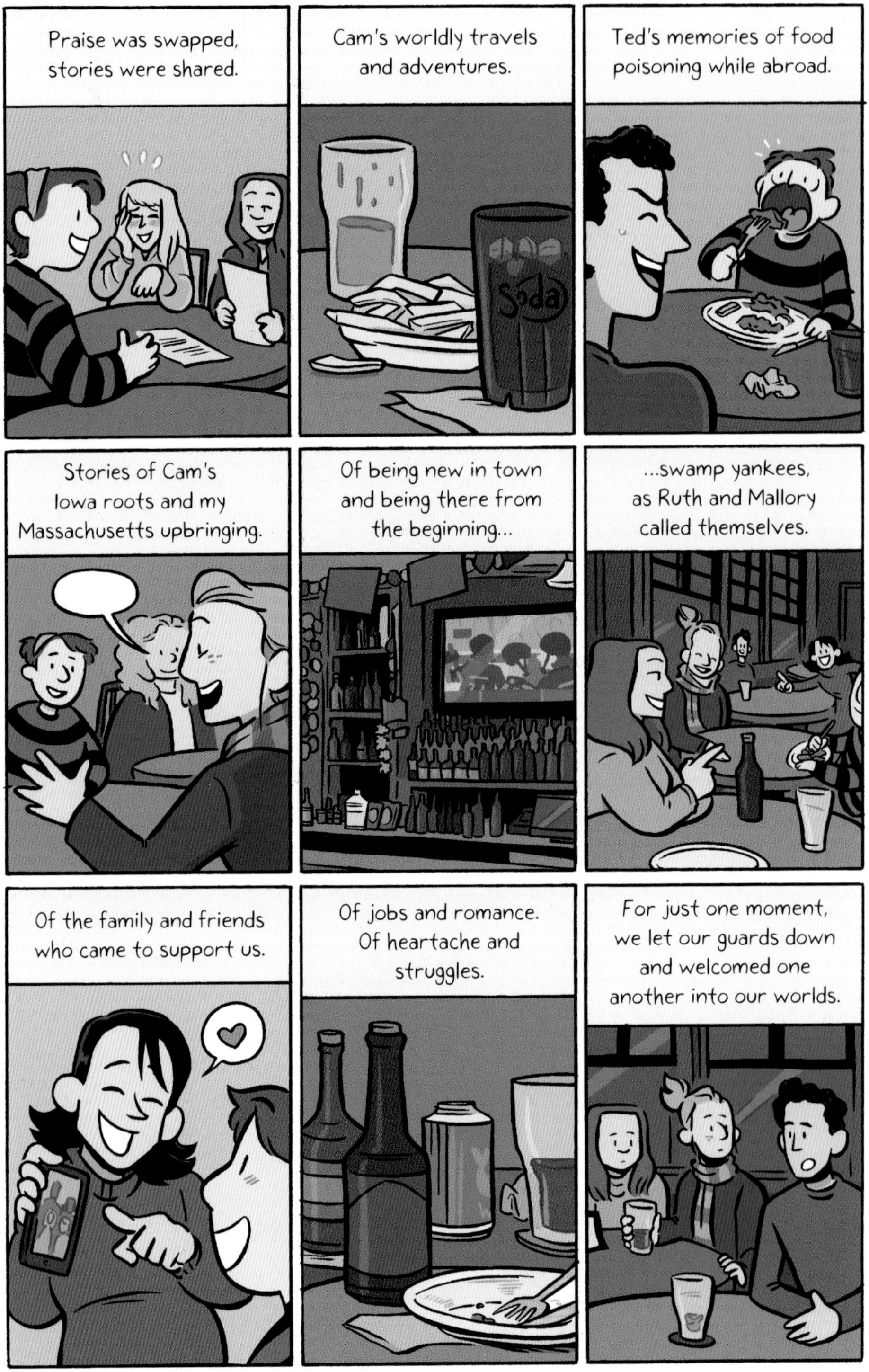

Praise was swapped, stories were shared.
Cam's worldly travels and adventures.
Soda
Ted's memories of food poisoning while abroad.
Stories of Cam's Iowa roots and my Massachusetts upbringing.
Of being new in town and being there from the beginning...
...swamp yankees, as Ruth and Mallory called themselves.
Of the family and friends who came to support us.
Of jobs and romance. Of heartache and struggles.
For just one moment, we let our guards down and welcomed one another into our worlds.

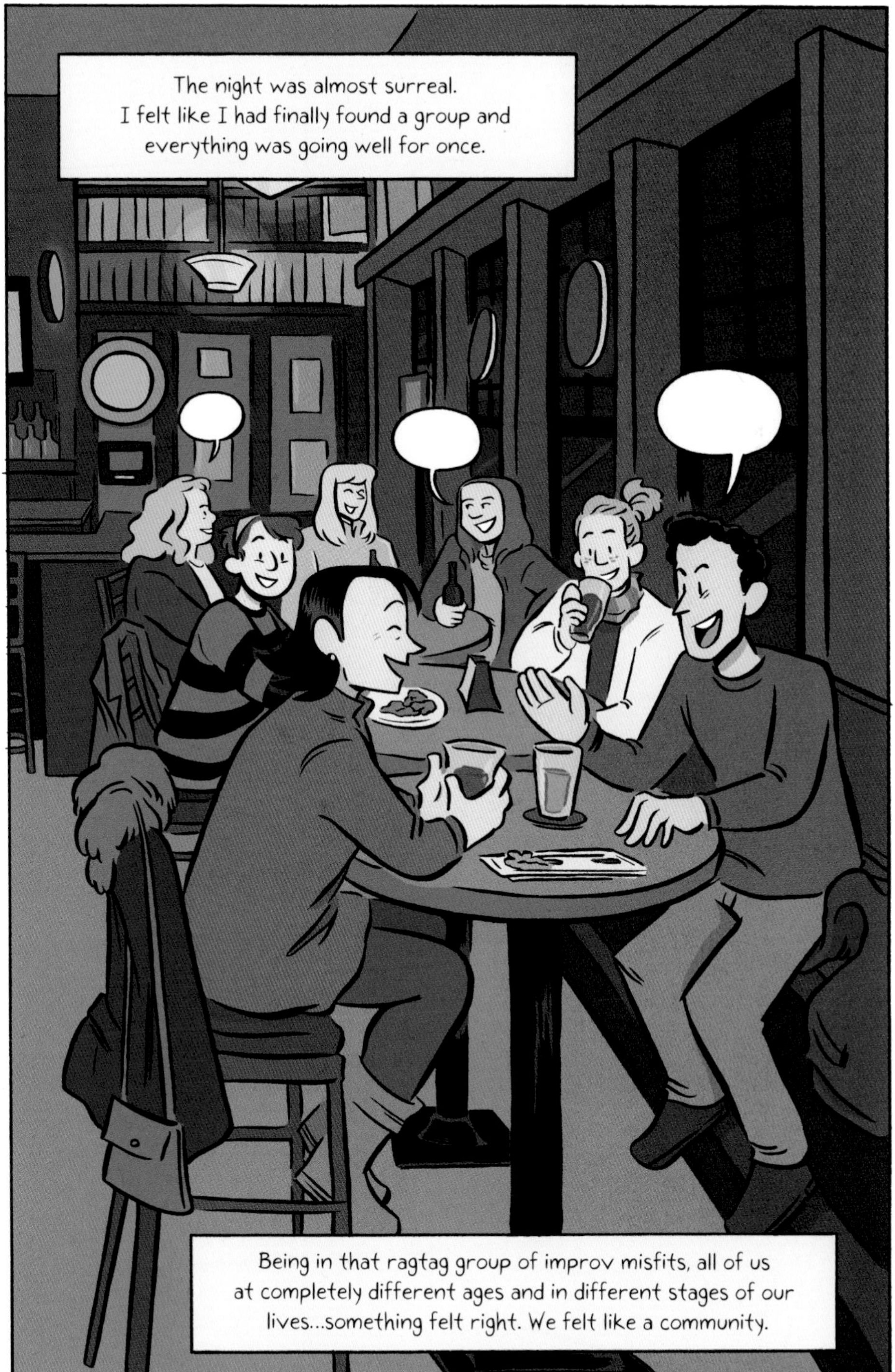
The night was almost surreal.
I felt like I had finally found a group and
everything was going well for once.
Being in that ragtag group of improv misfits, all of us
at completely different ages and in different stages of our
lives...something felt right. We felt like a community.

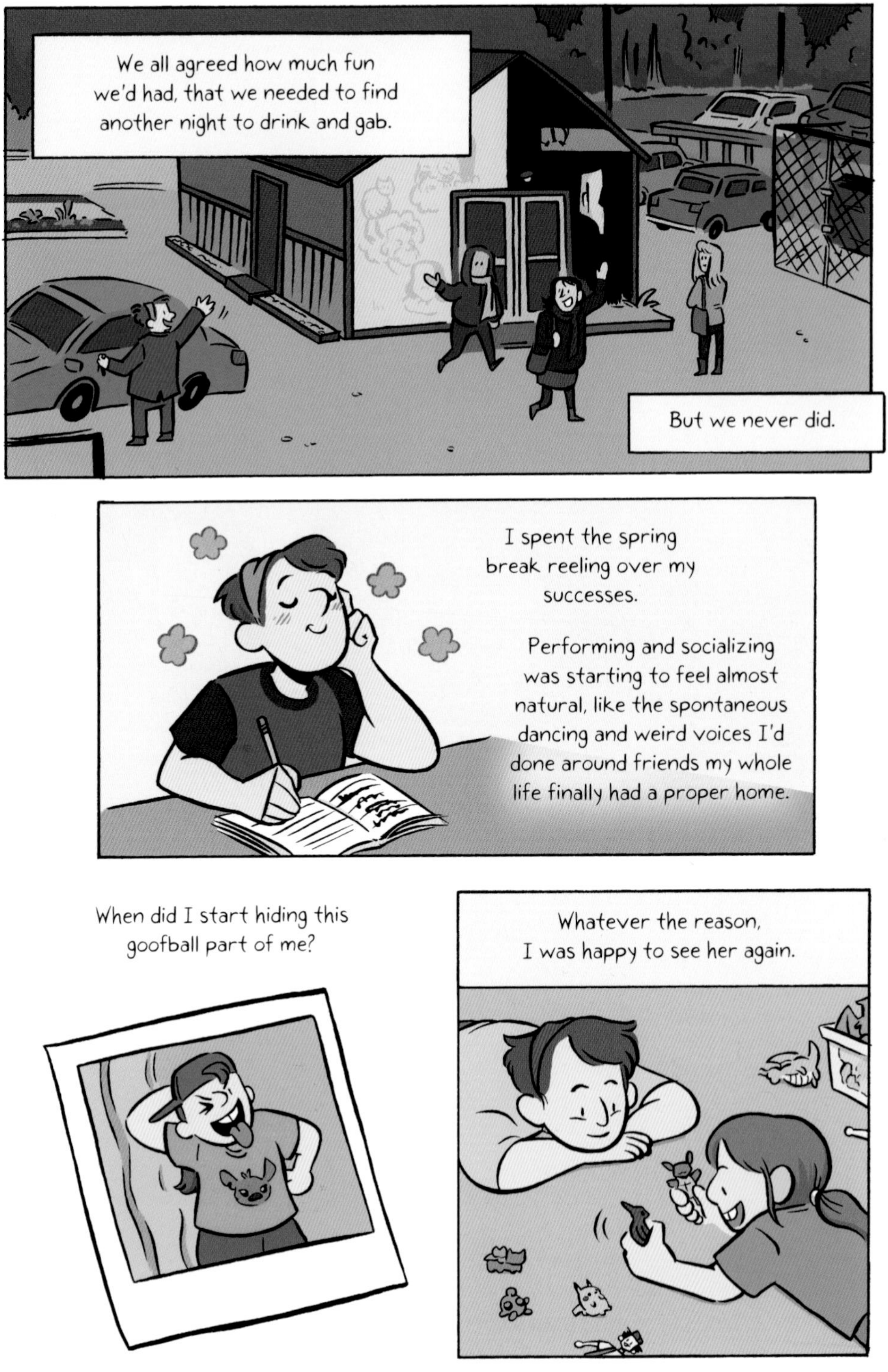
We all agreed how much fun we'd had, that we needed to find another night to drink and gab.
But we never did.
I spent the spring break reeling over my successes.
Performing and socializing was starting to feel almost natural, like the spontaneous dancing and weird voices I'd done around friends my whole life finally had a proper home.
When did I start hiding this goofball part of me?
Whatever the reason, I was happy to see her again.

PART 3

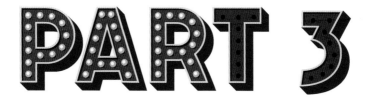

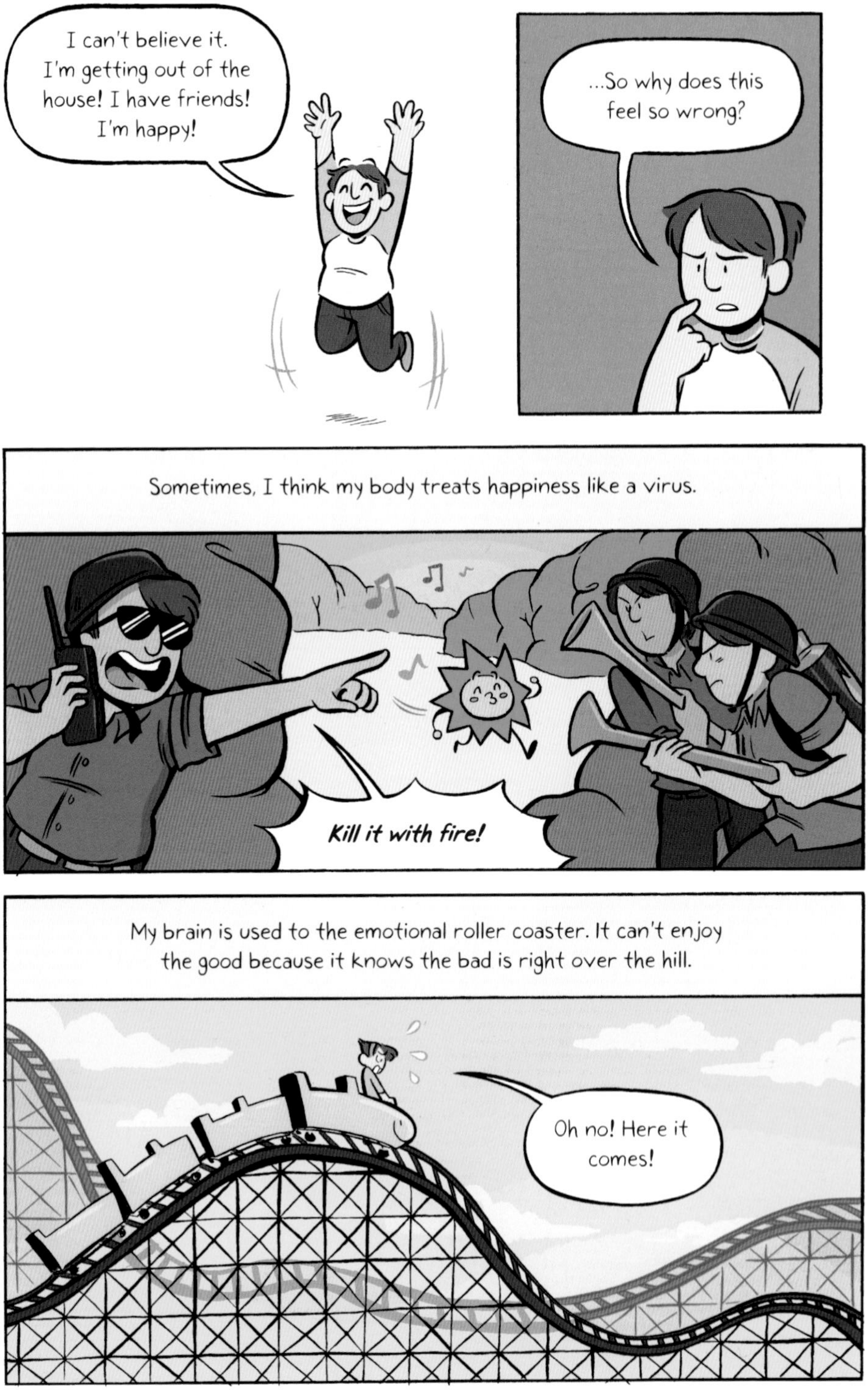
I can't believe it. I'm getting out of the house! I have friends! I'm happy!
...So why does this feel so wrong?
Sometimes, I think my body treats happiness like a virus.
Kill it with fire!
My brain is used to the emotional roller coaster. It can't enjoy the good because it knows the bad is right over the hill.
Oh no! Here it comes!

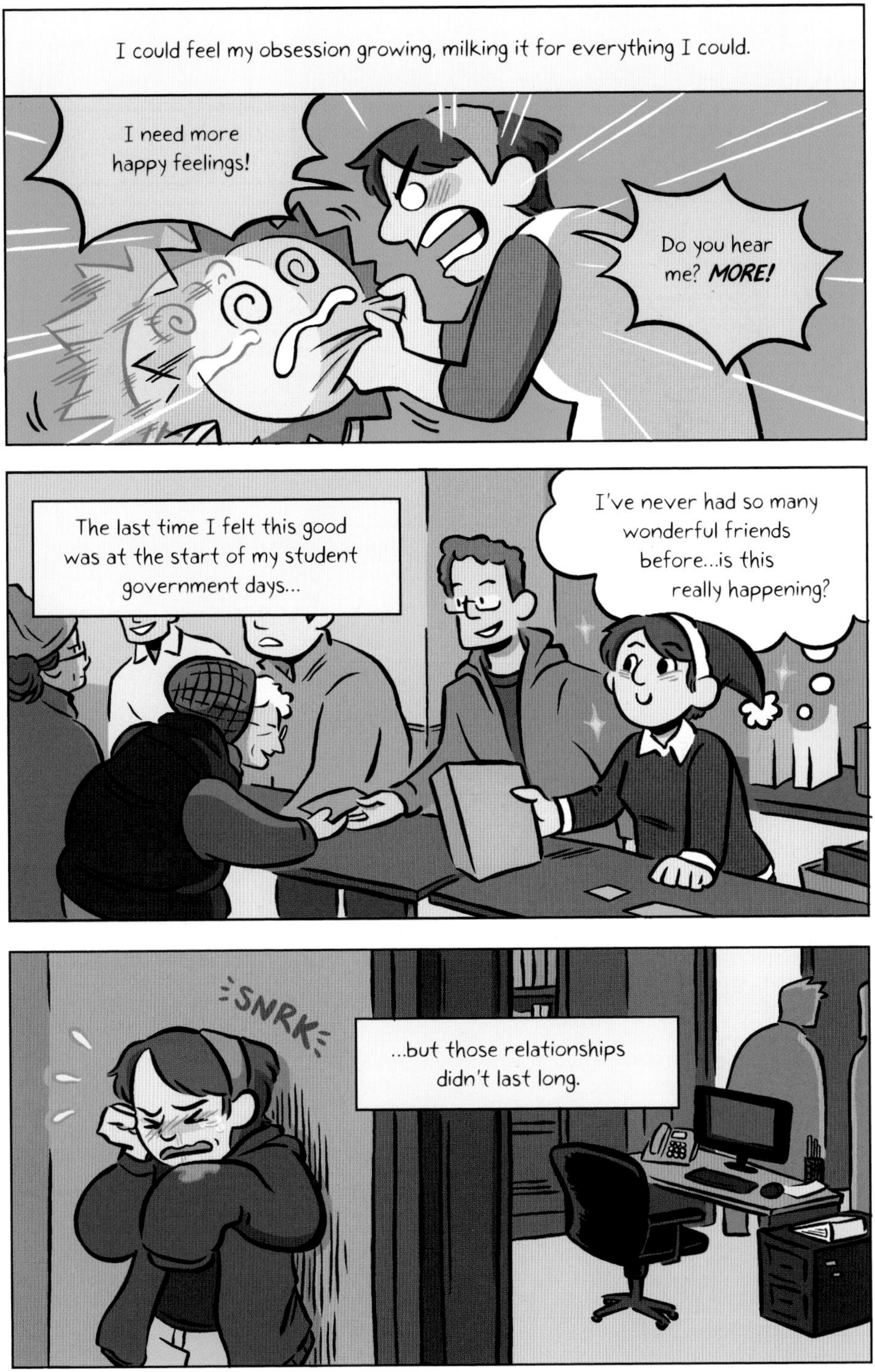
I could feel my obsession growing, milking it for everything I could.
I need more happy feelings!
Do you hear me? MORE!
The last time I felt this good was at the start of my student government days...
I've never had so many wonderful friends before...is this really happening?
SNRK
...but those relationships didn't last long.

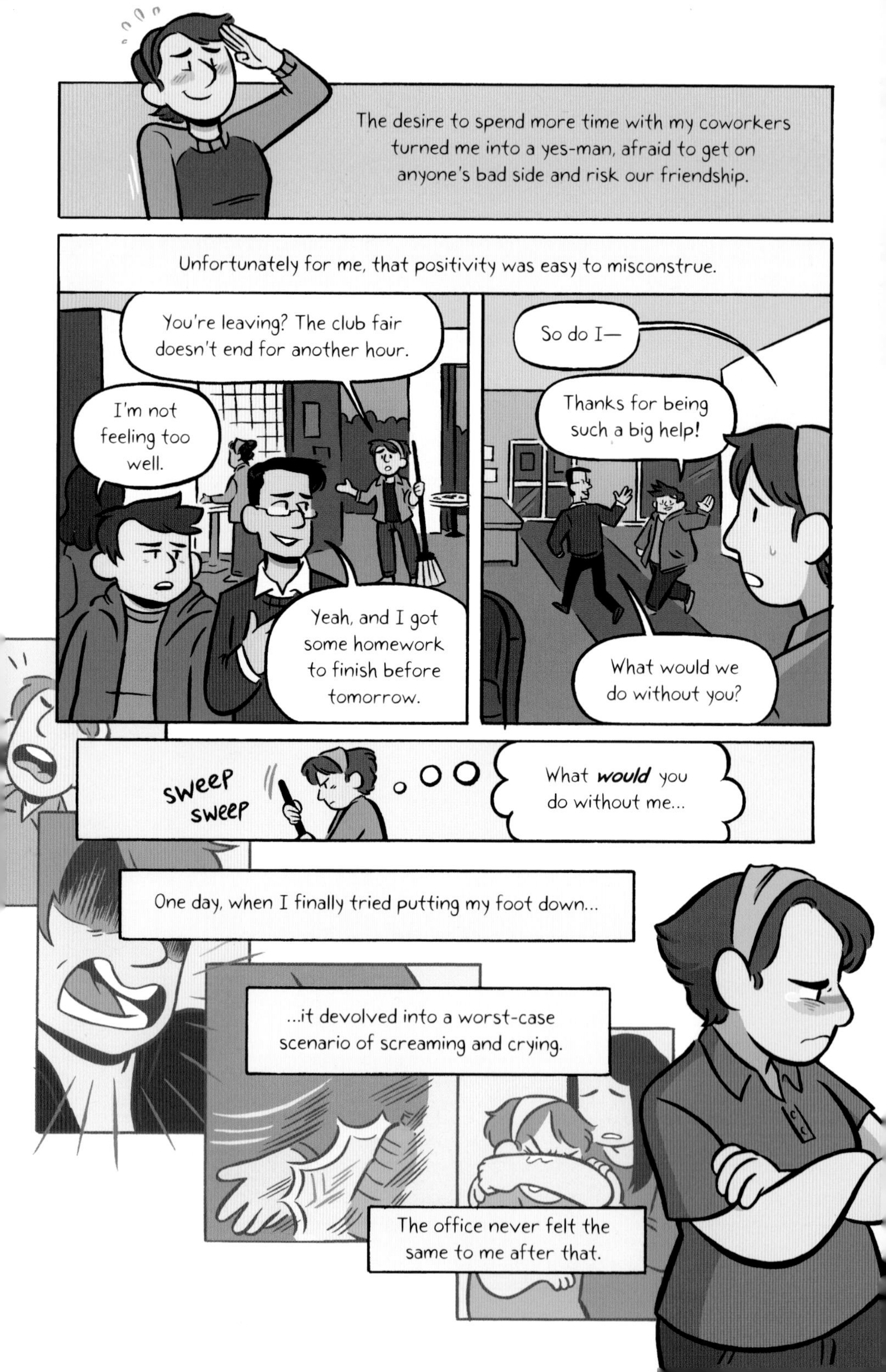

The desire to spend more time with my coworkers turned me into a yes-man, afraid to get on anyone's bad side and risk our friendship.
Unfortunately for me, that positivity was easy to misconstrue.
You're leaving? The club fair doesn't end for another hour.
I'm not feeling too well.
Yeah, and I got some homework to finish before tomorrow.
So do I—
Thanks for being such a big help!
What would we do without you?
sweep sweep
What *would* you do without me...
One day, when I finally tried putting my foot down...
...it devolved into a worst-case scenario of screaming and crying.
The office never felt the same to me after that.

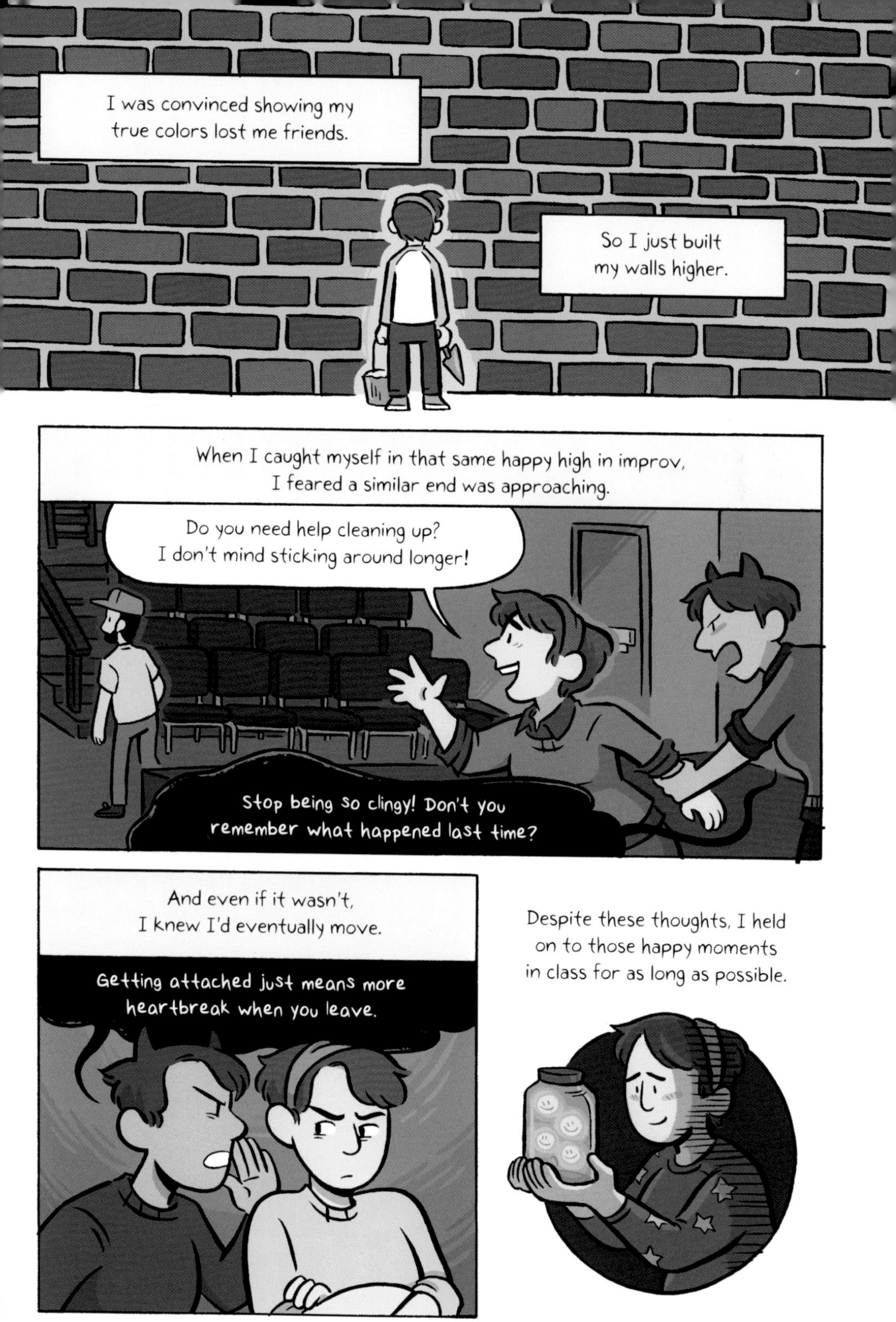

I was convinced showing my true colors lost me friends.
So I just built my walls higher.
When I caught myself in that same happy high in improv, I feared a similar end was approaching.
Do you need help cleaning up? I don't mind sticking around longer!
Stop being so clingy! Don't you remember what happened last time?
And even if it wasn't, I knew I'd eventually move.
Getting attached just means more heartbreak when you leave.
Despite these thoughts, I held on to those happy moments in class for as long as possible.

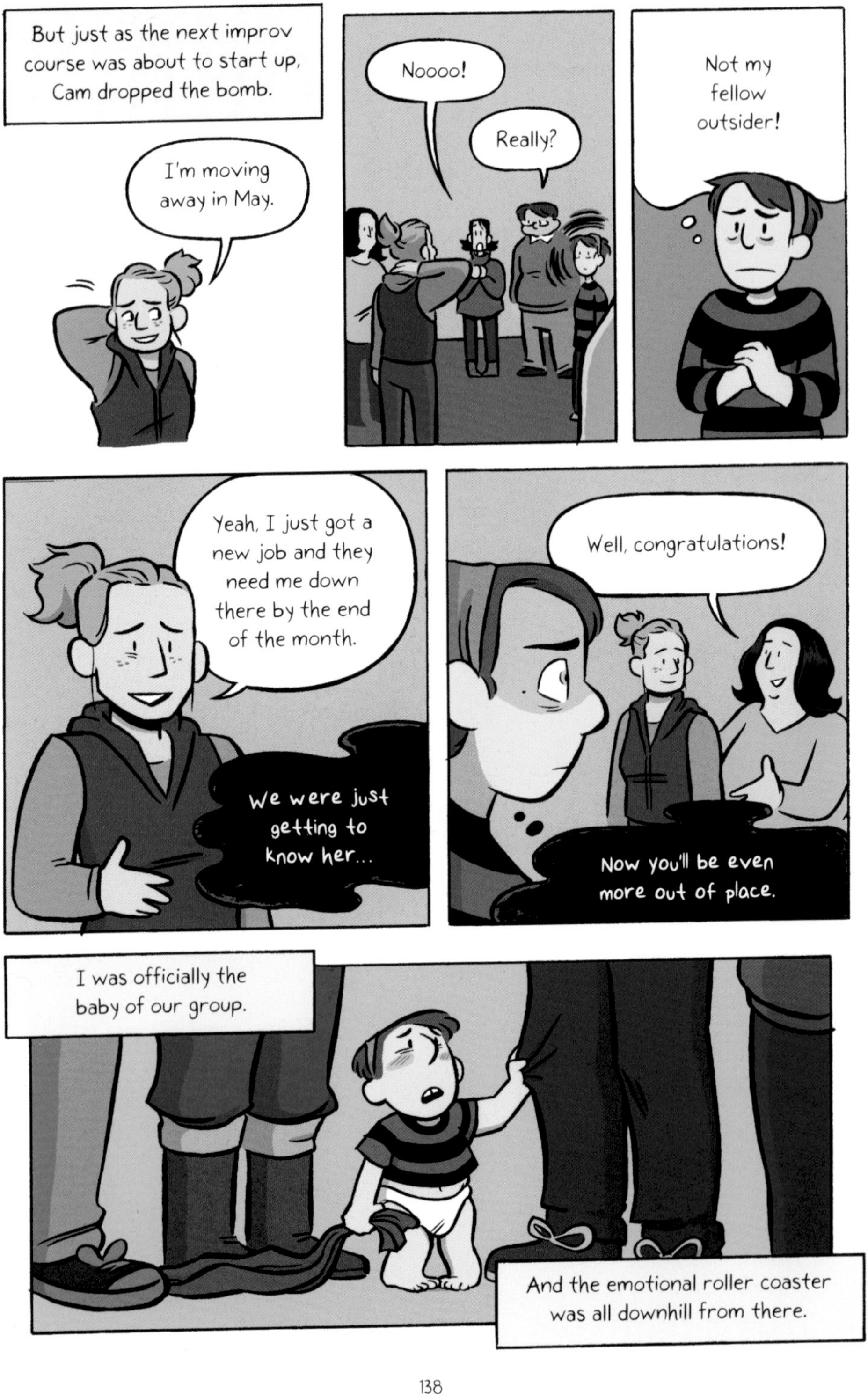
But just as the next improv course was about to start up, Cam dropped the bomb.
I'm moving away in May.
Noooo!
Really?
Not my fellow outsider!
Yeah, I just got a new job and they need me down there by the end of the month.
We were just getting to know her...
Well, congratulations!
Now you'll be even more out of place.
I was officially the baby of our group.
And the emotional roller coaster was all downhill from there.

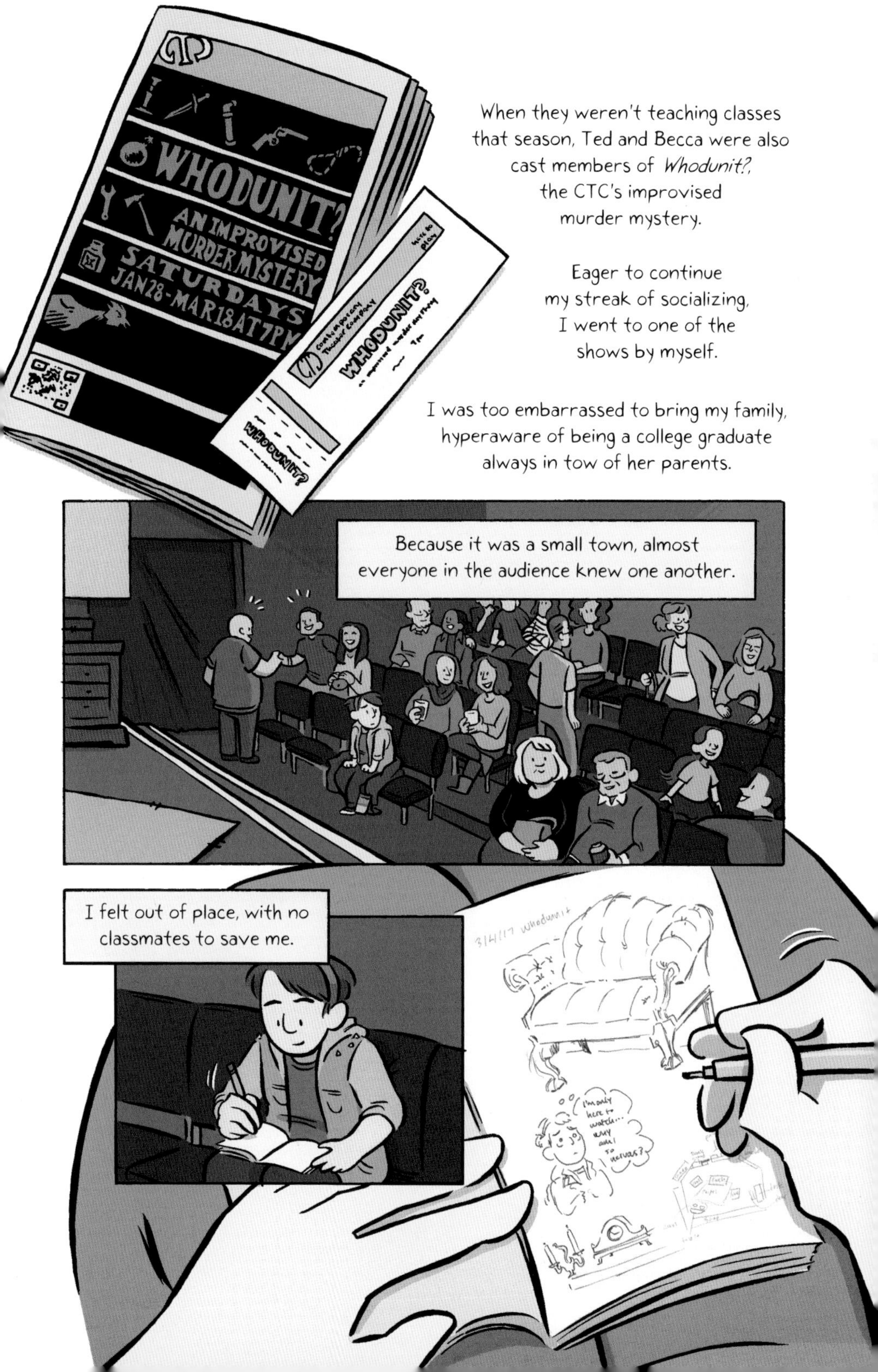
WHODUNIT?
AN IMPROVISED MURDER MYSTERY
SATURDAYS
JAN28-MAR18 AT 7PM
WHODUNIT?
WHODUNIT?
When they weren't teaching classes that season, Ted and Becca were also cast members of *Whodunit?*, the CTC's improvised murder mystery.
Eager to continue my streak of socializing, I went to one of the shows by myself.
I was too embarrassed to bring my family, hyperaware of being a college graduate always in tow of her parents.
Because it was a small town, almost everyone in the audience knew one another.
I felt out of place, with no classmates to save me.
3/4/17 whodunit
I'm only here to watch... why am I so nervous?

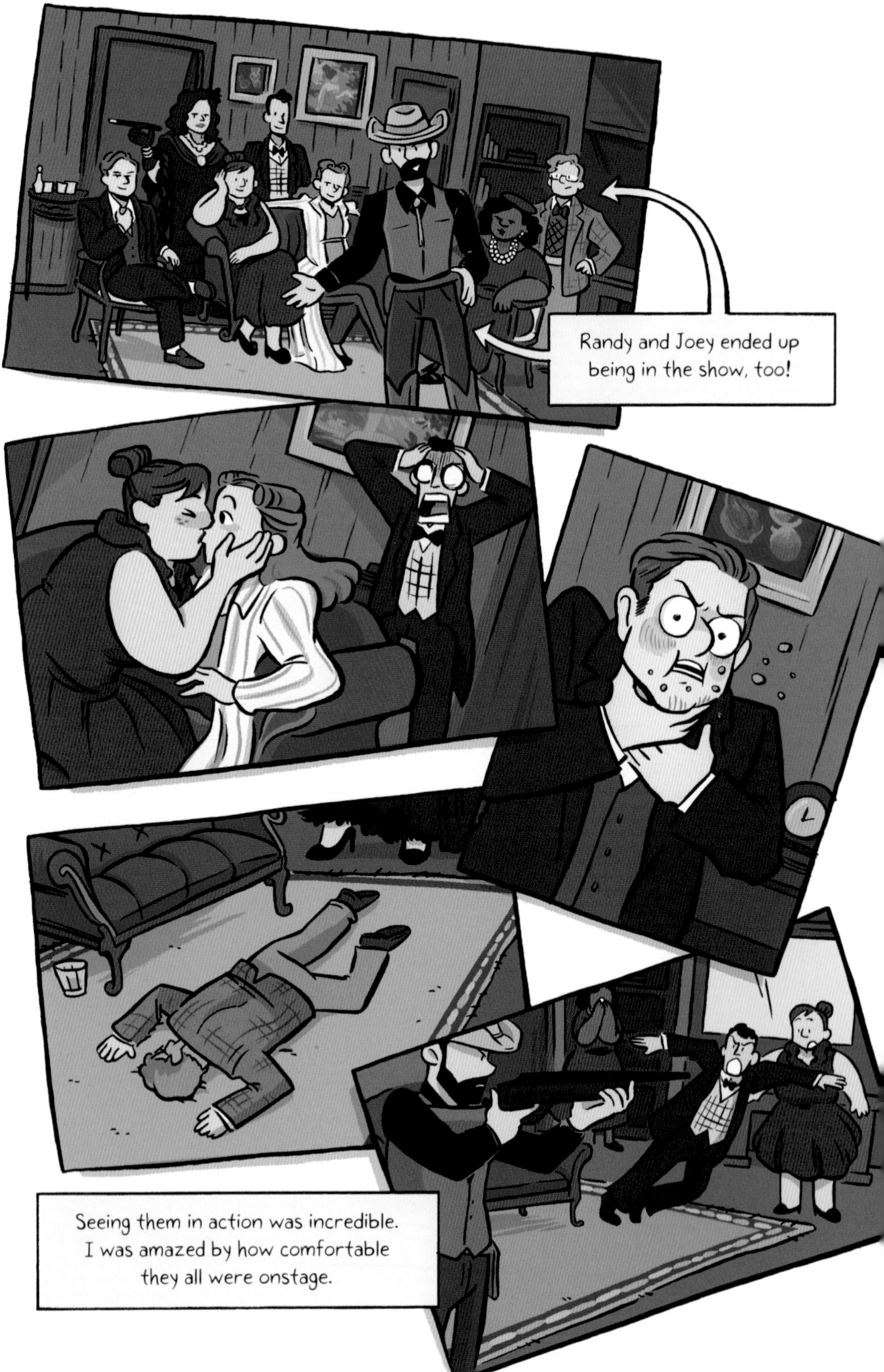
Randy and Joey ended up being in the show, too!
Seeing them in action was incredible. I was amazed by how comfortable they all were onstage.

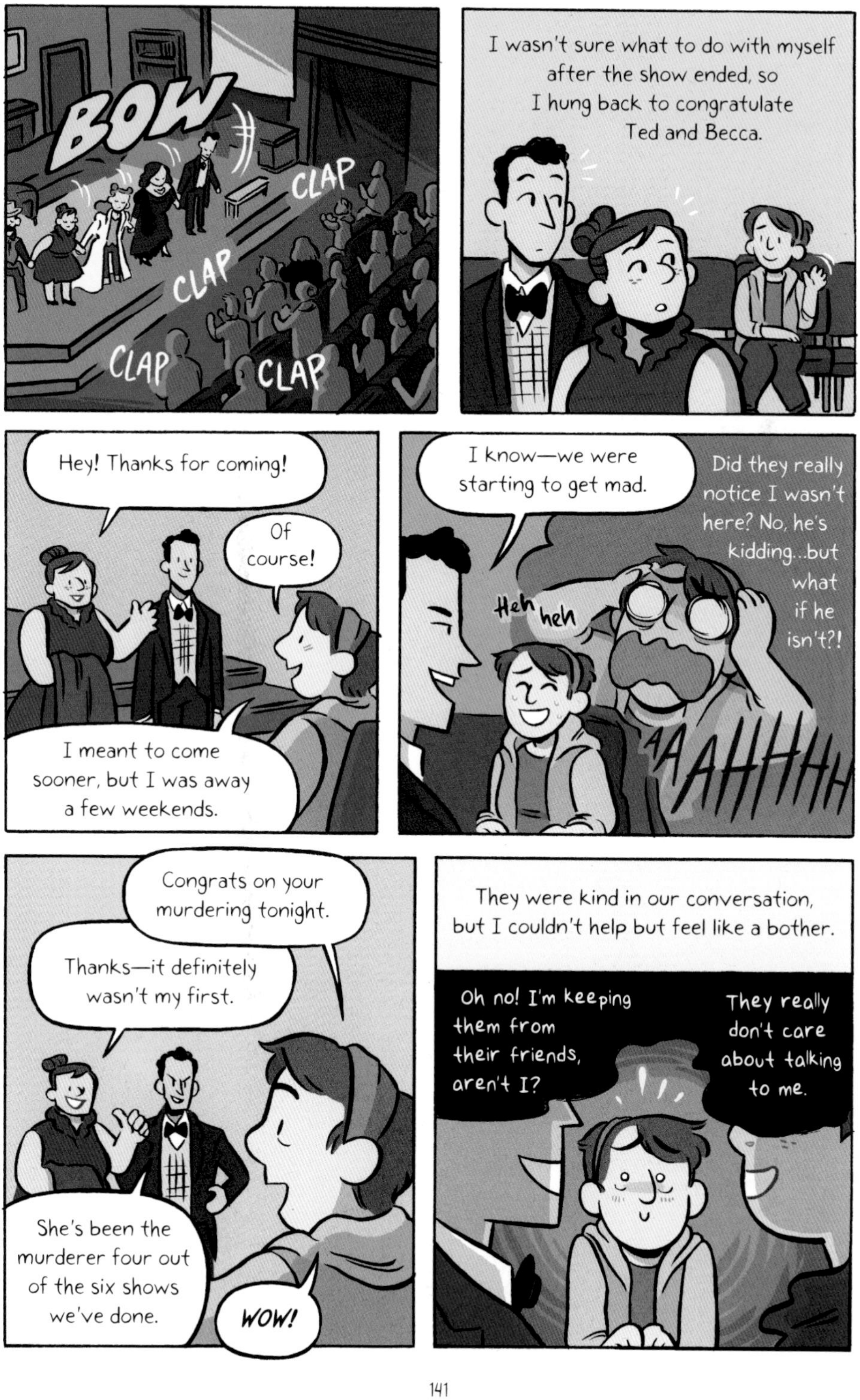
BOW
CLAP
CLAP
CLAP
CLAP
I wasn't sure what to do with myself after the show ended, so I hung back to congratulate Ted and Becca.
Hey! Thanks for coming!
Of course!
I meant to come sooner, but I was away a few weekends.
I know—we were starting to get mad.
Did they really notice I wasn't here? No, he's kidding...but what if he isn't?!
Heh heh
AAAHHHHH
Congrats on your murdering tonight.
Thanks—it definitely wasn't my first.
She's been the murderer four out of the six shows we've done.
WOW!
They were kind in our conversation, but I couldn't help but feel like a bother.
Oh no! I'm keeping them from their friends, aren't I?
They really don't care about talking to me.

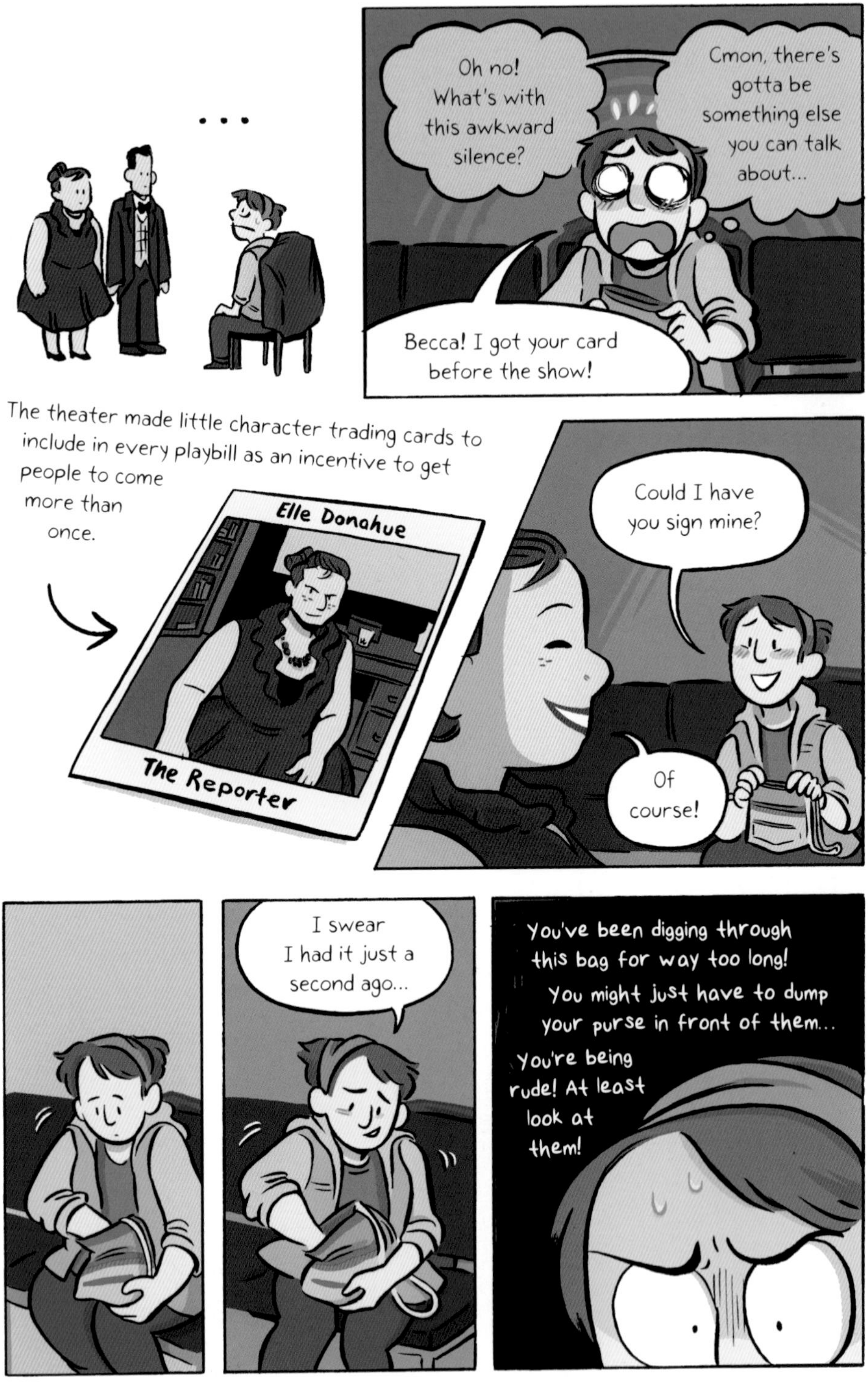
. . .
Oh no! What's with this awkward silence?
Cmon, there's gotta be something else you can talk about...
Becca! I got your card before the show!
The theater made little character trading cards to include in every playbill as an incentive to get people to come more than once.
Elle Donahue
The Reporter
Could I have you sign mine?
Of course!
I swear I had it just a second ago...
You've been digging through this bag for way too long!
You might just have to dump your purse in front of them...
You're being rude! At least look at them!

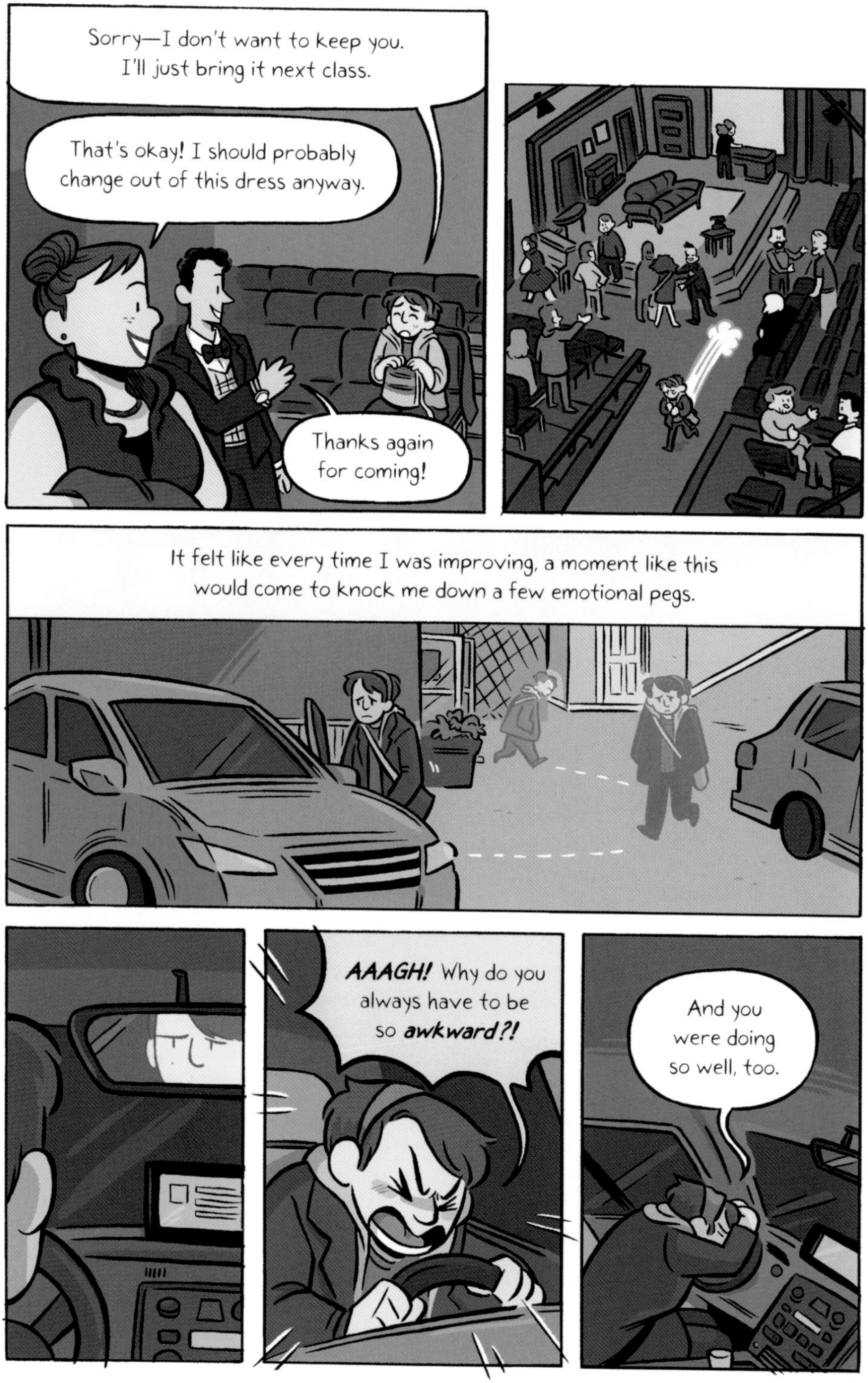

Sorry—I don't want to keep you. I'll just bring it next class.
That's okay! I should probably change out of this dress anyway.
Thanks again for coming!
It felt like every time I was improving, a moment like this would come to knock me down a few emotional pegs.
AAAGH! Why do you always have to be so ***awkward?!***
And you were doing so well, too.

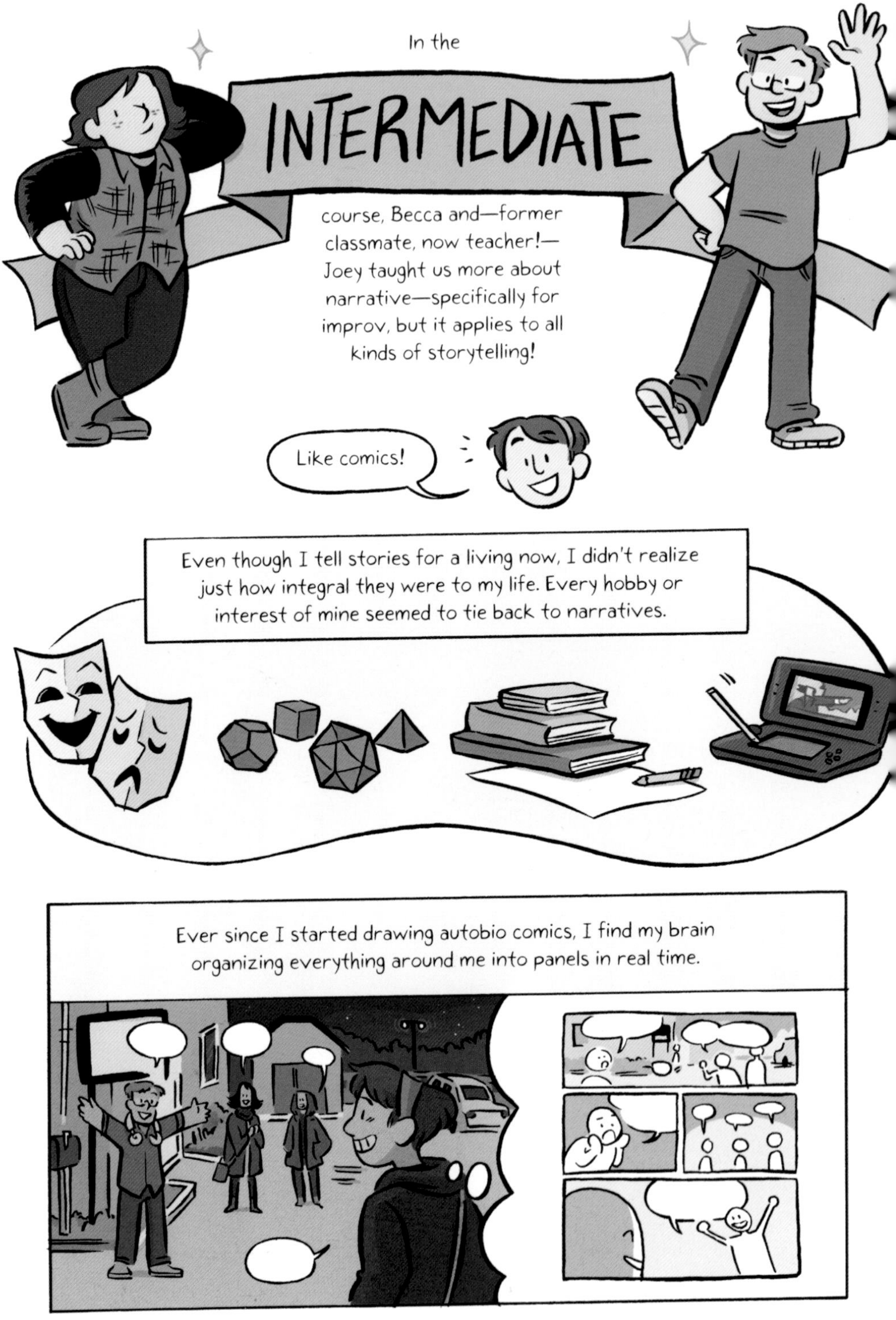
In the
INTERMEDIATE
course, Becca and—former classmate, now teacher!—Joey taught us more about narrative—specifically for improv, but it applies to all kinds of storytelling!
Like comics!
Even though I tell stories for a living now, I didn't realize just how integral they were to my life. Every hobby or interest of mine seemed to tie back to narratives.
Ever since I started drawing autobio comics, I find my brain organizing everything around me into panels in real time.

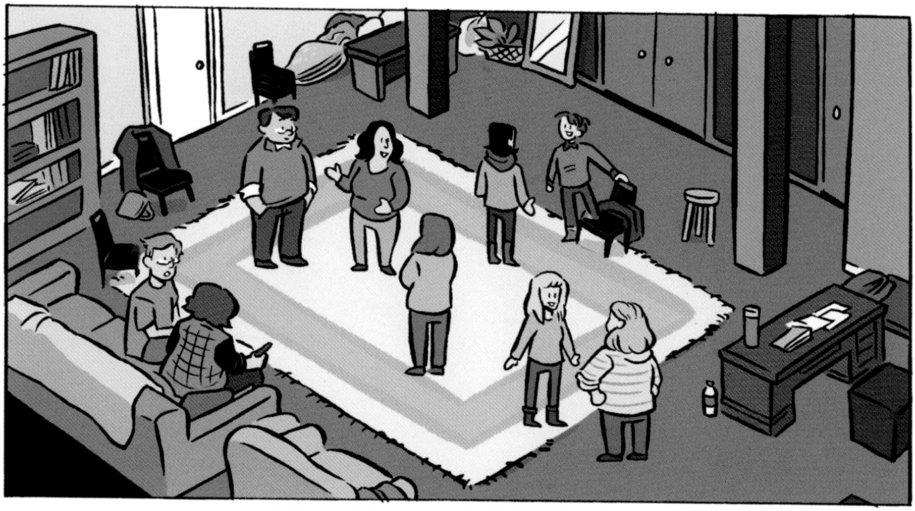

We were a bit hard to wrangle at the start of class, but
we were all just so happy to see one another and catch up!

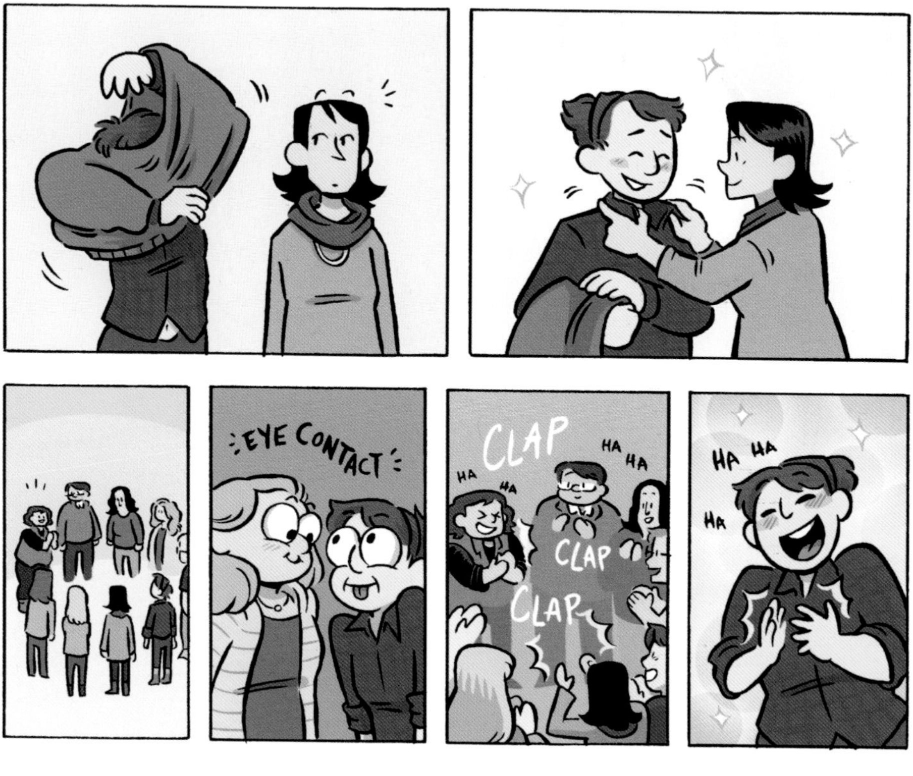
EYE CONTACT
CLAP
HA HA
HA HA
CLAP
CLAP
HA HA
HA

Let's work genre into some **8-Beat Stories.**

8-BEAT STORY AKA STORY SPINE

is a narrative circle game
where each person forwards the story based on the given structure.

1 Once upon a time...

2 And every day...

3 Until one day...

4-6 And because of that...
And because of that...
And because of that...

7 Until finally...

8 And ever since then...

Stories don't always have to follow this format—though you could certainly outline any piece of media with this template—but it's useful for improv when you're not quite sure where a scene should be heading.

1. **Once upon a time,** there was a mermaid named Ariel.
2. **And every day,** she dreamt of the human world.
3. **Until one day,** she saved Prince Eric from drowning and fell in love.
4. **And because of that,** she traded her voice to a sea witch to make her human.
5. **And because of that,** Eric struggled to remember her.
6. **And because of that,** the sea witch used Ariel's voice to hypnotize Eric into loving her instead.
7. **Until finally,** Ariel broke the witch's hold on her voice, and Eric recognized her as the girl who saved him.
8. **And ever since then,** Ariel has lived on land with her human prince.

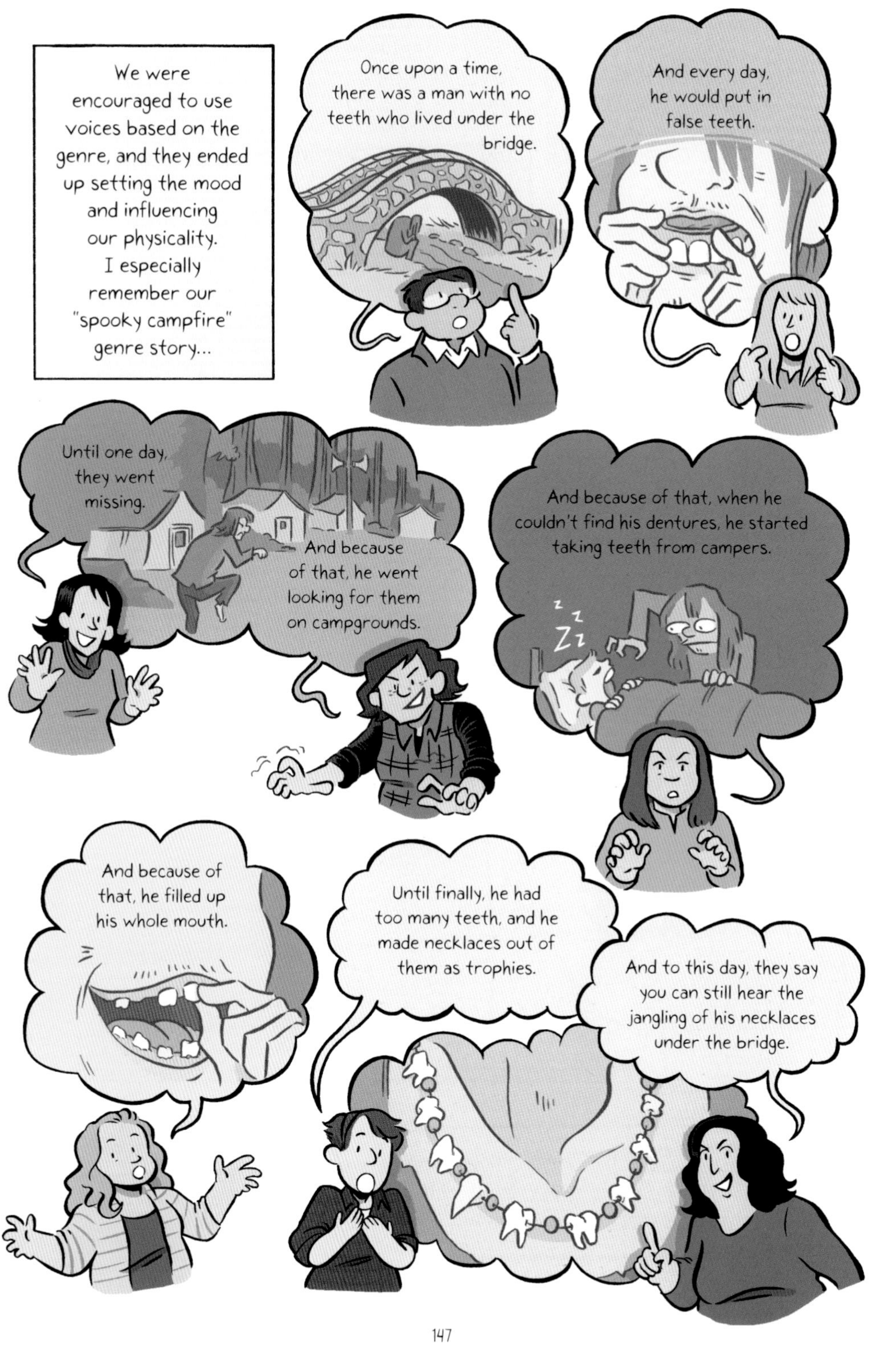
We were encouraged to use voices based on the genre, and they ended up setting the mood and influencing our physicality. I especially remember our "spooky campfire" genre story...
Once upon a time, there was a man with no teeth who lived under the bridge.
And every day, he would put in false teeth.
Until one day, they went missing.
And because of that, he went looking for them on campgrounds.
And because of that, when he couldn't find his dentures, he started taking teeth from campers.
Z z Z z
And because of that, he filled up his whole mouth.
Until finally, he had too many teeth, and he made necklaces out of them as trophies.
And to this day, they say you can still hear the jangling of his necklaces under the bridge.

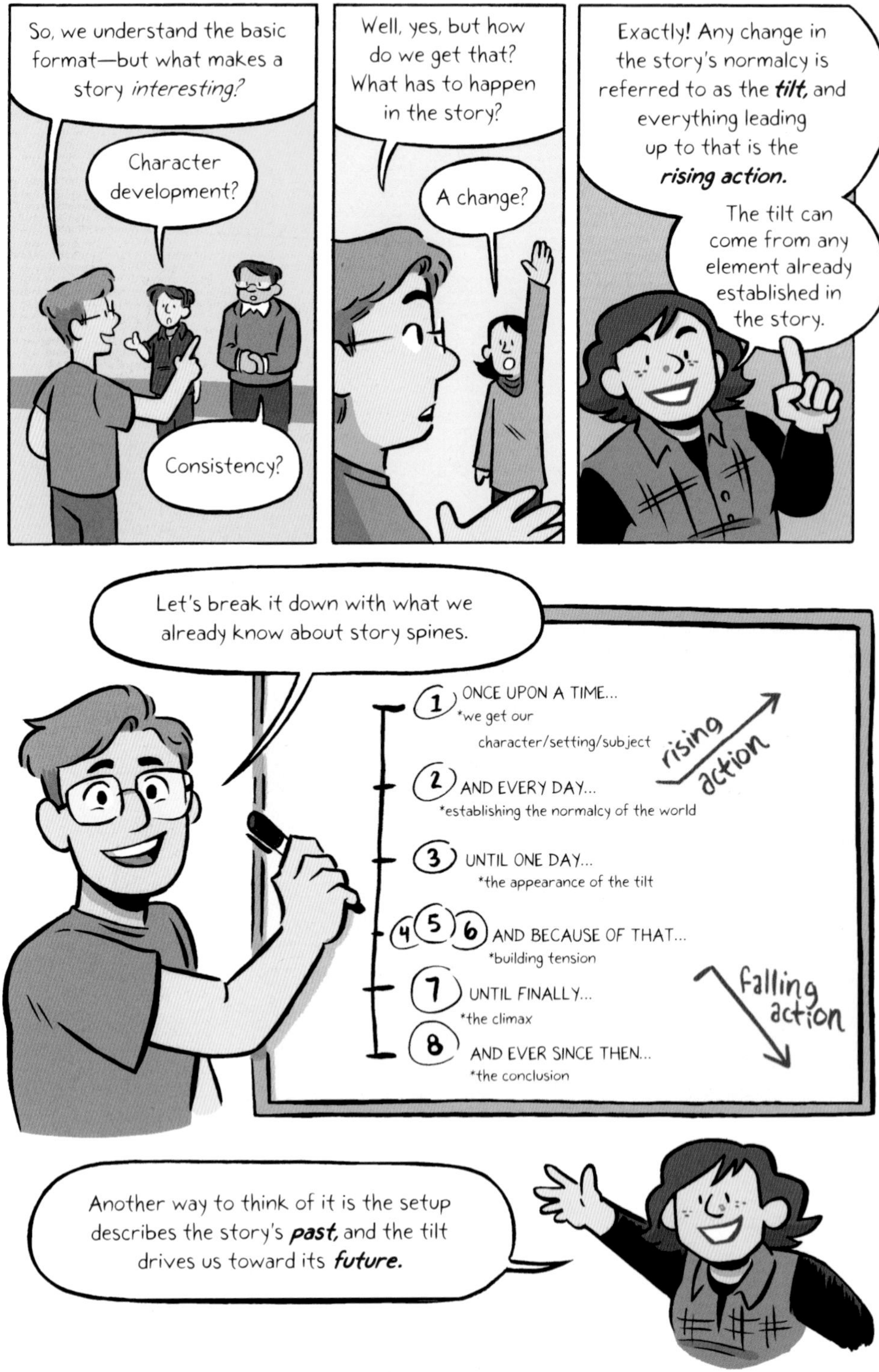
So, we understand the basic format—but what makes a story *interesting?*
Character development?
Consistency?
Well, yes, but how do we get that? What has to happen in the story?
A change?
Exactly! Any change in the story's normalcy is referred to as the ***tilt,*** and everything leading up to that is the ***rising action.***
The tilt can come from any element already established in the story.
Let's break it down with what we already know about story spines.
1 ONCE UPON A TIME...
*we get our character/setting/subject
2 AND EVERY DAY...
*establishing the normalcy of the world
3 UNTIL ONE DAY...
*the appearance of the tilt
4 5 6 AND BECAUSE OF THAT...
*building tension
7 UNTIL FINALLY...
*the climax
8 AND EVER SINCE THEN...
*the conclusion
rising action
falling action
Another way to think of it is the setup describes the story's ***past,*** and the tilt drives us toward its ***future.***

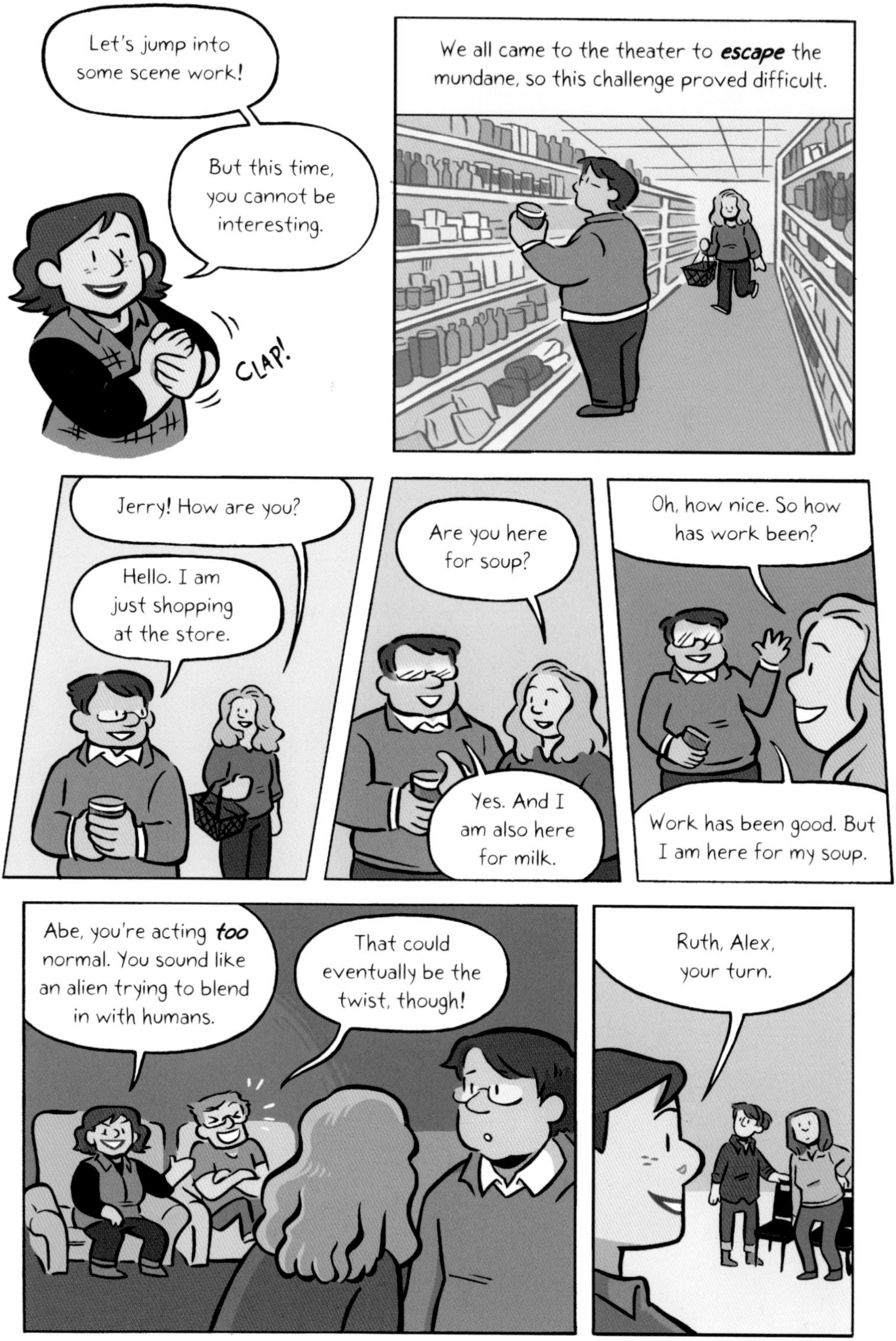
Let's jump into some scene work!
But this time, you cannot be interesting.
CLAP!
We all came to the theater to ***escape*** the mundane, so this challenge proved difficult.
Jerry! How are you?
Hello. I am just shopping at the store.
Are you here for soup?
Yes. And I am also here for milk.
Oh, how nice. So how has work been?
Work has been good. But I am here for my soup.
Abe, you're acting ***too*** normal. You sound like an alien trying to blend in with humans.
That could eventually be the twist, though!
Ruth, Alex, your turn.

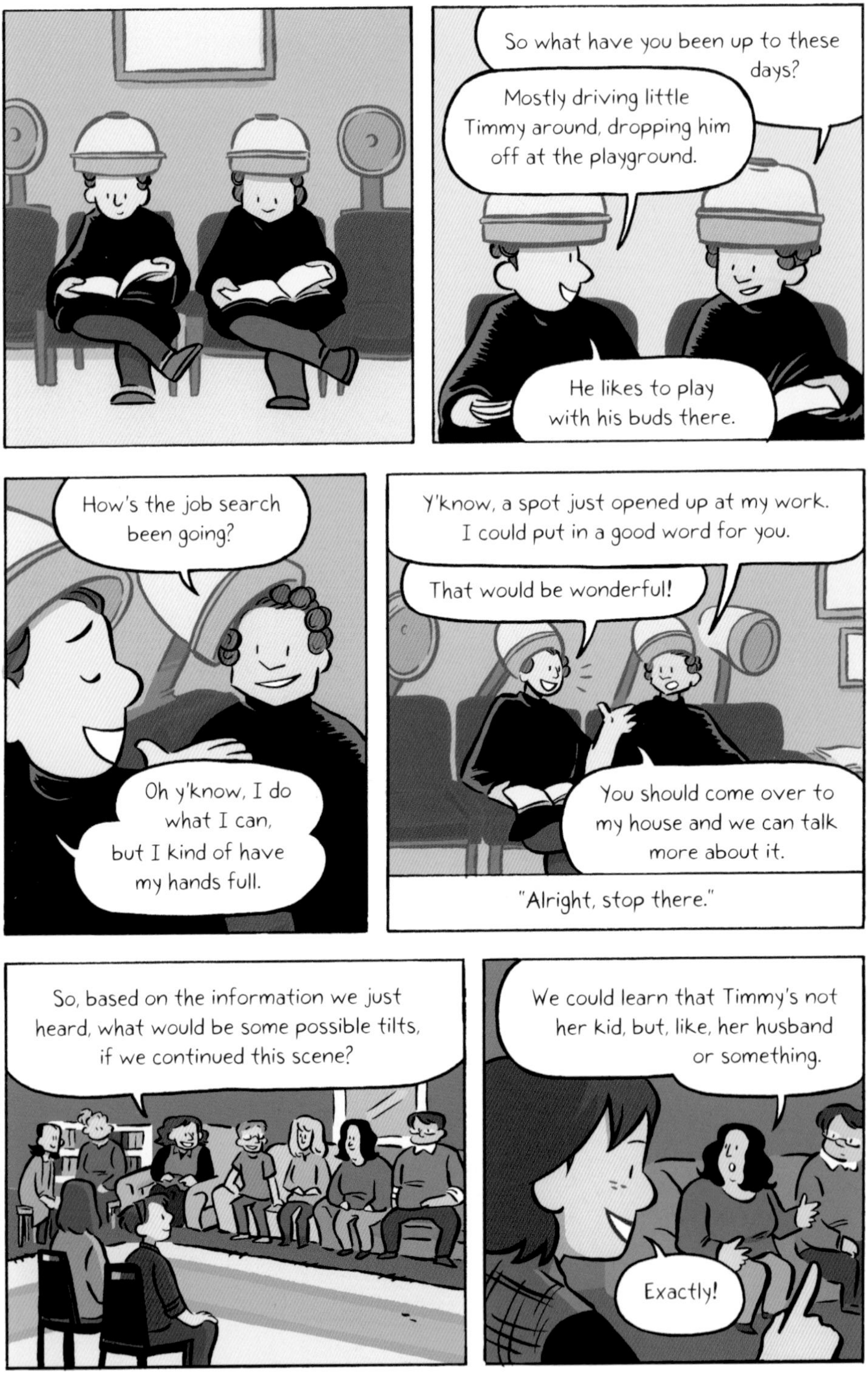

So what have you been up to these days?
Mostly driving little Timmy around, dropping him off at the playground.
He likes to play with his buds there.
How's the job search been going?
Oh y'know, I do what I can, but I kind of have my hands full.
Y'know, a spot just opened up at my work. I could put in a good word for you.
That would be wonderful!
You should come over to my house and we can talk more about it.
"Alright, stop there."
So, based on the information we just heard, what would be some possible tilts, if we continued this scene?
We could learn that Timmy's not her kid, but, like, her husband or something.
Exactly!

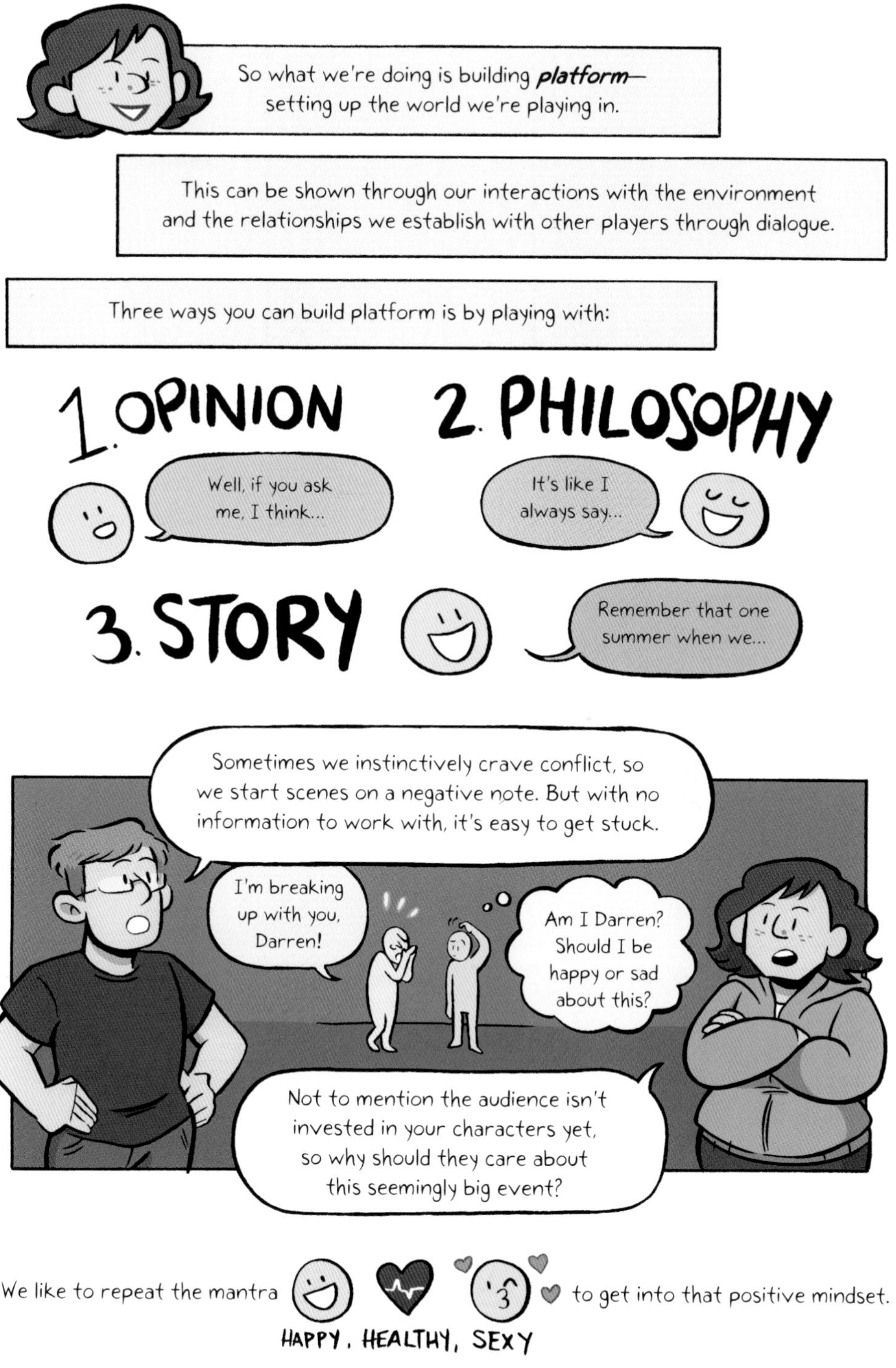

So what we're doing is building ***platform***— setting up the world we're playing in.
This can be shown through our interactions with the environment and the relationships we establish with other players through dialogue.
Three ways you can build platform is by playing with:
1. OPINION
Well, if you ask me, I think...
2. PHILOSOPHY
It's like I always say...
3. STORY
Remember that one summer when we...
Sometimes we instinctively crave conflict, so we start scenes on a negative note. But with no information to work with, it's easy to get stuck.
I'm breaking up with you, Darren!
Am I Darren? Should I be happy or sad about this?
Not to mention the audience isn't invested in your characters yet, so why should they care about this seemingly big event?
We like to repeat the mantra
HAPPY, HEALTHY, SEXY
to get into that positive mindset.

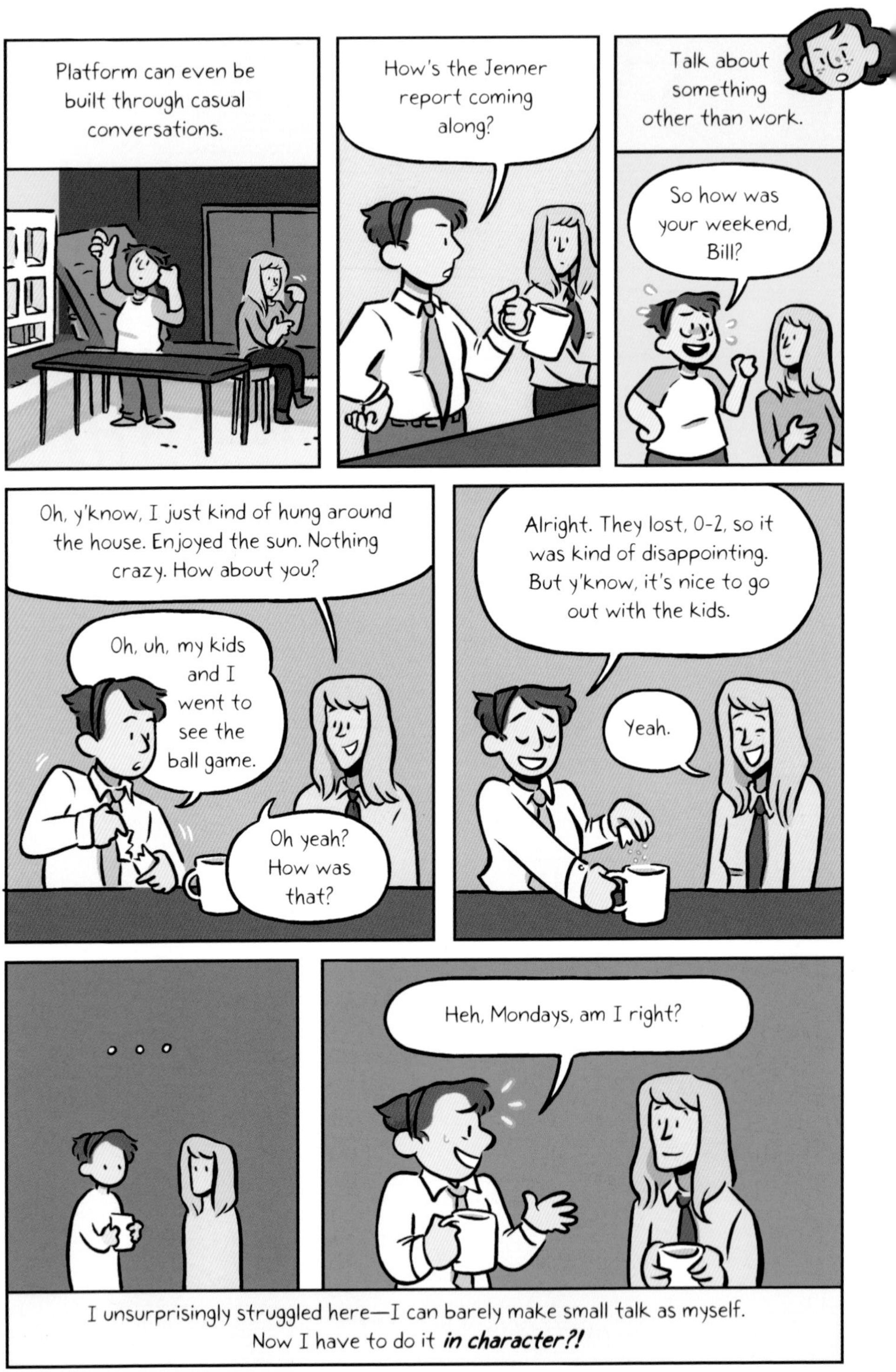
Platform can even be built through casual conversations.
How's the Jenner report coming along?
Talk about something other than work.
So how was your weekend, Bill?
Oh, y'know, I just kind of hung around the house. Enjoyed the sun. Nothing crazy. How about you?
Oh, uh, my kids and I went to see the ball game.
Oh yeah? How was that?
Alright. They lost, 0-2, so it was kind of disappointing. But y'know, it's nice to go out with the kids.
Yeah.
. . .
Heh, Mondays, am I right?
I unsurprisingly struggled here—I can barely make small talk as myself. Now I have to do it ***in character?!***

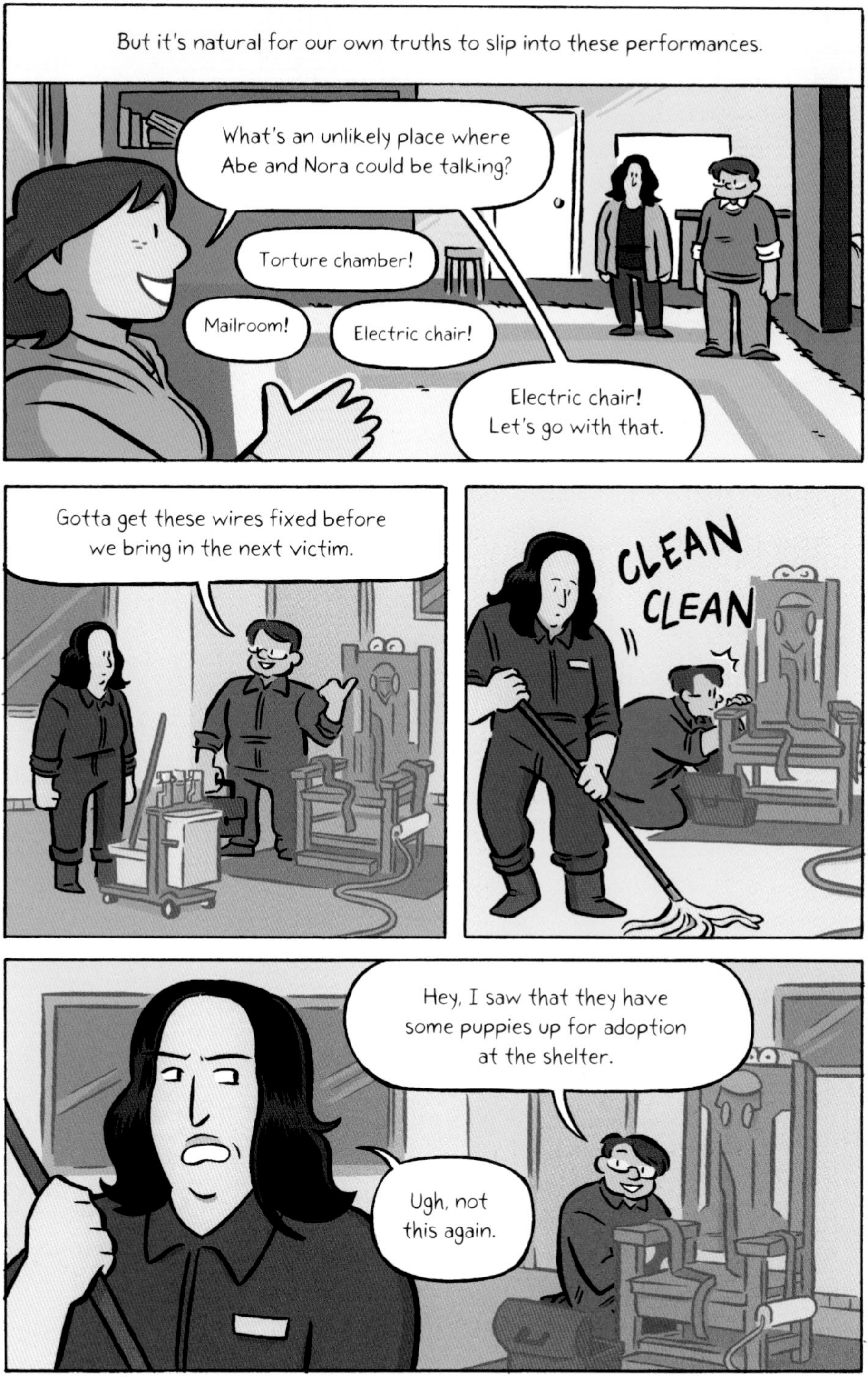
But it's natural for our own truths to slip into these performances.
What's an unlikely place where Abe and Nora could be talking?
Torture chamber!
Mailroom!
Electric chair!
Electric chair! Let's go with that.
Gotta get these wires fixed before we bring in the next victim.
CLEAN
CLEAN
Hey, I saw that they have some puppies up for adoption at the shelter.
Ugh, not this again.

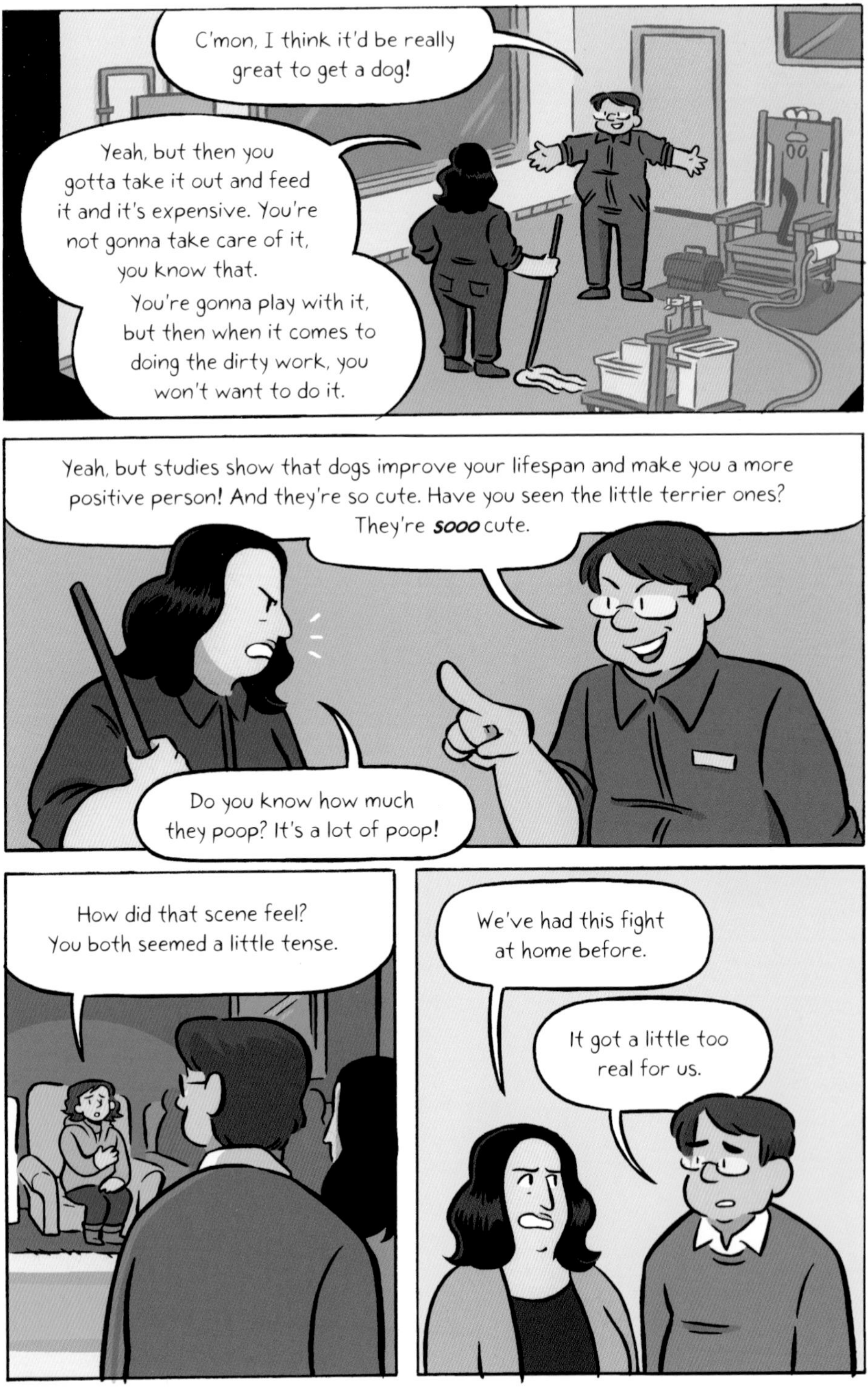
C'mon, I think it'd be really great to get a dog!
Yeah, but then you gotta take it out and feed it and it's expensive. You're not gonna take care of it, you know that.
You're gonna play with it, but then when it comes to doing the dirty work, you won't want to do it.
Yeah, but studies show that dogs improve your lifespan and make you a more positive person! And they're so cute. Have you seen the little terrier ones? They're ***sooo*** cute.
Do you know how much they poop? It's a lot of poop!
How did that scene feel? You both seemed a little tense.
We've had this fight at home before.
It got a little too real for us.

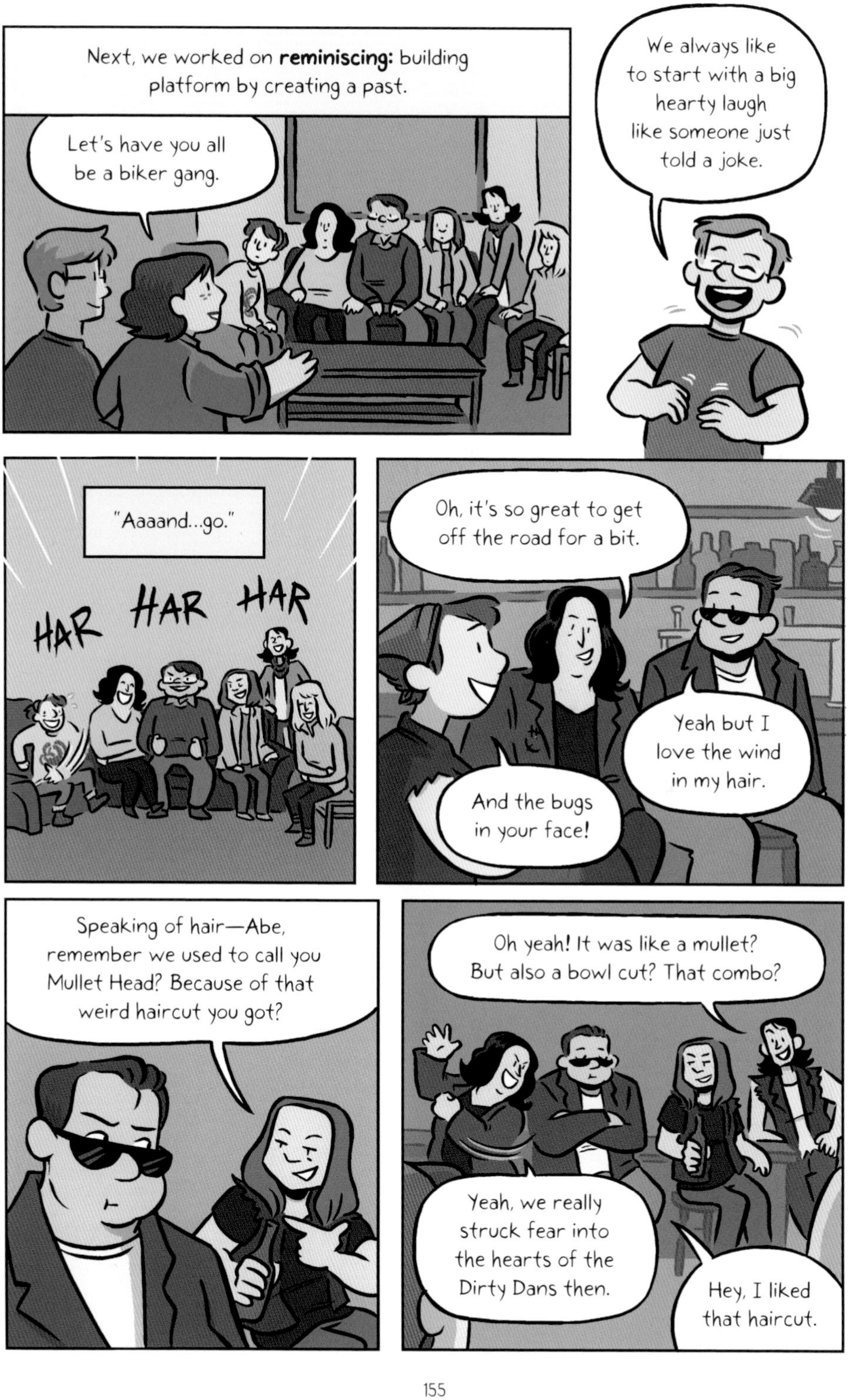
Next, we worked on **reminiscing:** building platform by creating a past.
Let's have you all be a biker gang.
We always like to start with a big hearty laugh like someone just told a joke.
"Aaaand...go."
HAR HAR HAR
Oh, it's so great to get off the road for a bit.
Yeah but I love the wind in my hair.
And the bugs in your face!
Speaking of hair—Abe, remember we used to call you Mullet Head? Because of that weird haircut you got?
Oh yeah! It was like a mullet? But also a bowl cut? That combo?
Yeah, we really struck fear into the hearts of the Dirty Dans then.
Hey, I liked that haircut.

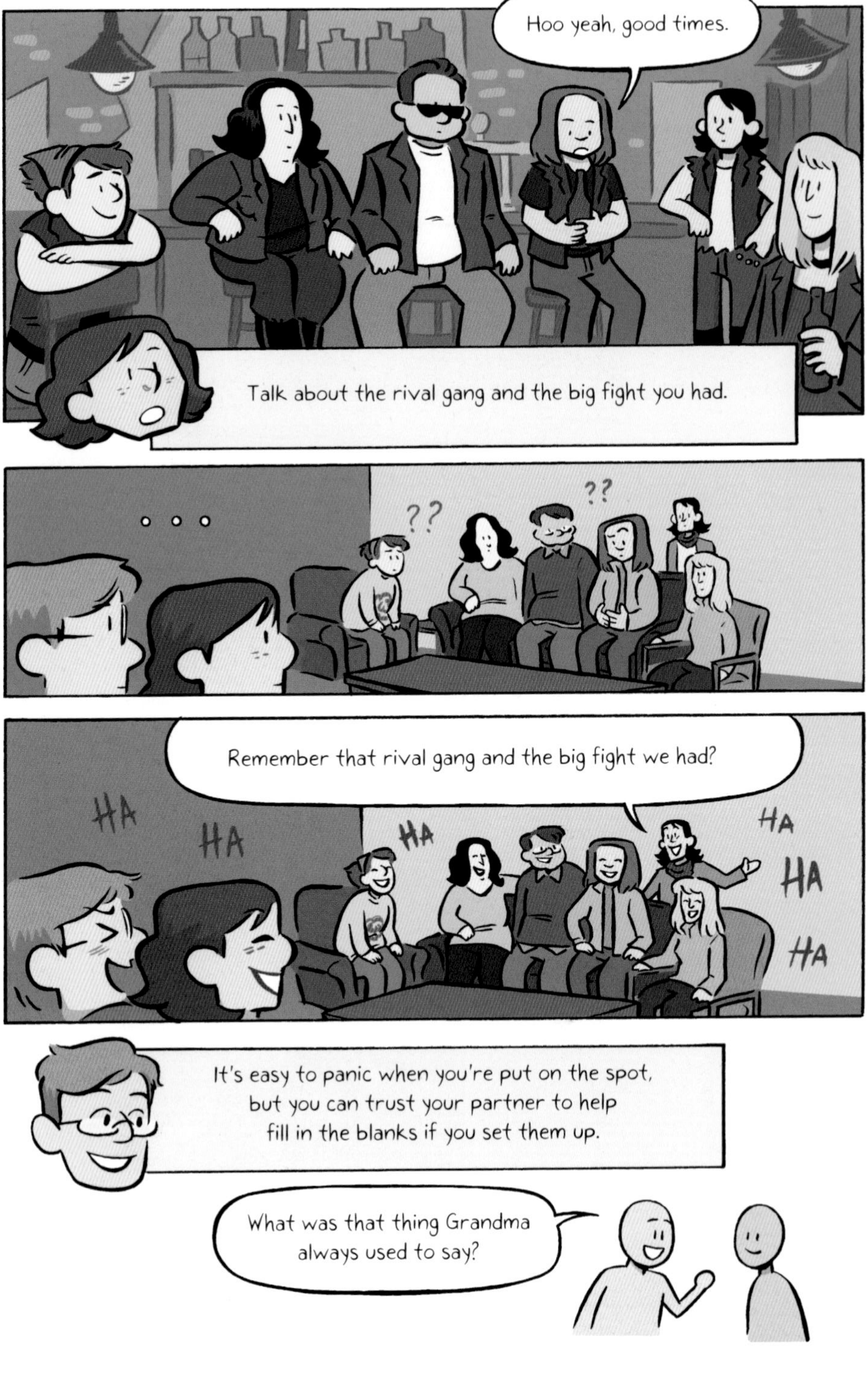
Hoo yeah, good times.
Talk about the rival gang and the big fight you had.
. . .
??
??
Remember that rival gang and the big fight we had?
HA
HA
HA
HA
HA
HA
It's easy to panic when you're put on the spot, but you can trust your partner to help fill in the blanks if you set them up.
What was that thing Grandma always used to say?

We moved on to implement our lessons in an exercise called

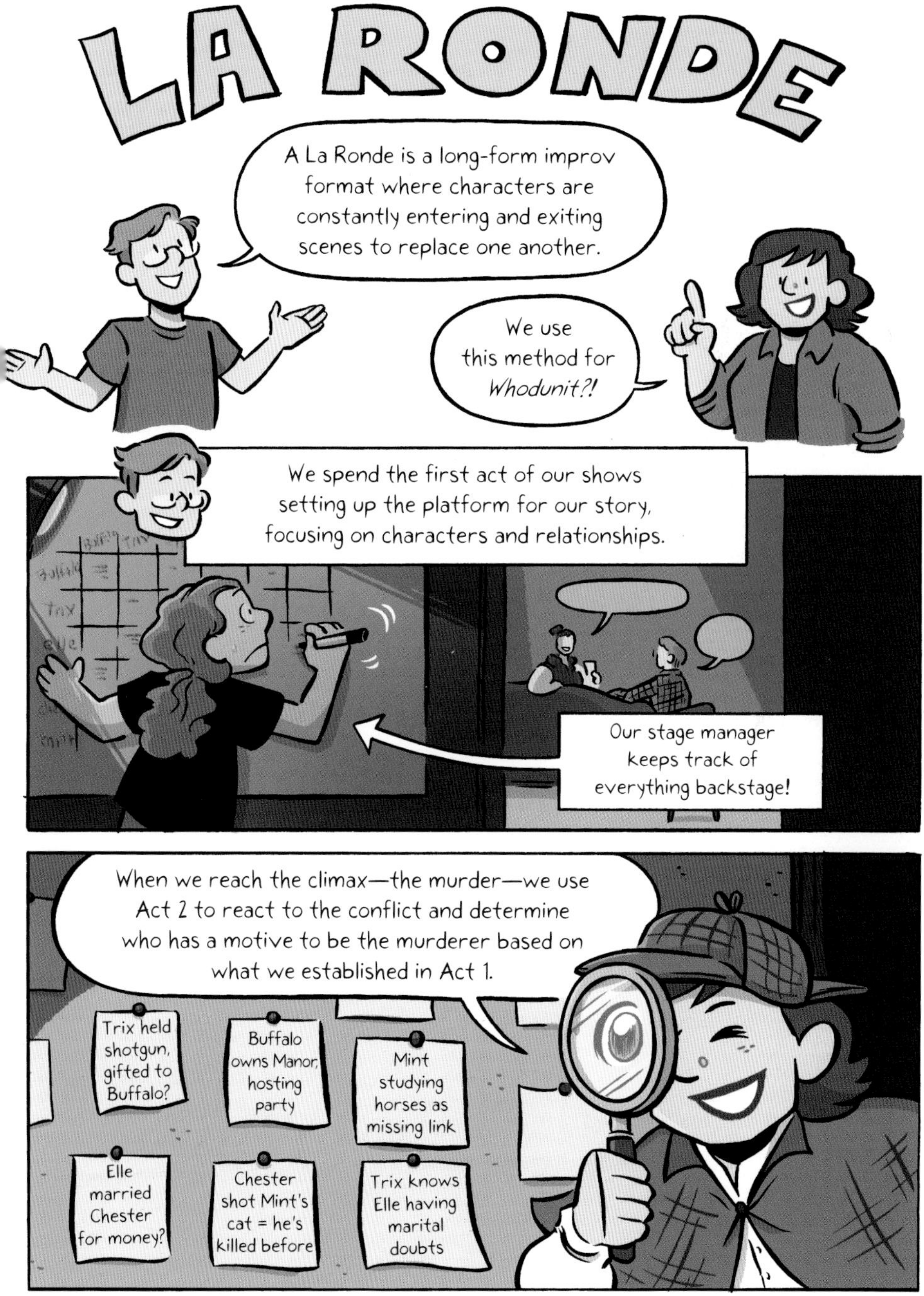
LA RONDE
A La Ronde is a long-form improv format where characters are constantly entering and exiting scenes to replace one another.
We use this method for *Whodunit?!*
We spend the first act of our shows setting up the platform for our story, focusing on characters and relationships.
Our stage manager keeps track of everything backstage!
When we reach the climax—the murder—we use Act 2 to react to the conflict and determine who has a motive to be the murderer based on what we established in Act 1.
Trix held shotgun, gifted to Buffalo?
Buffalo owns Manor, hosting party
Mint studying horses as missing link
Elle married Chester for money?
Chester shot Mint's cat = he's killed before
Trix knows Elle having marital doubts

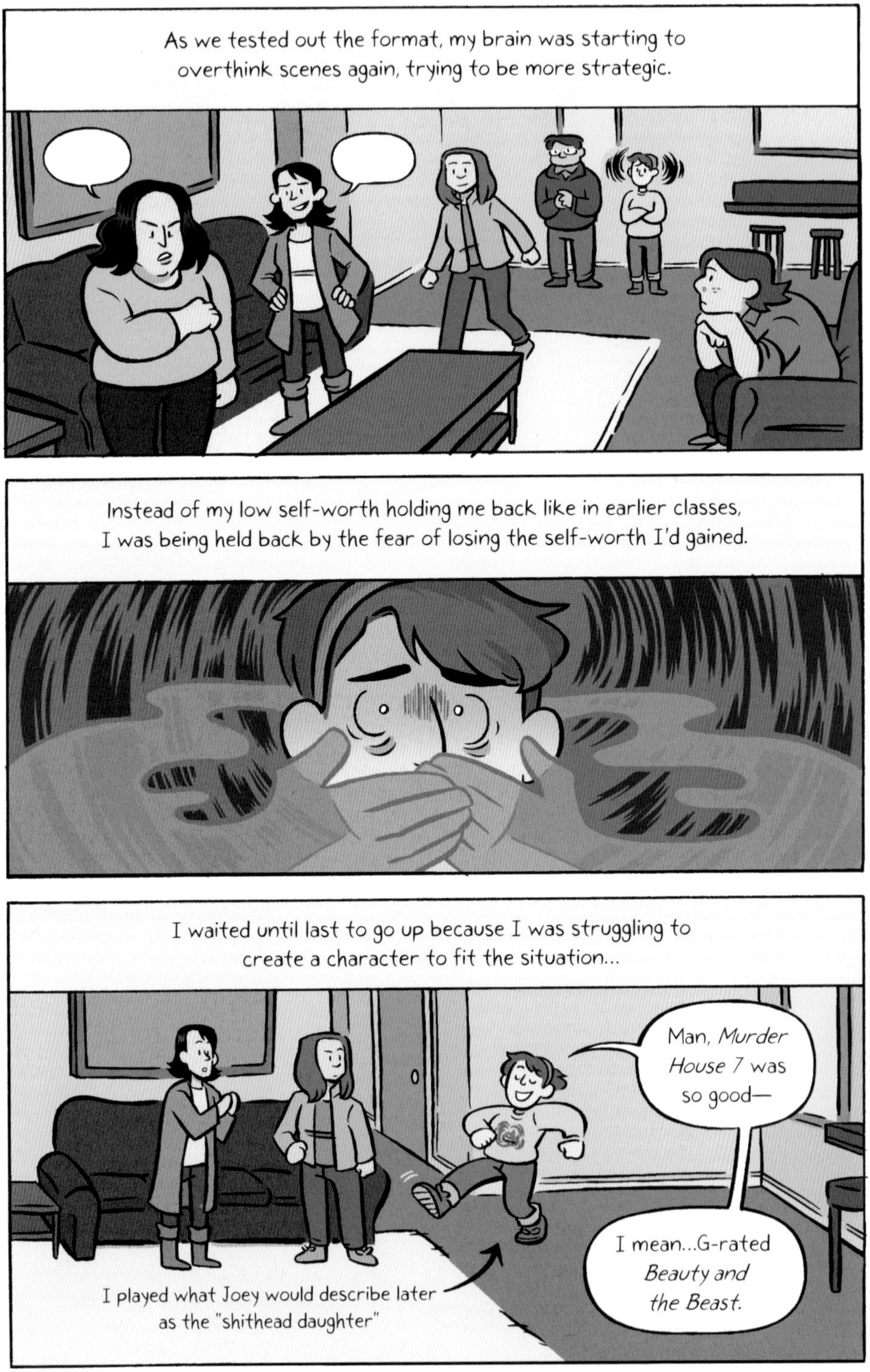
As we tested out the format, my brain was starting to overthink scenes again, trying to be more strategic.
Instead of my low self-worth holding me back like in earlier classes, I was being held back by the fear of losing the self-worth I'd gained.
I waited until last to go up because I was struggling to create a character to fit the situation...
Man, *Murder House 7* was so good—
I mean...G-rated *Beauty and the Beast.*
I played what Joey would describe later as the "shithead daughter"

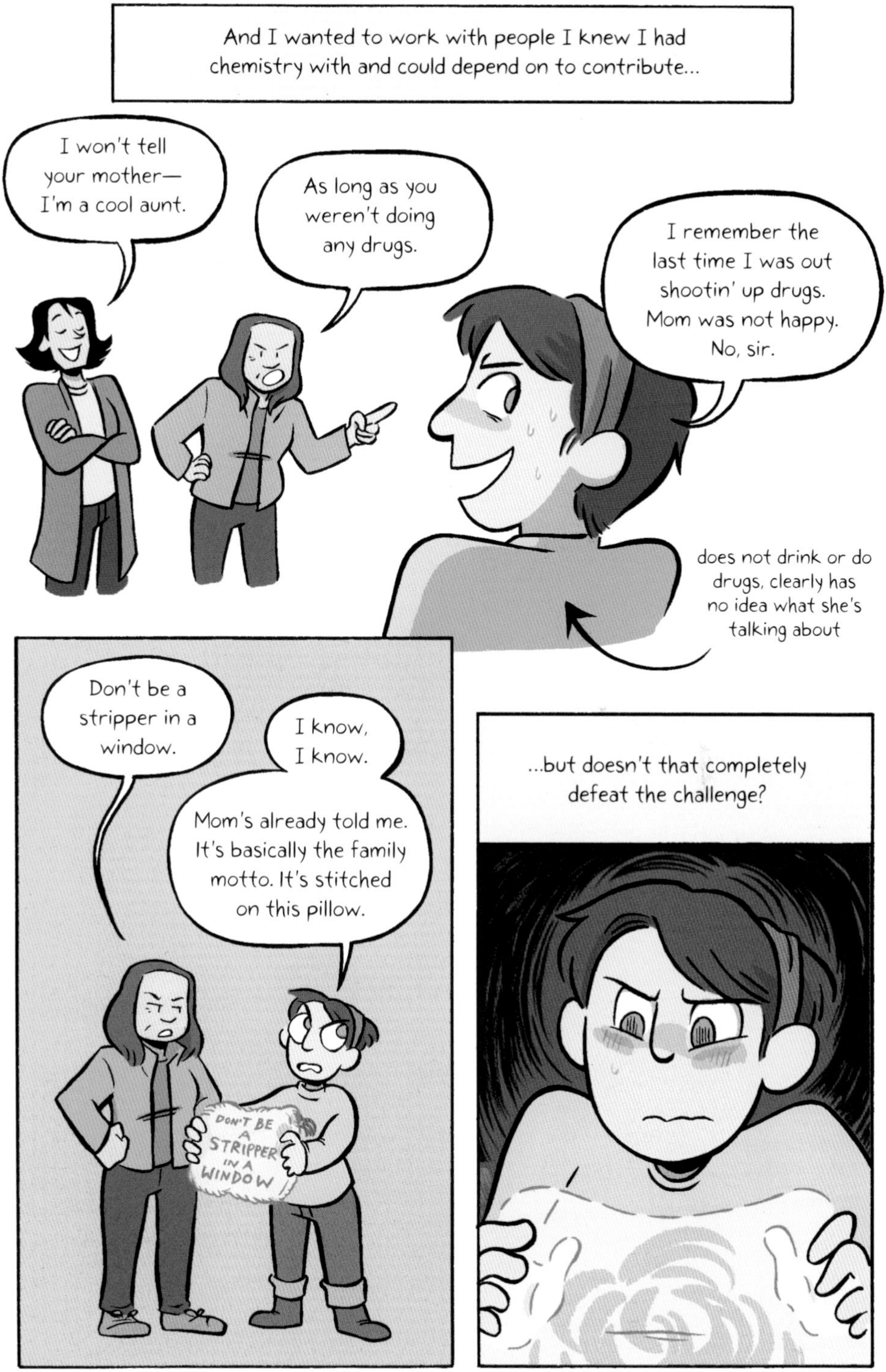
And I wanted to work with people I knew I had chemistry with and could depend on to contribute...
I won't tell your mother— I'm a cool aunt.
As long as you weren't doing any drugs.
I remember the last time I was out shootin' up drugs. Mom was not happy. No, sir.
does not drink or do drugs, clearly has no idea what she's talking about
Don't be a stripper in a window.
I know, I know.
Mom's already told me. It's basically the family motto. It's stitched on this pillow.
DON'T BE A STRIPPER IN A WINDOW
...but doesn't that completely defeat the challenge?

Character Circle

Brainstorming characters for one another
to use in scene work.

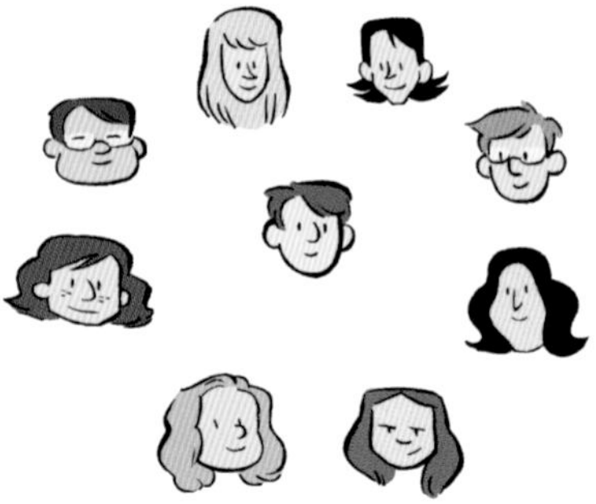

Go into the center of the circle. Your classmates will start throwing out names to you. Choose the one you like best.

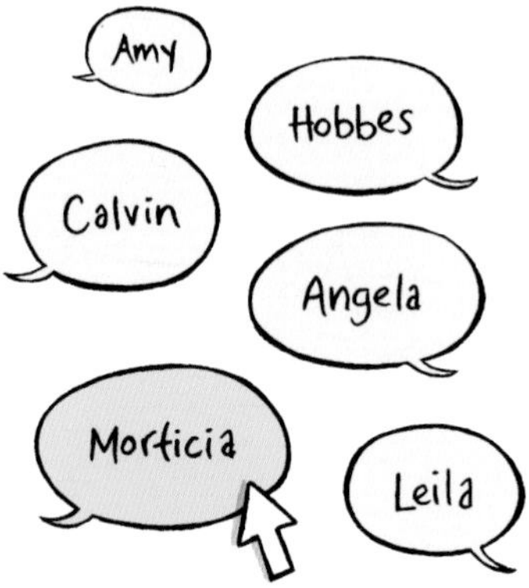
Amy
Hobbes
Calvin
Angela
Morticia
Leila

From there, the person who said that name will start the circle of endowments. Each person will add a new bit of information to the character. In the center, you can physically act it out if you're able to.

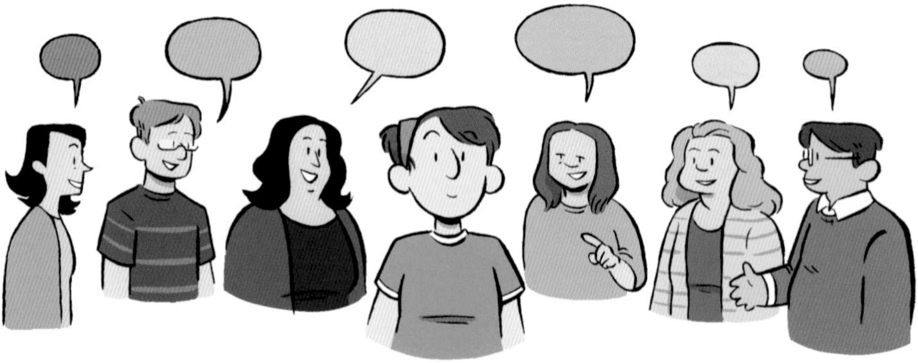

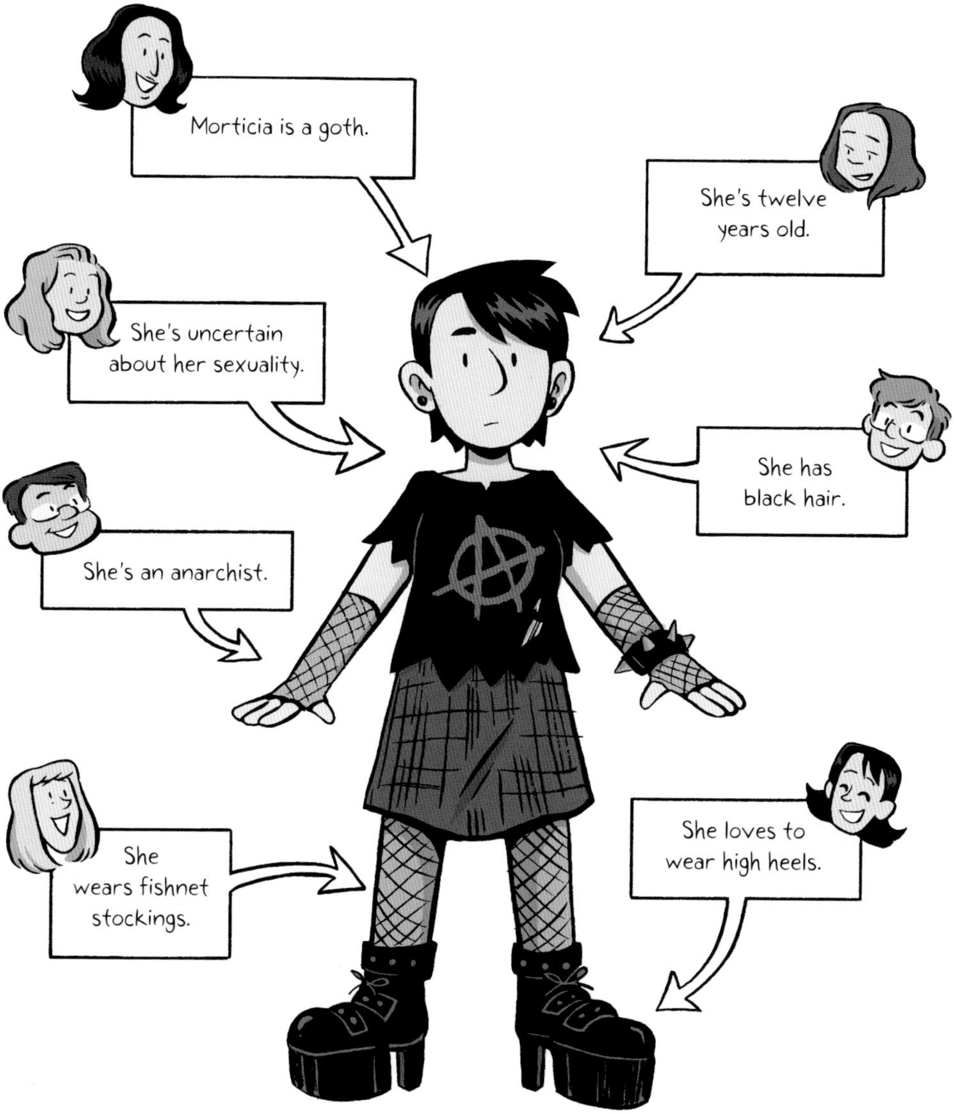
Morticia is a goth.
She's twelve years old.
She's uncertain about her sexuality.
She has black hair.
She's an anarchist.
She wears fishnet stockings.
She loves to wear high heels.

This method felt a lot more collaborative, which I enjoyed. But maybe I also liked it for its limitations. It took a lot of pressure off figuring how I could fit into a scene.

Mallory is
Sonny the Scam Artist

-missing two fingers
-talks loudly
-has a heart of gold

Ruth is
Pete the Cop

-has ESP
-smokes a lot of pot

Jill is
Monique the Psychic

-rival to Pete
-has six bratty kids

Abe is
Stewart the Janitor

-secretly a millionaire
-works as a janitor
-loves polishing floors
-looking for love

Helen is
Betty the Physician

-physician by night
-tattoo artist by day
-bodybuilder
-loves to show off and
 admire muscles

Nora is
Josie the Vet

-supermodel
-owns a pet store called
 "Josie and the Pussycats"
-owns ten cats, all
 named Josie

We played around with these characters
in a game of

CHANGE for CHANGE

a long-form improv format
developed by a CTC improviser.

All players start onstage with individual coins and flip to see
whether they are in the scene or not.

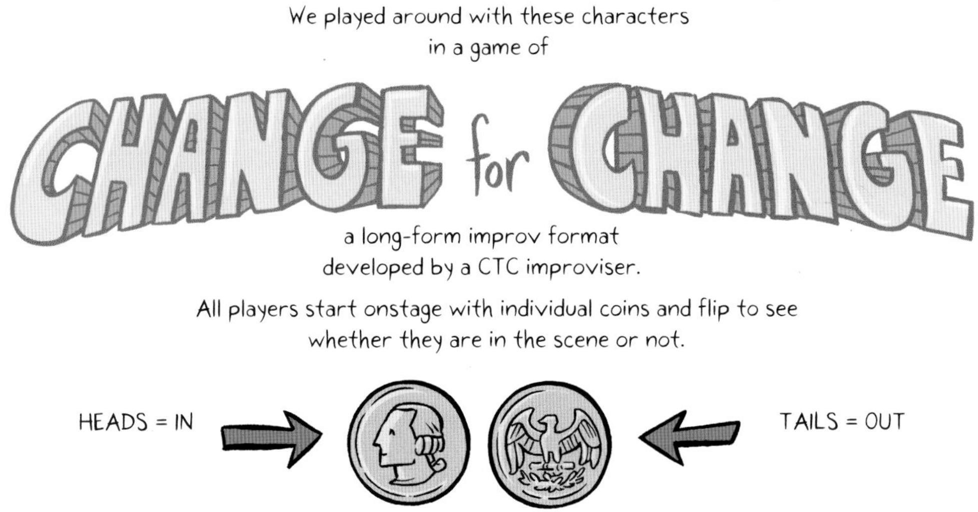
HEADS = IN
TAILS = OUT

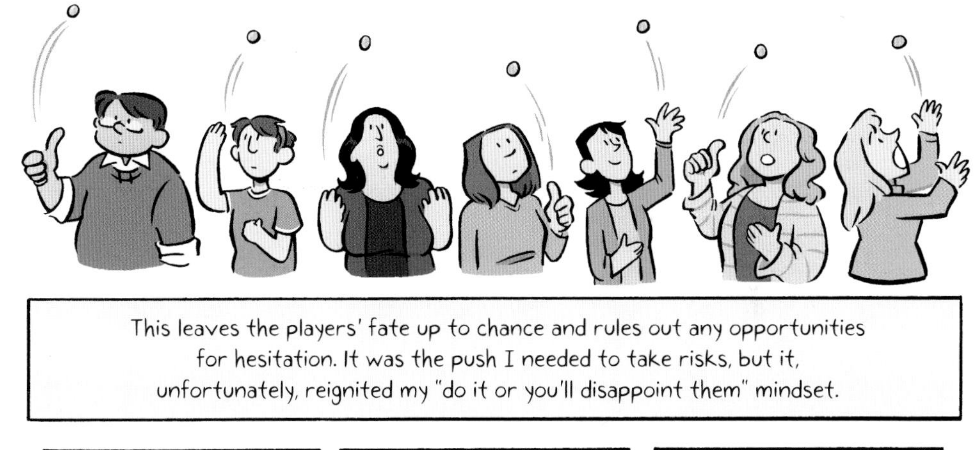

This leaves the players' fate up to chance and rules out any opportunities for hesitation. It was the push I needed to take risks, but it, unfortunately, reignited my "do it or you'll disappoint them" mindset.

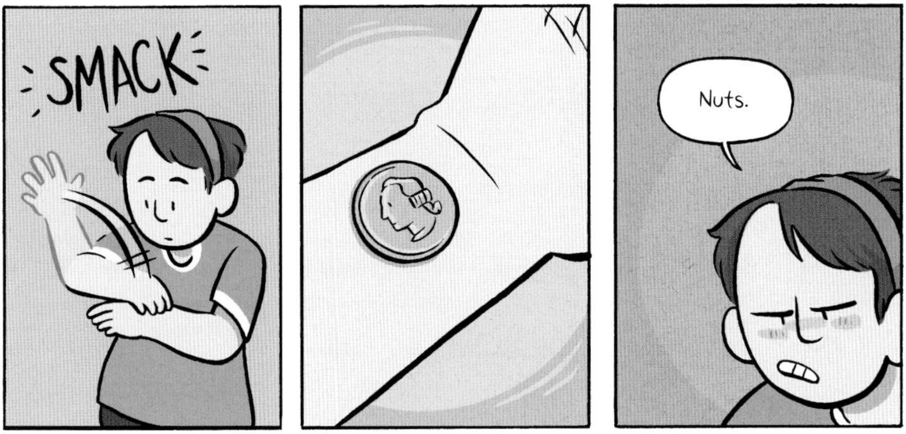
SMACK
Nuts.

☆ SCENE 1 ☆

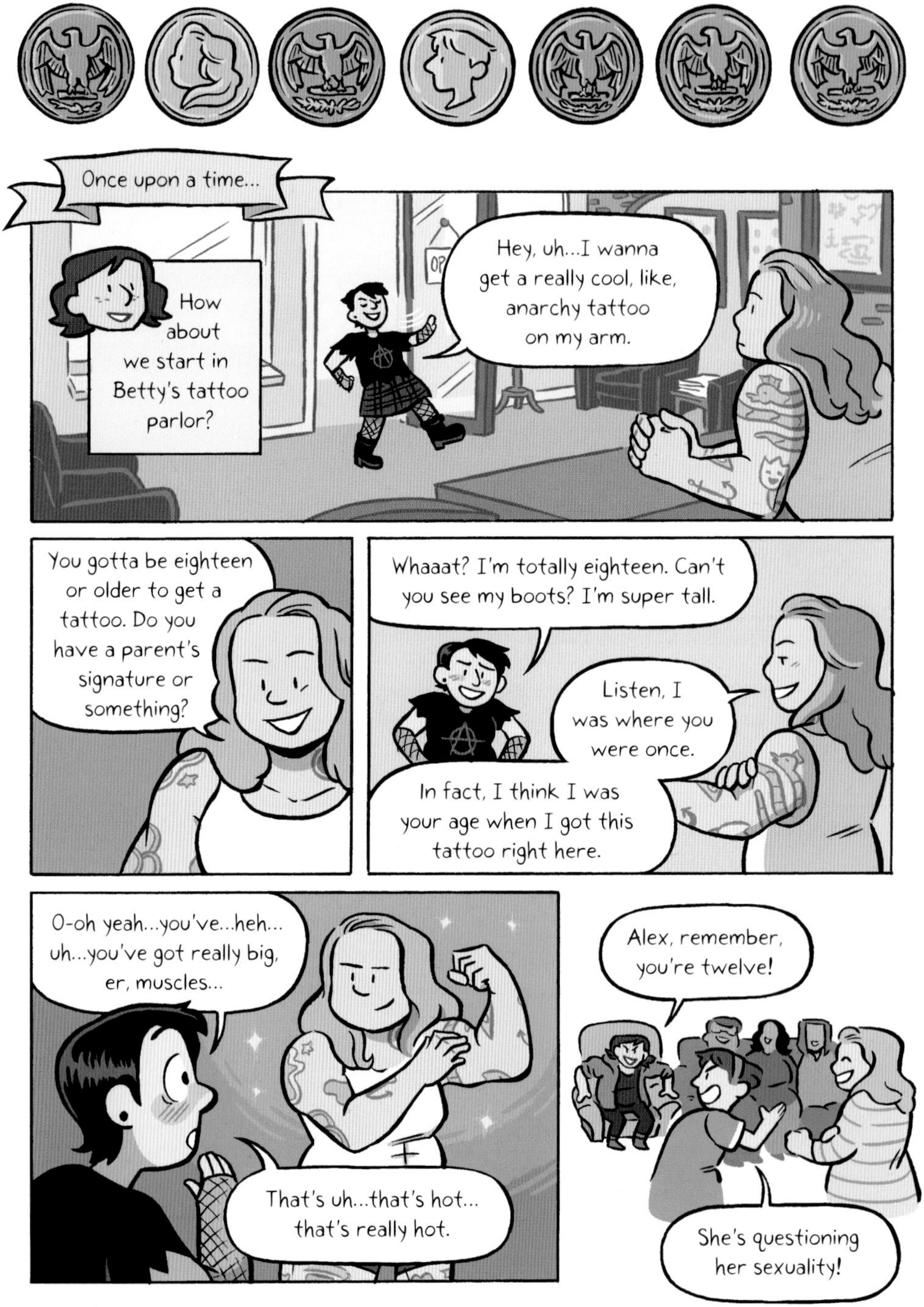
Once upon a time...
How about we start in Betty's tattoo parlor?
Hey, uh...I wanna get a really cool, like, anarchy tattoo on my arm.
You gotta be eighteen or older to get a tattoo. Do you have a parent's signature or something?
Whaaat? I'm totally eighteen. Can't you see my boots? I'm super tall.
Listen, I was where you were once.
In fact, I think I was your age when I got this tattoo right here.
O-oh yeah...you've...heh... uh...you've got really big, er, muscles...
That's uh...that's hot... that's really hot.
Alex, remember, you're twelve!
She's questioning her sexuality!

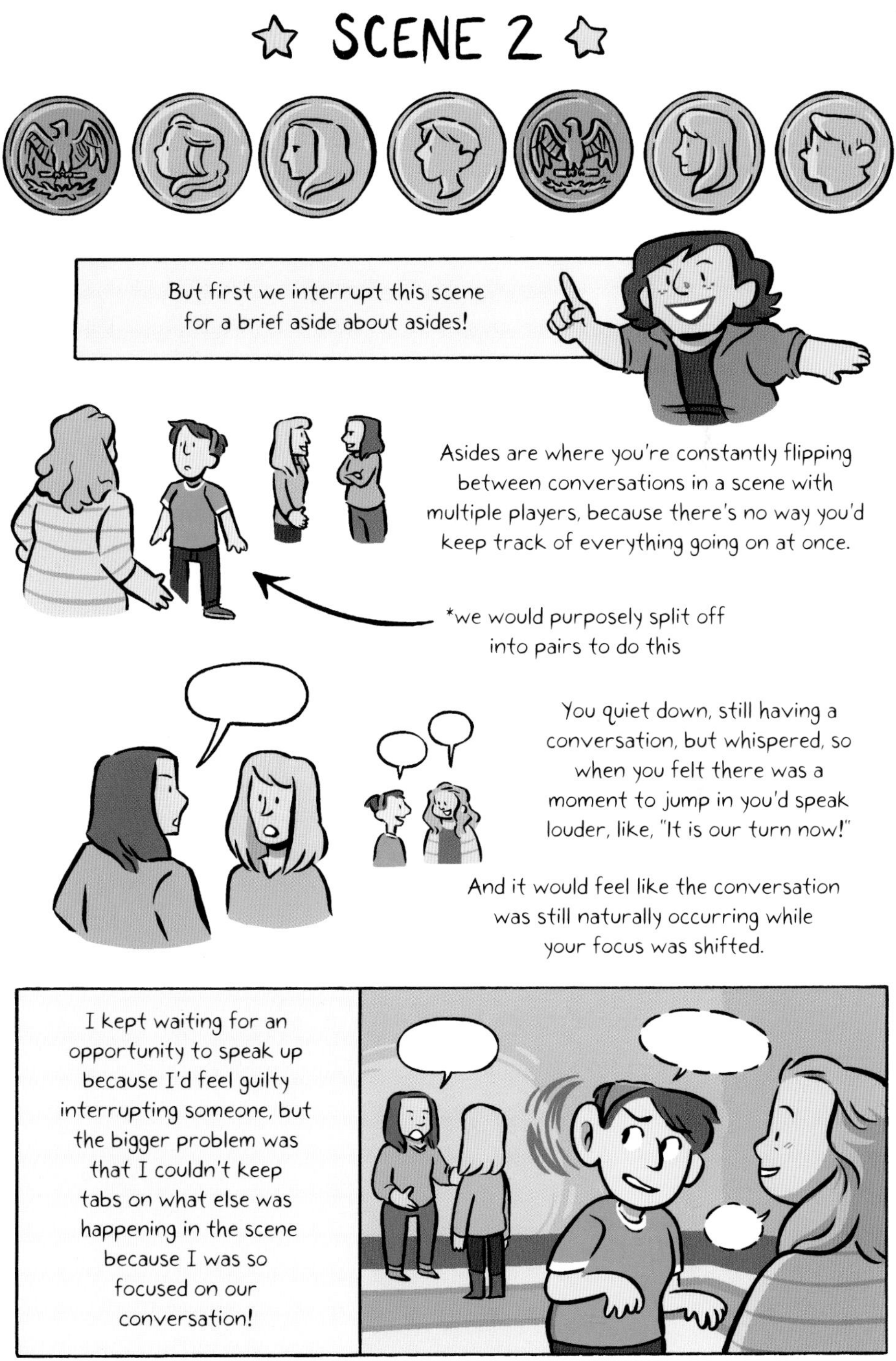
SCENE 2
But first we interrupt this scene for a brief aside about asides!
Asides are where you're constantly flipping between conversations in a scene with multiple players, because there's no way you'd keep track of everything going on at once.
*we would purposely split off into pairs to do this
You quiet down, still having a conversation, but whispered, so when you felt there was a moment to jump in you'd speak louder, like, "It is our turn now!"
And it would feel like the conversation was still naturally occurring while your focus was shifted.
I kept waiting for an opportunity to speak up because I'd feel guilty interrupting someone, but the bigger problem was that I couldn't keep tabs on what else was happening in the scene because I was so focused on our conversation!

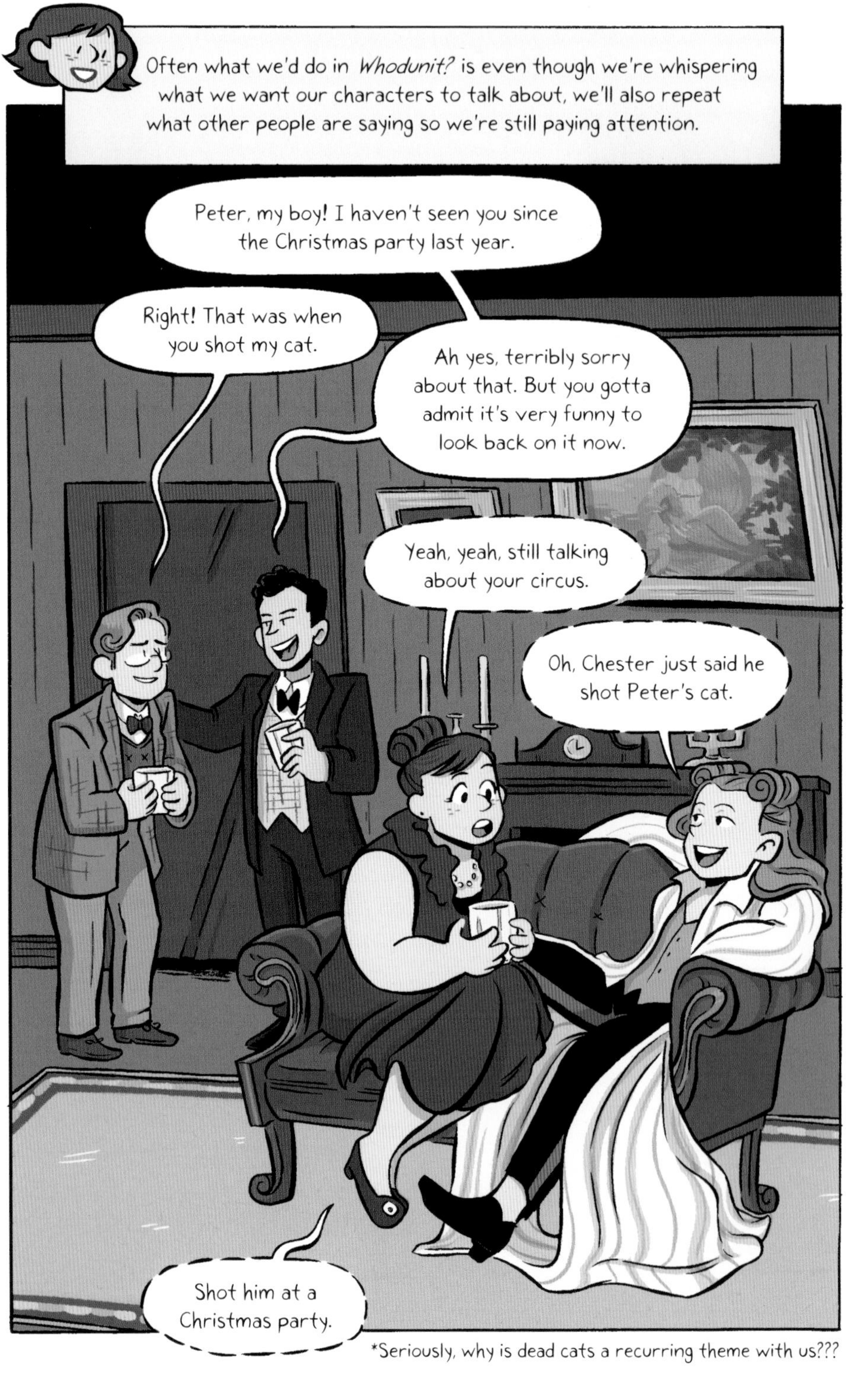
Often what we'd do in *Whodunit?* is even though we're whispering what we want our characters to talk about, we'll also repeat what other people are saying so we're still paying attention.
Peter, my boy! I haven't seen you since the Christmas party last year.
Right! That was when you shot my cat.
Ah yes, terribly sorry about that. But you gotta admit it's very funny to look back on it now.
Yeah, yeah, still talking about your circus.
Oh, Chester just said he shot Peter's cat.
Shot him at a Christmas party.
*Seriously, why is dead cats a recurring theme with us???

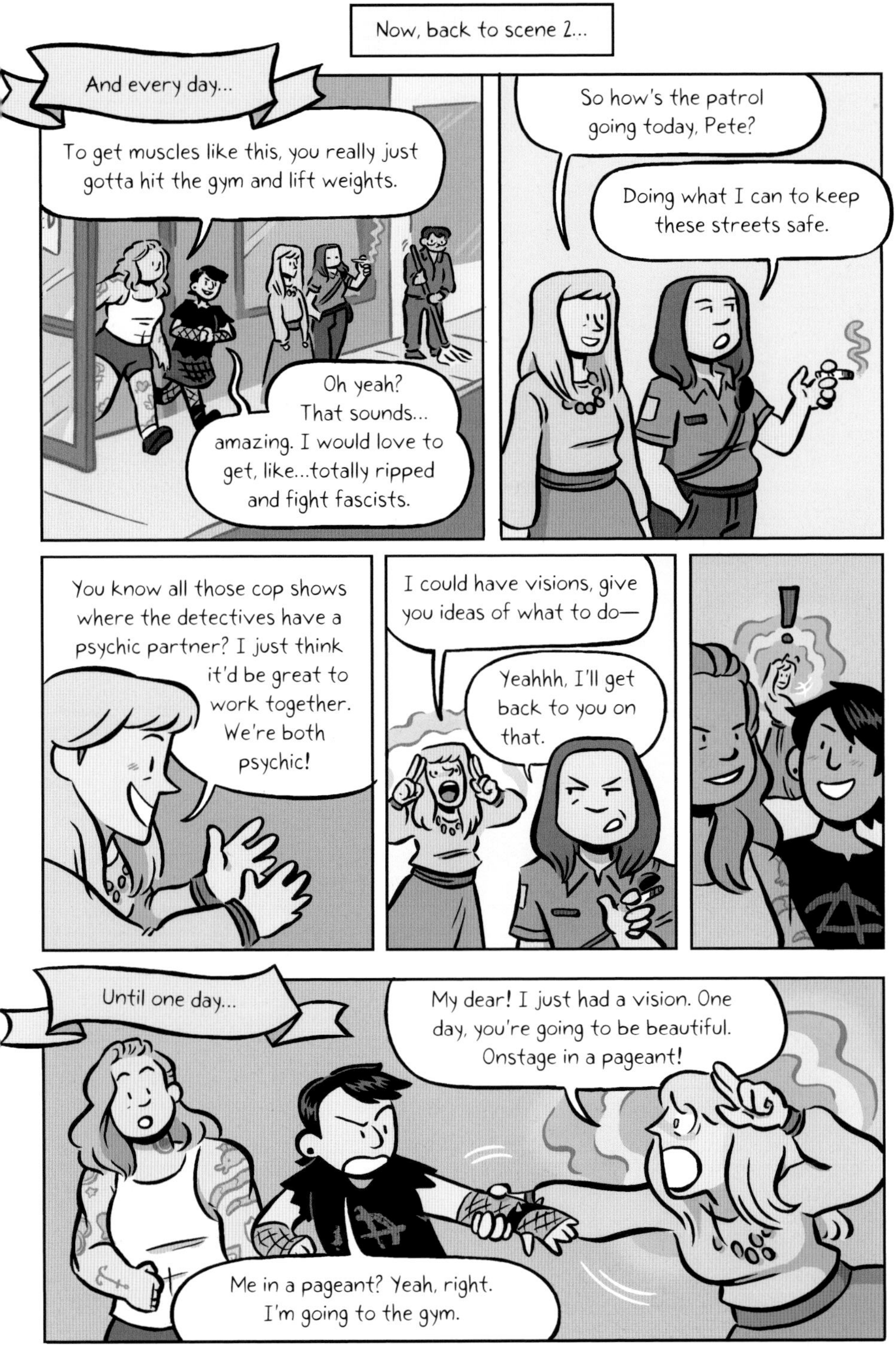
Now, back to scene 2...
And every day...
To get muscles like this, you really just gotta hit the gym and lift weights.
Oh yeah? That sounds... amazing. I would love to get, like...totally ripped and fight fascists.
So how's the patrol going today, Pete?
Doing what I can to keep these streets safe.
You know all those cop shows where the detectives have a psychic partner? I just think it'd be great to work together. We're both psychic!
I could have visions, give you ideas of what to do—
Yeahhh, I'll get back to you on that.
!
Until one day...
My dear! I just had a vision. One day, you're going to be beautiful. Onstage in a pageant!
Me in a pageant? Yeah, right. I'm going to the gym.

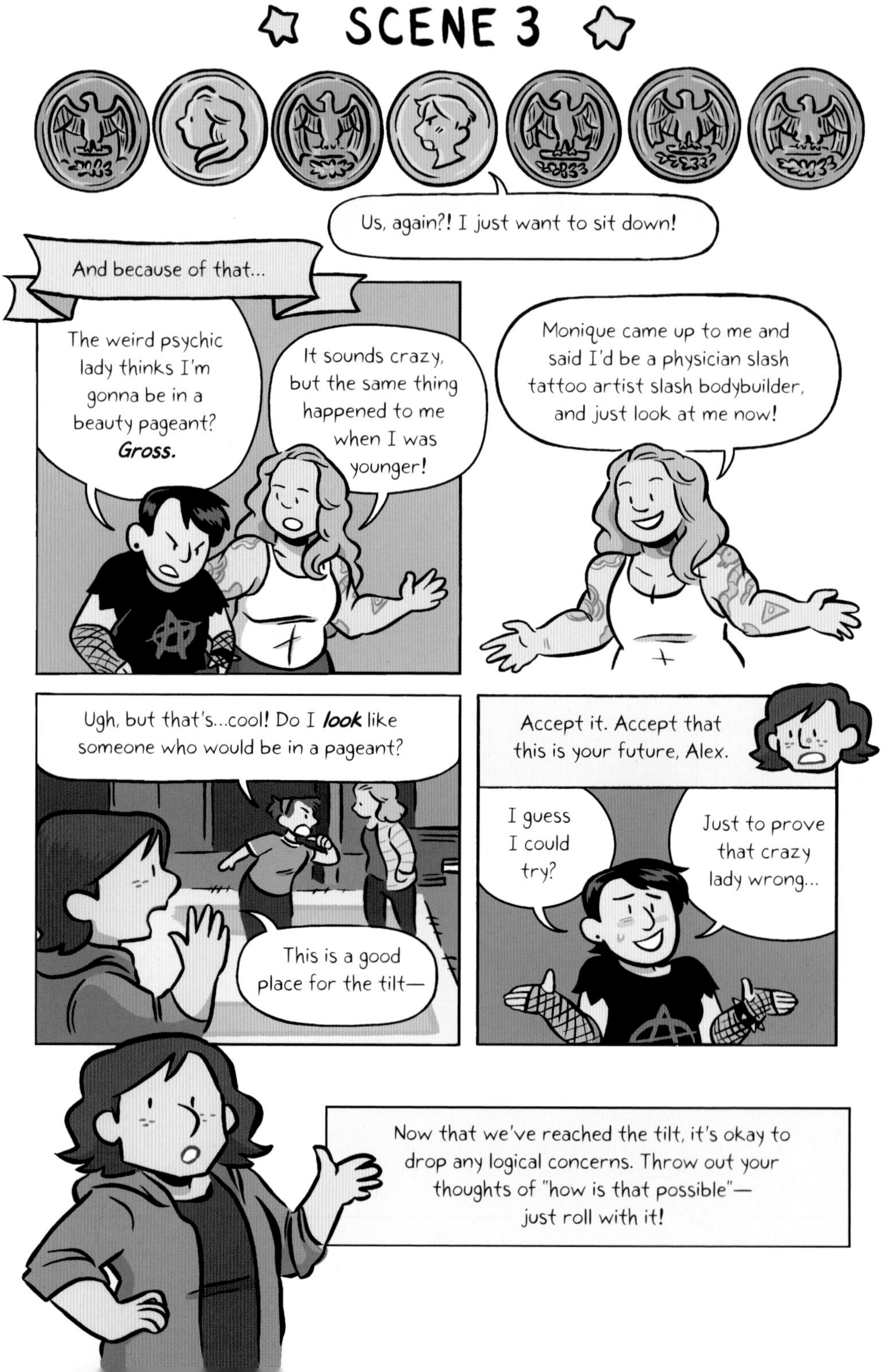
SCENE 3
Us, again?! I just want to sit down!
And because of that...
The weird psychic lady thinks I'm gonna be in a beauty pageant? **Gross.**
It sounds crazy, but the same thing happened to me when I was younger!
Monique came up to me and said I'd be a physician slash tattoo artist slash bodybuilder, and just look at me now!
Ugh, but that's...cool! Do I ***look*** like someone who would be in a pageant?
This is a good place for the tilt—
Accept it. Accept that this is your future, Alex.
I guess I could try?
Just to prove that crazy lady wrong...
Now that we've reached the tilt, it's okay to drop any logical concerns. Throw out your thoughts of "how is that possible"—just roll with it!

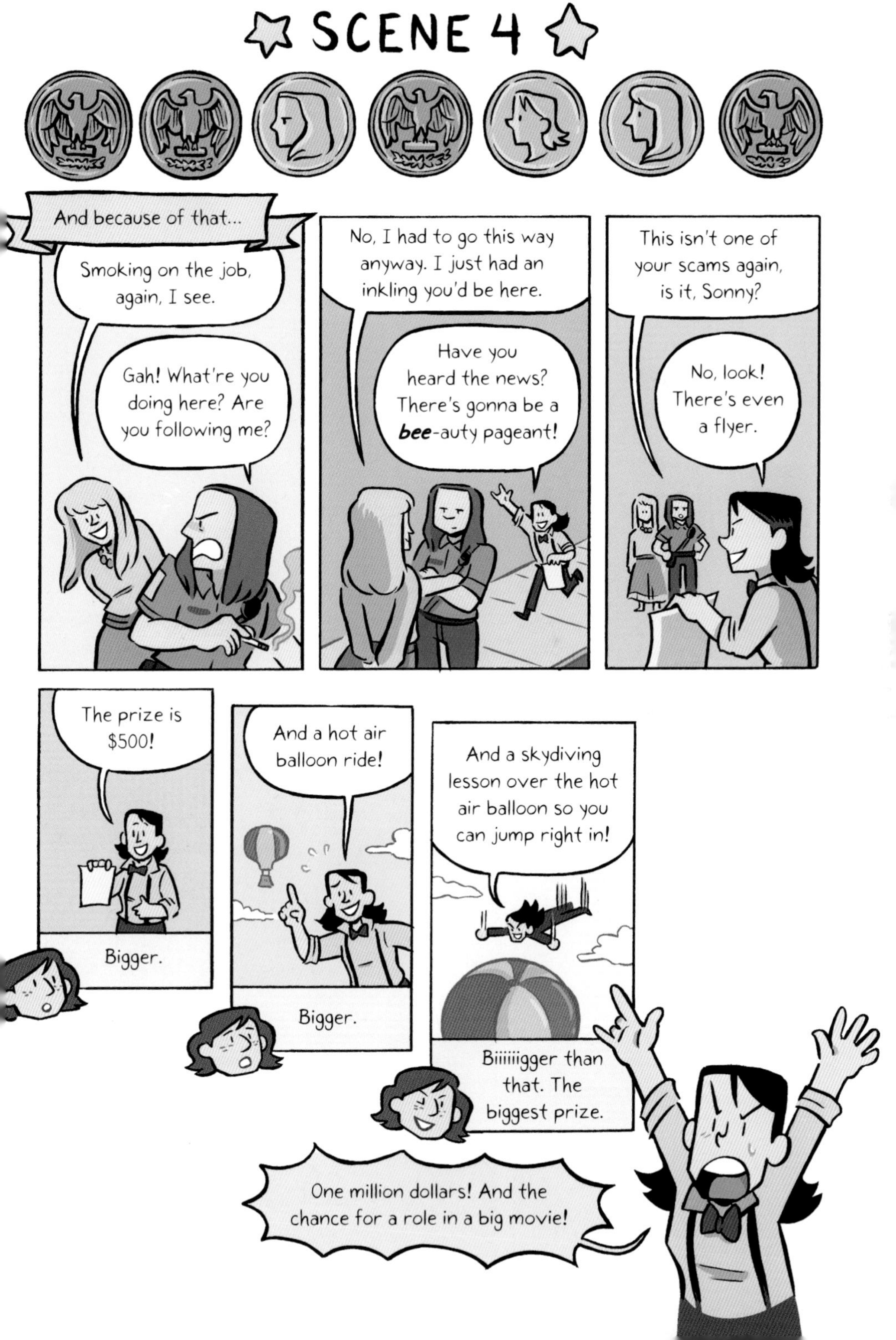
SCENE 4
And because of that...
Smoking on the job, again, I see.
Gah! What're you doing here? Are you following me?
No, I had to go this way anyway. I just had an inkling you'd be here.
Have you heard the news? There's gonna be a **bee**-auty pageant!
This isn't one of your scams again, is it, Sonny?
No, look! There's even a flyer.
The prize is $500!
Bigger.
And a hot air balloon ride!
Bigger.
And a skydiving lesson over the hot air balloon so you can jump right in!
Biiiiigger than that. The biggest prize.
One million dollars! And the chance for a role in a big movie!

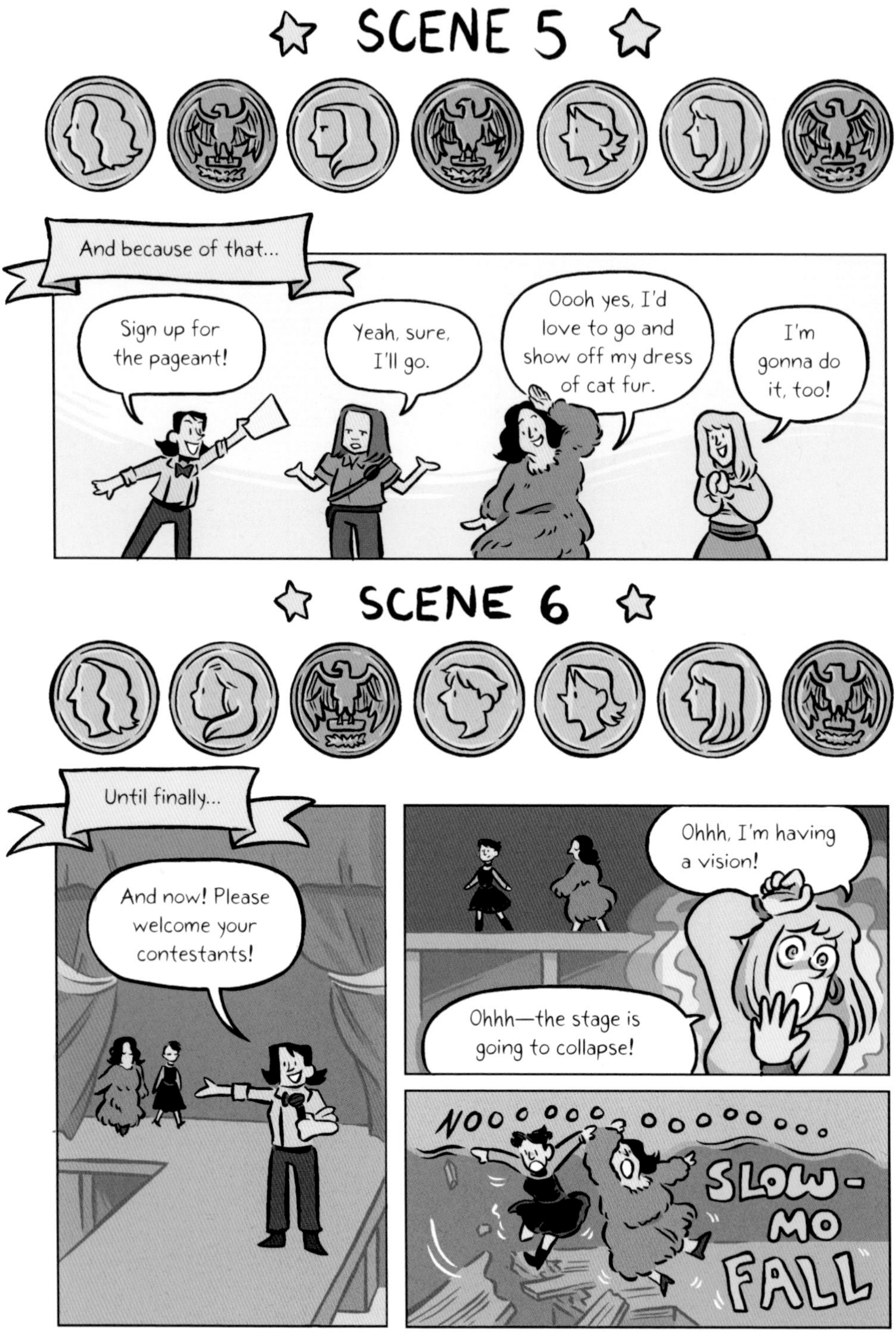
SCENE 5
And because of that...
Sign up for the pageant!
Yeah, sure, I'll go.
Oooh yes, I'd love to go and show off my dress of cat fur.
I'm gonna do it, too!
SCENE 6
Until finally...
And now! Please welcome your contestants!
Ohhh, I'm having a vision!
Ohhh—the stage is going to collapse!
NOOOOOOOOOOOOOO...
SLOW-MO FALL

SCENE 7

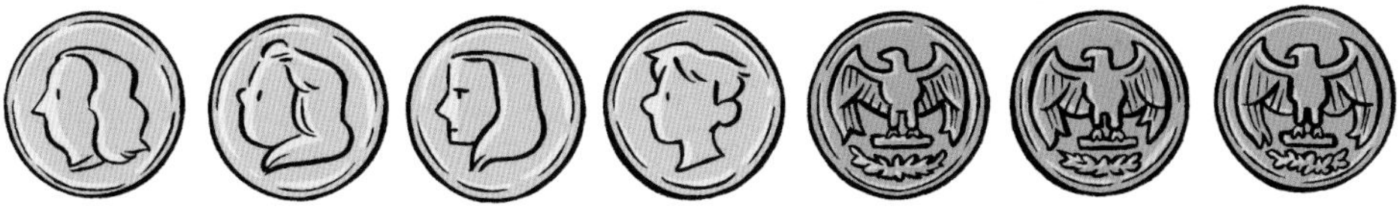

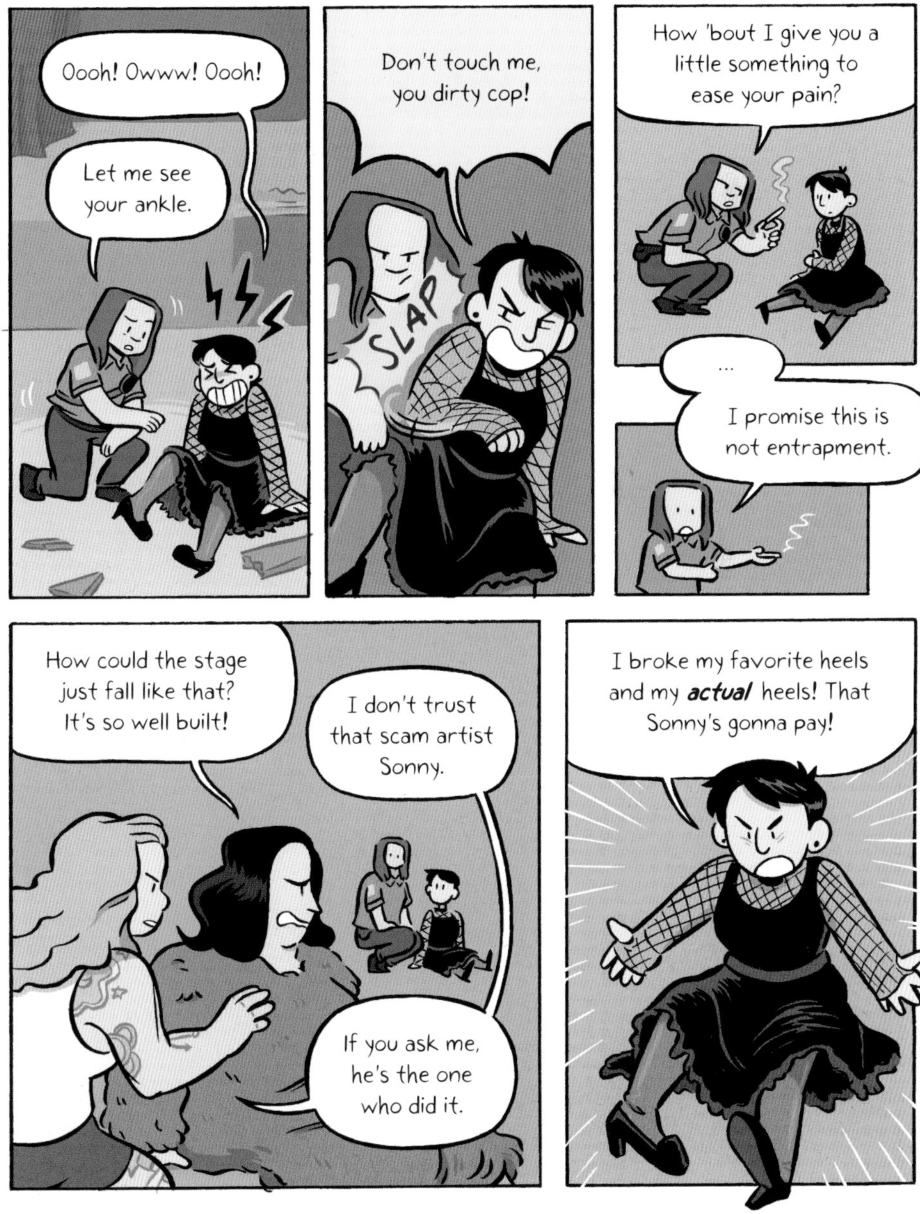

Oooh! Owww! Oooh!
Let me see your ankle.
Don't touch me, you dirty cop!
SLAP
How 'bout I give you a little something to ease your pain?
...
I promise this is not entrapment.
How could the stage just fall like that? It's so well built!
I don't trust that scam artist Sonny.
If you ask me, he's the one who did it.
I broke my favorite heels and my ***actual*** heels! That Sonny's gonna pay!

SCENE 8

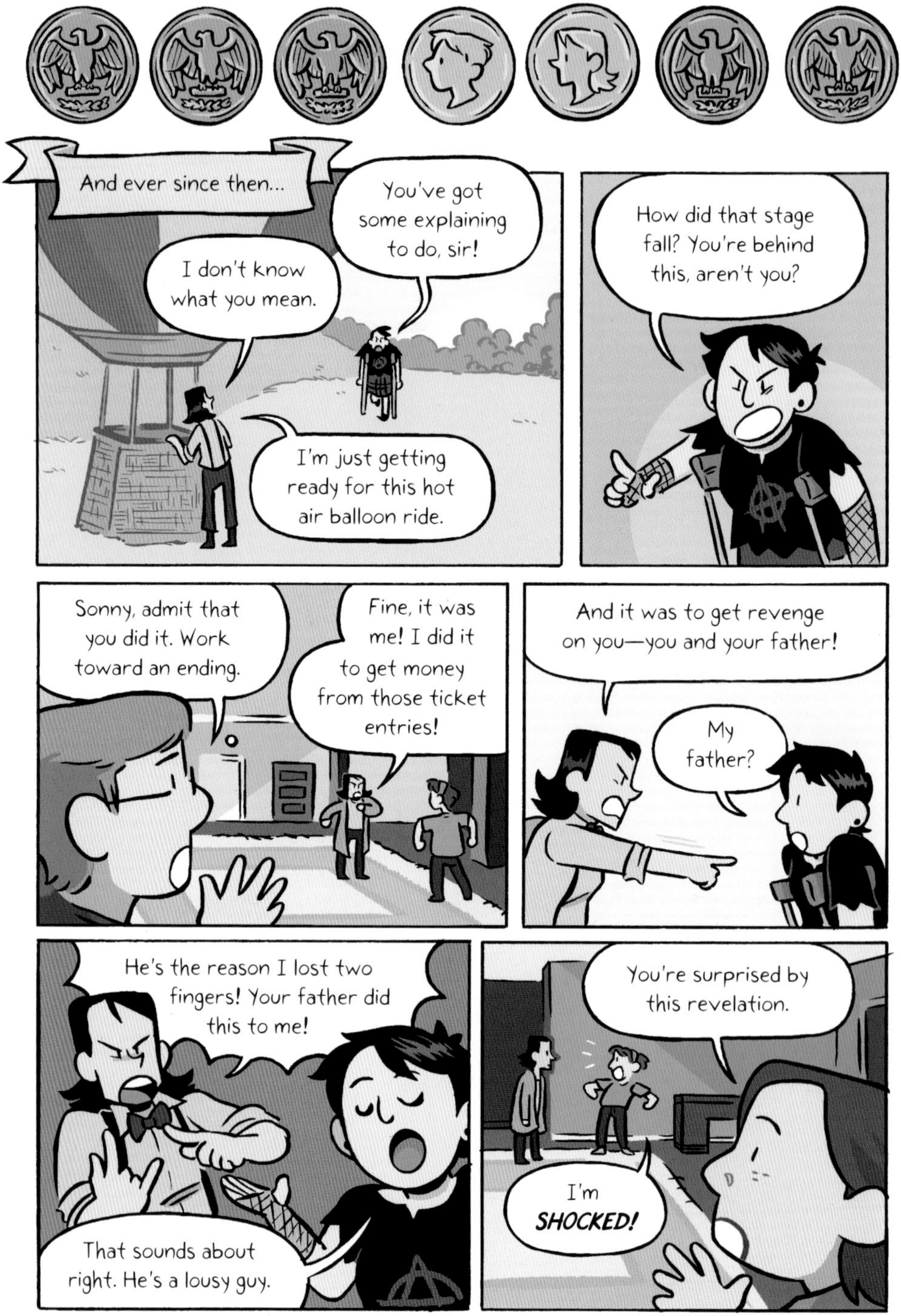

And ever since then...
You've got some explaining to do, sir!
I don't know what you mean.
I'm just getting ready for this hot air balloon ride.
How did that stage fall? You're behind this, aren't you?
Sonny, admit that you did it. Work toward an ending.
Fine, it was me! I did it to get money from those ticket entries!
And it was to get revenge on you—you and your father!
My father?
He's the reason I lost two fingers! Your father did this to me!
That sounds about right. He's a lousy guy.
You're surprised by this revelation.
I'm SHOCKED!

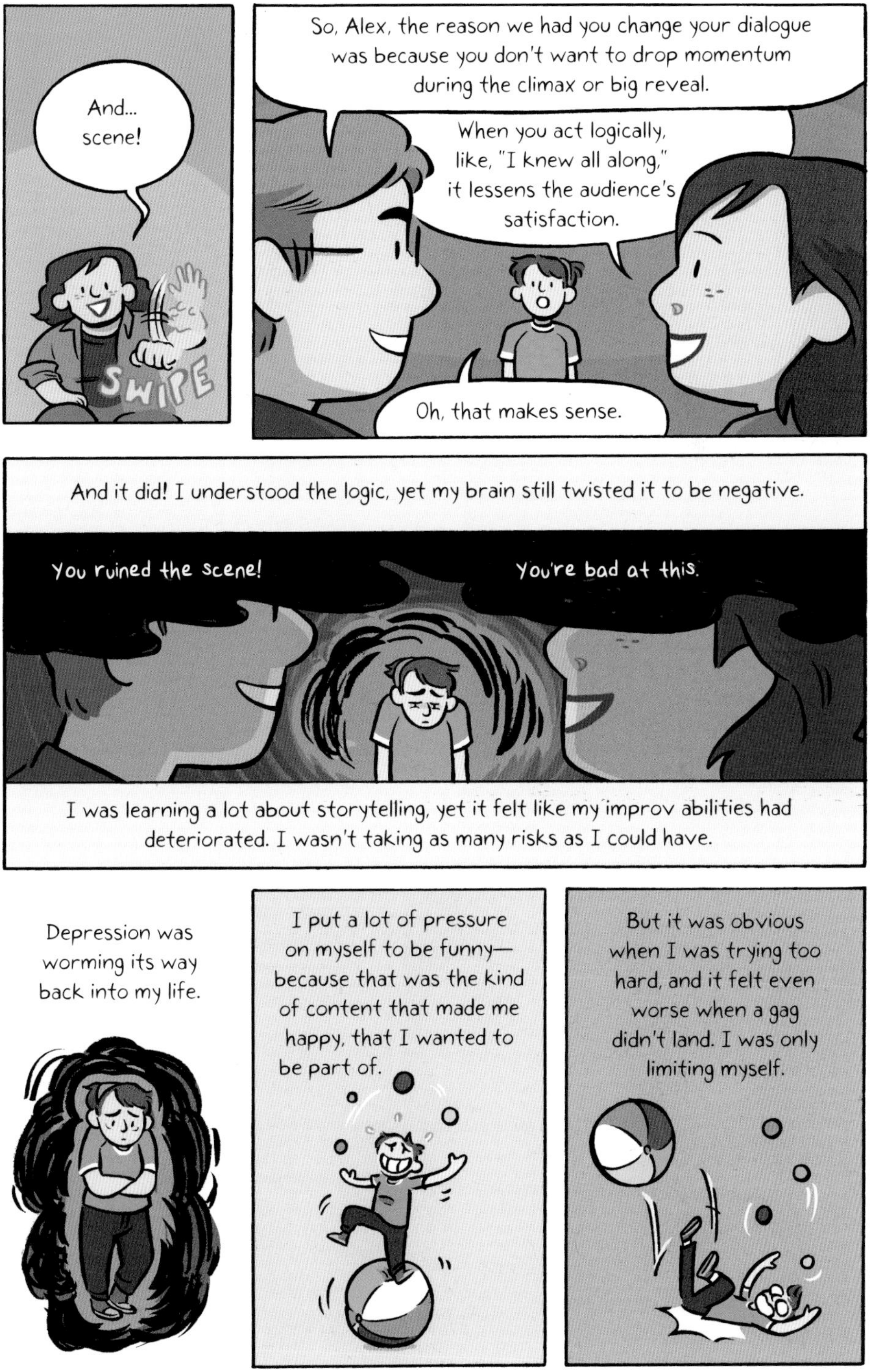
And... scene!
SWIPE
So, Alex, the reason we had you change your dialogue was because you don't want to drop momentum during the climax or big reveal.
When you act logically, like, "I knew all along," it lessens the audience's satisfaction.
Oh, that makes sense.
And it did! I understood the logic, yet my brain still twisted it to be negative.
You ruined the scene!
You're bad at this.
I was learning a lot about storytelling, yet it felt like my improv abilities had deteriorated. I wasn't taking as many risks as I could have.
Depression was worming its way back into my life.
I put a lot of pressure on myself to be funny—because that was the kind of content that made me happy, that I wanted to be part of.
But it was obvious when I was trying too hard, and it felt even worse when a gag didn't land. I was only limiting myself.

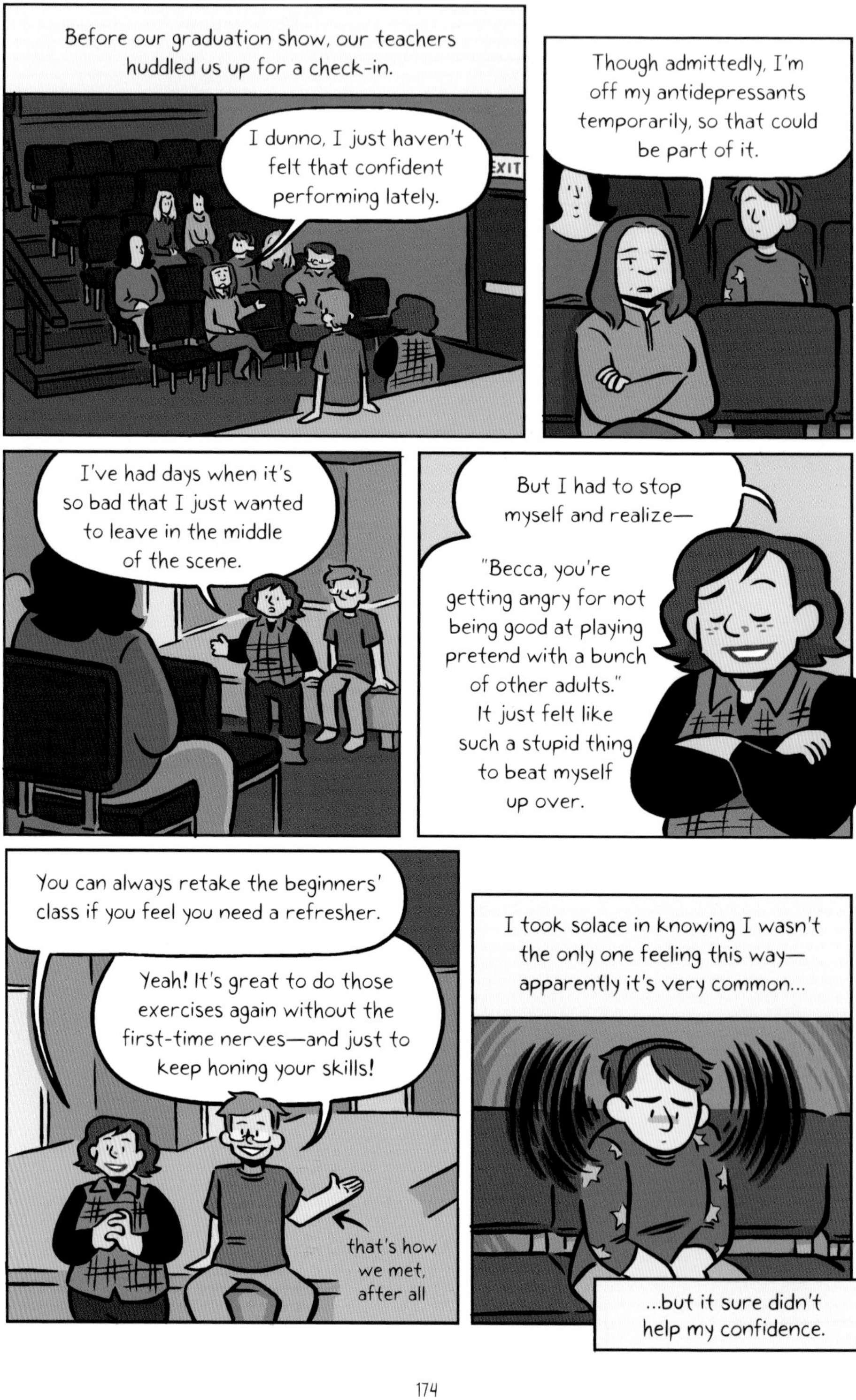
Before our graduation show, our teachers huddled us up for a check-in.
I dunno, I just haven't felt that confident performing lately.
EXIT
Though admittedly, I'm off my antidepressants temporarily, so that could be part of it.
I've had days when it's so bad that I just wanted to leave in the middle of the scene.
But I had to stop myself and realize—
"Becca, you're getting angry for not being good at playing pretend with a bunch of other adults." It just felt like such a stupid thing to beat myself up over.
You can always retake the beginners' class if you feel you need a refresher.
Yeah! It's great to do those exercises again without the first-time nerves—and just to keep honing your skills!
that's how we met, after all
I took solace in knowing I wasn't the only one feeling this way—apparently it's very common...
...but it sure didn't help my confidence.

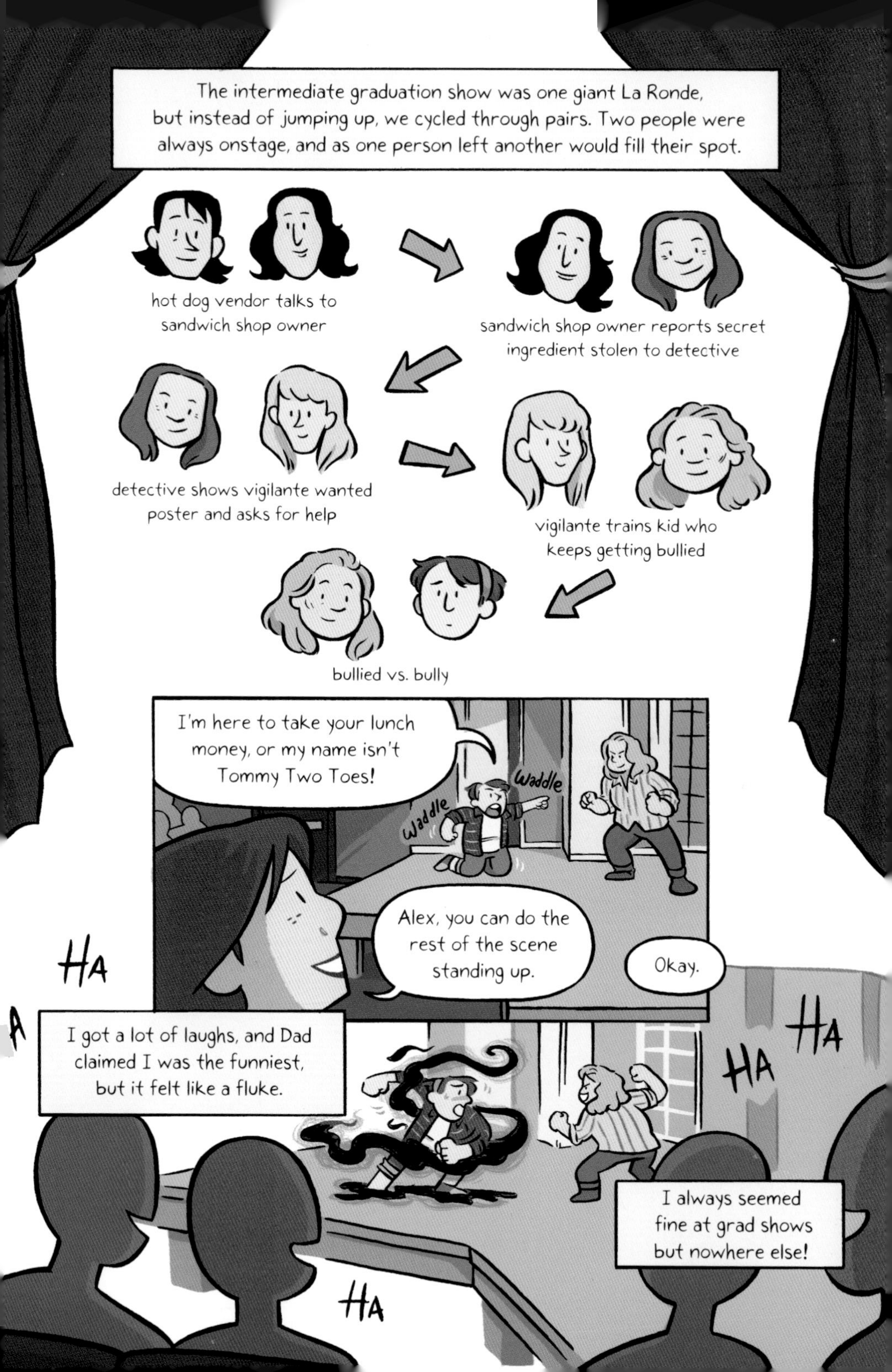
The intermediate graduation show was one giant La Ronde, but instead of jumping up, we cycled through pairs. Two people were always onstage, and as one person left another would fill their spot.
hot dog vendor talks to sandwich shop owner
sandwich shop owner reports secret ingredient stolen to detective
detective shows vigilante wanted poster and asks for help
vigilante trains kid who keeps getting bullied
bullied vs. bully
I'm here to take your lunch money, or my name isn't Tommy Two Toes!
Waddle
Waddle
Alex, you can do the rest of the scene standing up.
Okay.
HA
A
I got a lot of laughs, and Dad claimed I was the funniest, but it felt like a fluke.
HA
HA
I always seemed fine at grad shows but nowhere else!
HA

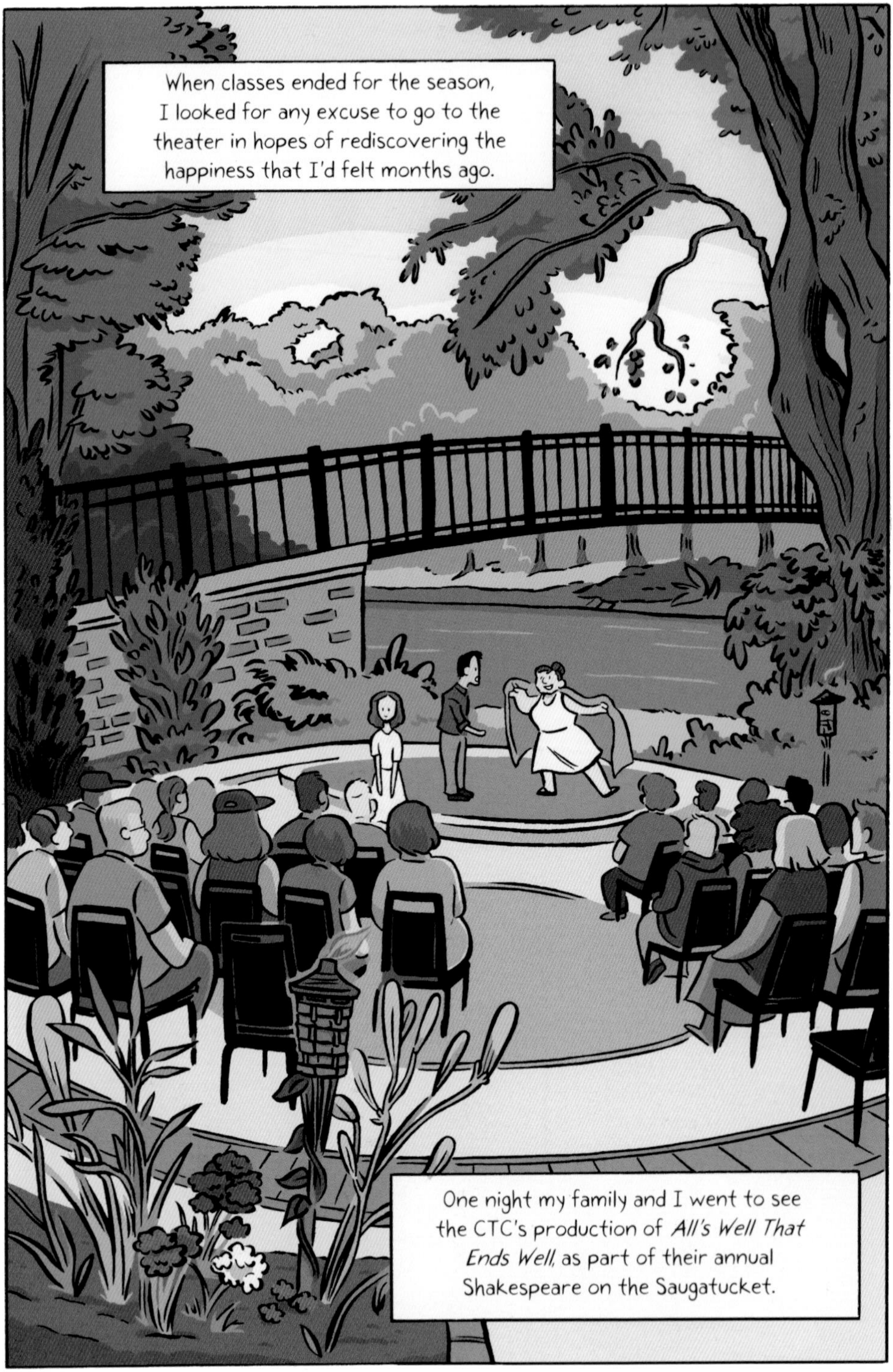
When classes ended for the season, I looked for any excuse to go to the theater in hopes of rediscovering the happiness that I'd felt months ago.
One night my family and I went to see the CTC's production of *All's Well That Ends Well*, as part of their annual Shakespeare on the Saugatucket.

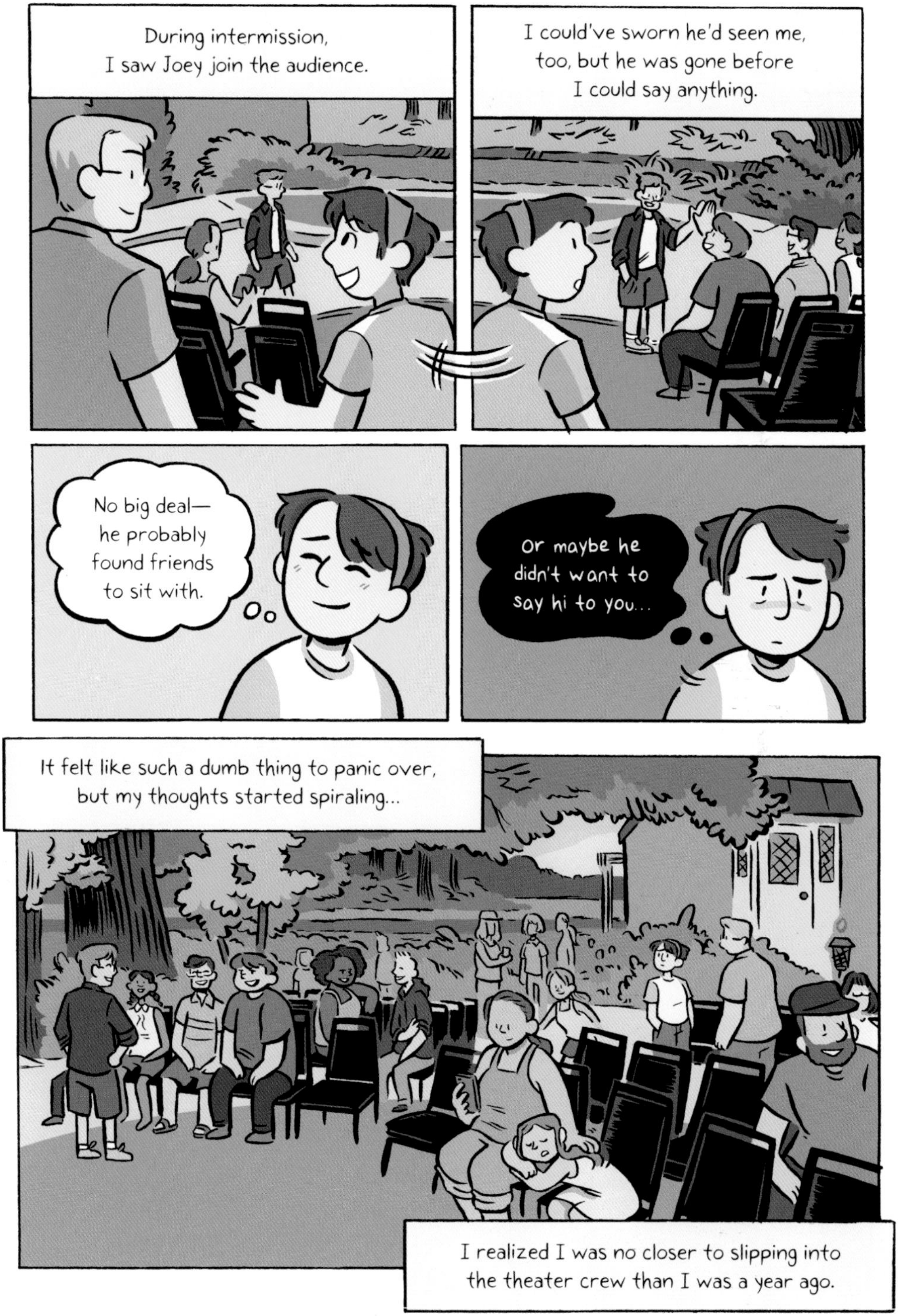
During intermission,
I saw Joey join the audience.
I could've sworn he'd seen me, too, but he was gone before I could say anything.
No big deal— he probably found friends to sit with.
Or maybe he didn't want to say hi to you...
It felt like such a dumb thing to panic over, but my thoughts started spiraling...
I realized I was no closer to slipping into the theater crew than I was a year ago.

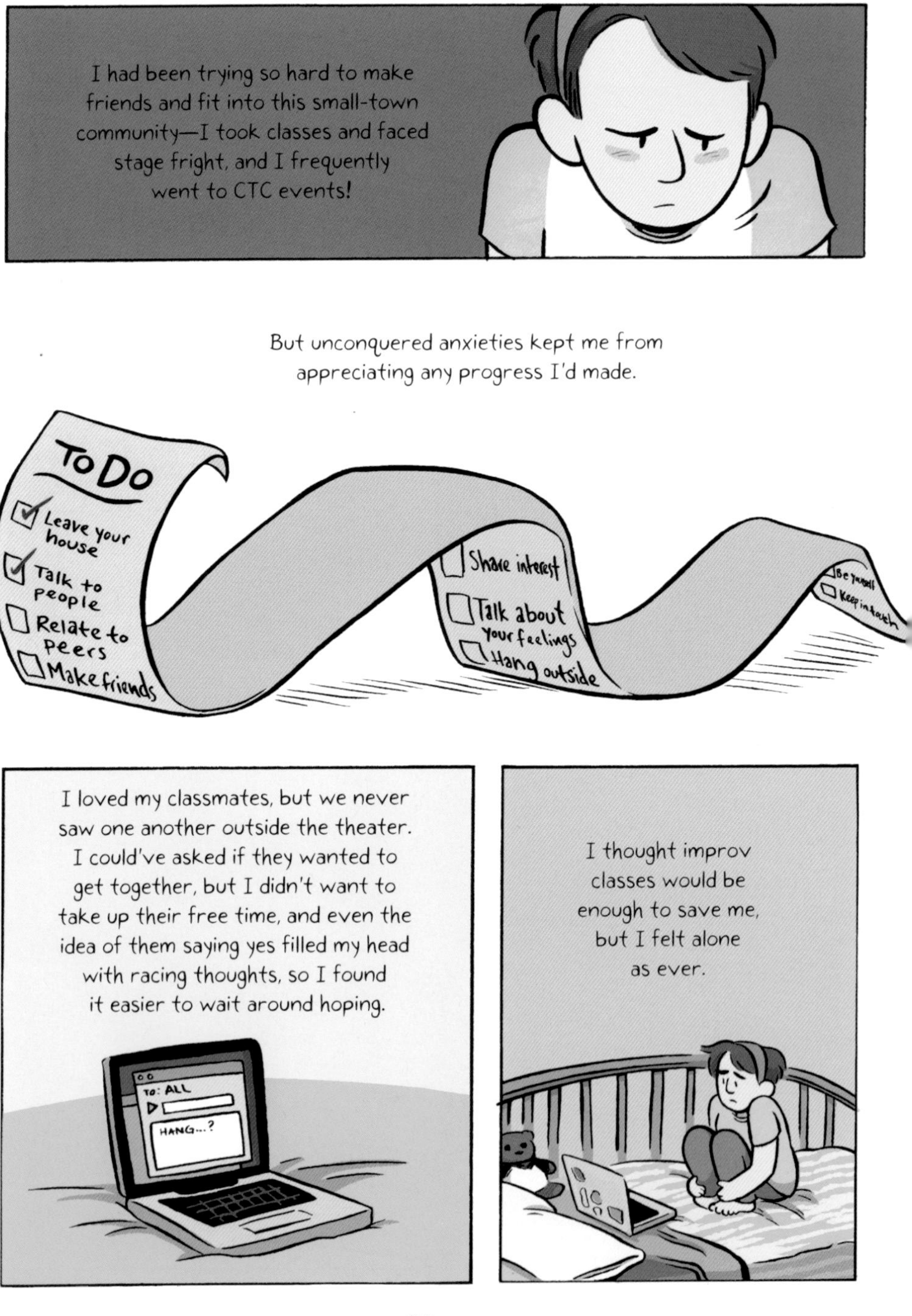
I had been trying so hard to make friends and fit into this small-town community—I took classes and faced stage fright, and I frequently went to CTC events!
But unconquered anxieties kept me from appreciating any progress I'd made.
To Do
Leave your house
Talk to people
Relate to peers
Make friends
Share interest
Talk about your feelings
Hang outside
Be yourself
Keep in touch
I loved my classmates, but we never saw one another outside the theater. I could've asked if they wanted to get together, but I didn't want to take up their free time, and even the idea of them saying yes filled my head with racing thoughts, so I found it easier to wait around hoping.
TO: ALL
HANG...?
I thought improv classes would be enough to save me, but I felt alone as ever.

PART 4

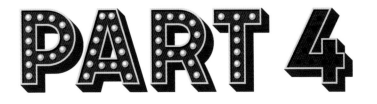

After spending most of the summer in my parents' basement,
I was glad to have reasons to get out of the house.

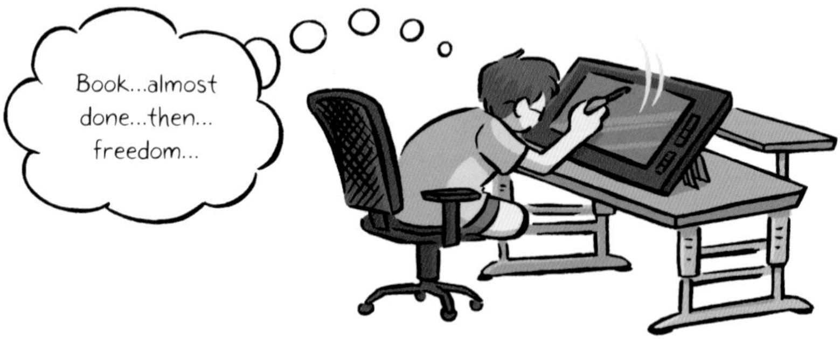
Book...almost done...then... freedom...

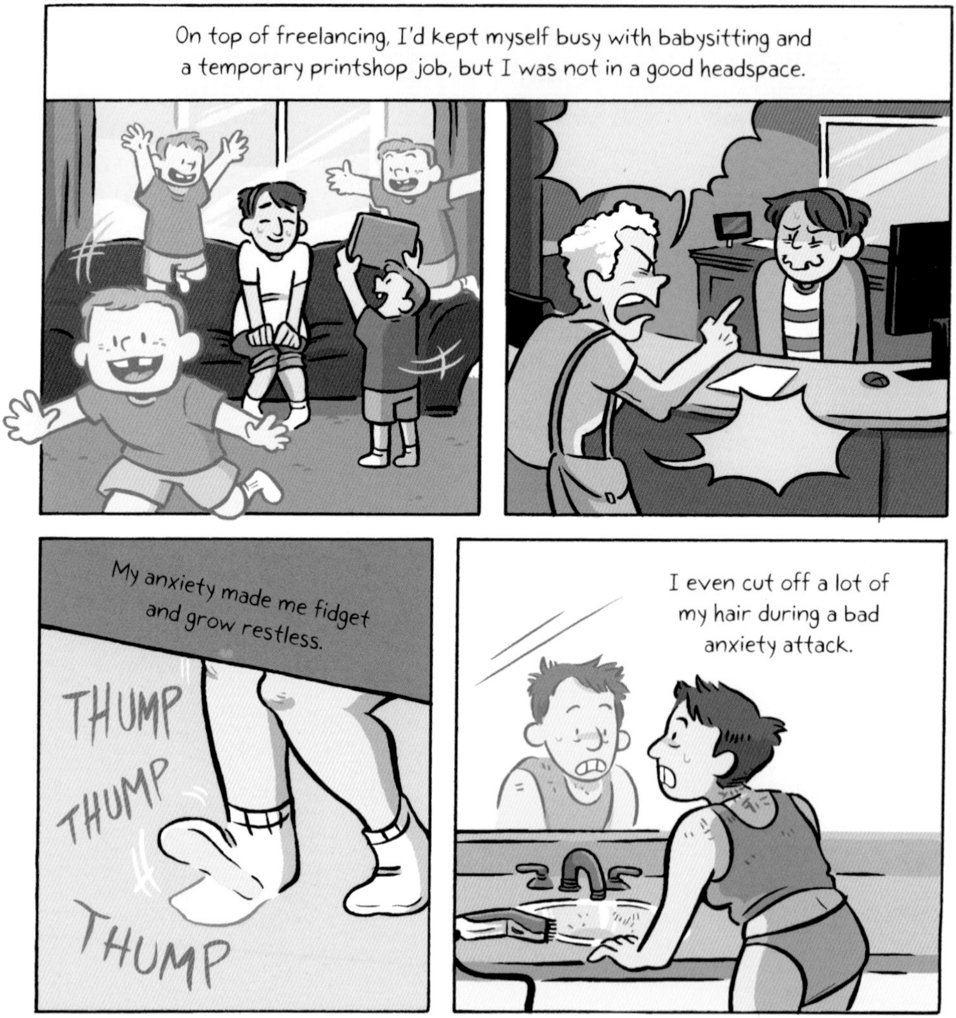
On top of freelancing, I'd kept myself busy with babysitting and a temporary printshop job, but I was not in a good headspace.
My anxiety made me fidget and grow restless.
THUMP
THUMP
THUMP
I even cut off a lot of my hair during a bad anxiety attack.

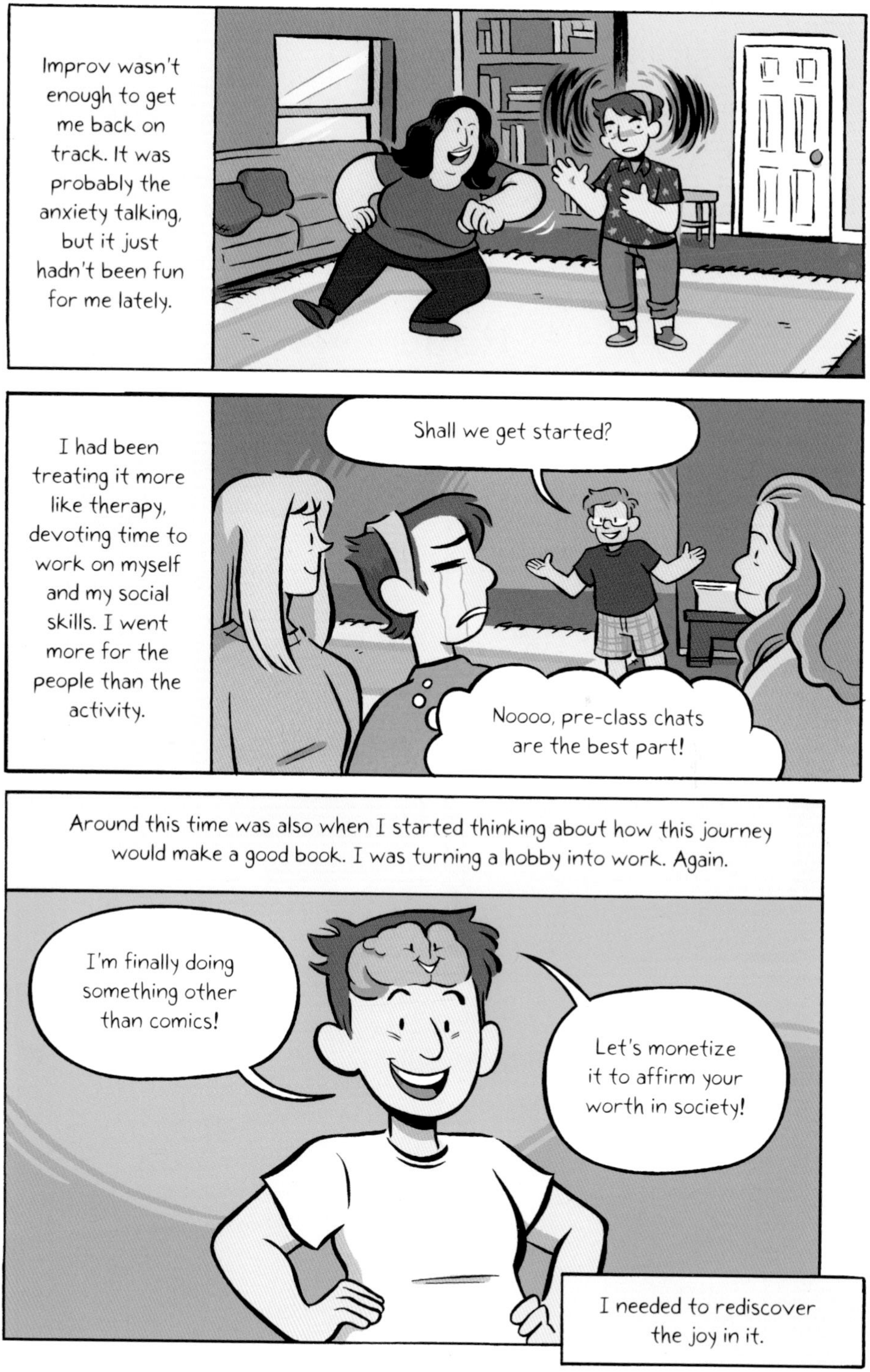
Improv wasn't enough to get me back on track. It was probably the anxiety talking, but it just hadn't been fun for me lately.
I had been treating it more like therapy, devoting time to work on myself and my social skills. I went more for the people than the activity.
Shall we get started?
Noooo, pre-class chats are the best part!
Around this time was also when I started thinking about how this journey would make a good book. I was turning a hobby into work. Again.
I'm finally doing something other than comics!
Let's monetize it to affirm your worth in society!
I needed to rediscover the joy in it.

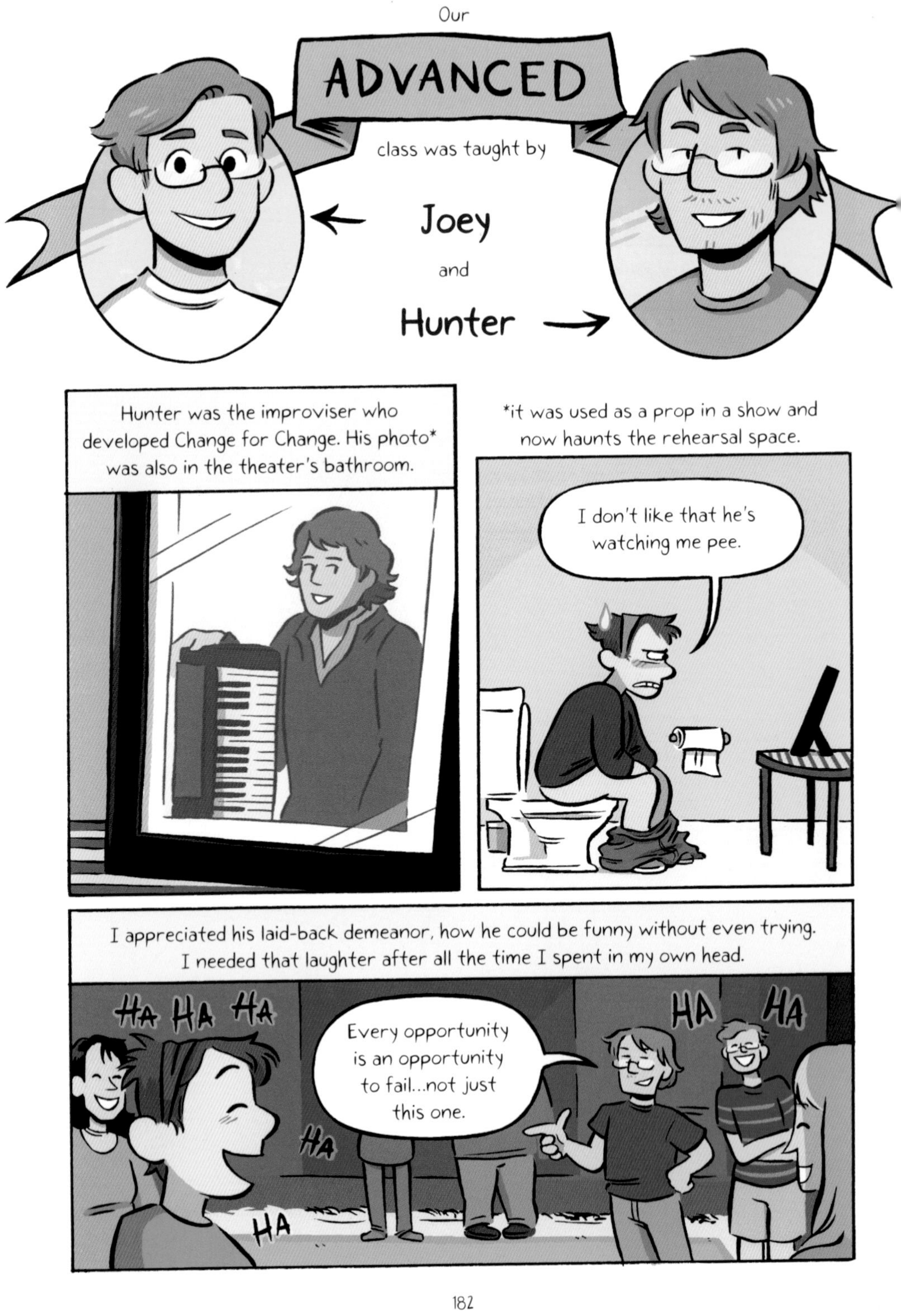
Our
ADVANCED
class was taught by
Joey
and
Hunter
Hunter was the improviser who developed Change for Change. His photo* was also in the theater's bathroom.
*it was used as a prop in a show and now haunts the rehearsal space.
I don't like that he's watching me pee.
I appreciated his laid-back demeanor, how he could be funny without even trying. I needed that laughter after all the time I spent in my own head.
HA HA HA
HA
HA
Every opportunity is an opportunity to fail...not just this one.
HA HA

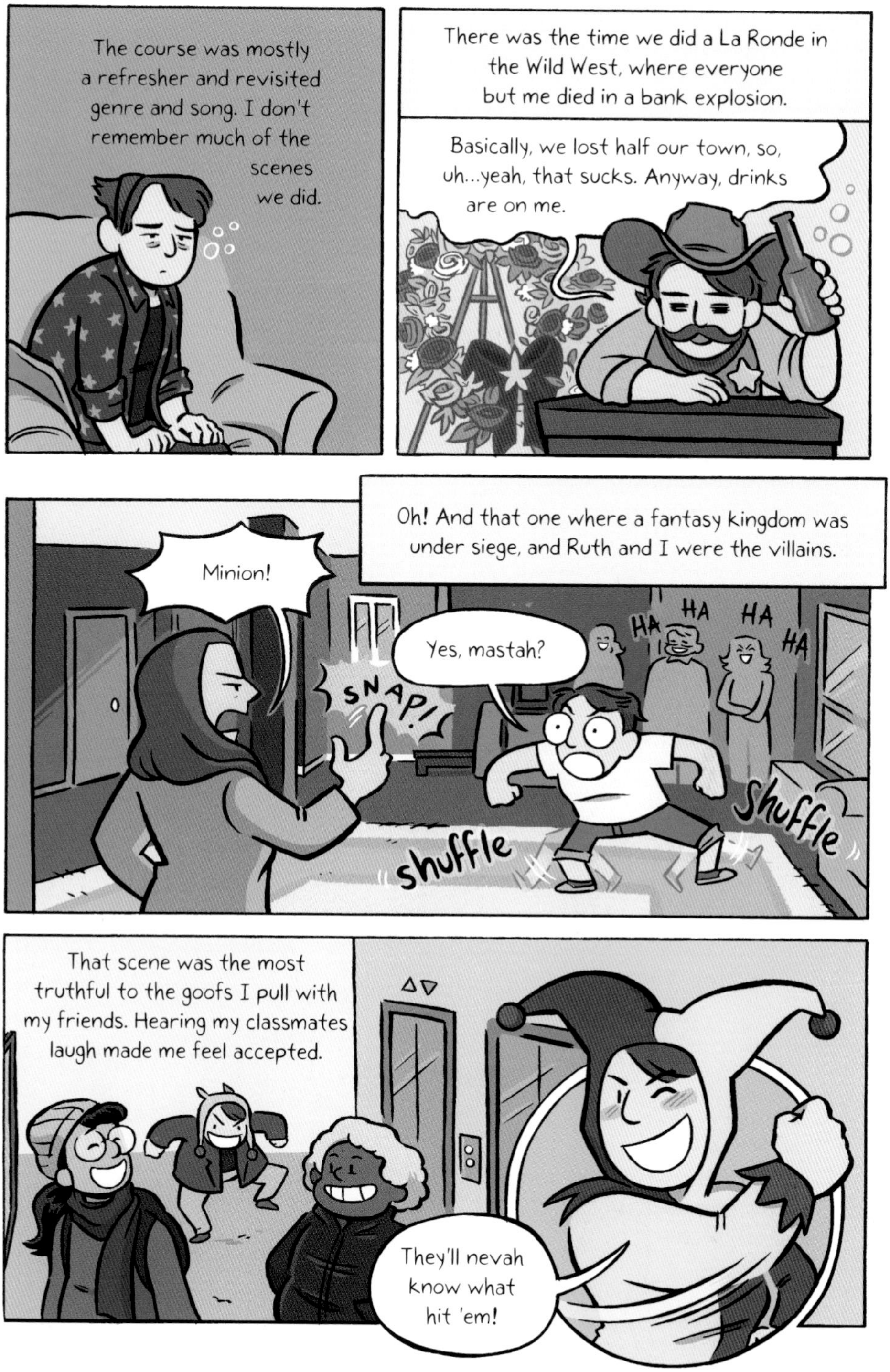
The course was mostly a refresher and revisited genre and song. I don't remember much of the scenes we did.
There was the time we did a La Ronde in the Wild West, where everyone but me died in a bank explosion.
Basically, we lost half our town, so, uh...yeah, that sucks. Anyway, drinks are on me.
Oh! And that one where a fantasy kingdom was under siege, and Ruth and I were the villains.
Minion!
SNAP!
Yes, mastah?
HA
HA
HA
HA
shuffle
shuffle
That scene was the most truthful to the goofs I pull with my friends. Hearing my classmates laugh made me feel accepted.
They'll nevah know what hit 'em!

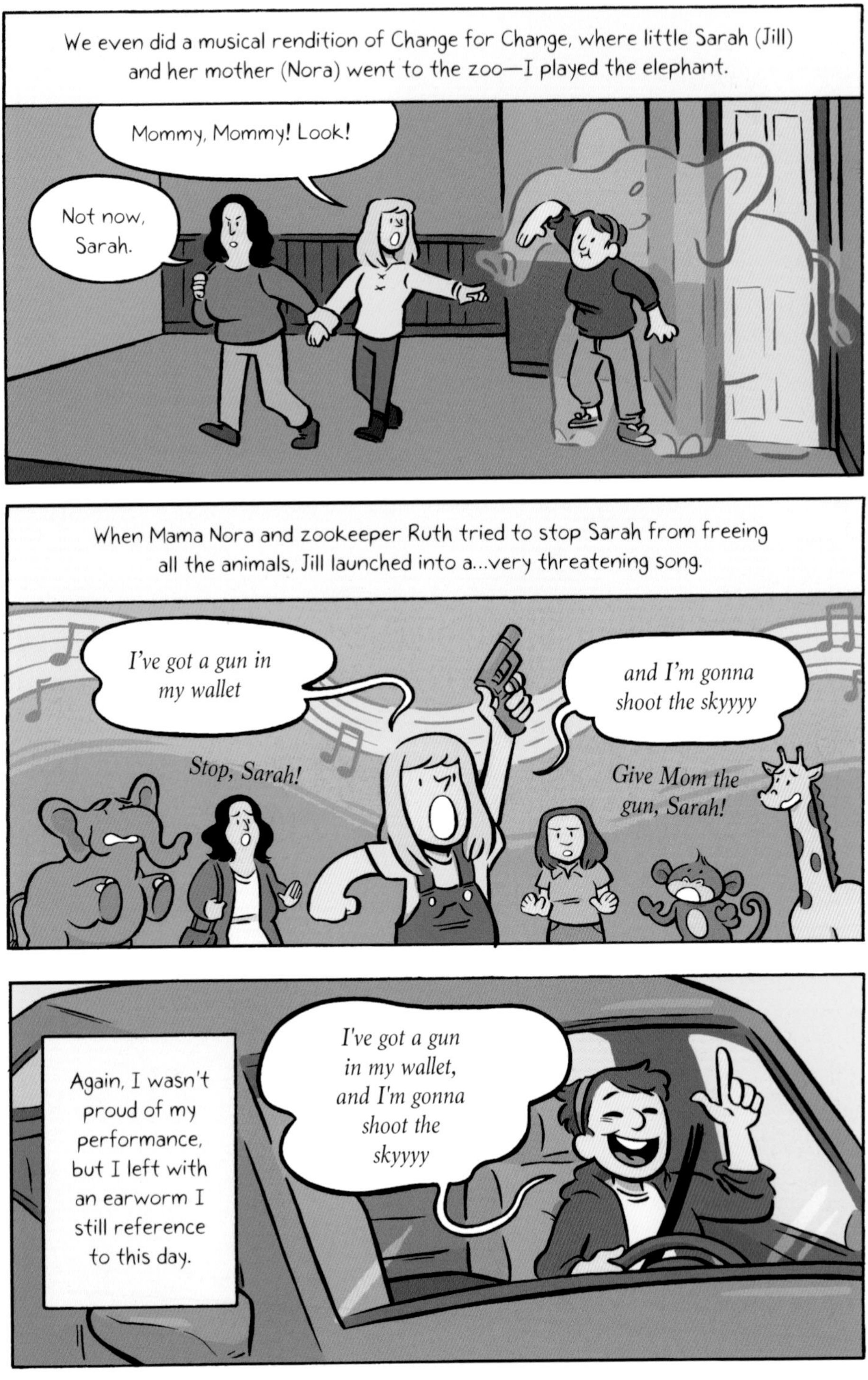
We even did a musical rendition of Change for Change, where little Sarah (Jill) and her mother (Nora) went to the zoo—I played the elephant.
Mommy, Mommy! Look!
Not now, Sarah.
When Mama Nora and zookeeper Ruth tried to stop Sarah from freeing all the animals, Jill launched into a...very threatening song.
I've got a gun in my wallet
and I'm gonna shoot the skyyyy
Stop, Sarah!
Give Mom the gun, Sarah!
Again, I wasn't proud of my performance, but I left with an earworm I still reference to this day.
I've got a gun in my wallet, and I'm gonna shoot the skyyyy

The course ran through a few more music games, albeit quickly.

ONE VERSE AT A TIME

is exactly what it sounds like...

Each player takes a turn to sing a verse about a topic (in this case, why parents hate their kids) while accompanied by a musician.

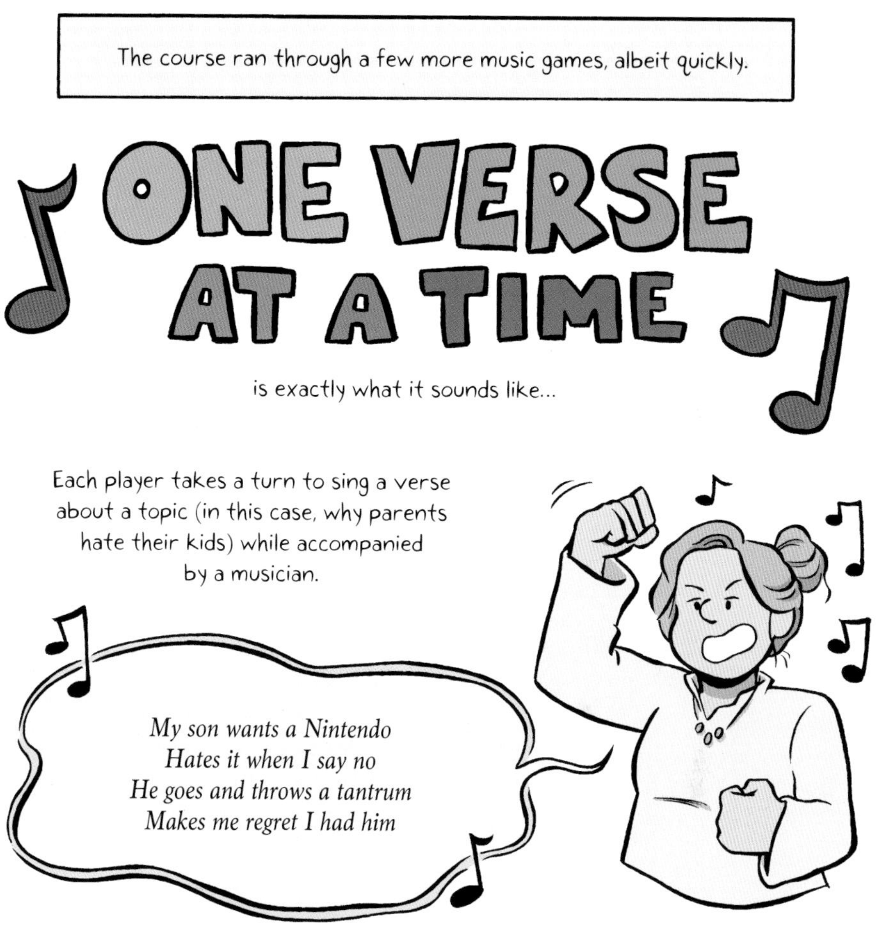
*My son wants a Nintendo
Hates it when I say no
He goes and throws a tantrum
Makes me regret I had him*

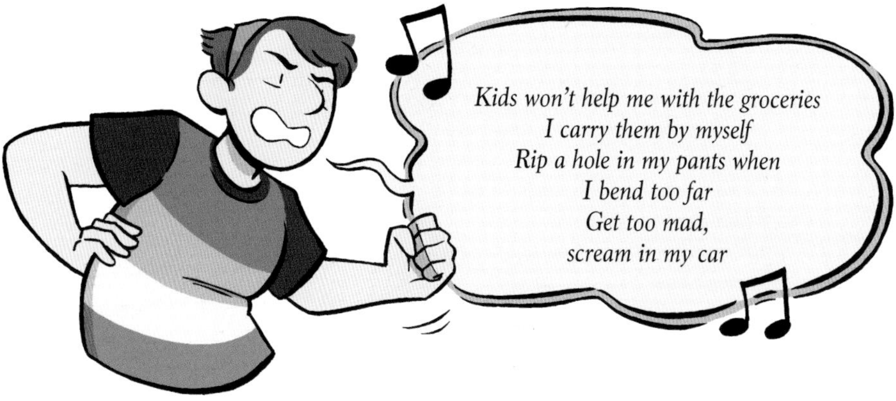
*Kids won't help me with the groceries
I carry them by myself
Rip a hole in my pants when
I bend too far
Get too mad,
scream in my car*

SHOWSTOPPER

better resembles musicals in that it begins with regular scene work.

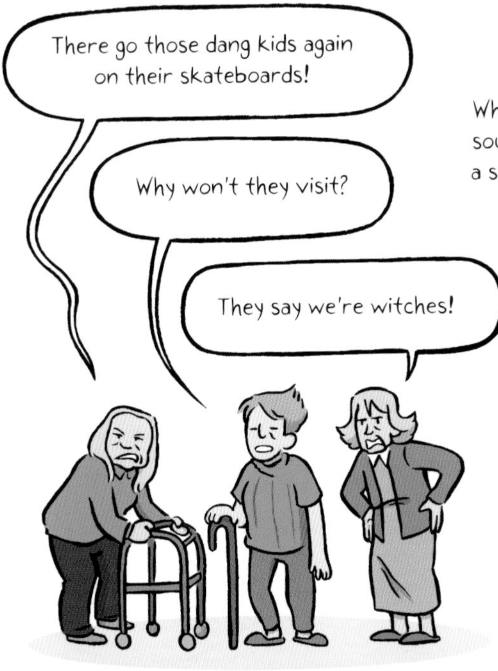
There go those dang kids again on their skateboards!
Why won't they visit?
They say we're witches!

When a character says something that sounds like it could be a title or line of a song, the director will usually cue the players to start singing.

(in our case, Hunter threw a rubber chicken onstage)

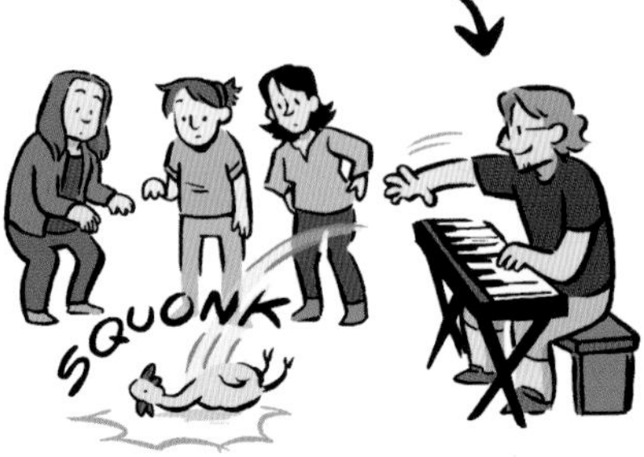
SQUONK

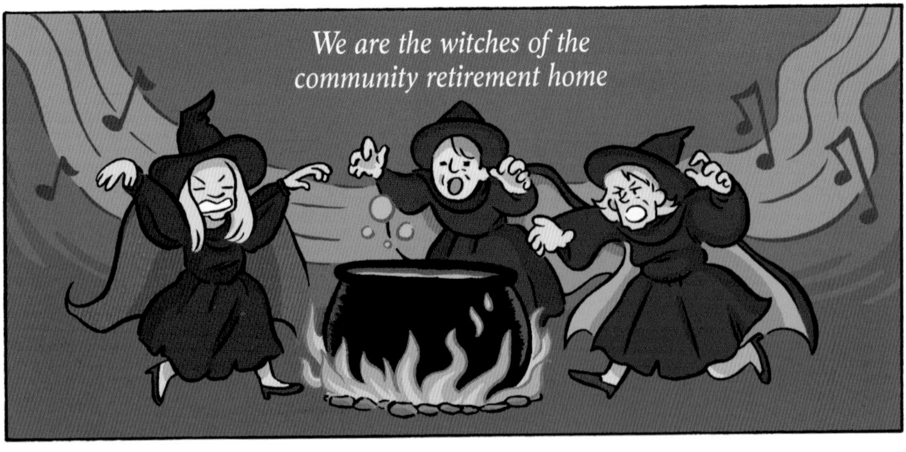
We are the witches of the community retirement home

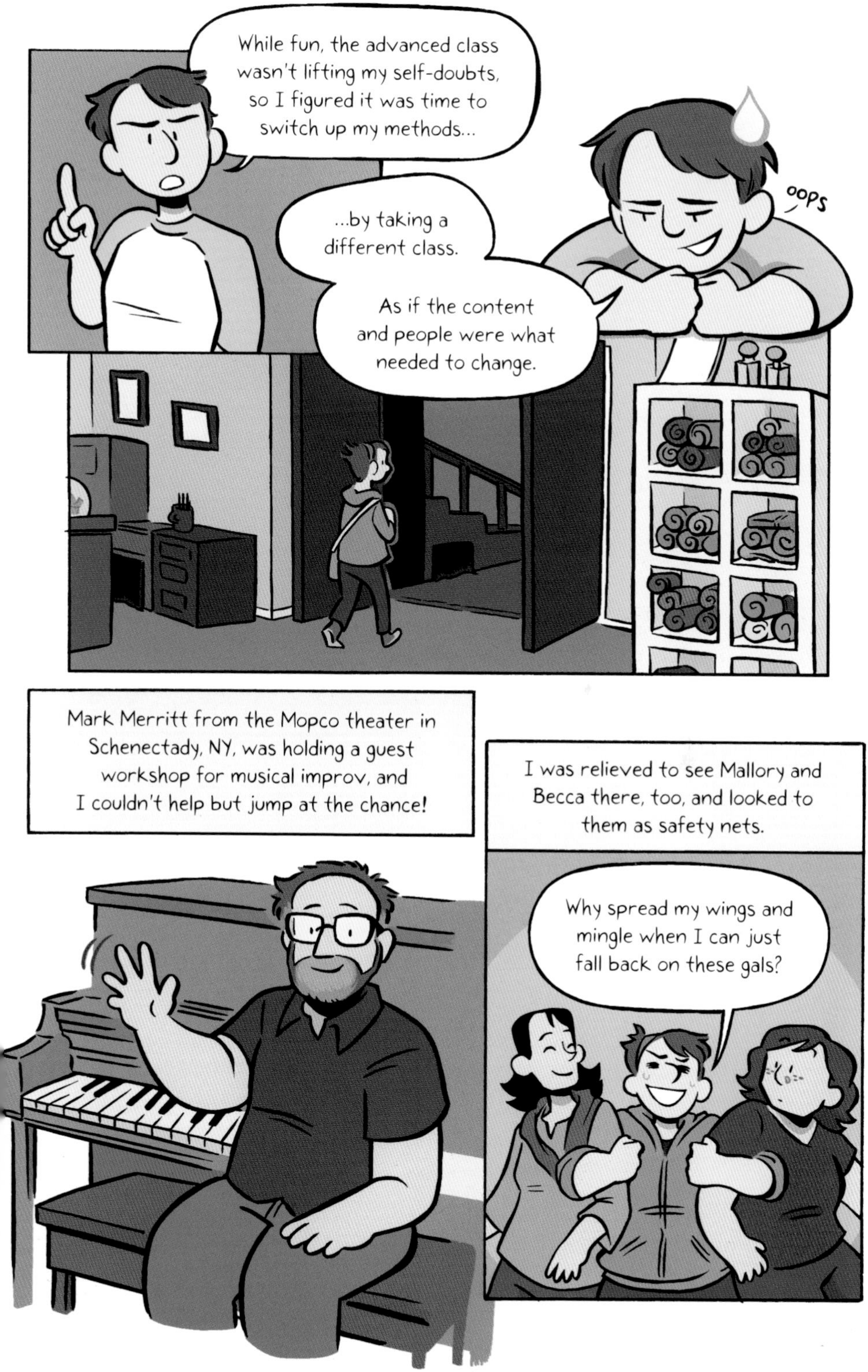
While fun, the advanced class wasn't lifting my self-doubts, so I figured it was time to switch up my methods...
...by taking a different class.
OOPS
As if the content and people were what needed to change.
Mark Merritt from the Mopco theater in Schenectady, NY, was holding a guest workshop for musical improv, and I couldn't help but jump at the chance!
I was relieved to see Mallory and Becca there, too, and looked to them as safety nets.
Why spread my wings and mingle when I can just fall back on these gals?

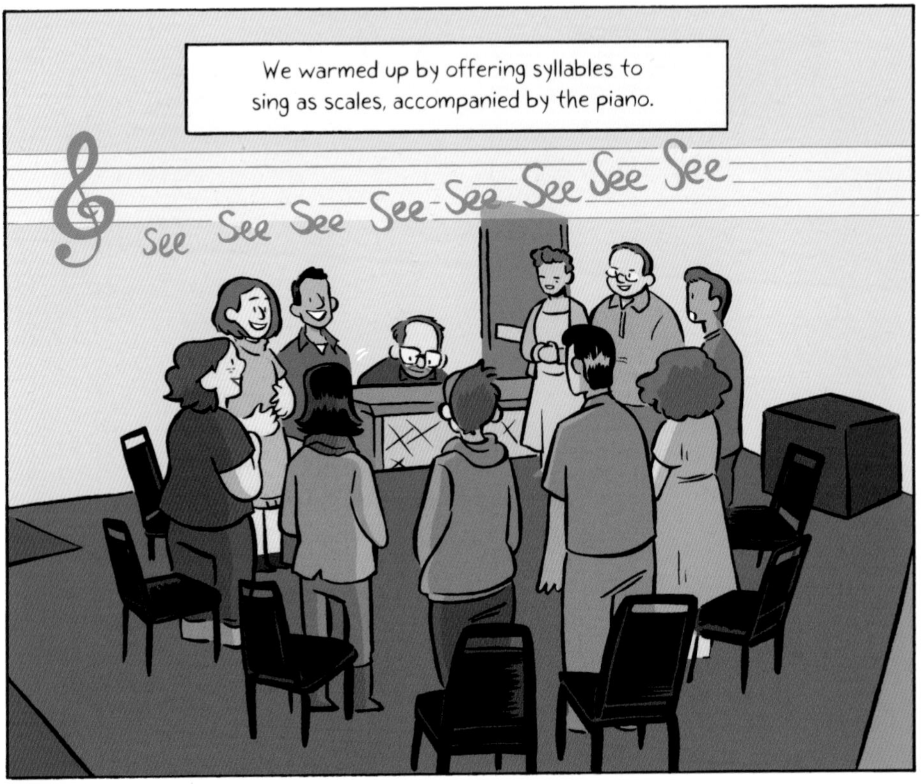
We warmed up by offering syllables to sing as scales, accompanied by the piano.
See See See See See See See See

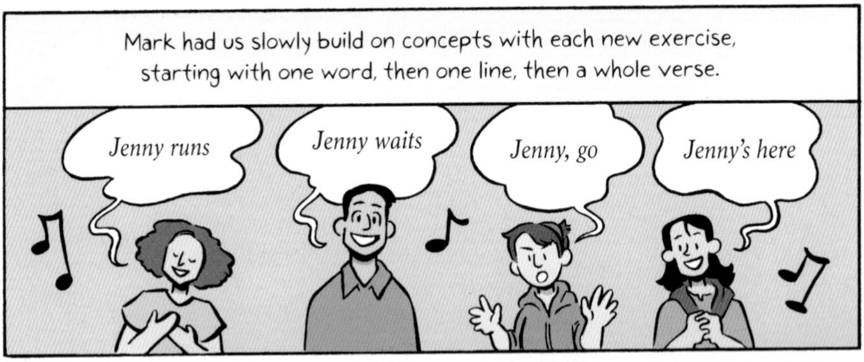
Mark had us slowly build on concepts with each new exercise, starting with one word, then one line, then a whole verse.
Jenny runs
Jenny waits
Jenny, go
Jenny's here

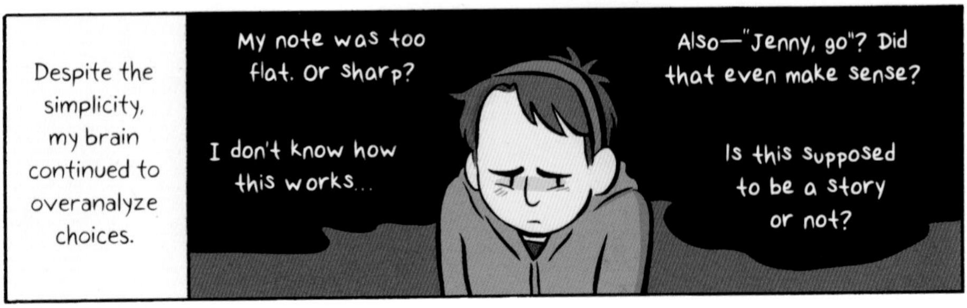
Despite the simplicity, my brain continued to overanalyze choices.
My note was too flat. Or sharp?
I don't know how this works...
Also—"Jenny, go"? Did that even make sense?
Is this supposed to be a story or not?

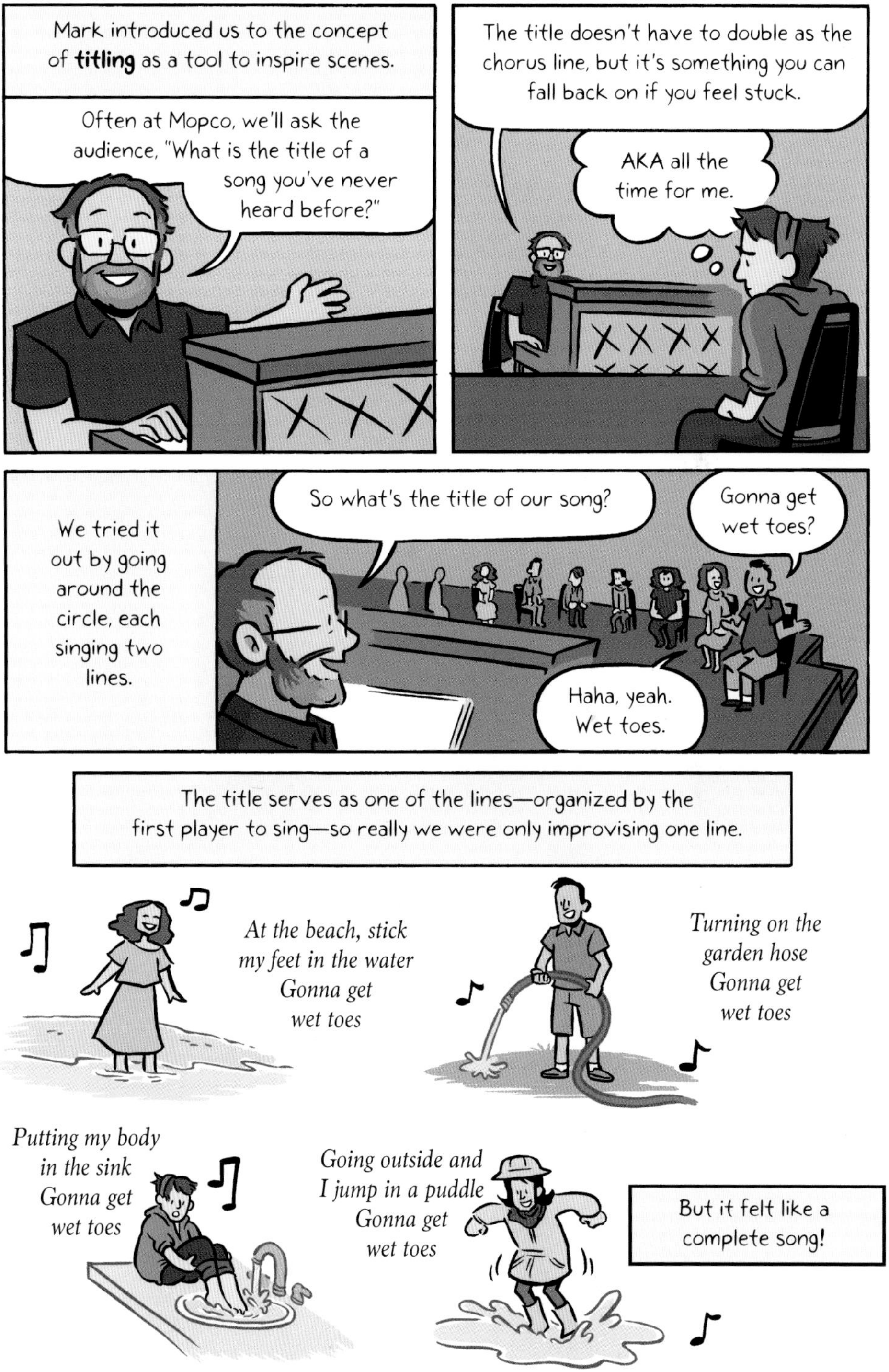
Mark introduced us to the concept of **titling** as a tool to inspire scenes.
Often at Mopco, we'll ask the audience, "What is the title of a song you've never heard before?"
The title doesn't have to double as the chorus line, but it's something you can fall back on if you feel stuck.
AKA all the time for me.
We tried it out by going around the circle, each singing two lines.
So what's the title of our song?
Gonna get wet toes?
Haha, yeah. Wet toes.
The title serves as one of the lines—organized by the first player to sing—so really we were only improvising one line.
At the beach, stick my feet in the water Gonna get wet toes
Turning on the garden hose Gonna get wet toes
Putting my body in the sink Gonna get wet toes
Going outside and I jump in a puddle Gonna get wet toes
But it felt like a complete song!

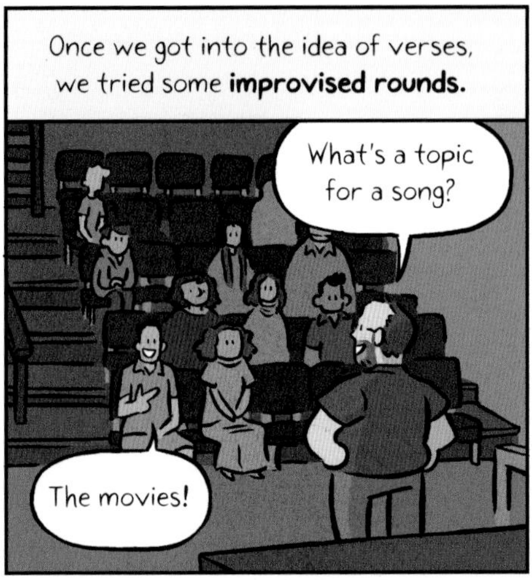
Once we got into the idea of verses, we tried some **improvised rounds.**
What's a topic for a song?
The movies!

A round is a musical composition where at least three singers follow the same melody, simultaneously singing different lyrics with different cues.

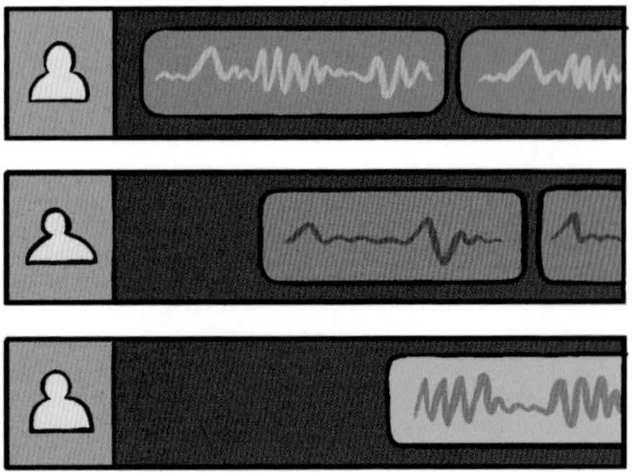

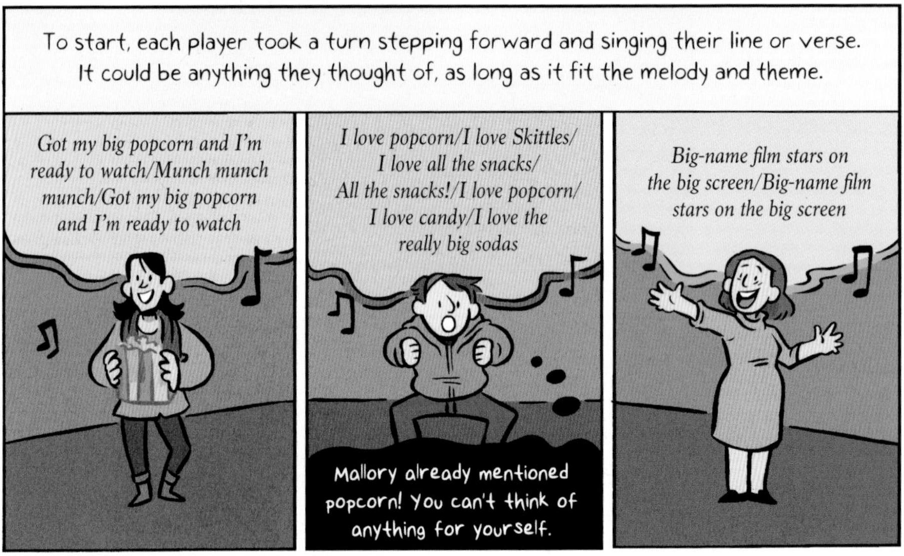
To start, each player took a turn stepping forward and singing their line or verse. It could be anything they thought of, as long as it fit the melody and theme.
Got my big popcorn and I'm ready to watch/Munch munch munch/Got my big popcorn and I'm ready to watch
I love popcorn/I love Skittles/I love all the snacks/All the snacks!/I love popcorn/I love candy/I love the really big sodas
Mallory already mentioned popcorn! You can't think of anything for yourself.
Big-name film stars on the big screen/Big-name film stars on the big screen

Once each player has an established role, player one starts singing their part until the conductor cues in player two, singing their verse while player one sings the first verse, and continuing with player three.

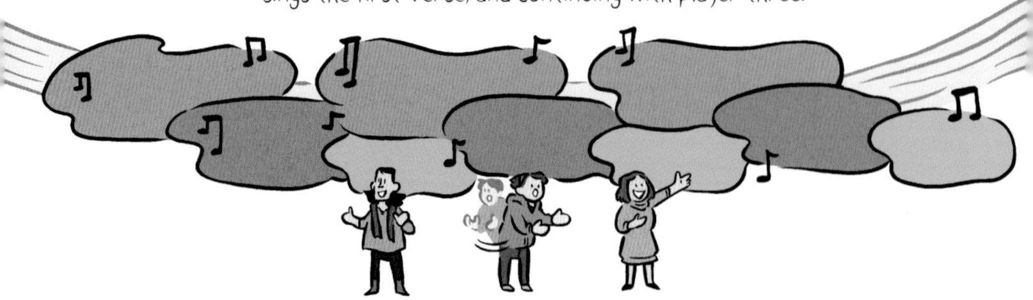

We ended the class with a **Song Circle** combining all we had learned in the past three hours. Each of us took turns singing to Mark's melody for our song called "Down by the River."

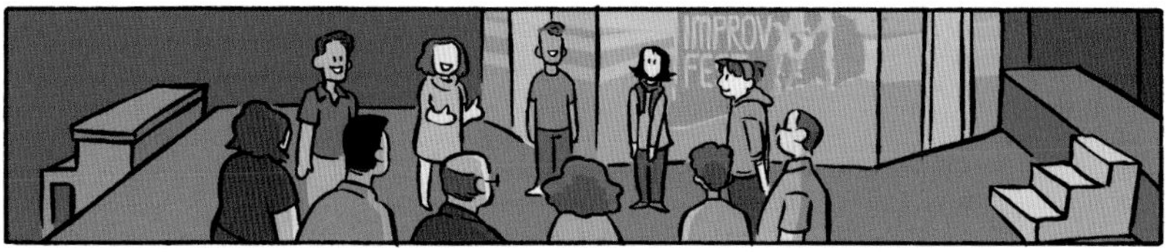
IMPROV
FE

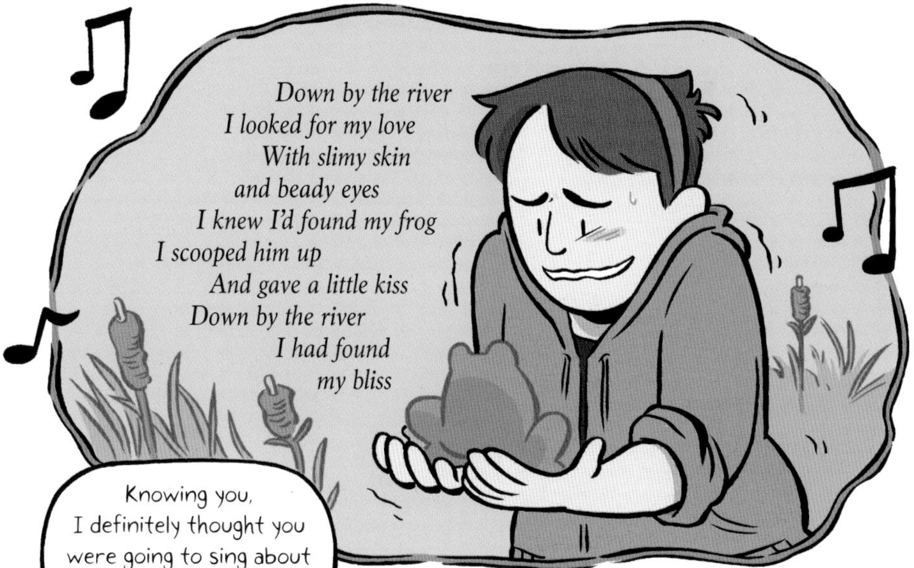
Down by the river
I looked for my love
With slimy skin
and beady eyes
I knew I'd found my frog
I scooped him up
And gave a little kiss
Down by the river
I had found
my bliss

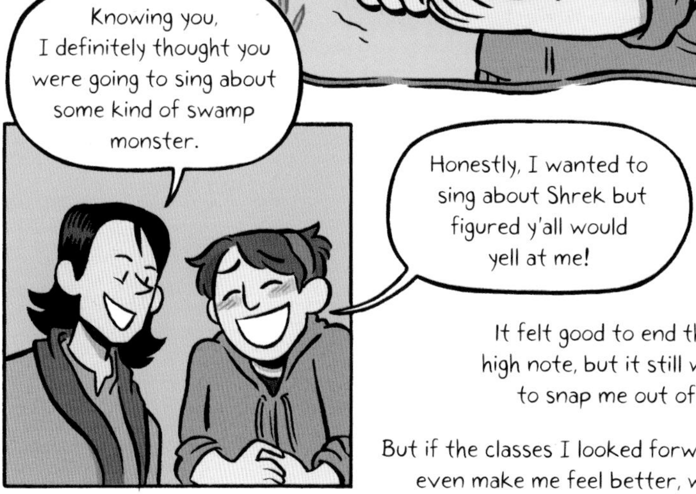
Knowing you, I definitely thought you were going to sing about some kind of swamp monster.
Honestly, I wanted to sing about Shrek but figured y'all would yell at me!

It felt good to end the class on a high note, but it still wasn't enough to snap me out of this funk.

But if the classes I looked forward to couldn't even make me feel better, what would? I had to try something new.

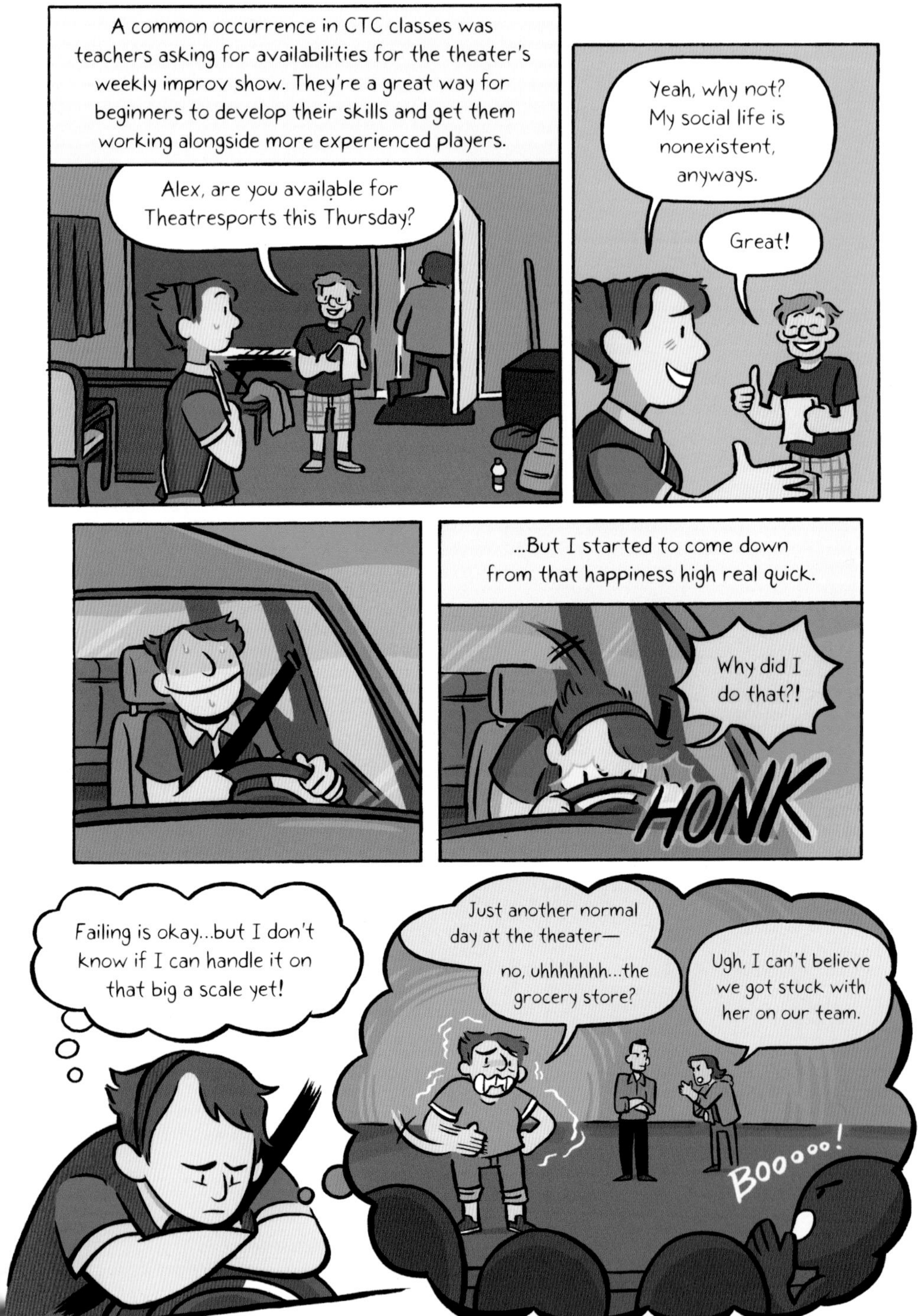
A common occurrence in CTC classes was teachers asking for availabilities for the theater's weekly improv show. They're a great way for beginners to develop their skills and get them working alongside more experienced players.
Alex, are you available for Theatresports this Thursday?
Yeah, why not? My social life is nonexistent, anyways.
Great!
...But I started to come down from that happiness high real quick.
Why did I do that?!
HONK
Failing is okay...but I don't know if I can handle it on that big a scale yet!
Just another normal day at the theater—
no, uhhhhhhh...the grocery store?
Ugh, I can't believe we got stuck with her on our team.
BOOooo!

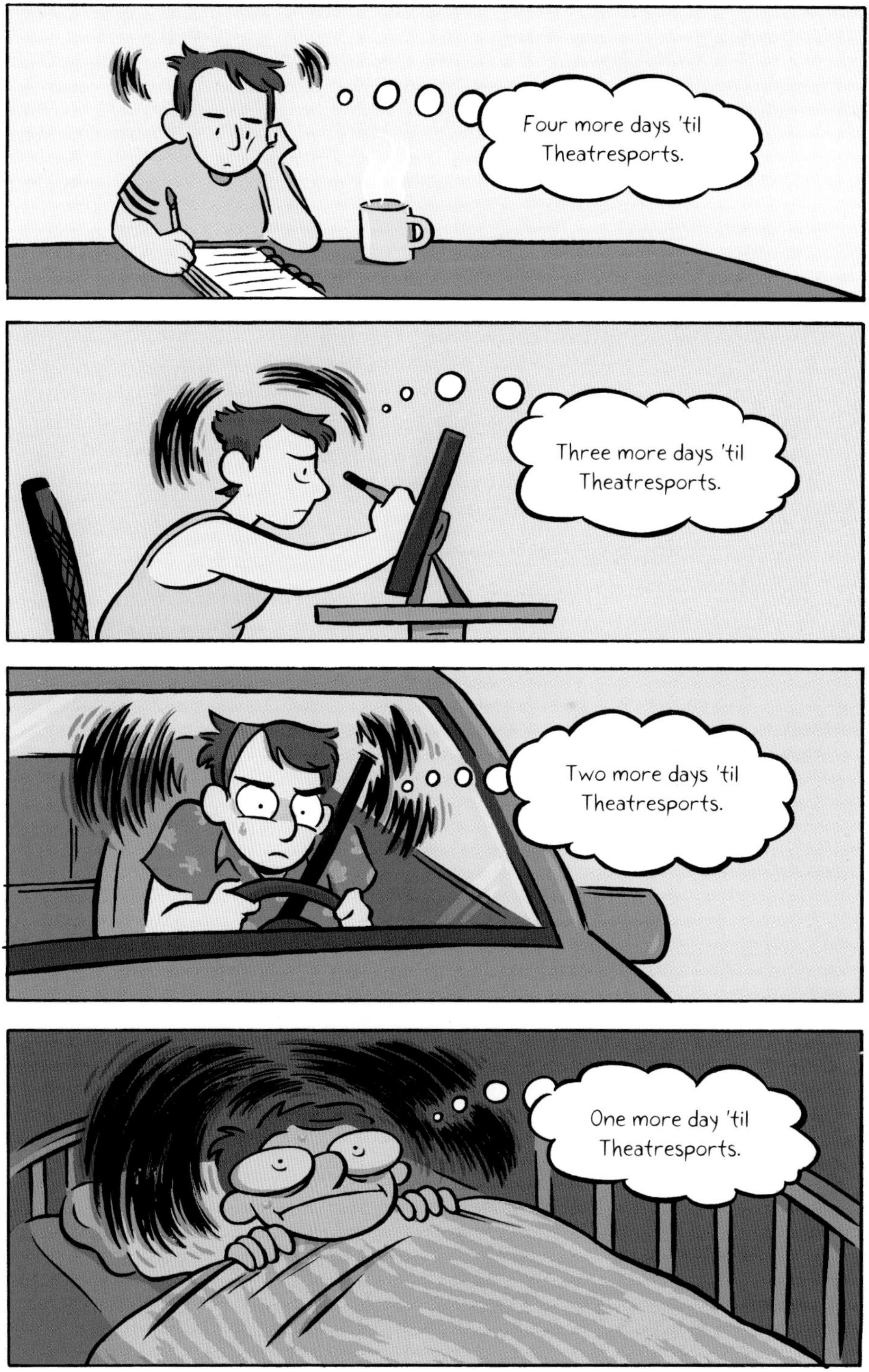
Four more days 'til Theatresports.
Three more days 'til Theatresports.
Two more days 'til Theatresports.
One more day 'til Theatresports.

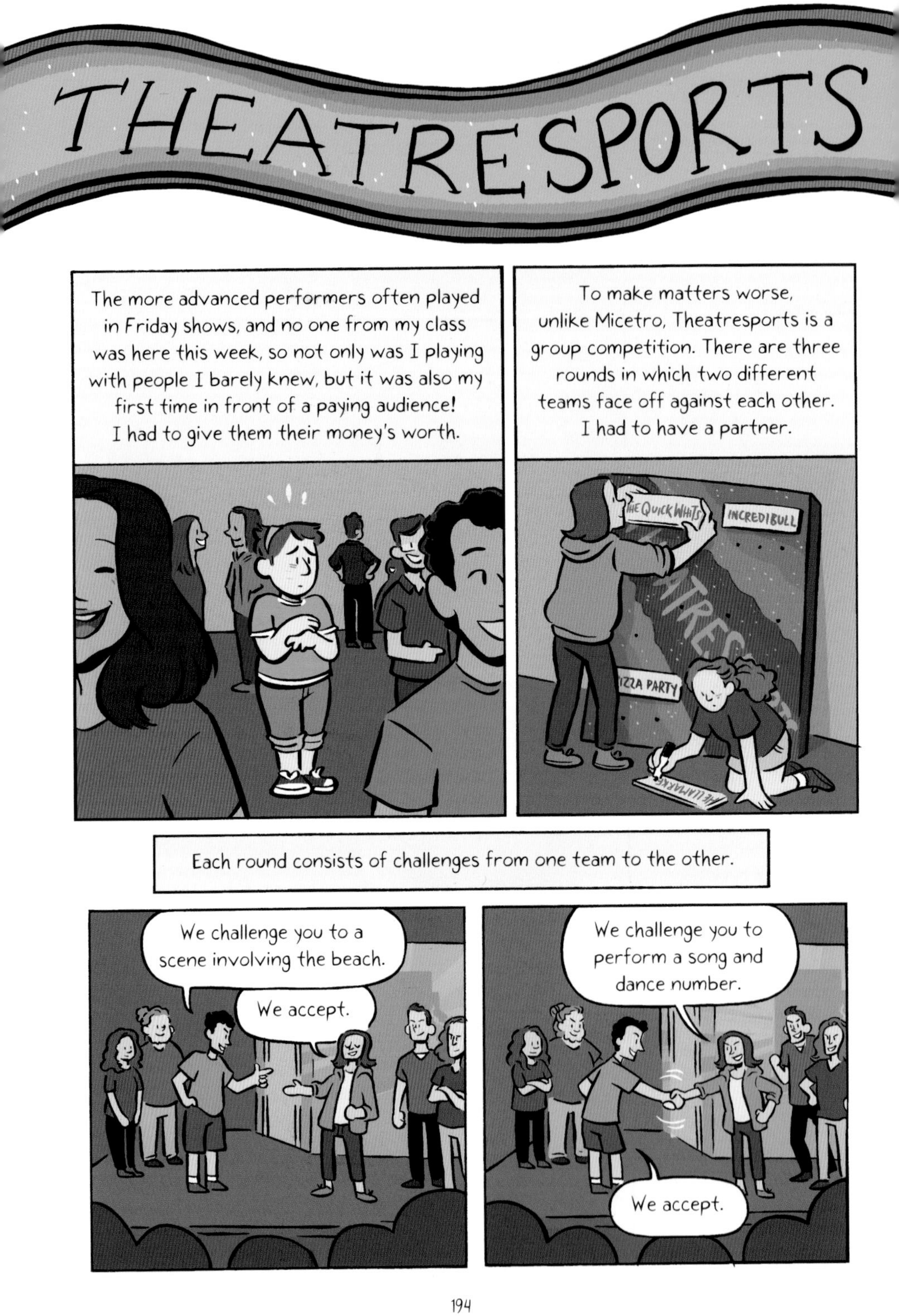
THEATRESPORTS
The more advanced performers often played in Friday shows, and no one from my class was here this week, so not only was I playing with people I barely knew, but it was also my first time in front of a paying audience! I had to give them their money's worth.
To make matters worse, unlike Micetro, Theatresports is a group competition. There are three rounds in which two different teams face off against each other. I had to have a partner.
THE QUICK WHITS
INCREDIBULL
IZZA PARTY
Each round consists of challenges from one team to the other.
We challenge you to a scene involving the beach.
We accept.
We challenge you to perform a song and dance number.
We accept.

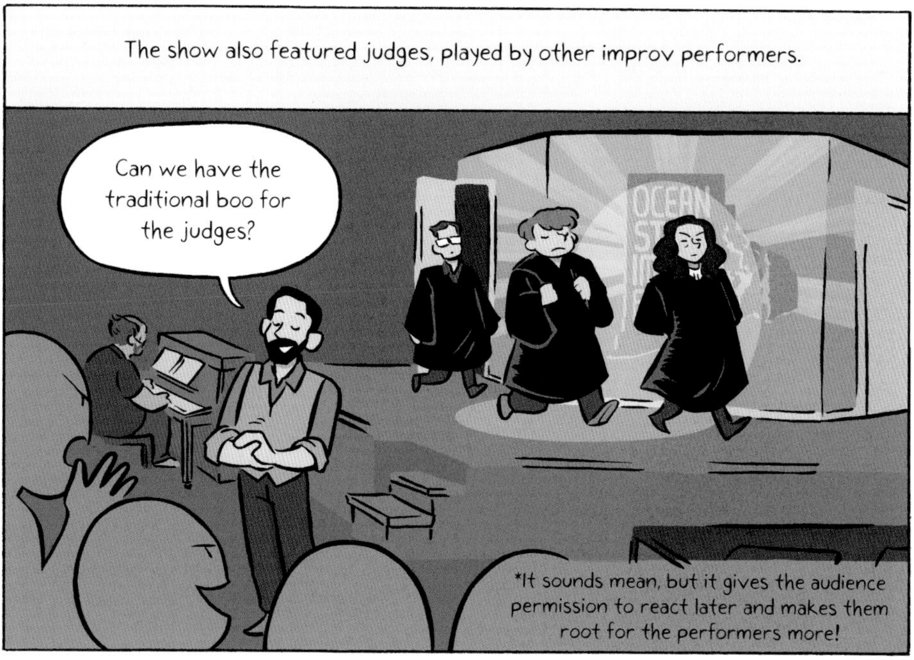
The show also featured judges, played by other improv performers.
Can we have the traditional boo for the judges?
OCEAN STATE
*It sounds mean, but it gives the audience permission to react later and makes them root for the performers more!

The judges rate each scene for points and honk their horn
if the team was boring or contradicted the challenge.

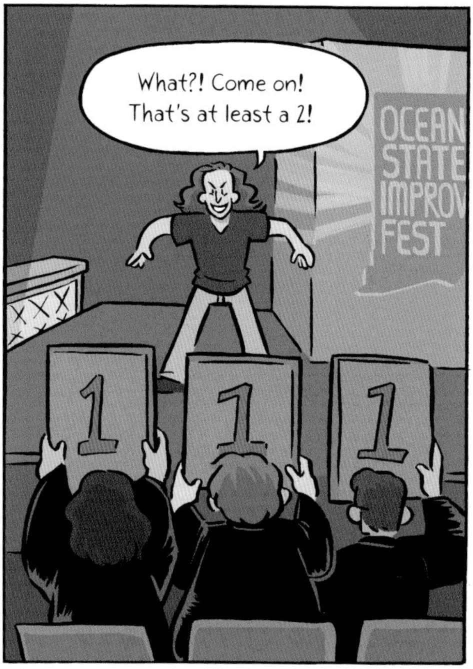
What?! Come on! That's at least a 2!
OCEAN STATE IMPROV FEST
1
1
1

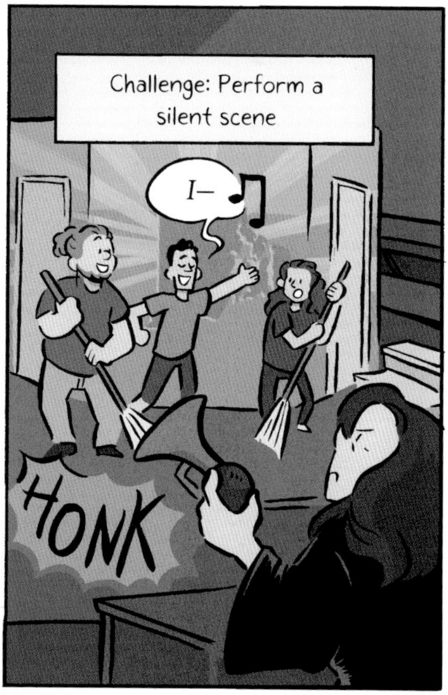
Challenge: Perform a silent scene
I–
HONK

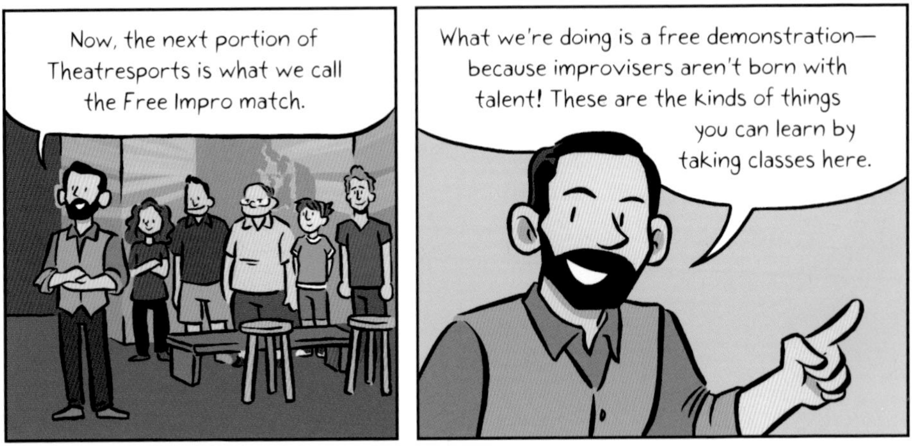
Now, the next portion of Theatresports is what we call the Free Impro match.
What we're doing is a free demonstration—because improvisers aren't born with talent! These are the kinds of things you can learn by taking classes here.

Our example for the night was a game called **Taxi Cab.**

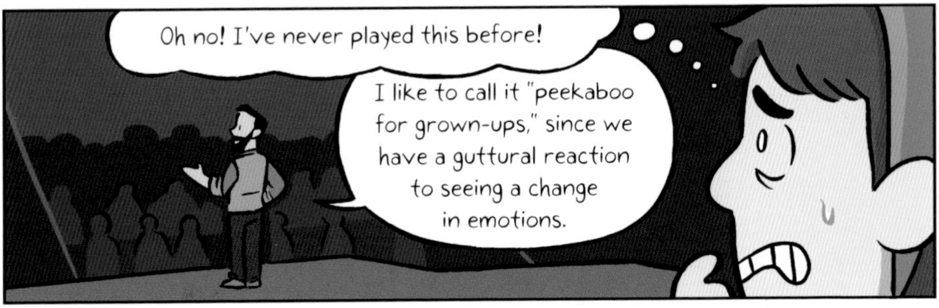
Oh no! I've never played this before!
I like to call it "peekaboo for grown-ups," since we have a guttural reaction to seeing a change in emotions.

With chairs set up to look like car seats, one player acts as the taxi driver. After establishing their personality, they pick up a customer with a wildly different personality, and the driver and fellow passengers adopt those traits.

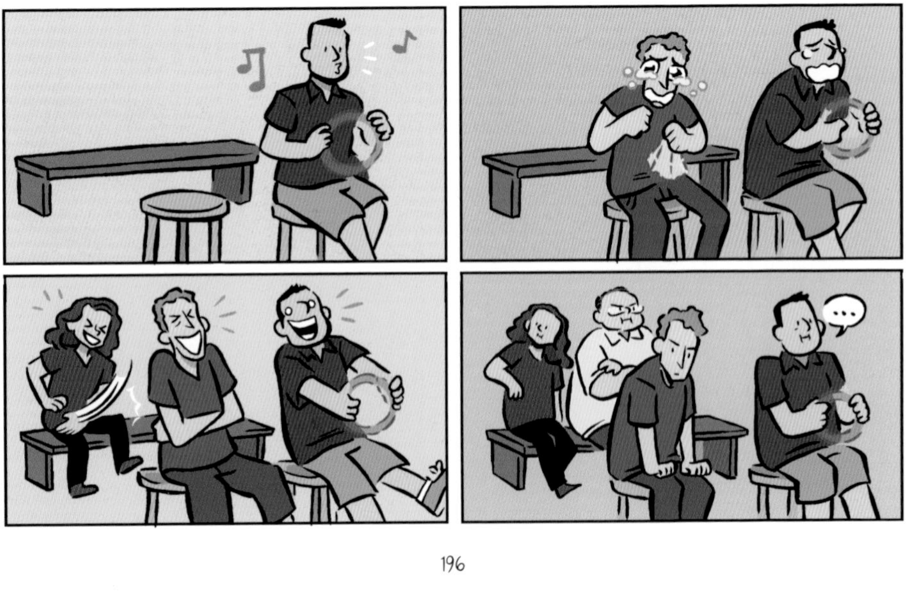
...

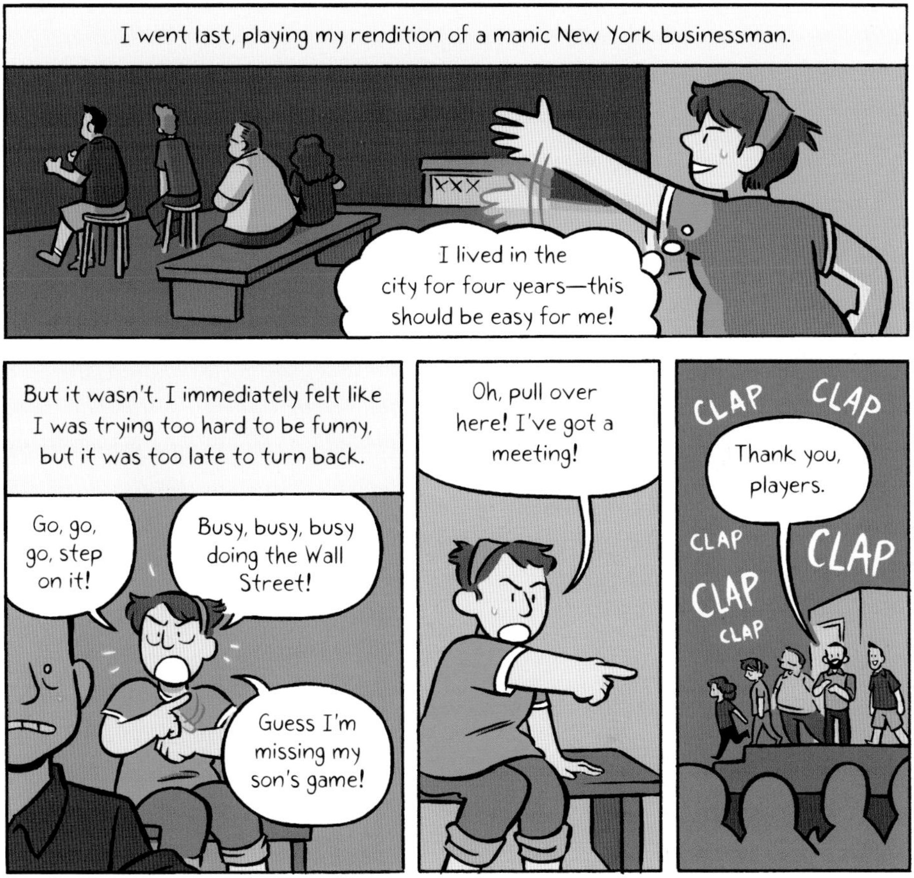
I went last, playing my rendition of a manic New York businessman.
I lived in the city for four years—this should be easy for me!
But it wasn't. I immediately felt like I was trying too hard to be funny, but it was too late to turn back.
Go, go, go, step on it!
Busy, busy, busy doing the Wall Street!
Guess I'm missing my son's game!
Oh, pull over here! I've got a meeting!
CLAP CLAP
Thank you, players.
CLAP CLAP CLAP CLAP

Once everyone has a chance to mimic each other's emotions, the driver drops off passengers in reverse order, reverting back to the previous player's personality until the driver is alone again.

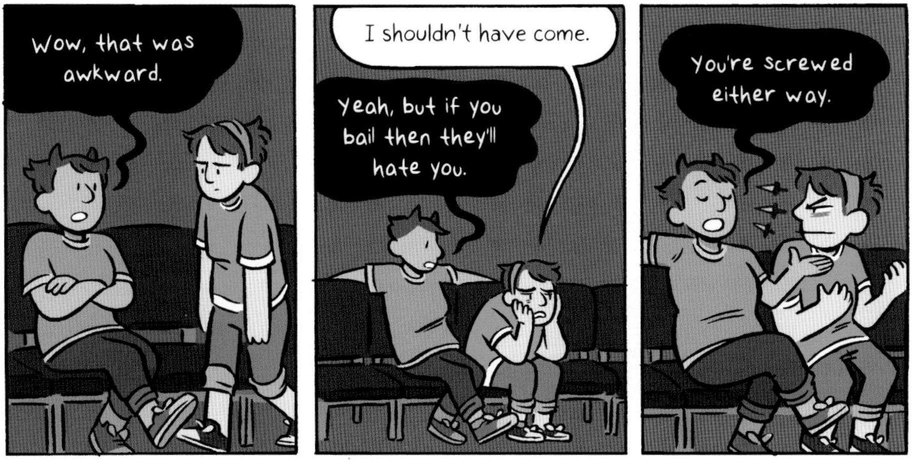
Wow, that was awkward.
I shouldn't have come.
Yeah, but if you bail then they'll hate you.
You're screwed either way.

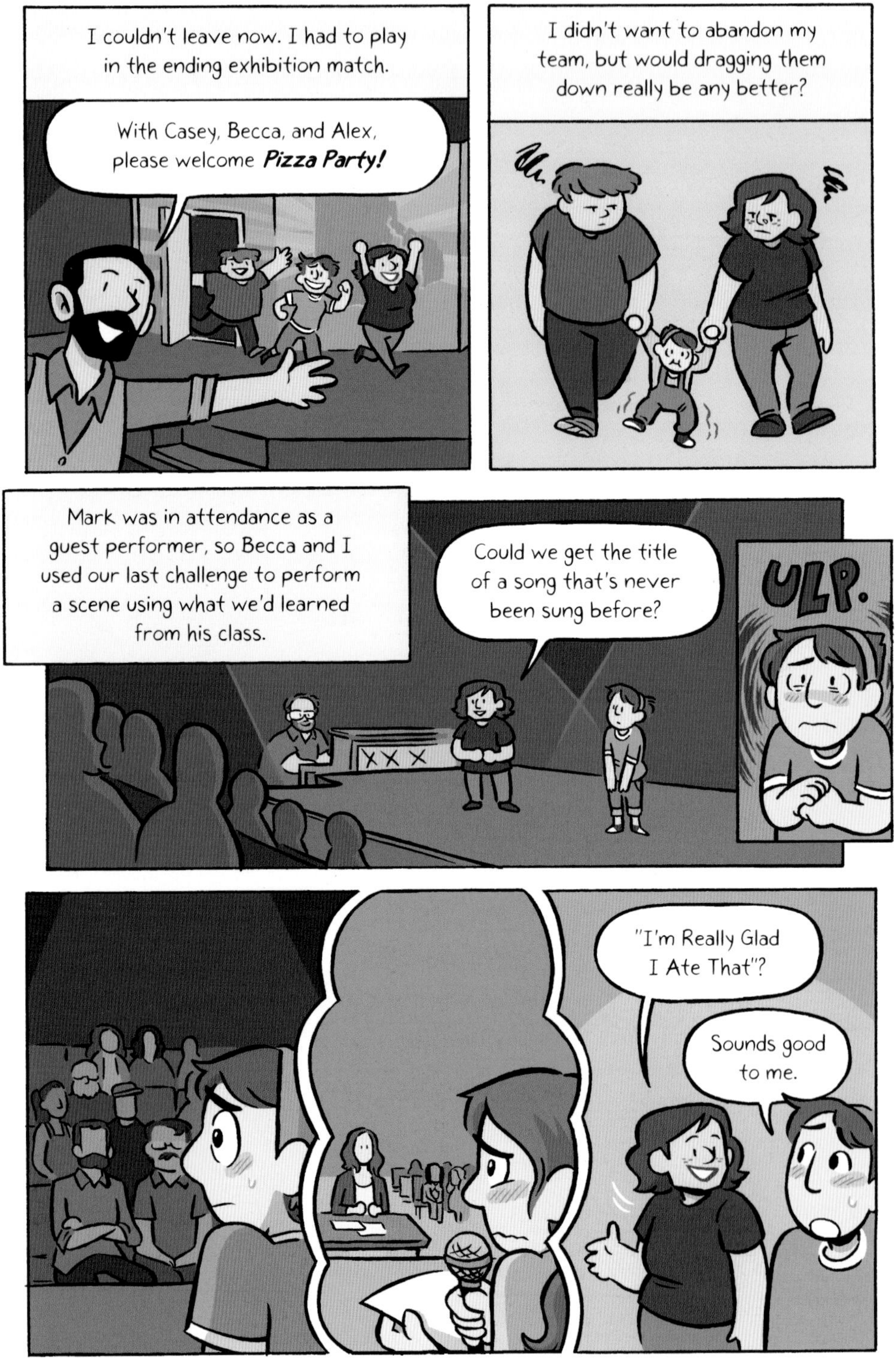

I couldn't leave now. I had to play in the ending exhibition match.
With Casey, Becca, and Alex, please welcome ***Pizza Party!***
I didn't want to abandon my team, but would dragging them down really be any better?
Mark was in attendance as a guest performer, so Becca and I used our last challenge to perform a scene using what we'd learned from his class.
Could we get the title of a song that's never been sung before?
ULP.
"I'm Really Glad I Ate That"?
Sounds good to me.

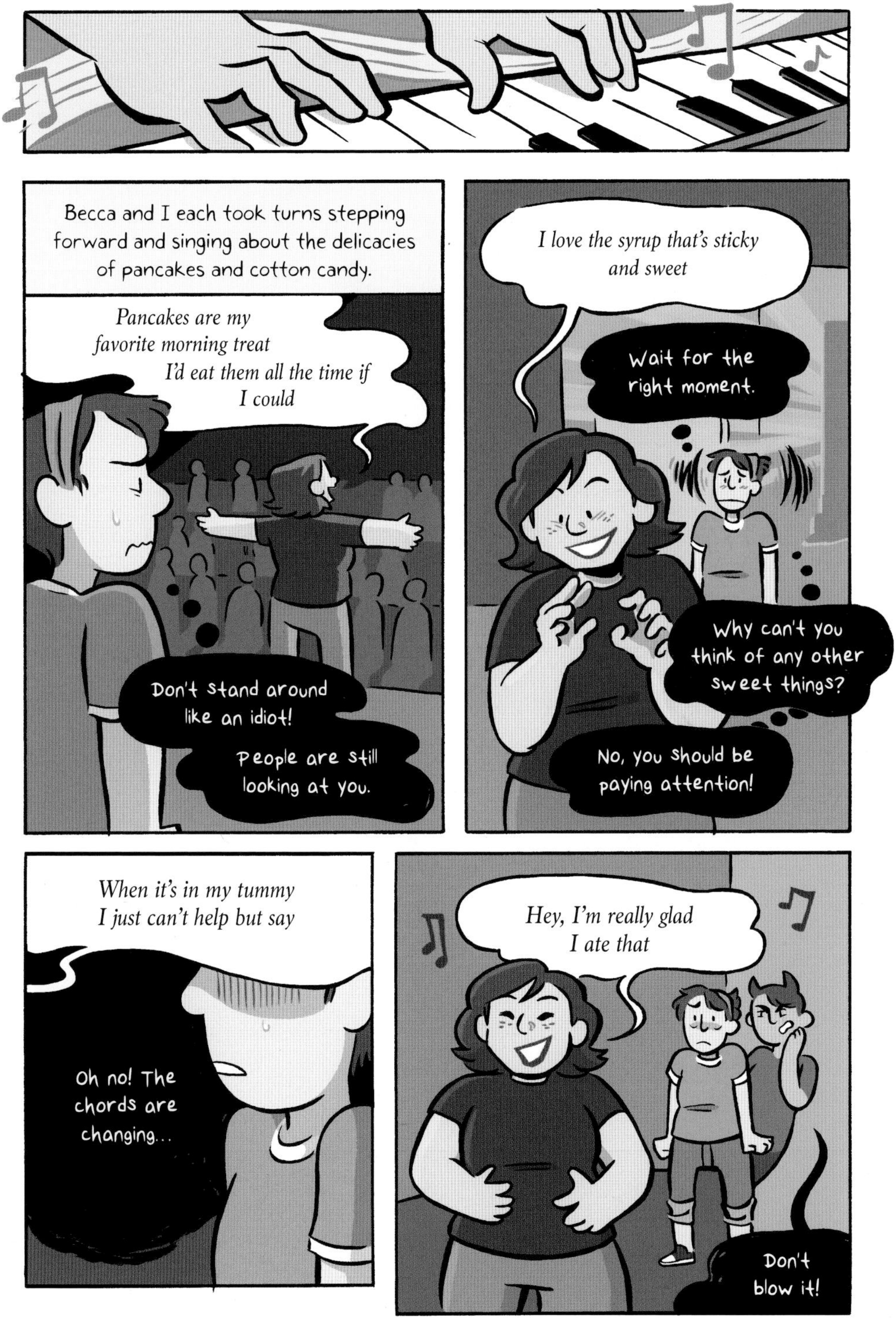
Becca and I each took turns stepping forward and singing about the delicacies of pancakes and cotton candy.
Pancakes are my favorite morning treat
I'd eat them all the time if I could
Don't stand around like an idiot!
People are still looking at you.
I love the syrup that's sticky and sweet
Wait for the right moment.
Why can't you think of any other sweet things?
No, you should be paying attention!
When it's in my tummy I just can't help but say
Oh no! The chords are changing...
Hey, I'm really glad I ate that
Don't blow it!

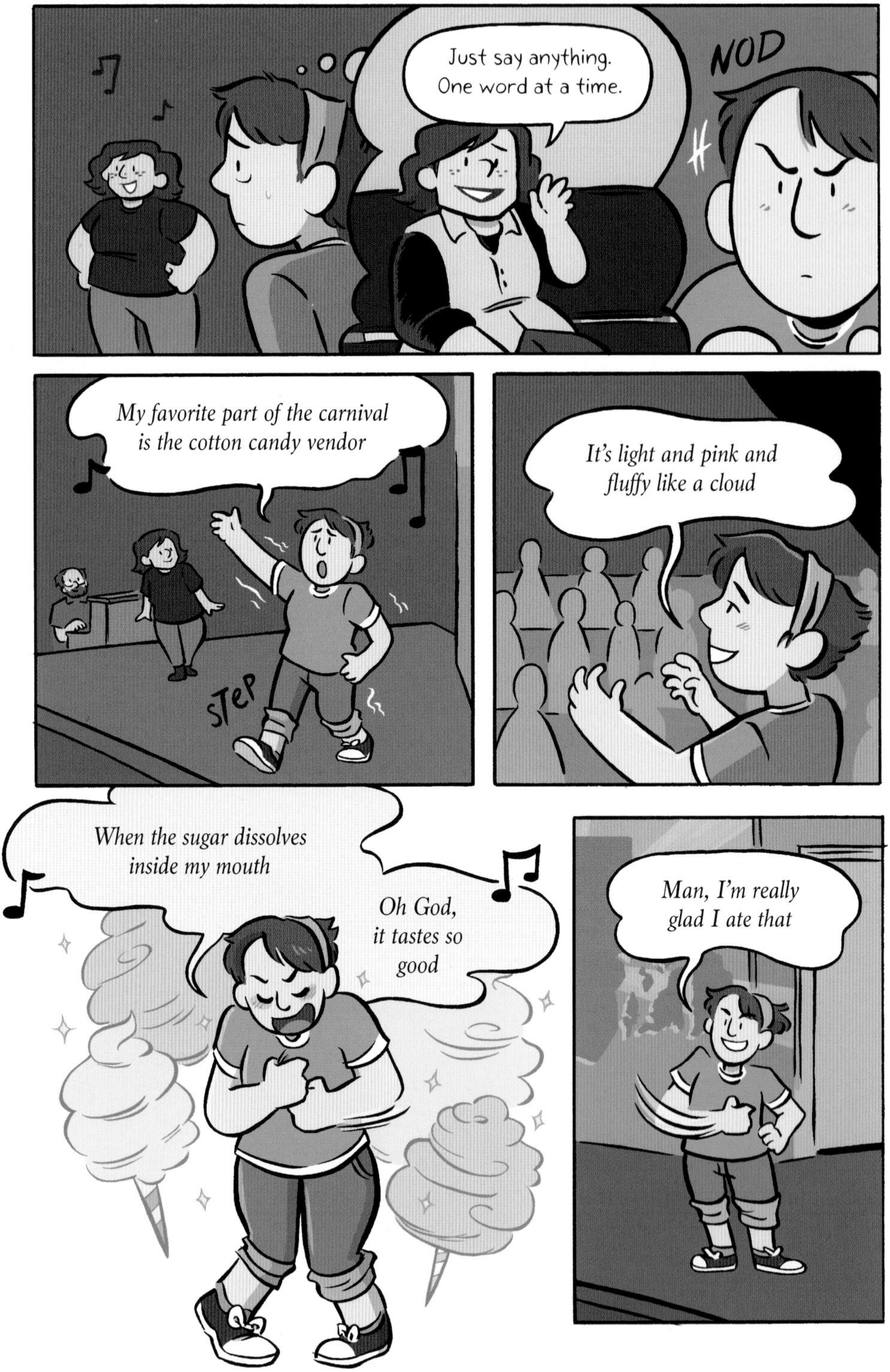
Just say anything. One word at a time.
NOD
My favorite part of the carnival is the cotton candy vendor
STEP
It's light and pink and fluffy like a cloud
When the sugar dissolves inside my mouth
Oh God, it tastes so good
Man, I'm really glad I ate that

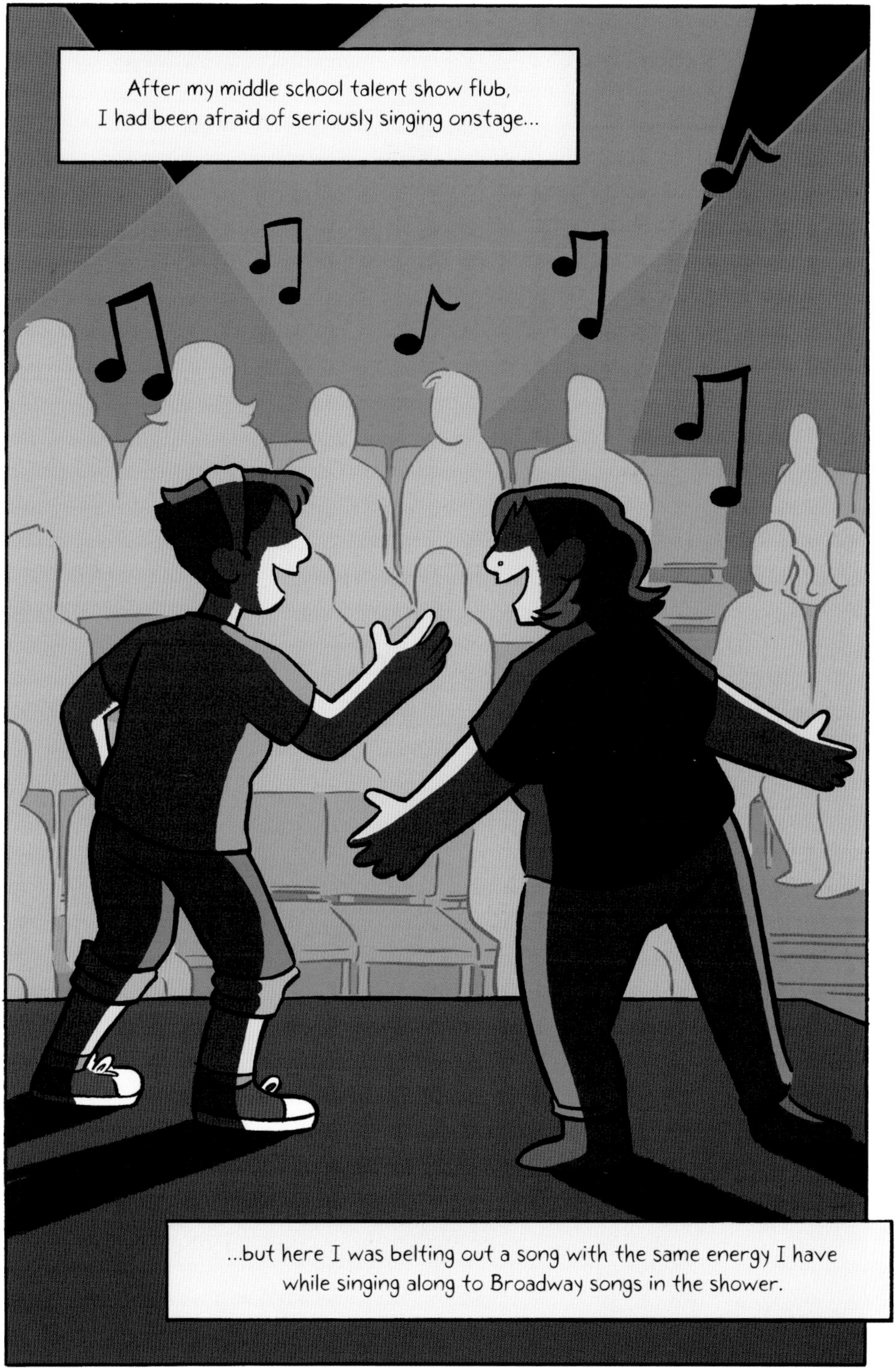
After my middle school talent show flub,
I had been afraid of seriously singing onstage...
...but here I was belting out a song with the same energy I have
while singing along to Broadway songs in the shower.

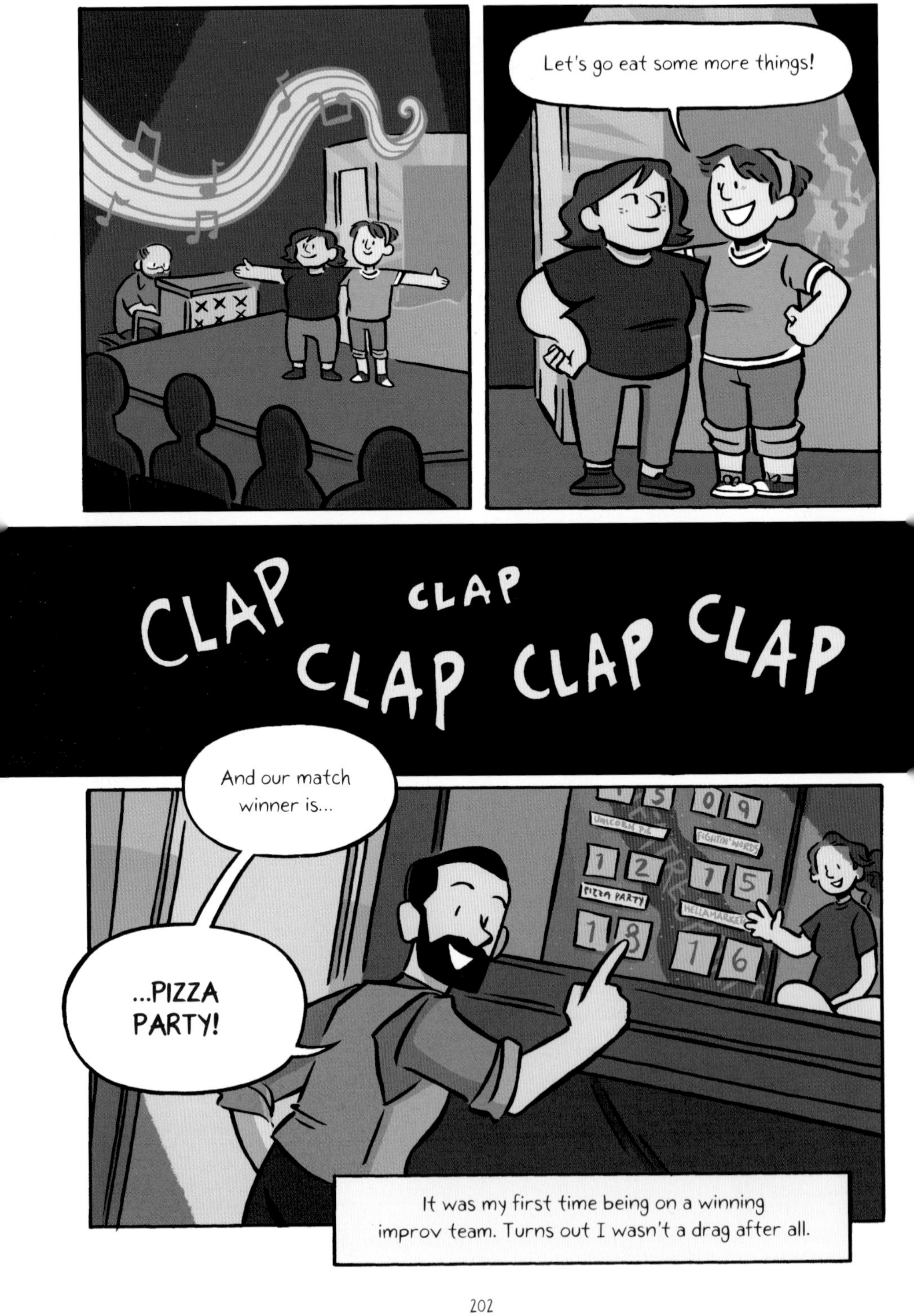
Let's go eat some more things!
CLAP
CLAP
CLAP
CLAP
CLAP
And our match winner is...
UNICORN PIE
FIGHTIN' WORDS
PIZZA PARTY
...PIZZA PARTY!
It was my first time being on a winning improv team. Turns out I wasn't a drag after all.

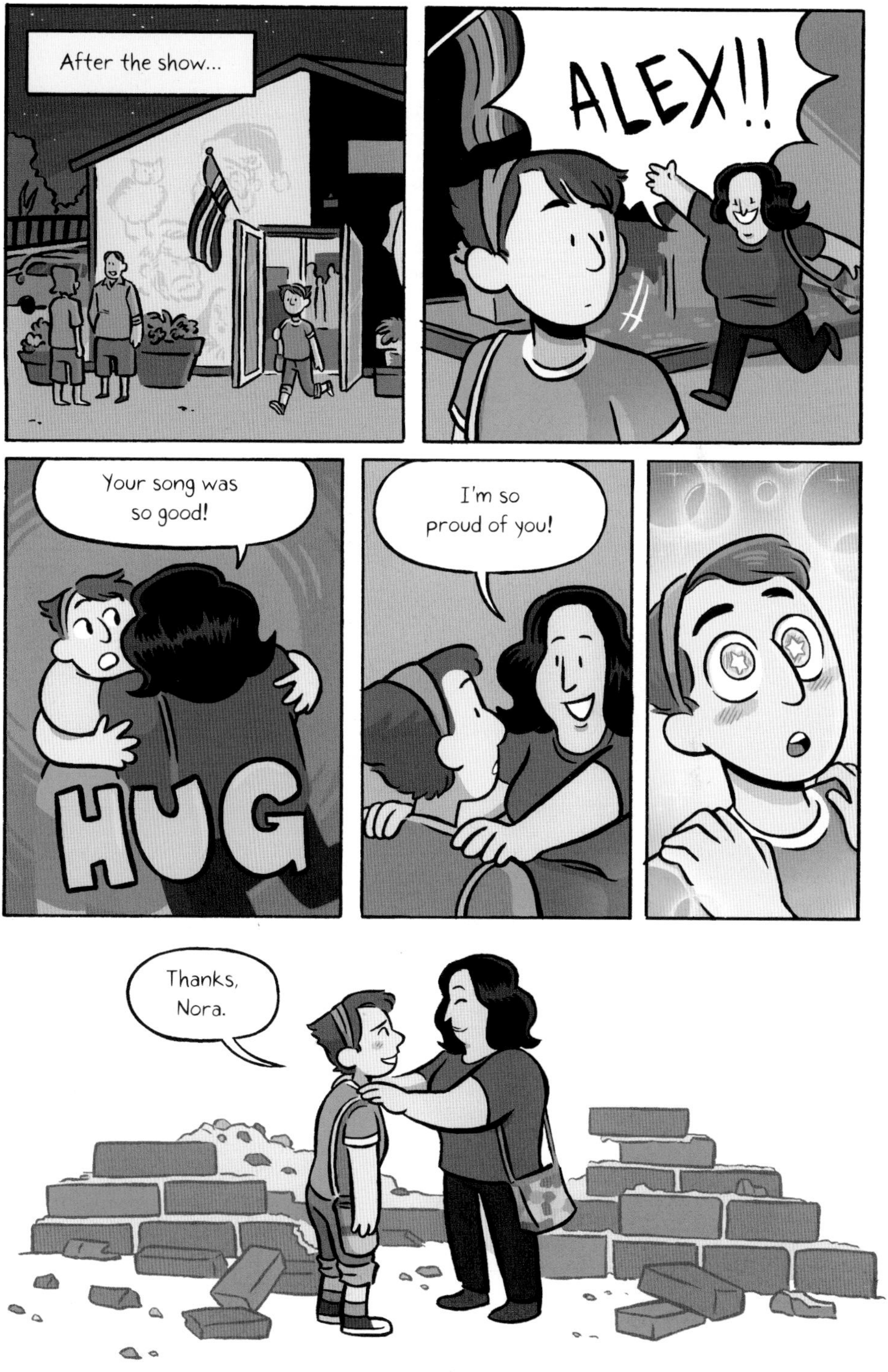
After the show...
ALEX!!
Your song was so good!
HUG
I'm so proud of you!
Thanks, Nora.

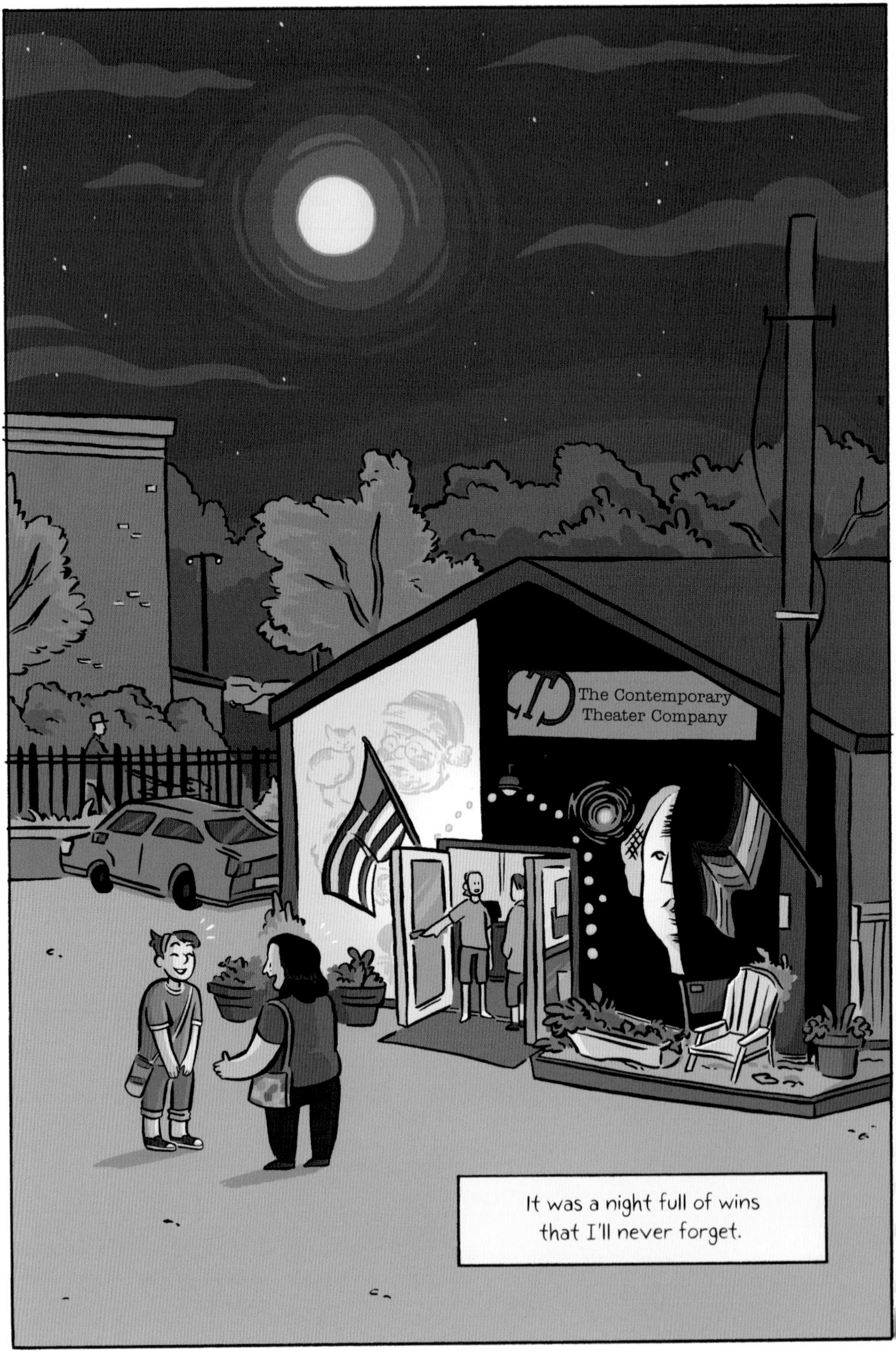
The Contemporary Theater Company
It was a night full of wins that I'll never forget.

PART 5

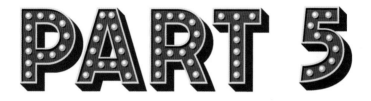

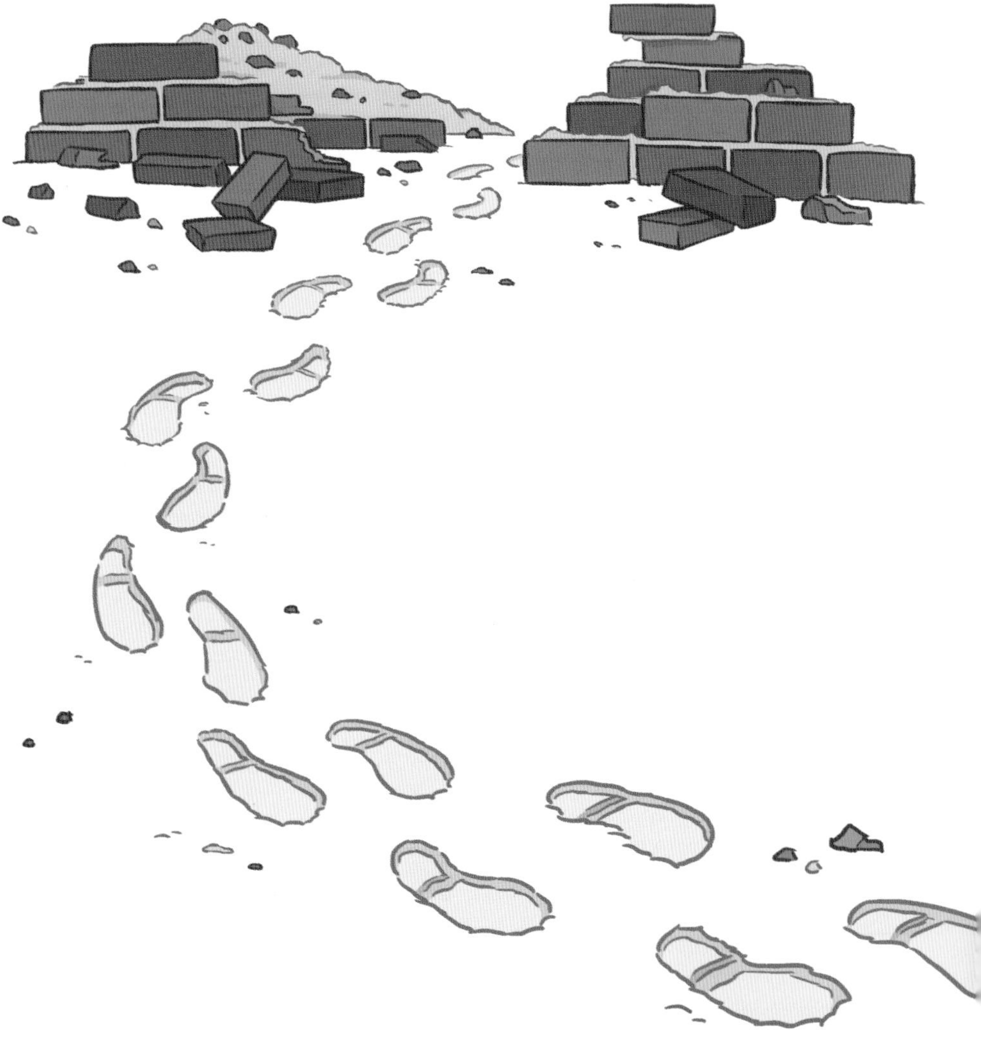

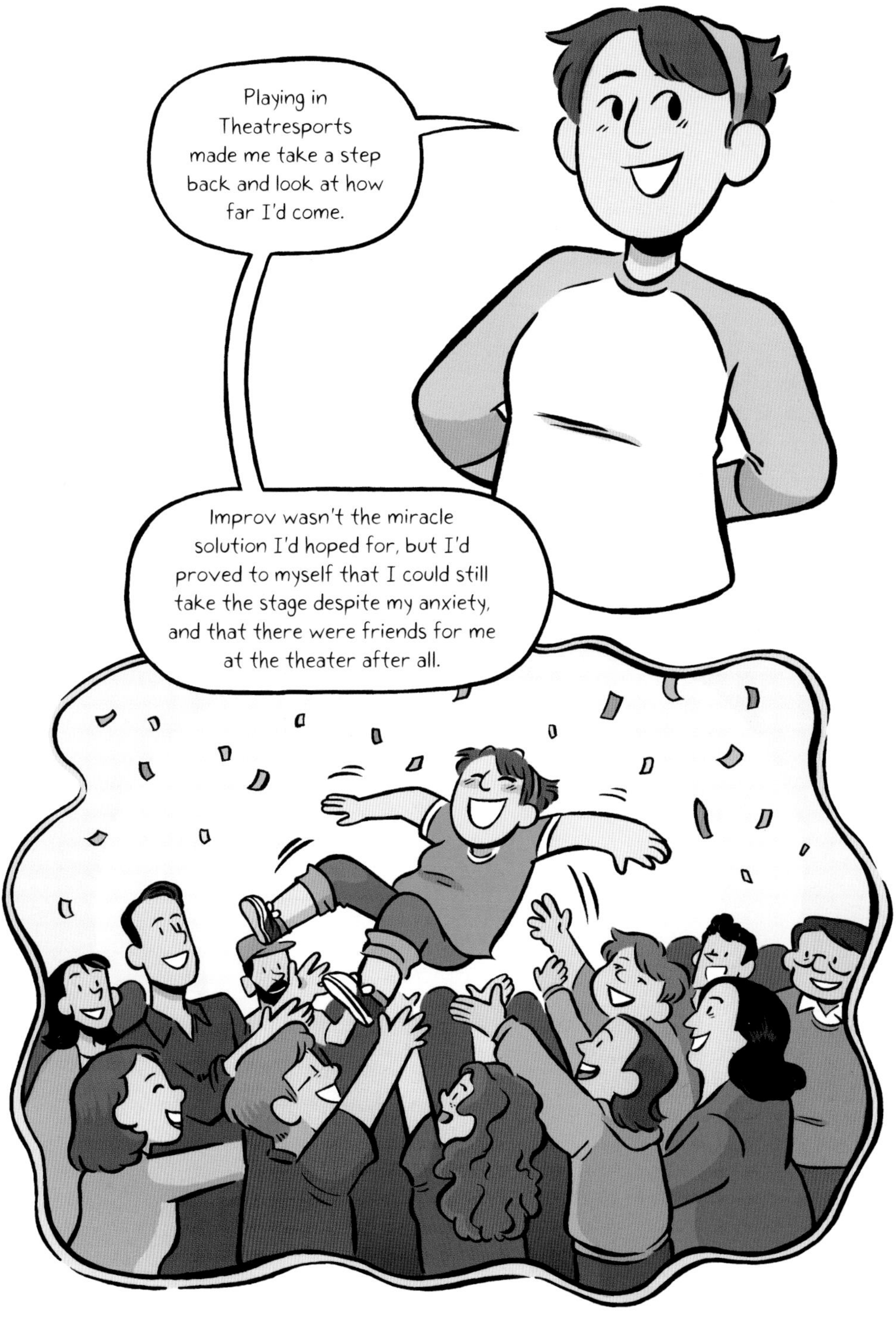
Playing in Theatresports made me take a step back and look at how far I'd come.
Improv wasn't the miracle solution I'd hoped for, but I'd proved to myself that I could still take the stage despite my anxiety, and that there were friends for me at the theater after all.

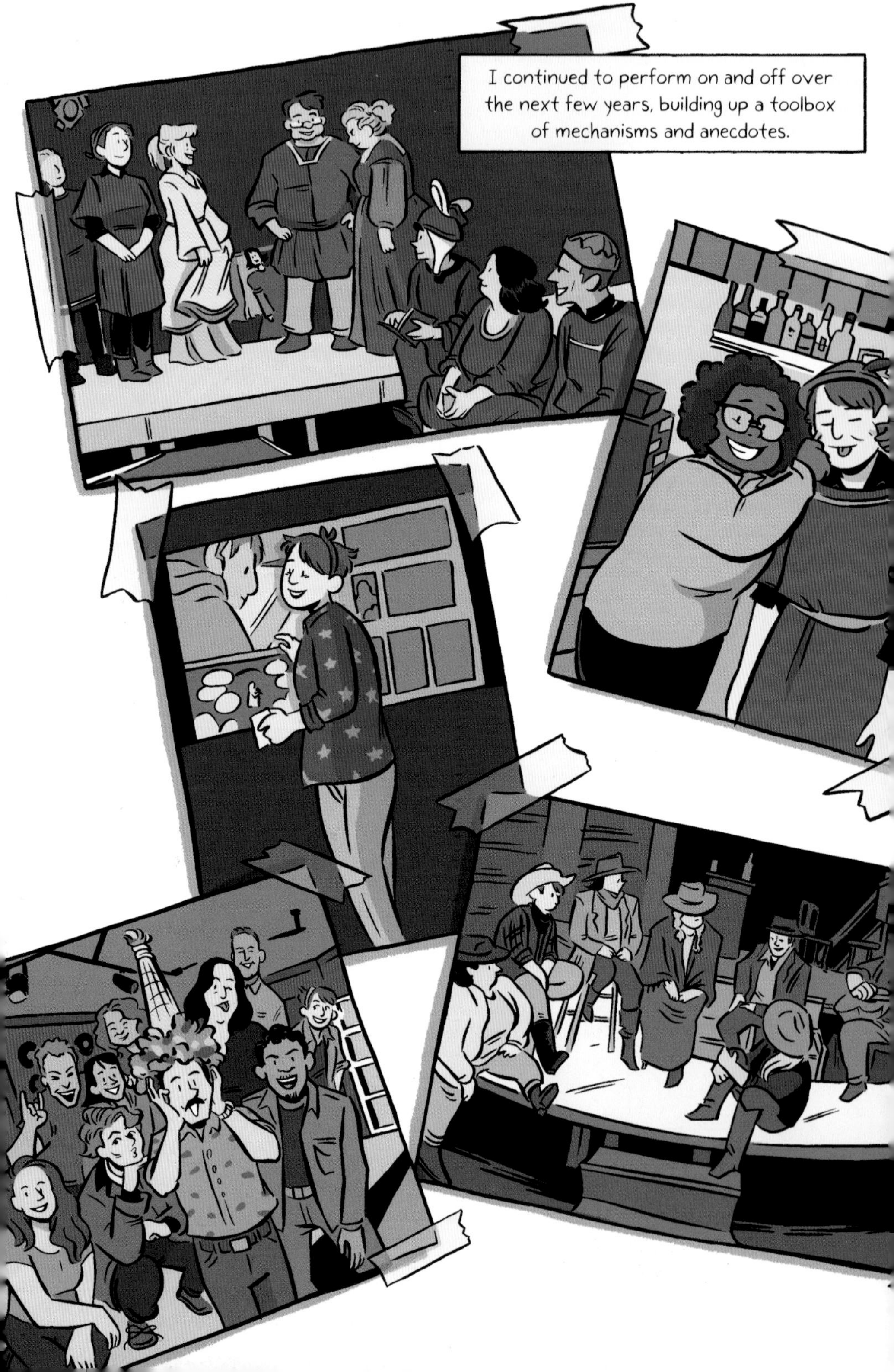
I continued to perform on and off over the next few years, building up a toolbox of mechanisms and anecdotes.

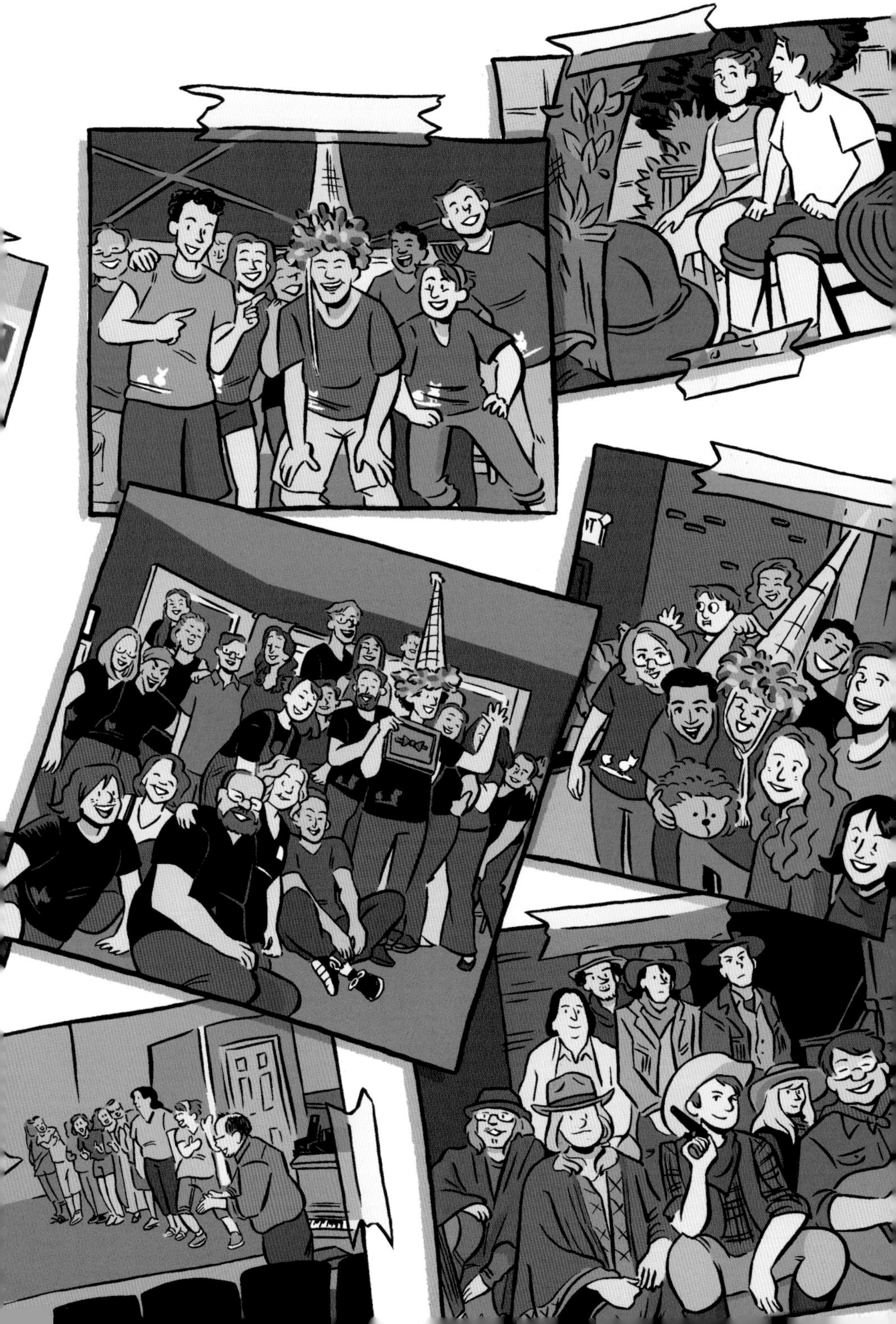

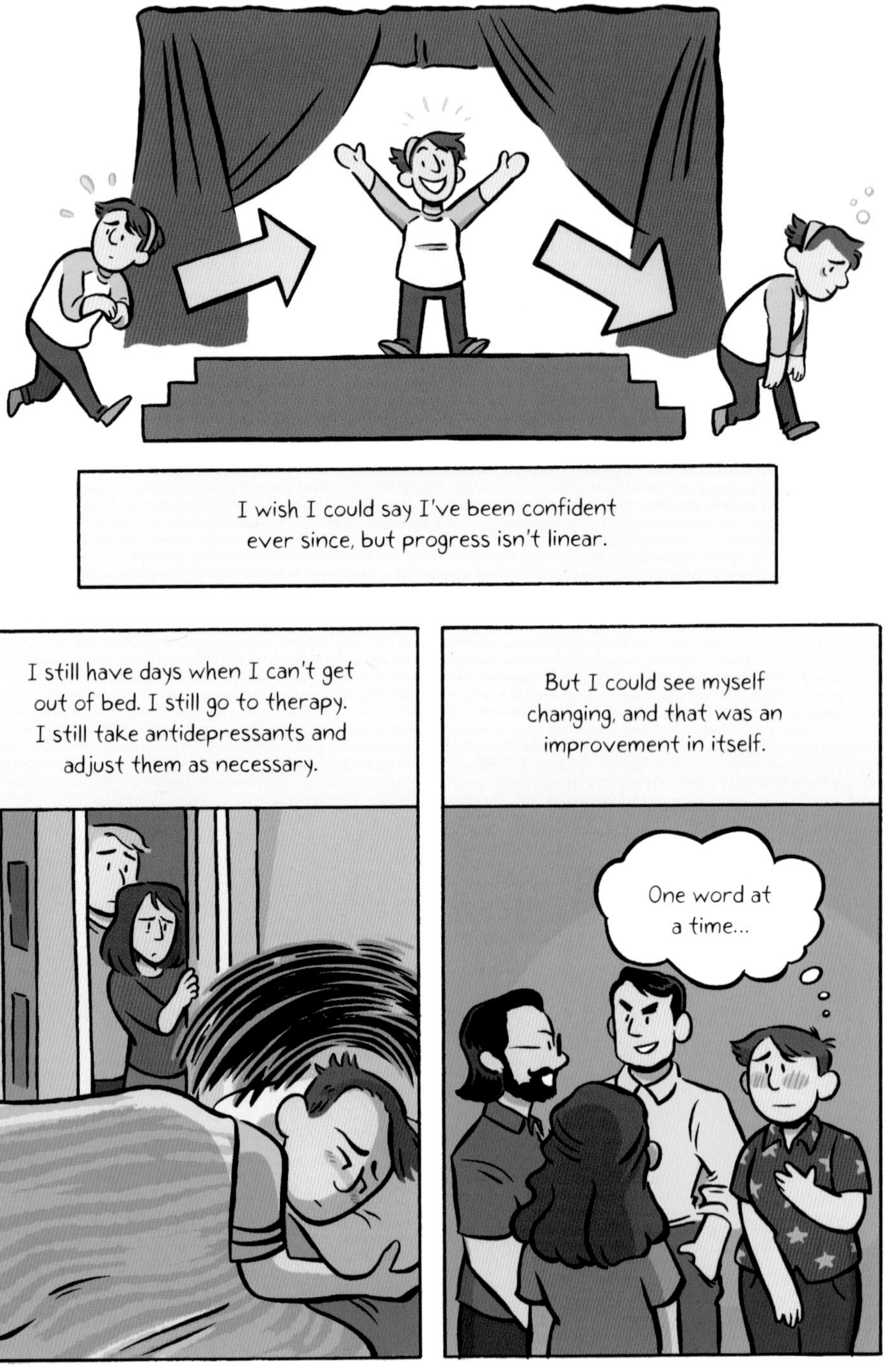
I wish I could say I've been confident ever since, but progress isn't linear.
I still have days when I can't get out of bed. I still go to therapy. I still take antidepressants and adjust them as necessary.
But I could see myself changing, and that was an improvement in itself.
One word at a time...

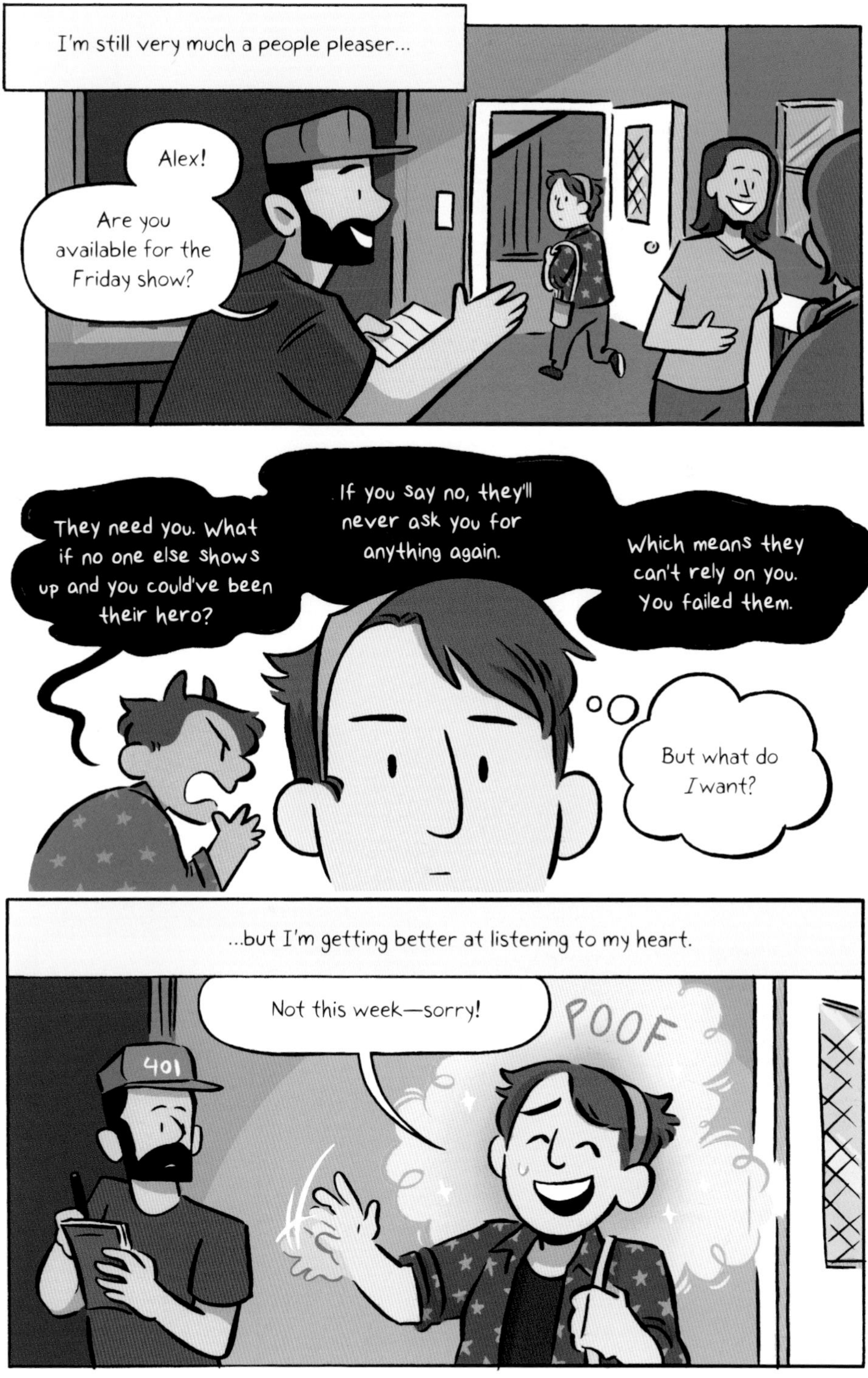
I'm still very much a people pleaser...
Alex!
Are you available for the Friday show?
They need you. What if no one else shows up and you could've been their hero?
If you say no, they'll never ask you for anything again.
Which means they can't rely on you. You failed them.
But what do *I* want?
...but I'm getting better at listening to my heart.
Not this week—sorry!
POOF
401

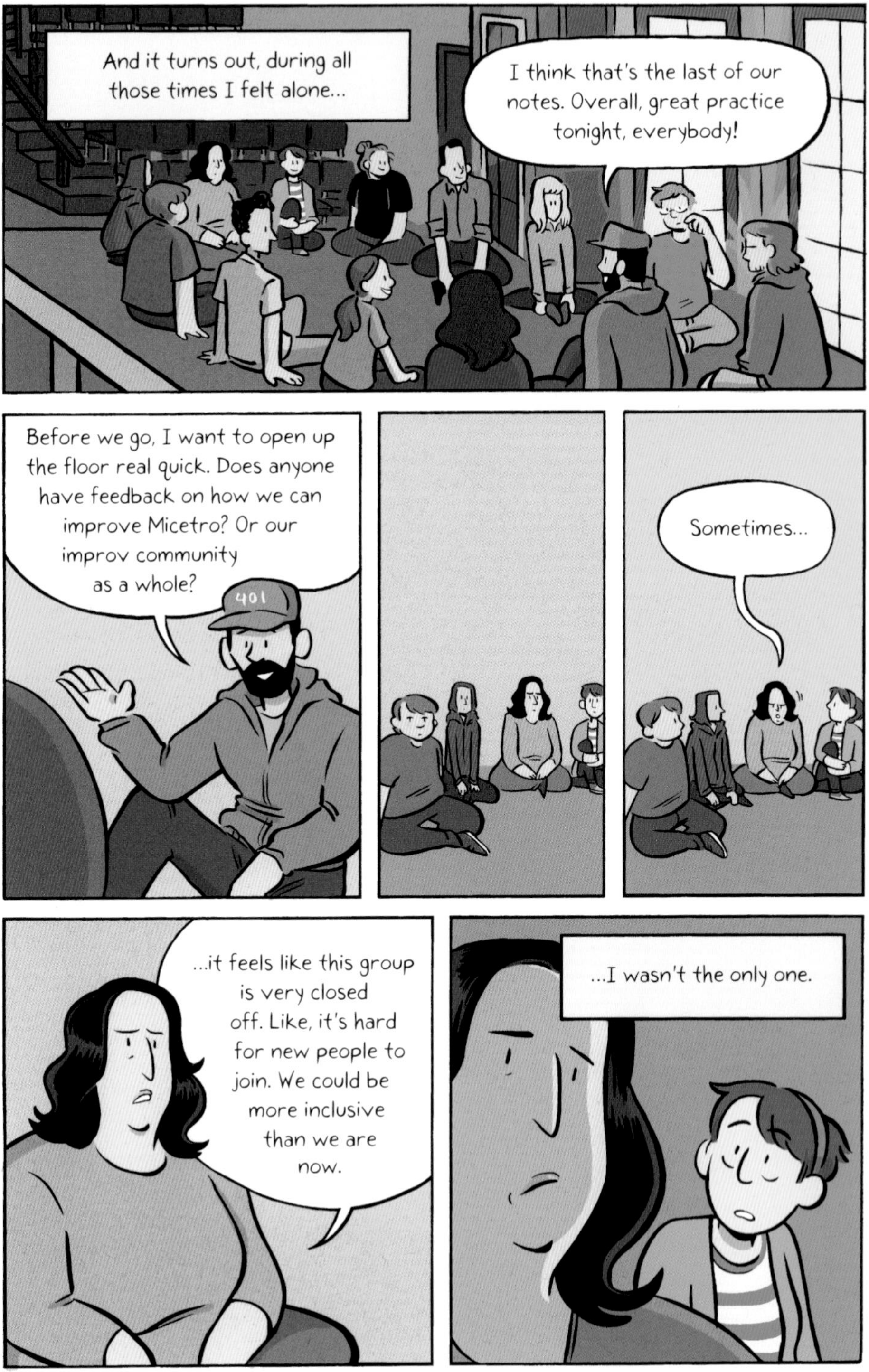
And it turns out, during all those times I felt alone...
I think that's the last of our notes. Overall, great practice tonight, everybody!
Before we go, I want to open up the floor real quick. Does anyone have feedback on how we can improve Micetro? Or our improv community as a whole?
401
Sometimes...
...it feels like this group is very closed off. Like, it's hard for new people to join. We could be more inclusive than we are now.
...I wasn't the only one.

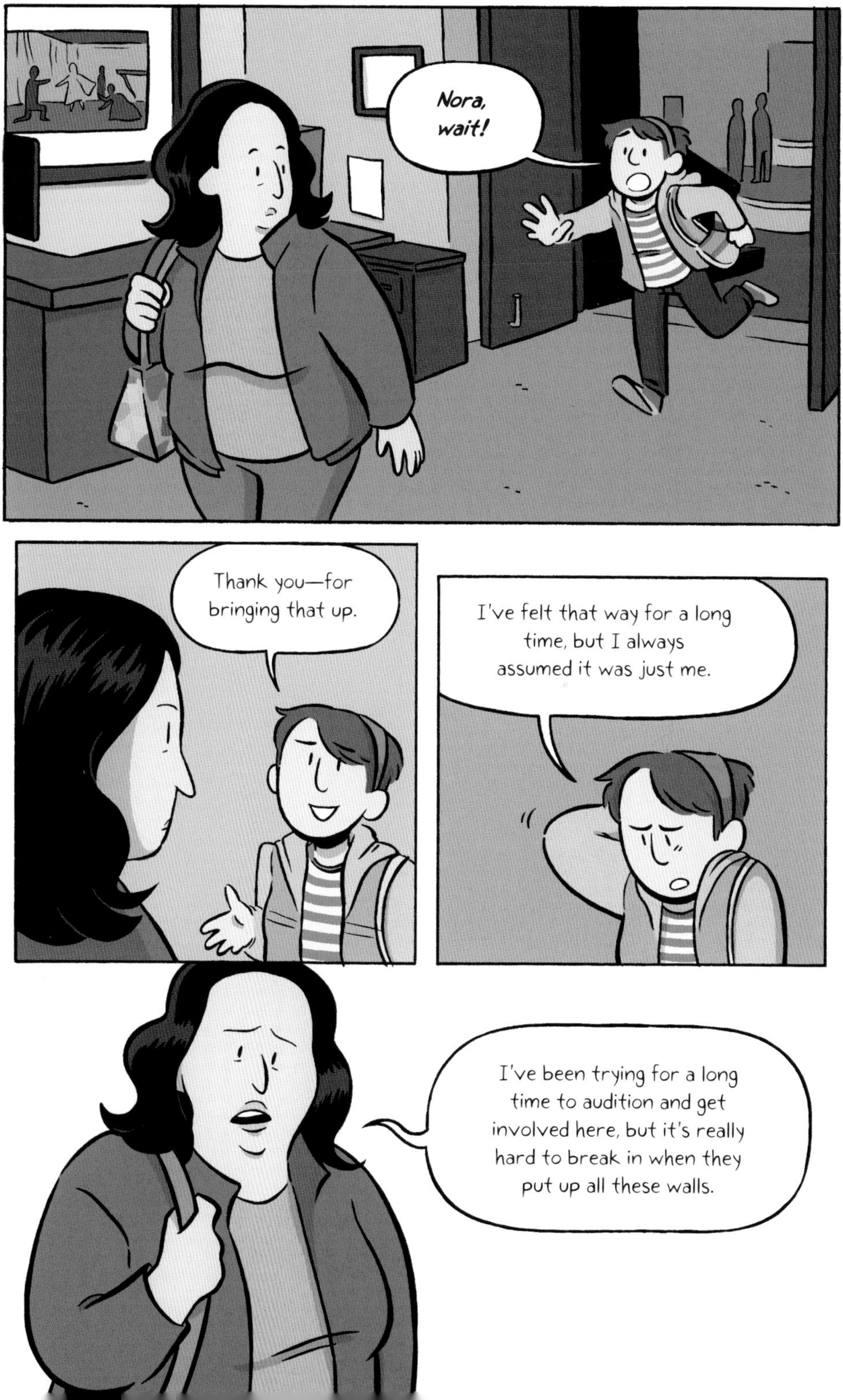

Nora, wait!
Thank you—for bringing that up.
I've felt that way for a long time, but I always assumed it was just me.
I've been trying for a long time to audition and get involved here, but it's really hard to break in when they put up all these walls.

Fitting in with people my age was never my strong suit.

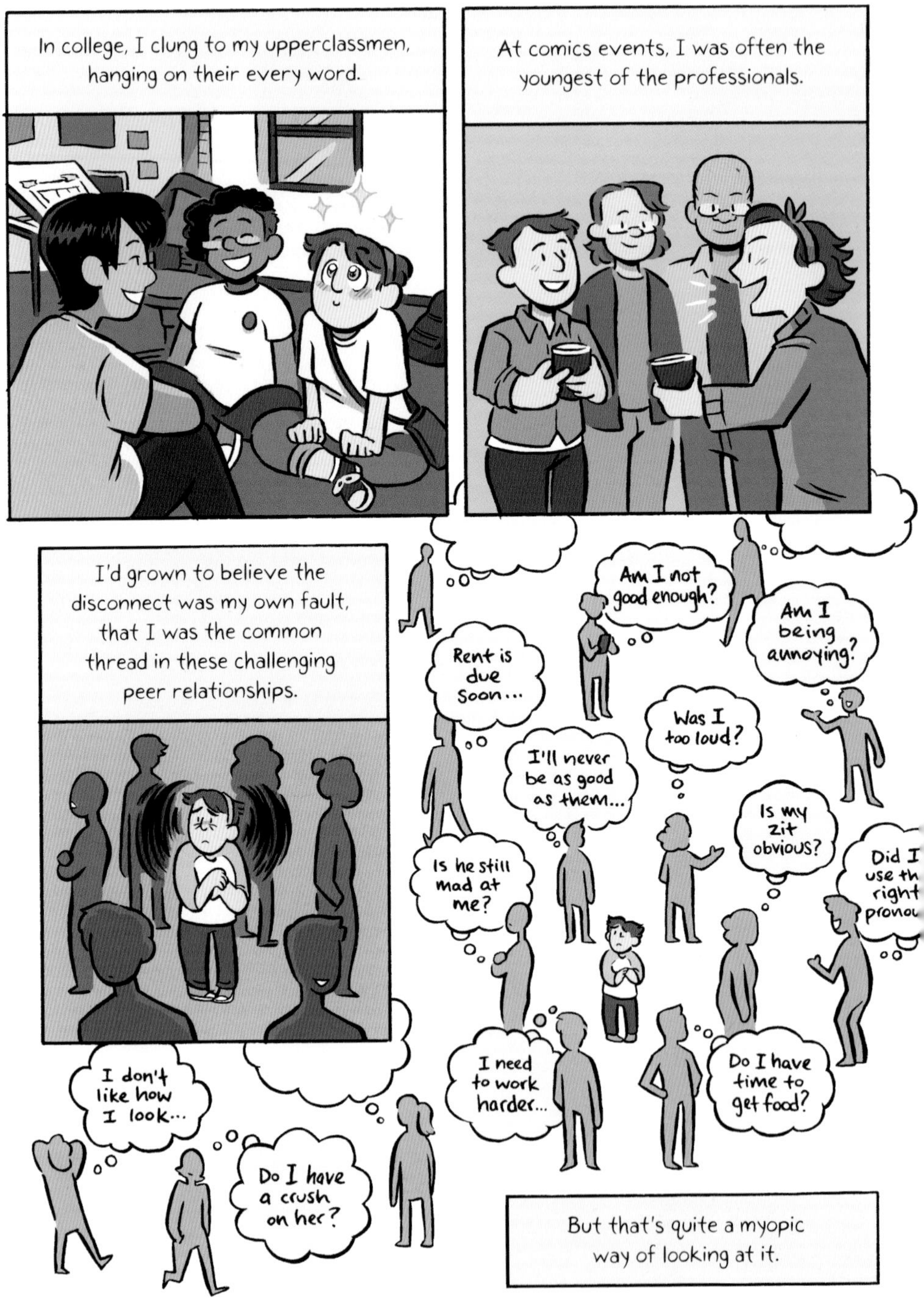
In college, I clung to my upperclassmen, hanging on their every word.
At comics events, I was often the youngest of the professionals.
I'd grown to believe the disconnect was my own fault, that I was the common thread in these challenging peer relationships.
Am I not good enough?
Am I being annoying?
Rent is due soon...
Was I too loud?
I'll never be as good as them...
Is my zit obvious?
Did I use th right pronou
Is he still mad at me?
I need to work harder...
Do I have time to get food?
I don't like how I look...
Do I have a crush on her?
But that's quite a myopic way of looking at it.

It's hard to be on the outside looking in.

But I understood the veterans' side, too.

At college events, I would retreat back to my friends for the rest of the night, exhausted from fighting the built-up anxiety all week.

I didn't mean to be cliquey, but it was easier to fall back on the people I knew best.

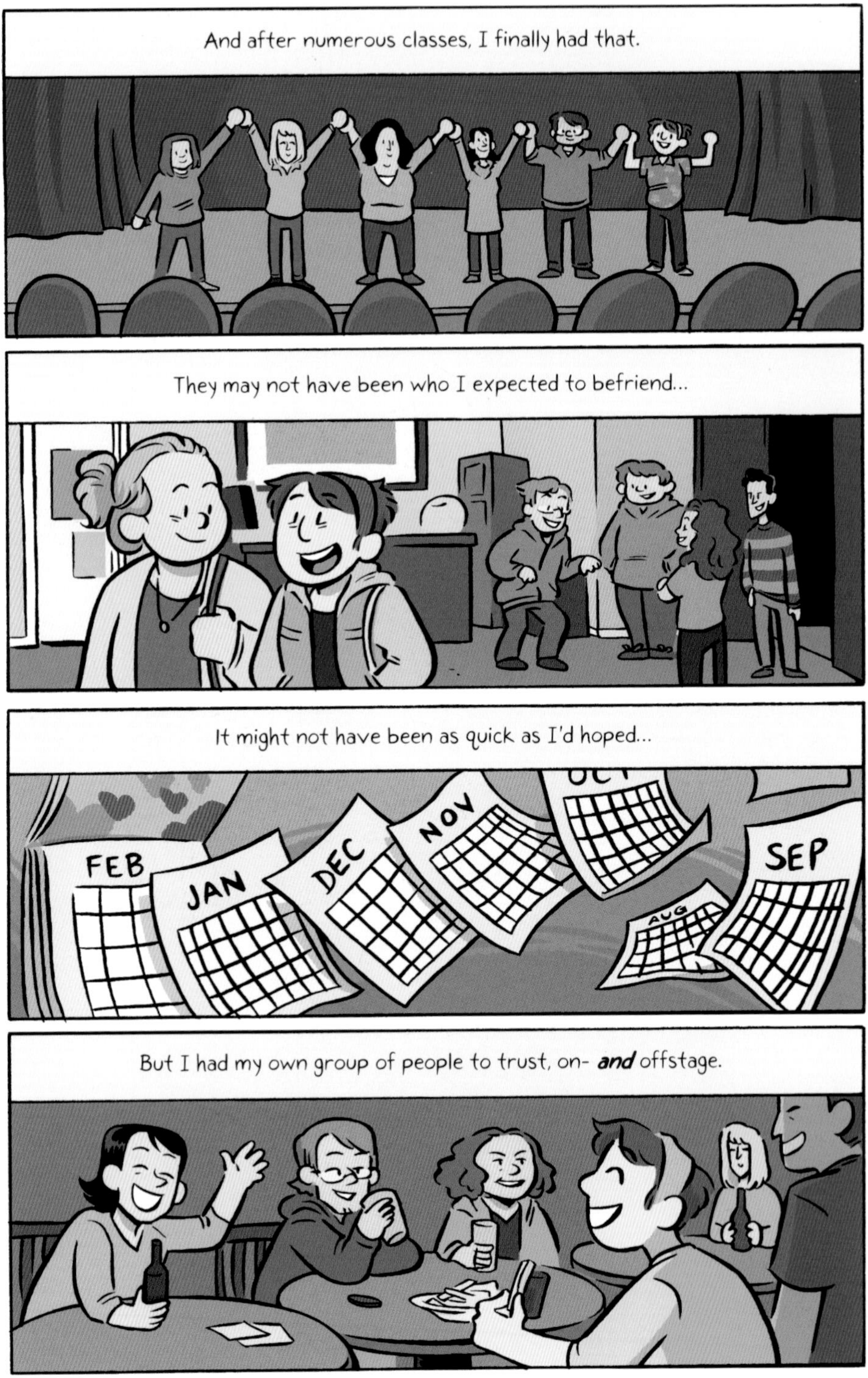
And after numerous classes, I finally had that.
They may not have been who I expected to befriend...
It might not have been as quick as I'd hoped...
FEB
JAN
DEC
NOV
AUG
SEP
But I had my own group of people to trust, on- *and* offstage.

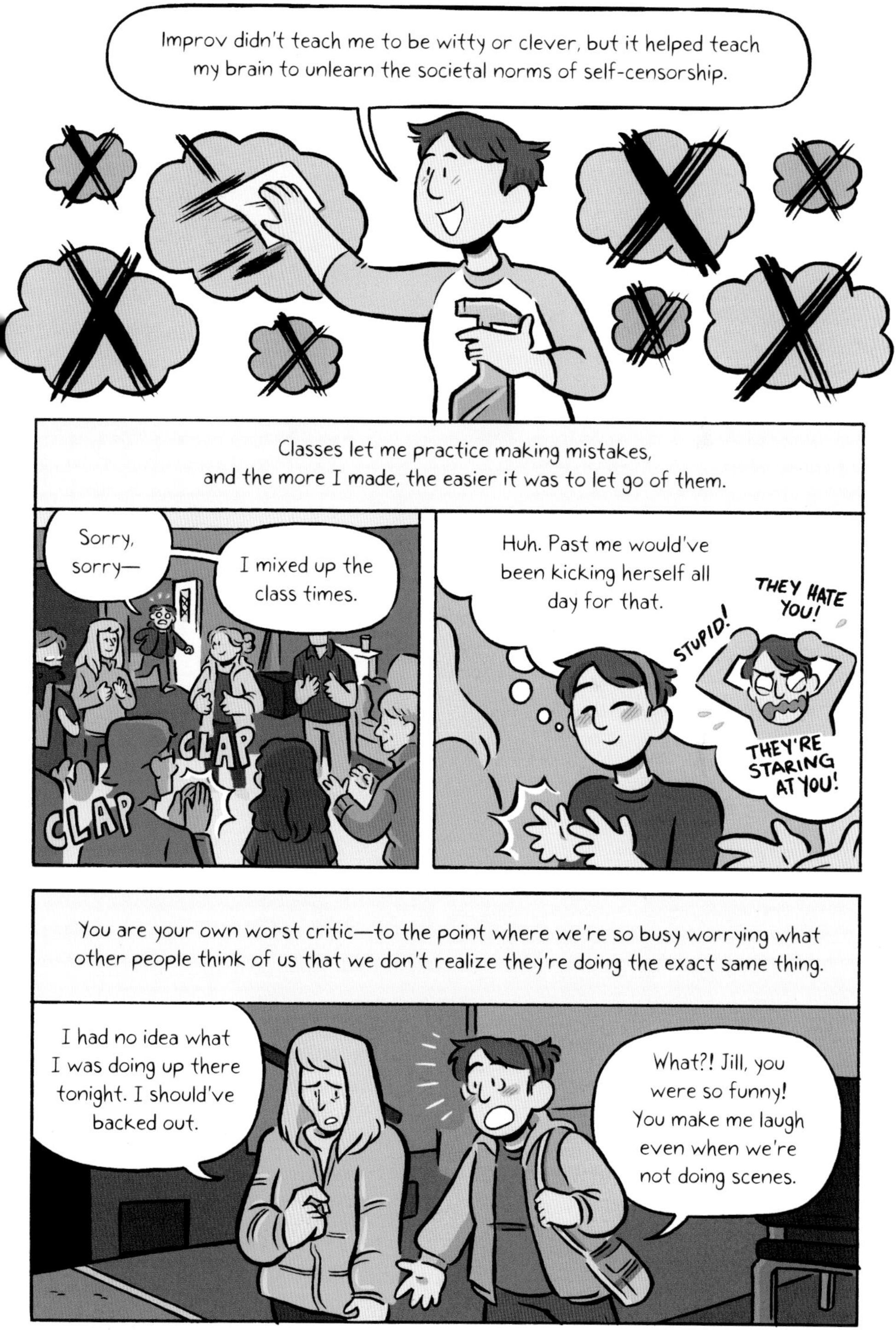
Improv didn't teach me to be witty or clever, but it helped teach my brain to unlearn the societal norms of self-censorship.
Classes let me practice making mistakes, and the more I made, the easier it was to let go of them.
Sorry, sorry—
I mixed up the class times.
CLAP
CLAP
Huh. Past me would've been kicking herself all day for that.
THEY HATE YOU!
STUPID!
THEY'RE STARING AT YOU!
You are your own worst critic—to the point where we're so busy worrying what other people think of us that we don't realize they're doing the exact same thing.
I had no idea what I was doing up there tonight. I should've backed out.
What?! Jill, you were so funny! You make me laugh even when we're not doing scenes.

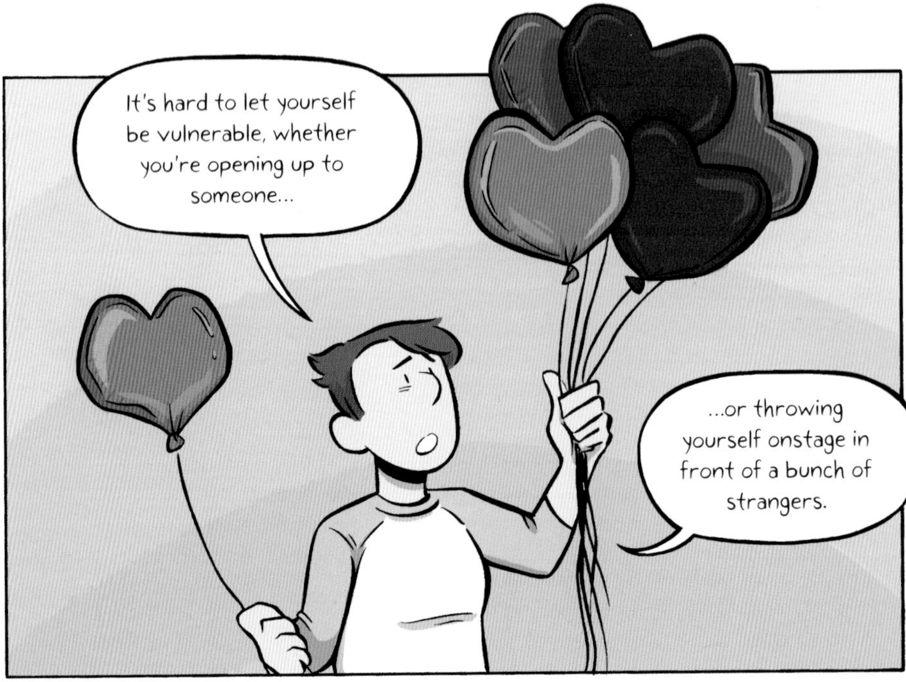
It's hard to let yourself be vulnerable, whether you're opening up to someone...
...or throwing yourself onstage in front of a bunch of strangers.

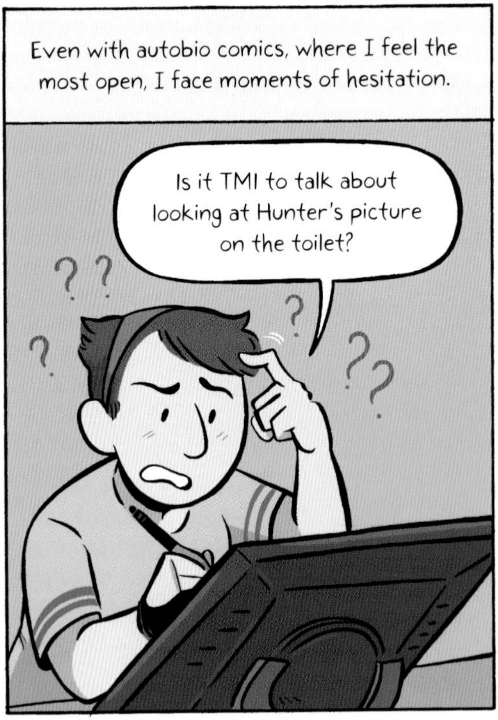
Even with autobio comics, where I feel the most open, I face moments of hesitation.
Is it TMI to talk about looking at Hunter's picture on the toilet?

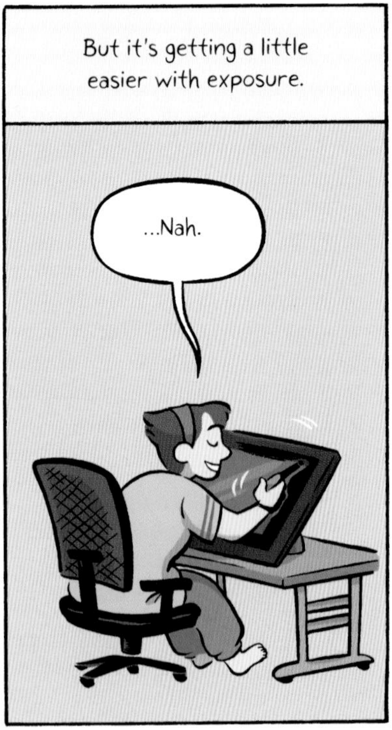
But it's getting a little easier with exposure.
...Nah.

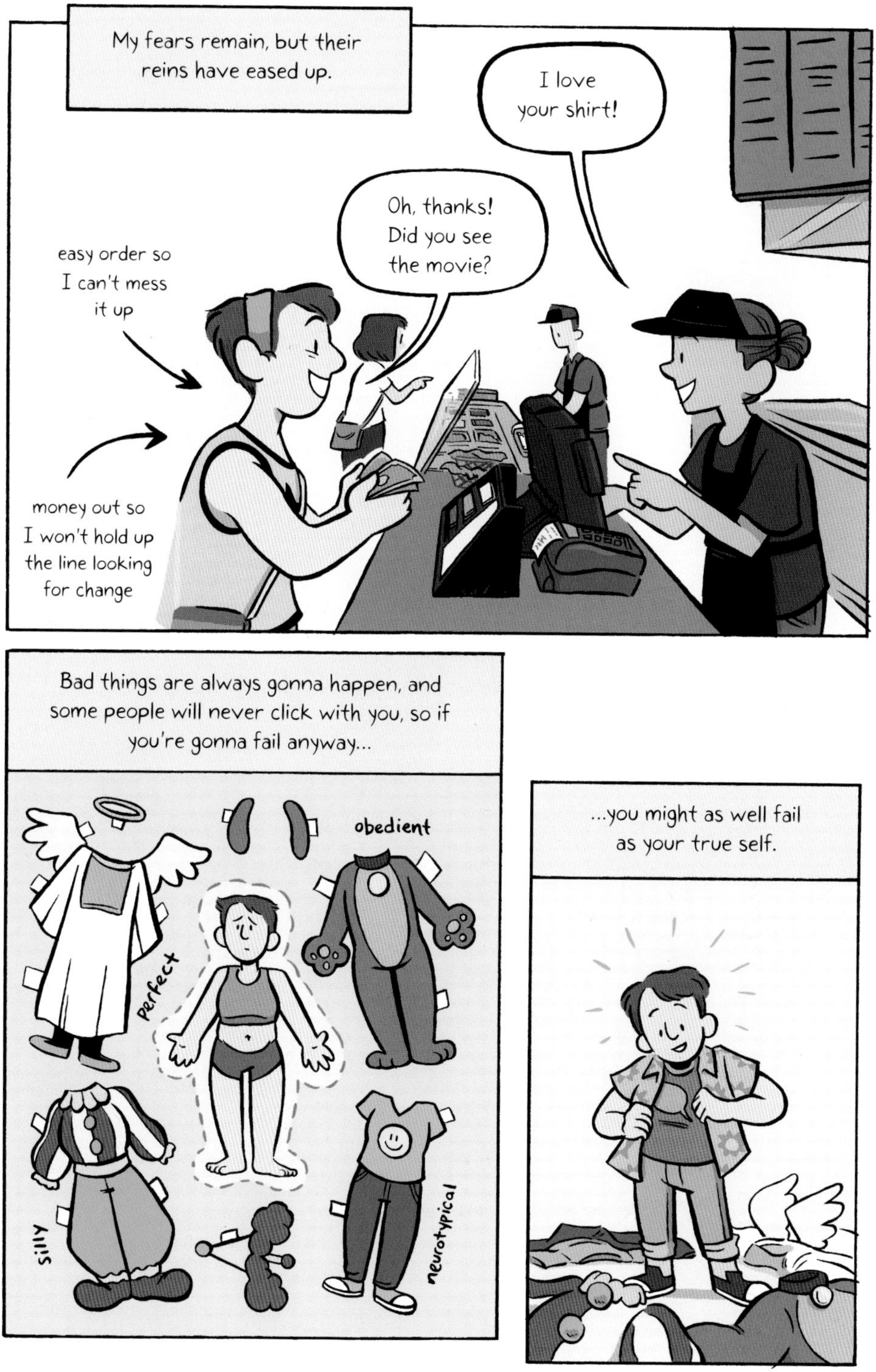
My fears remain, but their reins have eased up.
I love your shirt!
Oh, thanks! Did you see the movie?
easy order so I can't mess it up
money out so I won't hold up the line looking for change
Bad things are always gonna happen, and some people will never click with you, so if you're gonna fail anyway...
obedient
perfect
silly
neurotypical
...you might as well fail as your true self.

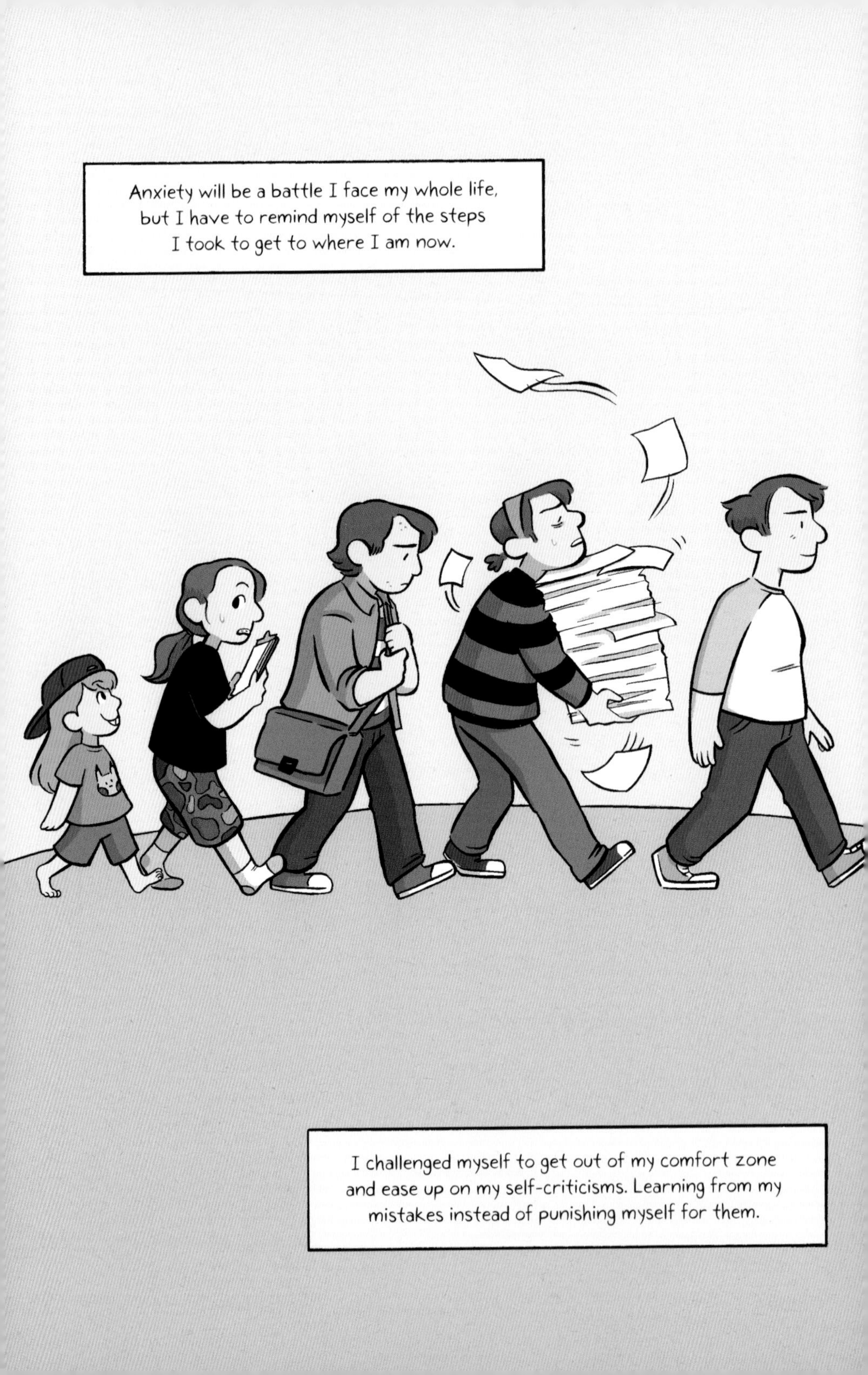
Anxiety will be a battle I face my whole life, but I have to remind myself of the steps I took to get to where I am now.
I challenged myself to get out of my comfort zone and ease up on my self-criticisms. Learning from my mistakes instead of punishing myself for them.

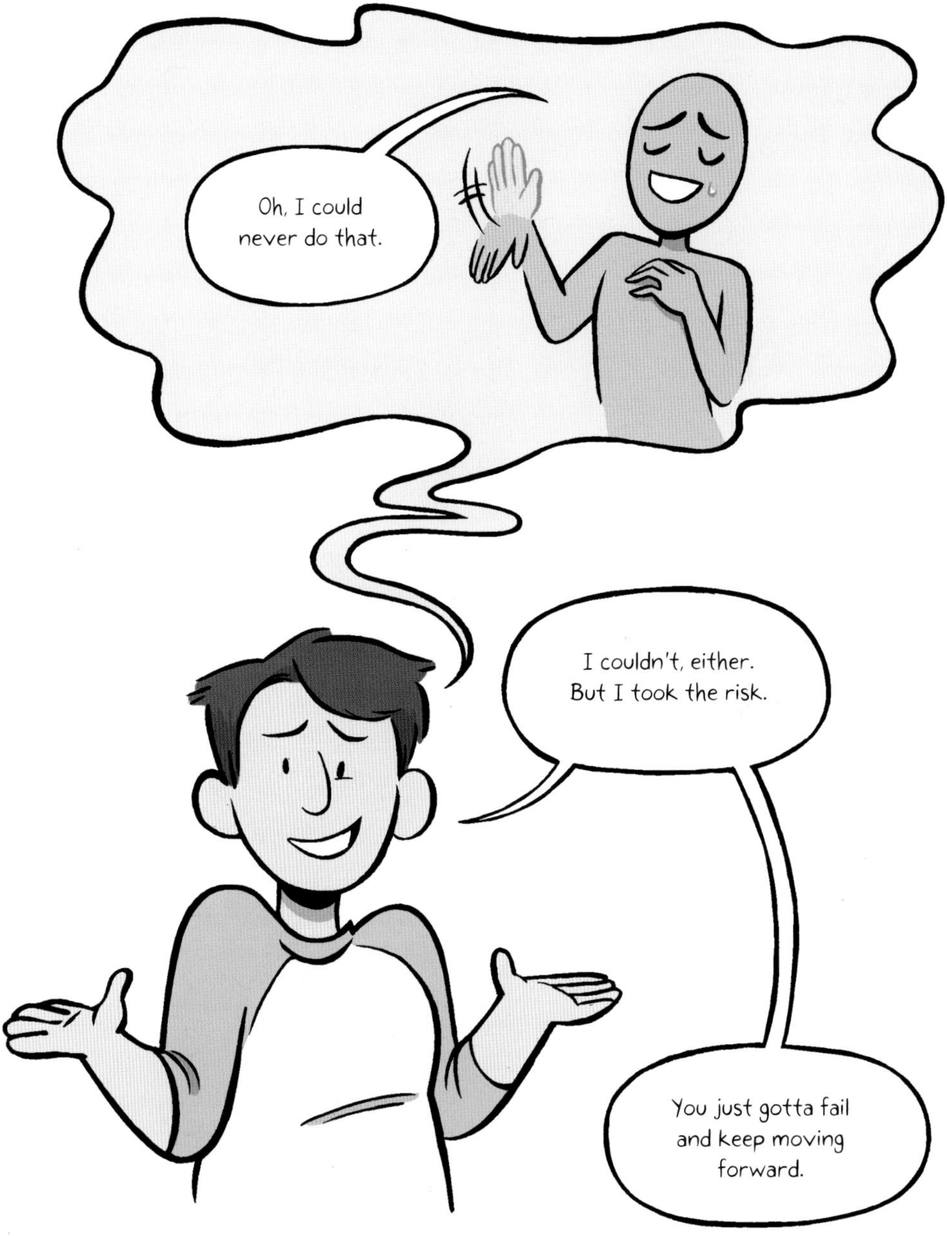
Oh, I could never do that.
I couldn't, either. But I took the risk.
You just gotta fail and keep moving forward.

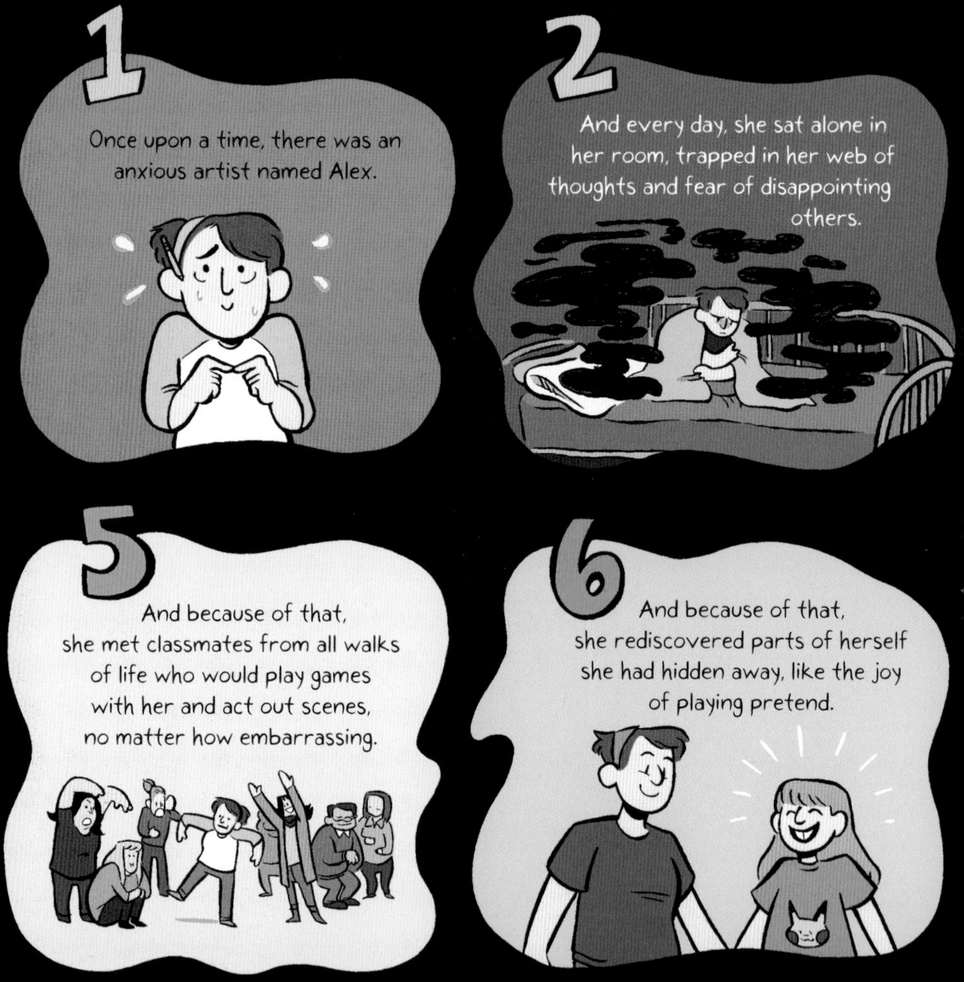
1
Once upon a time, there was an anxious artist named Alex.
2
And every day, she sat alone in her room, trapped in her web of thoughts and fear of disappointing others.
5
And because of that, she met classmates from all walks of life who would play games with her and act out scenes, no matter how embarrassing.
6
And because of that, she rediscovered parts of herself she had hidden away, like the joy of playing pretend.

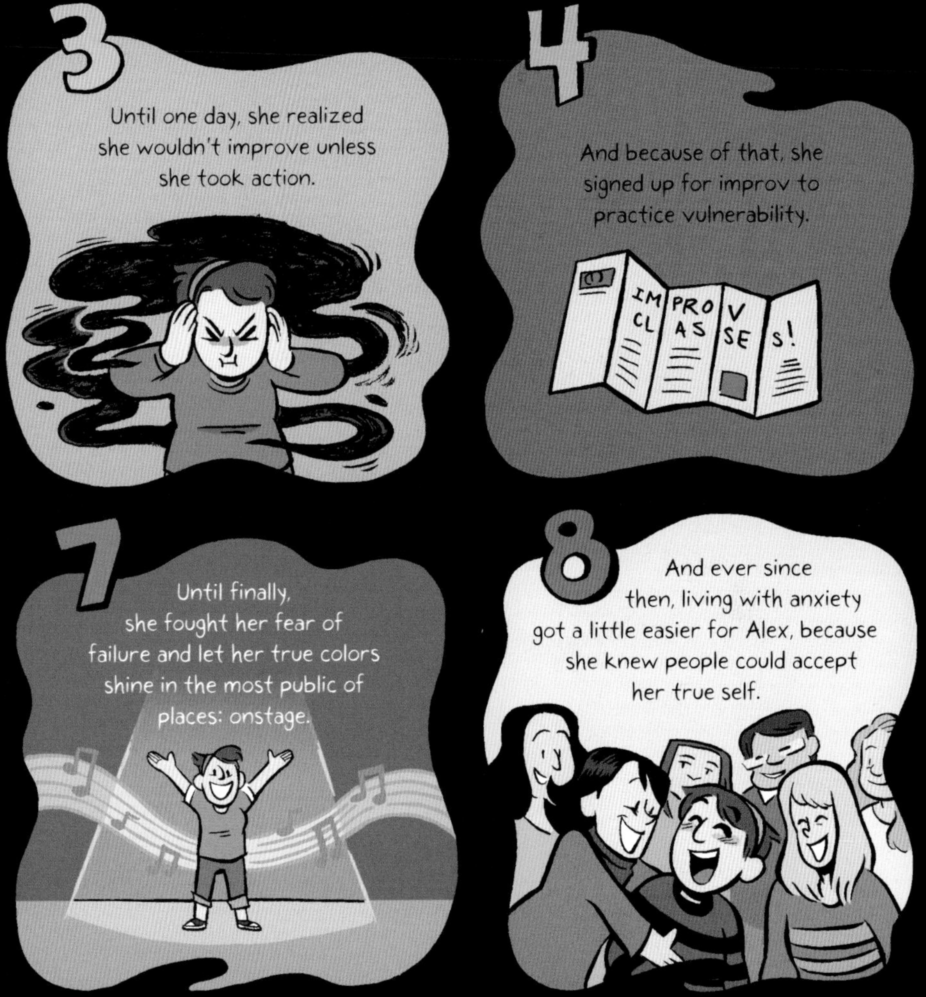
3
Until one day, she realized she wouldn't improve unless she took action.
4
And because of that, she signed up for improv to practice vulnerability.
IMPROV
CLASSES!
7
Until finally, she fought her fear of failure and let her true colors shine in the most public of places: onstage.
8
And ever since then, living with anxiety got a little easier for Alex, because she knew people could accept her true self.

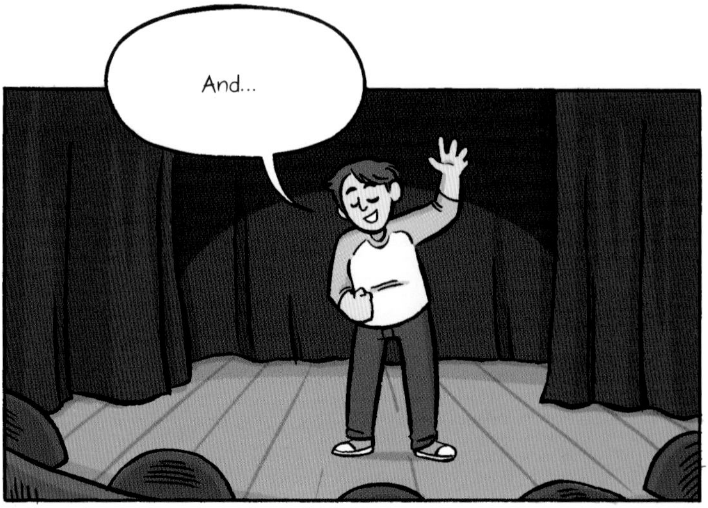
And...

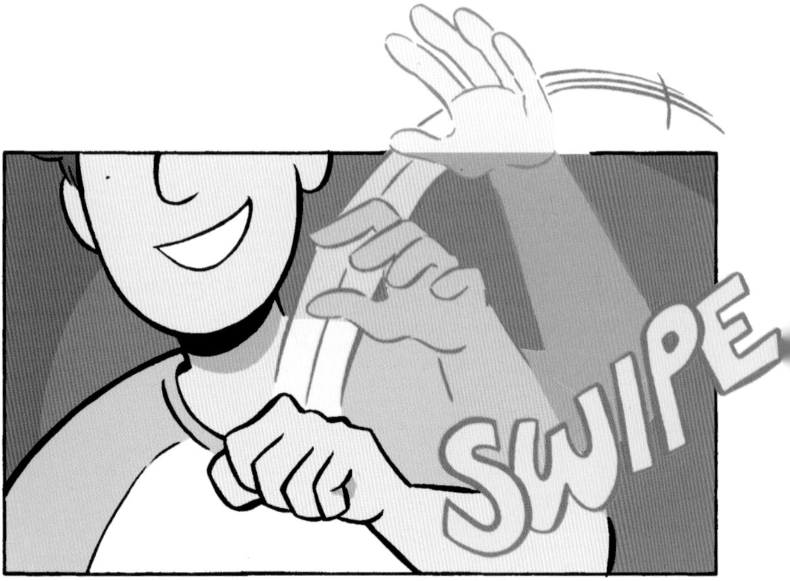
SWIPE

...scene.

Author's Note

When reading memoirs, it's important to remember that characters often are, or are based on, real people, with their own version of events. By only hearing the author's side of the story, many facts can slip through the cracks. In the case of *Improve*, this limited perspective also applies to my personal improv endeavors.

Being a white person in a predominantly white environment, my experiences differ greatly from most marginalized folks', and it feels callous to disregard the misogyny and racism that plague the history of improvisation, comedy, and theater. Improvisation is an act of vulnerability, so how can we open up to strangers when it feels unsafe to do so? Performing is great for pushing us out of our comfort zones, but it should never be at the expense of someone's well-being.

As always, we must work to be anti-racist, anti-ableist, and queer-affirming; to educate ourselves; and to stop microaggressions from betraying theater's promise of inclusivity. Inevitably, a joke or scene will feel off, but as long as players hold one another and themselves accountable while taking risks, I believe improv can continue to find success in its failures.

For further reading on the subject, I recommend:

Whose Improv Is It Anyway? by Amy Seham

"Yes, and...that joke is sexist: Improv troupes, unchecked creepiness and the toll that being 'cool with it' takes" by Arthur Chu (*Salon*, 2016)

"'This room's not ready for me': improv as a BAME comic" by Jamal Khadar (*The Guardian*, 2020)

BONUS GAMES!

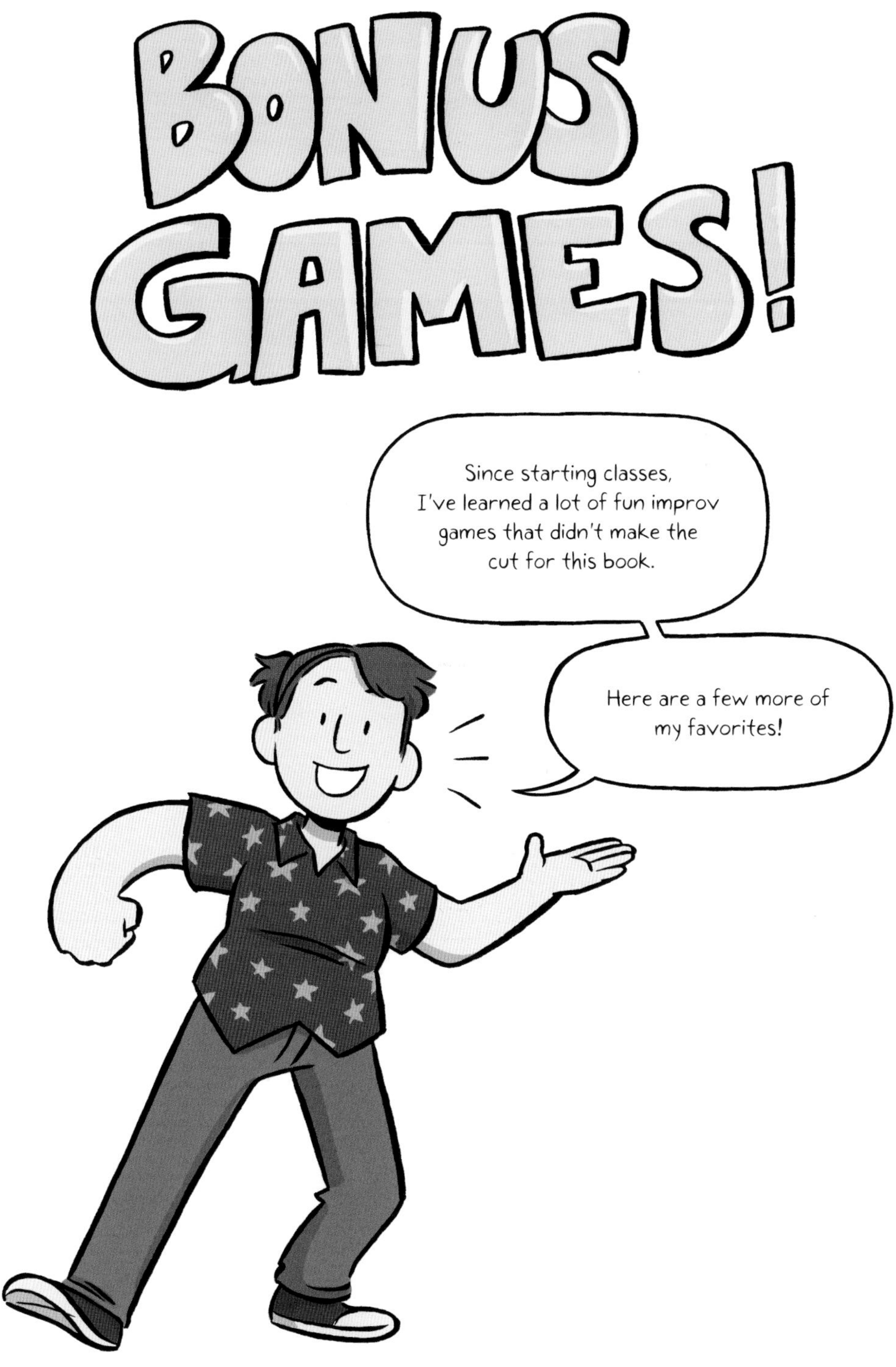
Since starting classes, I've learned a lot of fun improv games that didn't make the cut for this book.
Here are a few more of my favorites!

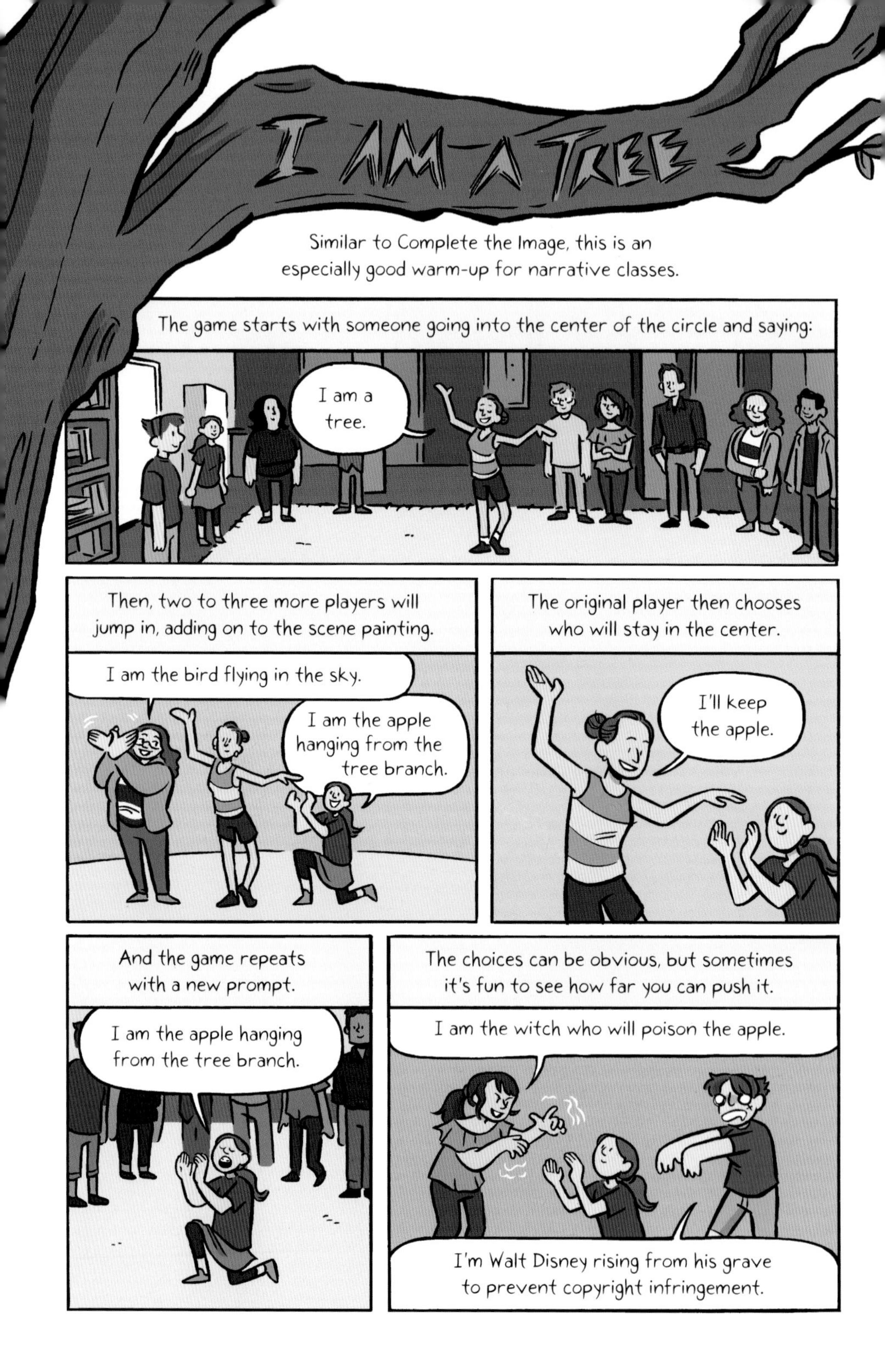
I AM A TREE
Similar to Complete the Image, this is an especially good warm-up for narrative classes.
The game starts with someone going into the center of the circle and saying:
I am a tree.
Then, two to three more players will jump in, adding on to the scene painting.
I am the bird flying in the sky.
I am the apple hanging from the tree branch.
The original player then chooses who will stay in the center.
I'll keep the apple.
And the game repeats with a new prompt.
I am the apple hanging from the tree branch.
The choices can be obvious, but sometimes it's fun to see how far you can push it.
I am the witch who will poison the apple.
I'm Walt Disney rising from his grave to prevent copyright infringement.

WHOOSH! BANG! POW!

A circle warm-up where players pass around the aforementioned sounds (WHOOSH, BANG, POW), but each sound has its own rule.

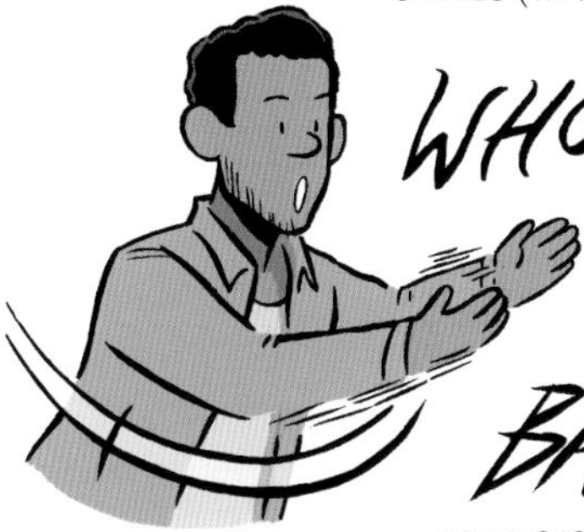

WHOOSH! can pass to the player on your left or right.

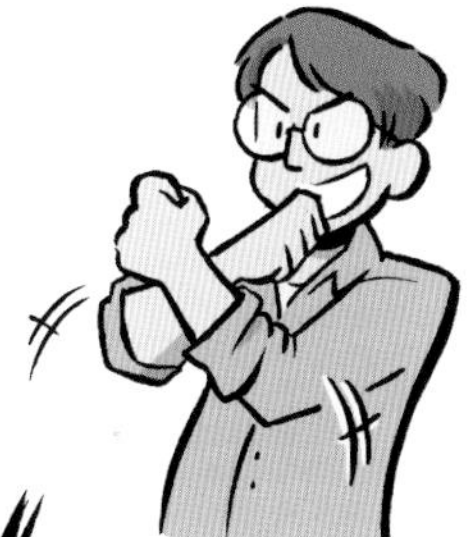

BANG! reverses the WHOOSH, sending it back to the previous player.

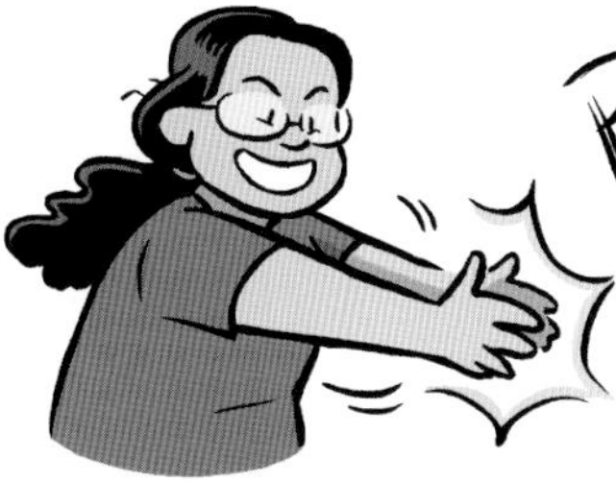

POW! passes it across the circle to the player you're pointing at.

Depending on whom you play with, a few additional options are:

* **BRIDGE!** skips two people, who have to duck.

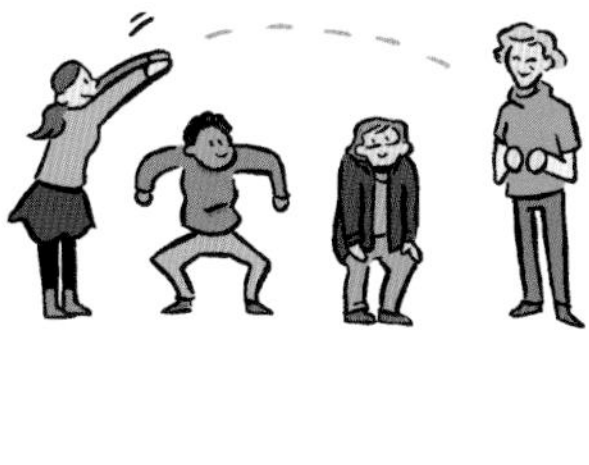

* **TUNNEL!** skips three people, who have to jump, as though the sound is traveling underneath them.

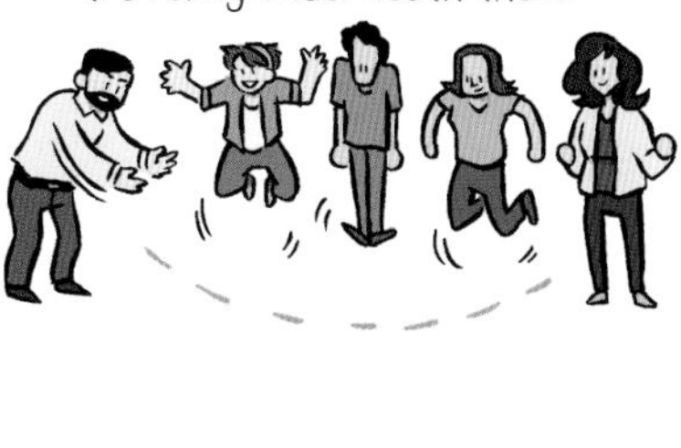

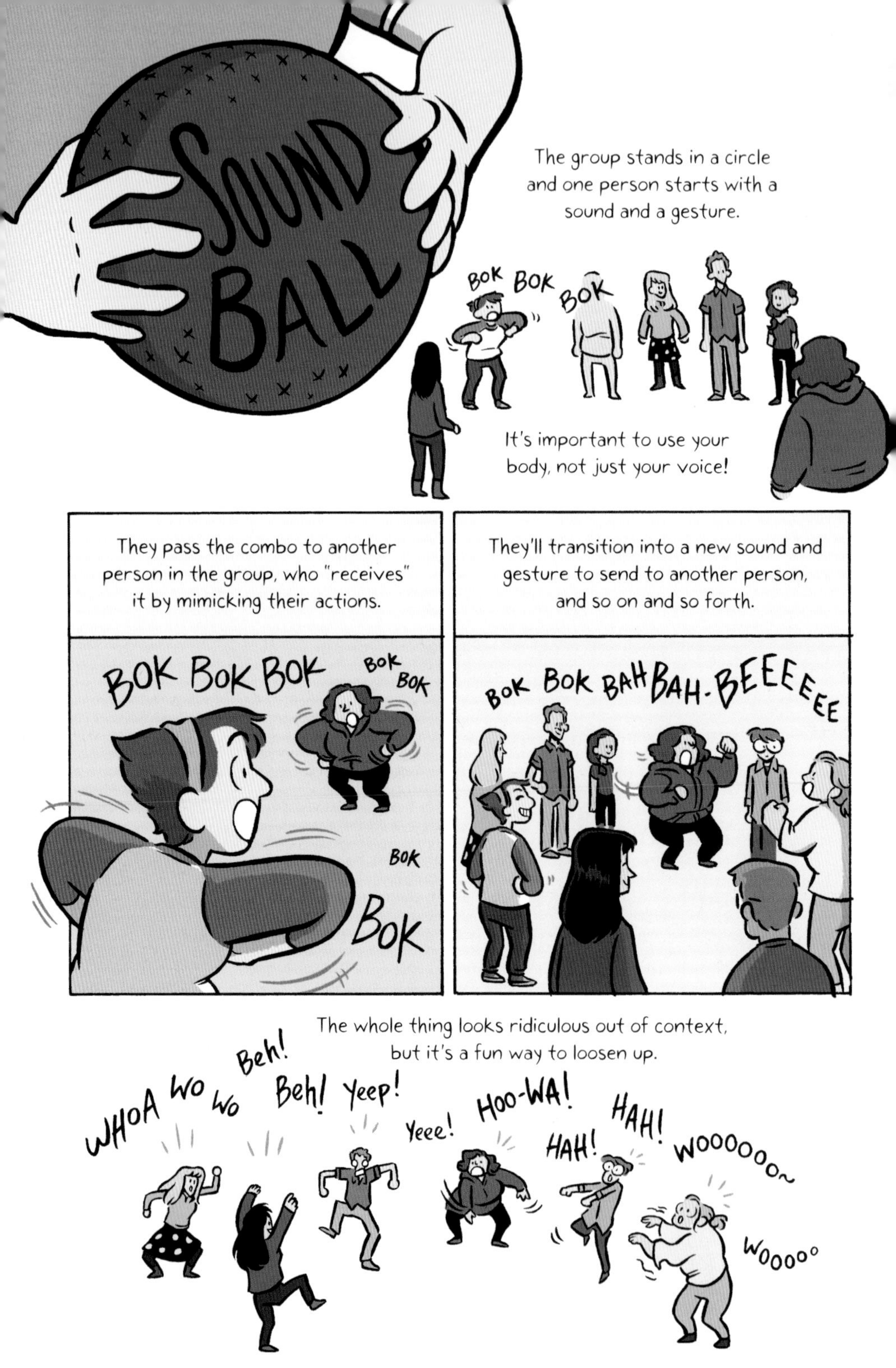
SOUND BALL
The group stands in a circle and one person starts with a sound and a gesture.
BOK BOK BOK
It's important to use your body, not just your voice!
They pass the combo to another person in the group, who "receives" it by mimicking their actions.
BOK BOK BOK
BOK BOK
BOK
BOK
They'll transition into a new sound and gesture to send to another person, and so on and so forth.
BOK BOK BAH BAH-BEEEEEEE
The whole thing looks ridiculous out of context, but it's a fun way to loosen up.
WHOA WO WO
Beh! Beh!
Yeep!
Yeee!
HOO-WA!
HAH! HAH!
WOOOOOO~
WOOOOO

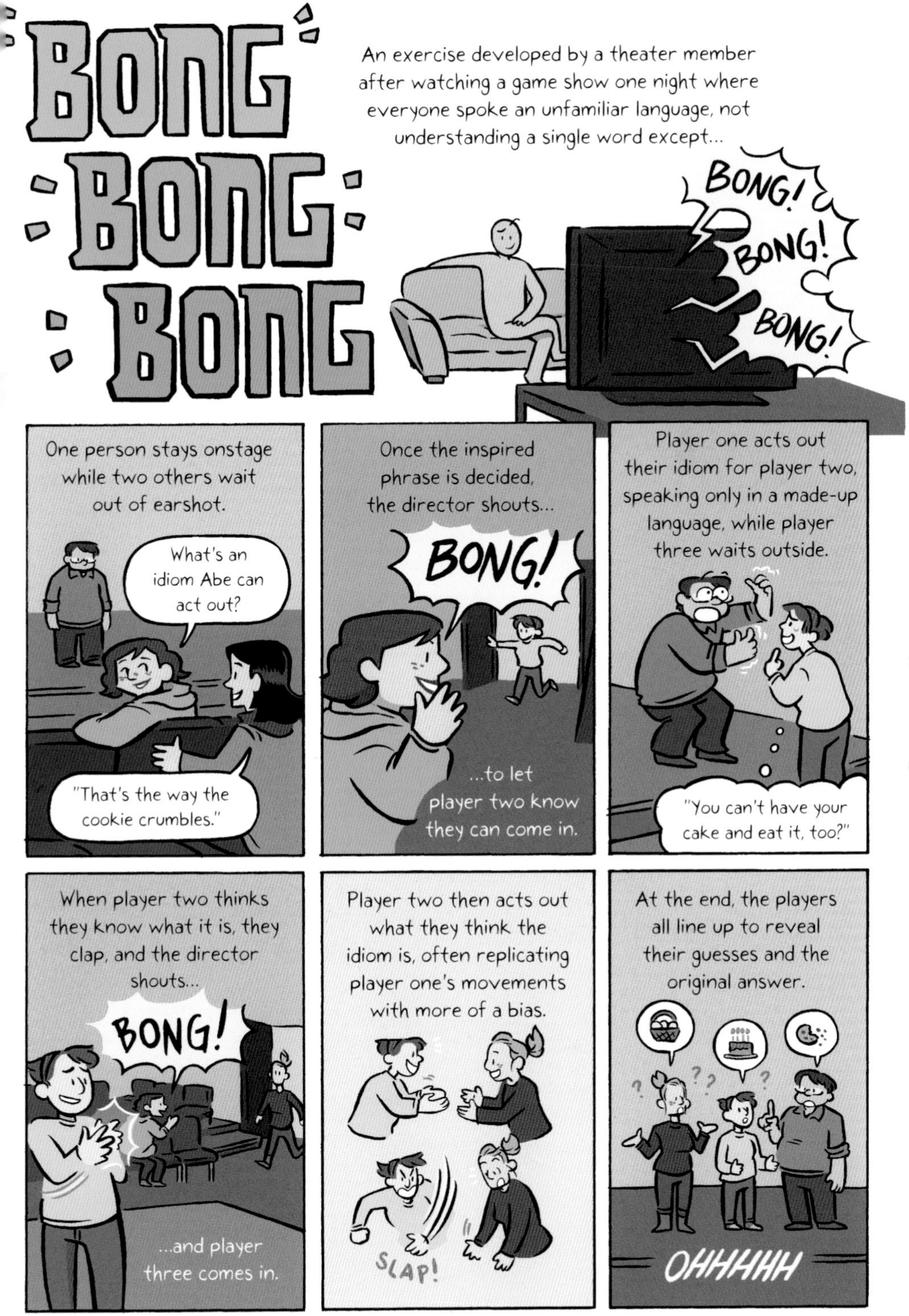
BONG BONG BONG
An exercise developed by a theater member after watching a game show one night where everyone spoke an unfamiliar language, not understanding a single word except...
BONG!
BONG!
BONG!
One person stays onstage while two others wait out of earshot.
What's an idiom Abe can act out?
"That's the way the cookie crumbles."
Once the inspired phrase is decided, the director shouts...
BONG!
...to let player two know they can come in.
Player one acts out their idiom for player two, speaking only in a made-up language, while player three waits outside.
"You can't have your cake and eat it, too?"
When player two thinks they know what it is, they clap, and the director shouts...
BONG!
...and player three comes in.
Player two then acts out what they think the idiom is, often replicating player one's movements with more of a bias.
SLAP!
At the end, the players all line up to reveal their guesses and the original answer.
OHHHHH

*It's basically Telephone but in gibberish.

YEARBOOK

After getting suggestions from the audience, the players pose onstage as though they are taking a school club photo.

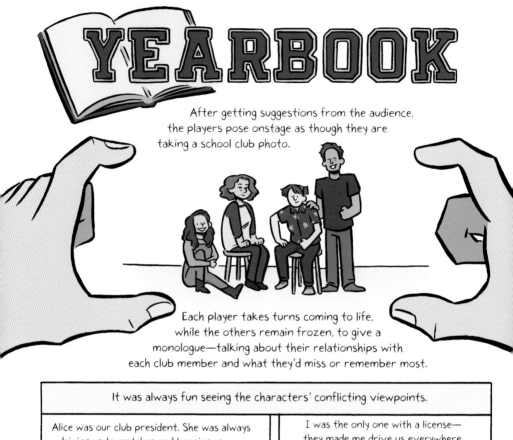

Each player takes turns coming to life, while the others remain frozen, to give a monologue—talking about their relationships with each club member and what they'd miss or remember most.

It was always fun seeing the characters' conflicting viewpoints.

Alice was our club president. She was always driving us to matches and keeping us organized.

She was the only one I trusted in this club.

I was the only one with a license—they made me drive us everywhere, and they were always late!

I never wanted to be in this stupid club in the first place!

The last member wraps up the scene with their final note, and once they return to their spot, the director pretends to finish taking the photo and the scene ends.

:CLICK!:
Thanks, kids.

TONY-WINNING MOMENT

This game isn't much different from other ones I've played, but I'm a sucker for musicals, so I'm biased!

The idea is that you're performing excerpts from a musical that has been nominated for all the Tony awards this year.

we made a musical called "Under the Stairs," about goblins hiding in a human house

Two people begin the scene normally, until the director yells, "This is your Tony-winning moment!"

Marty, I've always loved ya like a brother.

I love you like a lover—

What?

Alex, this is your Tony-winning moment!

HA HA HA HA HA

Aw poopy.

HA

This cues the last person to sing the song that got them nominated for Best Actor.

fifteen years under the stairs

is a long, long time

The game continues until every player has had their own Tony-winning moment, so everyone gets a chance in the limelight!

HAT GAME

A staple of Micetro improv—and a lot harder than it sounds!

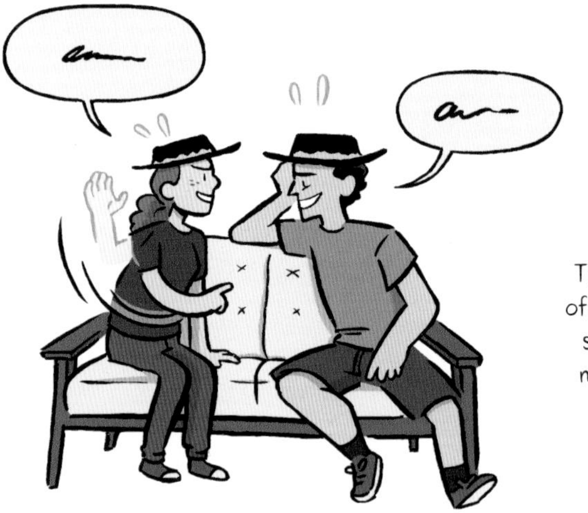

Two partners play a scene while wearing wide-brimmed hats.

The goal is to snatch the hat off your partner's head: if you succeed, you win, but if you miss, you automatically lose.

It's a practice in mindfulness, in staying alert in the scene but not overplanning.

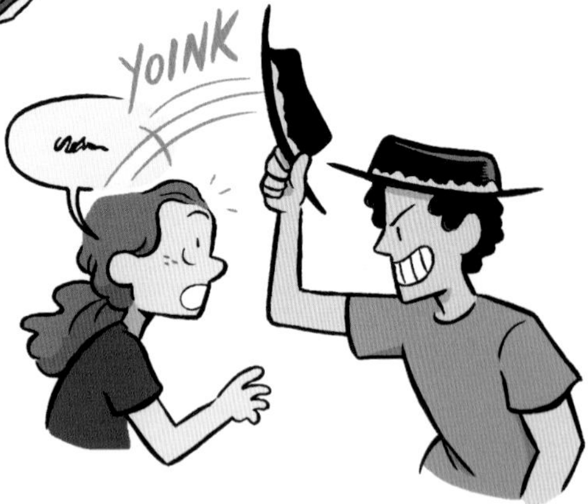
YOINK

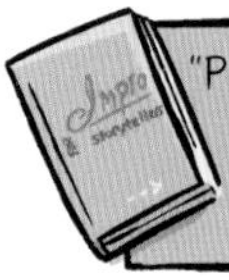

"Part of the mind plays the scene, while another part watches attentively."
Impro for Storytellers, p. 159

Often your partner makes their move when you become "absent."

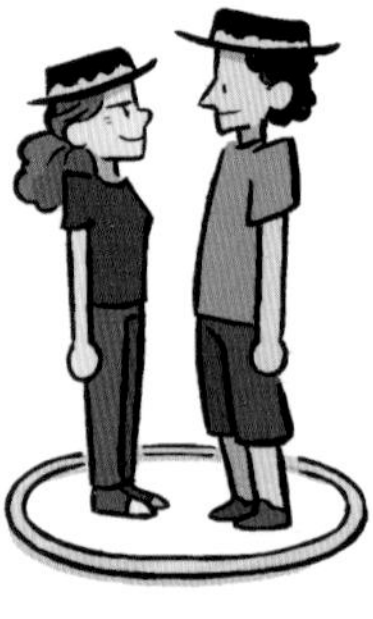

If the players are being too cautious, backing away to protect their own hats, the director will push them closer to one another.

← the CTC makes them do the scene inside a hula hoop!

Acknowledgments

My peers and friends inspire me every day, but these people especially
deserve thanks for making this book possible:

Mom and Dad, for their housing and endless support in both my artistic endeavors
and mental health. Thank you for learning alongside me—I know it wasn't always easy.

My editor, Tim Stout, for his patience, perspective, and cute family photos.
(Double thanks to Katherine, Jackson, and Tristan for letting me borrow him!)

My agent, Charlie Olsen, who believed in this book the moment I pitched it.

Molly Johanson, Kirk Benshoff, Calista Brill, Samia Fakih, Robyn Chapman,
and everyone at First Second, who produce amazing work behind the scenes.

Alex Lu, for his thoughtful sensitivity read-through.

Wren Chavers, Veronica Agarwal, and Anthony Kim, the best friends a gal could ask for,
who provided constant support and critique, even when I messaged them at ungodly hours.

Veronica Agarwal (again!) and Kyla Smith, for their generous assistance with
flatting and line art cleanup when I found I was in over my head.

Sam, whose extroversion always ends up looking mean in my comics (sorry!)
when in reality she is the coolest and smartest seestor ever.

All the mental health professionals who have assisted me over the years,
but especially my current therapist, who encouraged this theatrical journey.

Tory Woollcott and Kean Soo, my Canadian comics parents, who have shown me nothing but
kindness since we met and endured many improv stories when I'd visit them up north.

Raina Telgemeier, for her considerate memoir advice and well-wishes.

The Alaska Robotics Comics Camp of 2019, who dealt with my nonstop
improv talk as I dreamed up a book four years in the making.

The Comics Support Group Discord server, for their feedback and assurance.

The Bone Squad, for their friendship and fantastical escapism.

And of course, the inspiration for this book: my classmates and community at the
Contemporary Theater Company, including but not limited to Chris S., Chris H., Charlie, Riley,
Christine, Verne, Tina, Miriam, Gayle, Jess, Tyler, Brian, Neal, Maggie, Ashley, Maddie, Amanda,
Eddie, Sarah, Kathy, and the fine folks that make up Mopco, the Electric City Puppets, and
Broke Gravy. Thank you for lifting me up and not letting me fall.